WITHDRAWN

INTRODUCTION TO THE SCIENCE
OF ETHICS

INTRODUCTION TO THE SCIENCE OF ETHICS

BY

THEODORE DE LAGUNA

BOOKS FOR LIBRARIES PRESS
FREEPORT, NEW YORK

First Published 1914
Reprinted 1972

Library of Congress Cataloging in Publication Data

De Laguna, Theodore de Leo, 1876-1930.
  Introduction to the science of ethics.

  ([BCL/select bibliographies reprint series])
  Reprint of the 1914 ed.
  Includes bibliographies.
  1. Ethics. I. Title.
BJ1025.D4 1972   170   72-4166
ISBN 0-8369-6887-5

PRINTED IN THE UNITED STATES OF AMERICA

PREFACE

THE title of this book is intended to be fairly descriptive of it. It treats of ethics as a science, which if not wholly independent of metaphysical considerations — and of no science can that be said — is sufficiently independent to permit of separate positive treatment. And under the broad license of an 'introduction' it presents not only an outline of the science as we find it to-day, but some account of the past which has made it what it is.

Part I contains brief chapters upon the scope and methods of the science and upon one metaphysical topic (the freedom of the will) which cannot well be passed over in silence. But it is mainly given up to a discussion of the subjects of moral judgments and a survey of the various kinds of standards according to which, under the conditions of savage or of civilized life, moral judgments are made. It is thus intended to present a broad background of facts against which the explanatory theories, old and new, may be the better appreciated.

Part II is a review of the principal Greek and English ethical theories. In an introductory note I have given my reasons for including this review. It does not purport to be a history of ethics, even for the periods which it covers. By neglecting much that is important to the historian, I have gained space for a fuller and, I trust, more interesting and instructive treatment of the men and movements that are included. In connection with Part II a selection from the ethical classics should certainly be read; and this, however meager, should not fail to comprise Books I, II, and X of the *Nicomachean Ethics*.

Especially in the case of the Greek ethicists, I have not always found it possible to separate the moral theories entirely from their metaphysical basis; indeed, to have done so would in some cases have amounted to a falsification. But I have at least relegated the metaphysics to a strictly subordinate place.

In Part III a positive treatment of moral problems is presented in connection with the elements of the general theory of values. So far as I know, this is the first attempt at an elementary presentation of any of the newer phases of the latter subject. Not that the theory of values as such is new. It is as old as ethics itself. But in recent years it has undergone a great development, and one of unusual interest — a development, however, which has remained buried in monographs and treatises that are wholly inaccessible to the undergraduate student as well as to the educated public generally.

It should be observed that Part III is intelligible — I would not say equally intelligible — without the previous reading of Part II, which may therefore be omitted if time requires or the instructor so prefers. Parts I and III will then serve as an 'Elements of Ethics.' I hope, however, that this extreme course may not often be taken. It may, however, often be necessary to omit some passages of Part II; and it is not so closely written but that omissions can easily be made. I would suggest that Chapter X and the account of the stimuli of the moral sense in Chapter XI, while dealing of matters of great importance in themselves, may be most easily spared by the beginner.

I should not know how to record the debts which I have incurred in writing this book; and I shall not attempt it. The great debts, of which I remain ever conscious, are, naturally enough, to my own teachers of ethics, Professor Howison of California and Professor McGilvary of Cornell and Wisconsin; but such debts are more easily felt than set forth. I should, however, mention that in the writing of Chapter XI I received several suggestions from Dr. Edna Shearer (a pupil of the late David Irons), whose unpublished dissertation on Hume's ethics was completed under my supervision.

CAMBRIDGE, ENGLAND,
November 14, 1914.

CONTENTS

PART I. THE FIELD OF ETHICS

CHAPTER		PAGE
I.	SCOPE AND RELATIONS OF THE SCIENCE OF ETHICS	3

    I. THE PROBLEMS OF ETHICS, 3.
    II. THE RELATIONS OF ETHICS, 8.
    III. ETHICS AS A THEORETICAL SCIENCE AND AS THE PHILOSOPHY OF PRACTICE, 11.

II. THE METHODS OF ETHICS 13

III. THE FIELD OF MORAL JUDGMENTS 23

    I. CHARACTER AND CONDUCT, 23.
    II. THE MORAL AGENT, 26.
    III. EXTENT OF MORAL CONDUCT, 29.
    IV. CONTENT OF THE MORAL ACT, 31. *1. The Problem,* 31. *2. Status of Unforeseen Consequences,* 33. *3. Motive vs. Intention,* 39.
    APPENDIX: THE INTENTION TO DO RIGHT, 42.

IV. RESPONSIBILITY AND FREEDOM 50

    I. RESPONSIBILITY, 50.
    II. THE RELATION BETWEEN FREEDOM AND RESPONSIBILITY, 51.
    III. FURTHER ARGUMENTS FOR INDETERMINISM, 56.
    IV. FURTHER ARGUMENTS FOR DETERMINISM, 58.
    V. PHYSICAL AND QUASI-PHYSICAL DETERMINISM, 63.

V. GENERAL SURVEY OF MORAL STANDARDS . . . 66

    I *a.* THE STANDARDS OF DUTY, 67. *1. Instinctive and Customarg Standards,* 67. *2. Personal Authority,* 73. *3. The Authority of Law,* 77.

I b. THE STANDARDS OF BENEVOLENCE, 80. *1. Ideality of Benevolence and Virtue*, 80. *2. Benevolence in General*, 82. *3. The Objects of Benevolence*, 83. (1) Benevolence to Individuals, 83. (2) Devotion to an Institution, 85. (3) Devotion to a Cause, 86. (4) Devotion to a Representative, 87.

II. THE STANDARDS OF VIRTUE, 88. *1. The Kinds of Virtue*, 88. (1) Courage, 89. (2) Temperance, 91. (3) Wisdom, 93. *2. Virtue without Effort*, 96. *3. The Imitation of the Ideal*, 97.

PART II. THE CLASSICAL SCHOOLS

INTRODUCTORY NOTE 101

VI. THE BEGINNINGS OF ETHICS 105
    I. THE SOPHISTS, 105.
    II. SOCRATES, 112. *1. Fundamental Assumptions*, 113. *2. Theory of Virtue*, 115.

VII. HEDONISM 123
    I. ARISTIPPUS, 124.
    II. OTHER HEDONISTS, 126.

VIII. ENERGISM 131
    I. GENERAL FEATURES OF ANCIENT ENERGISM, 131.
    II. PLATO, 133. *1. The Virtues in General*, 135. *2. Wisdom*, 138. *3. Pleasure*, 142.
    III. ARISTOTLE, 144. *1. Metaphysical Basis*, 145. *2. Happiness*, 147. *3. Virtue*, 149. *4. The Supremacy of Pure Reason*, 153.
    IV. CONCLUDING COMMENTS, 154.

IX. RIGORISM 158
    I. THE CYNICS, 158.
    II. THE STOICS, 163. *1. The Background*, 163. *2. The Relation of Morality to Instinct*, 164. *3. The Stoic Paradoxes*, 167. *4. The Virtuous Life*, 169.

CONTENTS

CHAPTER		PAGE
X.	THE BEGINNINGS OF MODERN ETHICS	175
	I. THE POINT OF DEPARTURE, 175.	
	II. HOBBES, 177. *1. Fundamental Principles*, 177. *2. The State of Nature*, 182. *3. The Conditions of Peace*, 185. *4. The Function of the State*, 187.	
	III. CUDWORTH, 189.	
	IV. CUMBERLAND, 190.	
XI.	THE CLASSICAL SCHOOLS OF THE EIGHTEENTH CENTURY	198
	I. PRELIMINARY REMARKS, 198.	
	II. INTUITIONALISM, 200. *1. The Mathematical Analogy*, 200. *2. Obligation — Reward and Punishment*, 203. *3. The Universality of Moral Laws*, 206.	
	III. SENTIMENTALISM, 207. *1. Empirical Standpoint*, 207. *2. The Analogy of Beauty*, 208. *3. Obligation*, 215. *4. The Stimuli*, 217.	
	IV. UTILITARIANISM, 223. *1. The Utilitarian Program*, 223. *2. Obligation*, 226. *3. Approbation and Disapprobation*, 230.	
	V. CONCLUDING REMARKS, 232.	
XII.	THE NINETEENTH CENTURY AND GERMAN INFLUENCE	235
	I. THE NEW UTILITARIANISM, 235.	
	II. KANT, 238.	
	III. FICHTE, 242.	
	IV. HEGEL, 243.	
	V. THE ENGLISH CONTROVERSIES, 245.	
XIII.	THE HEDONISTIC CONTROVERSY	247
	I. THE KINDS OF HEDONISM, 247.	
	II. THE SELFISH THEORY, 252.	
	III. THE THEORY OF ORIGINAL SELFISHNESS, 259.	
	IV. THE HEDONISTIC THEORY OF VALUES IN GENERAL, 261.	
	V. ETHICAL HEDONISM, 271.	

PART III. THE EVOLUTIONARY THEORY OF MORAL VALUES

CHAPTER   PAGE
XIV. THE SIGNIFICANCE OF MORALITY FOR SOCIETY   281
    I. INTRODUCTION, 281.
    II. MORALITY AND SOCIAL WELFARE, 282.
    III. SOCIAL INTERCOURSE, 286.
    IV. THE RELATION OF MORALITY TO SOCIAL INTERCOURSE, 292.

XV. CHARACTER, SENTIMENT, AND VALUE   296
    I. MORALITY AND INDIVIDUAL WELFARE, 296.
    II. CHARACTER, 298.
    III. THE SENTIMENTS, 304.
    IV. VALUATION, 311.
    V. THE VALUE OF A SUM OF THINGS, 315.
    VI. VIRTUE AND HAPPINESS, 318. *1. Indirect Value of Morality*, 318. *2. Direct Value of Morality*, 320.

XVI. THE SOCIAL CHARACTER OF SENTIMENTS, AND THE OBJECTIVITY OF VALUES   324
    I. INTRODUCTION, 324.
    II. THE EXCITATION OF SYMPATHY, 325.
    III. ADMIRATION AND CONTEMPT. PRIDE AND SHAME, 329.
    IV. THE EDUCATION OF THE SENTIMENTS, 330.
    V. THE OBJECTIVITY OF VALUES, 335.
    VI. THE FUNCTION OF THE ÉLITE, 340.
    VII. ABSOLUTE VALUES, 347.
    VIII. HISTORICAL CONTINUITY, 350.
    IX. INDIVIDUAL DIFFERENCES, 354.
    X. VALUES PECULIAR TO MINOR SOCIAL GROUPS, 358.

XVII. THE SIGNIFICANCE OF DARWINISM   360
    I. EVOLUTION IN GENERAL, 360.
    II. DARWINISM, 363.

CONTENTS

CHAPTER			PAGE
	III.	APPLICATION OF DARWINISM TO ETHICS, 367.	
	IV.	CONGENITAL BASIS OF MORALITY, 372.	
	V.	THE ANALOGY OF LANGUAGE, 376.	
XVIII.	THE EVOLUTION OF MORAL STANDARDS		379
	I.	CONDITIONS OF MORAL EVOLUTION, 379.	
	II.	THE PROBLEM, 381.	
	III.	THE MODIFICATION OF STANDARDS OF VALUE, 382.	
	IV.	CONVENTIONALITY IN MORAL STANDARDS, 388.	
	V.	DOUBT AND REFLECTION, 391.	
	VI.	THE RISE OF DISCONTENT, 394.	
	VII.	DUTY AND BENEVOLENCE IN EVOLUTION, 398.	
	VIII.	THE PROGRESS OF BENEVOLENCE, 401.	
	IX.	THE RELATION OF VIRTUE TO DUTY AND BENEVOLENCE, 404.	
CONCLUSION			407
INDEX			413

GENERAL REFERENCES

ELEMENTARY WORKS.
  MACKENZIE, J. S., *Manual of Ethics.*
  MUIRHEAD, J. H., *Elements of Ethics.*
  SETH, J., *A Study of Ethical Principles.*
  THILLY, F., *Introduction to Ethics.*
  FITE, W., *An Introductory Study of Morals.*
  MEZES, S. E., *Ethics, Descriptive and Explanatory.*
  BOWNE, B. P., *The Principles of Ethics.*
  PERRY, R. B., *The Moral Economy.*
  DEWEY and TUFTS, *Ethics.*
  PALMER, G. H., *The Field of Ethics,* and *The Nature of Goodness.*
  PAULSEN, F., *System of Ethics.*
  ROYCE, J., *The Philosophy of Loyalty.*
  RASHDALL, H., *Ethics.*
  SORLEY, W. R., *The Moral Life.*
  MOORE, G. E., *Ethics.*

TREATISES:
  WUNDT, W., *Ethics.*
  STEPHEN, L., *Science of Ethics.*
  JANET, P., *The Theory of Morals.*
  LADD, G., *The Philosophy of Conduct.*
  MOORE, G. E., *Principia Ethica.*
  TAYLOR, A. E., *The Problem of Conduct.*
  RASHDALL, H., *The Theory of Good and Evil.*
  HOBHOUSE, L. T., *Morals in Evolution.*
  WESTERMARCK, E., *The Origin and Development of the Moral Ideas.*
  READ, C., *Natural and Social Morals.*
  WALLACE, W., *Lectures and Essays on Natural Theology and Ethics.*

PART I
THE FIELD OF ETHICS

CHAPTER I

SCOPE AND RELATIONS OF THE SCIENCE OF ETHICS

I. THE PROBLEMS OF ETHICS

Double Origin of the Science. — The science of ethics has grown principally out of the attempts to solve two sets of problems, which at first sight may not appear to be closely connected with each other. On the one hand it has been asked: *What is happiness? What would be the highest or most complete happiness? What can a man do toward securing happiness for himself or for others?* On the other hand the inquiry has been raised: *What is the meaning of 'right' and 'wrong,' 'good' and 'bad,' as applied to men's conduct and character? How do we make these distinctions and what validity do they possess?* But however different their starting-points, the two inquiries are apt to run together very speedily. The study of the conditions of happiness usually reveals the fact that virtue, or good character — the sort of character that shows itself in right conduct — is by far the most important condition. Some moralists have even identified virtue and happiness. And the study of moral distinctions has either led to the conclusion that their meaning is somehow bound up with the happy or unhappy consequences of conduct; or, at least, the study has involved some consideration of reward and punishment, and thus the problem of the relation between virtue and happiness has come into view.

Preliminary Definition. — Ethics thus constitutes a unified body of doctrine, which may be defined as the science of

4 INTRODUCTION TO THE SCIENCE OF ETHICS

morality, or the science of moral distinctions.[1] Such a definition will not apply perfectly to every system that has passed under the name of 'ethics'; but that is not to be expected. One can never give a logically perfect definition of an historical growth. One cannot, for example, define socialism or Christianity in such a way as to include all who have ever been regarded as socialists or as Christians, without making the terms so broad that scarcely any one would be excluded. Now it is one of the best approved maxims of science, that one should be content with the degree of exactness which the given subject-matter admits of. To strain beyond this is to make oneself liable to serious error. The definitions which we give here must be taken simply as preliminary indications, which may give the student a fair idea of what to expect, and may help him to thread his way through the discussions that are to follow.

Ambiguity of Terms. — If the attempt is made to amplify the definition of ethics by explaining the terms 'moral' and 'morality,' a curious difficulty arises. Almost all the familiar expressions that might be used for such an explanation are found to be fatally ambiguous. For instance, let us consider the adjectives 'good' and 'bad.' These are used to denote, not simply moral qualities, but any sort of worth or unworth whatsoever. Dogs and horses, houses and lands, groceries, pictures, scientific theories — anything that is capable of attracting human interest — may be good or bad. Men themselves may be thus described in more senses than one. "Antonio is a good man," may be a testimony to his virtue or an acknowledgment of his mer-

[1] The term 'ethics' is derived from the Greek ἠθικά (moral), from ἦθος (character), which Aristotle rightly surmised to be connected with ἔθος (custom). This connection seemed to him to be important, because he believed that the process of character-forming is essentially one of *habituation*. The term 'moral' is similarly derived from *moralia* (the Latin technical equivalent for ἠθικά), formed by analogy from *mos* (custom, manners). Aristotle, *Nichomachean Ethics*, II, 1; cf. Wundt, *Ethics*, vol. I, pp. 24–26.

cantile standing. Only the context can determine. So also with the other pair of adjectives, 'right' and 'wrong.' Anything that conforms, or fails to conform, to a standard of sufficiency or correctness is right or wrong accordingly. Conformity to moral standards is only one sort of rightness. To denote it plainly it must be set down as 'morally right.' Similarly of 'merit,' 'responsibility,' 'obligation.' They may be as wide or as narrow as you please. 'Ought,' like 'right' and 'wrong,' refers to conformity to a given standard. Everything *ought* to be *right*. 'Virtue' itself, though usually restricted to moral goodness, is sometimes applied to the valuable properties of inanimate substances. It must not be supposed that this ambiguity is due to any peculiar poverty of the English language. Other languages show a similar condition. Our language has, indeed, two important common terms that are regularly used in an ethical significance, — 'conscience' and 'duty.' But one hears too of an 'æsthetic conscience.' And the word 'duties' is often used to denote merely what a man is employed to perform — a sense far too narrow for ethical purposes. Consequently, if the student does not already know pretty well what 'morality' means, no definition that we can give is likely to be of much use to him. The only ready device that could be used to cure his ignorance would be a list of typical actions and traits of character to which moral predicates are applied.

Two Kinds of Moral Valuation. — The fact that our language, like many others, has two common pairs of terms by which to denote moral distinctions is significant. It points to two markedly different attitudes toward the moral problems of daily life, from which important differences in ethical theory have arisen. 'Good' and 'bad' are names for positive and negative values, which are attributed both to conduct and to character. Various grades of 'better' and 'worse' are recognized, with the zero-point of the

6 INTRODUCTION TO THE SCIENCE OF ETHICS

'indifferent' somewhere between. 'Right' and 'wrong' also express a kind of valuation; but they are directly applicable only to conduct, and only indirectly to the author of the conduct. 'Right' denotes agreement with a certain standard, and hence it is not properly susceptible of degrees. Furthermore, there is no zero-point: an act is either right or not right, and if not right it is wrong. There may be degrees of wrongness, but only in the sense of amount of departure from the standard of rightness.

Examples. — There is perhaps no way in which the student can better be introduced to the study of ethics than by setting before him examples of these two types of moral valuation — the *personal* and the *impersonal*, as we may call them. The examples which we shall use for this purpose would have been so familiar to the reader of a generation or two ago, that the barest reference would have been sufficient. One may wish that this were the case to-day. The first, illustrating the personal type of valuation, consists of the concluding words of a speech of a rude shepherd, whose younger brother — whom he has promised his aged father to protect — has been convicted of a serious theft and condemned to slavery:

" Now therefore when I come to thy servant my father, and the lad is not with us; seeing that his life is bound up with the lad's life; it will come to pass, when he seeth that the lad is not with us, that he will die: and thy servants will bring down the gray hairs of thy servant our father with sorrow to Sheol. For thy servant became surety for the lad unto my father, saying, If I bring him not unto thee, then shall I bear the blame to my father for ever. Now therefore, let thy servant, I pray thee, abide instead of the lad a bondman to my lord; and let the lad go up with his brethren. For how shall I go up to my father, if the lad is not with me? lest I see the evil that shall come on my father." [1]

[1] *Genesis* xliv. 30–34; American Standard Version.

The second example exhibits a contrast to the first, which is all the more striking because it too involves the fulfillment of a promise; not, however, to a man, but to a tribal God. A chieftain, going out to battle, has vowed that if he returns victorious he will offer up as a burnt sacrifice whatever first comes out of his house to meet him; and his daughter, an only child, is the first to appear:

"And it came to pass, when he saw her, that he rent his clothes, and said, Alas, my daughter! thou hast brought me very low, and thou art one of them that trouble me; for I have opened my mouth unto Jehovah, and I cannot go back. And she said unto him, My father, thou hast opened thy mouth unto Jehovah; do unto me that which hath proceeded out of thy mouth, forasmuch as Jehovah hath taken vengeance for thee on thine enemies, even on the children of Ammon." [1]

These examples might be paralleled without end; but we shall limit ourselves to a third example, in which the personal and impersonal types of moral valuation are seen *in conflict*. A religious teacher and certain of his followers are walking through the grainfields on the sabbath day; and the latter have plucked some of the ears, thus technically breaking an ancient and venerated law, and arousing the criticism of punctilious lovers of the law:

"And he said unto them, Did ye never read what David did, when he had need, and was hungry, he, and they that were with him? How he entered into the house of God when Abiathar was high priest, and ate the show-bread, which it is not lawful to eat save for the priests, and gave also to them that were with him?"

And the whole issue is immediately summed up in the sentence that has passed into a proverb: "The sabbath was made for man, and not man for the sabbath." [2]

[1] *Judges* xi. 35–36.   [2] *Mark* ii. 23 ff.

II. THE RELATIONS OF ETHICS

With Politics. — Ethics stands in very close relations with several other sciences. In the first place, it is intimately connected with political theory. (1) When ethics is regarded as primarily the theory of happiness, the investigator soon discovers that political conditions have much to do in determining the happiness or unhappiness of whole peoples. To distinguish between the two sciences, ethics may be regarded as treating of the conditions of happiness so far as these are under the control of the individual; while to politics is left the problem of determining how the general happiness may be determined by wise government. Sometimes, indeed, the two sciences are regarded as essentially one. Politics may be treated as a department of ethics; or ethics may be treated (as by Aristotle) as an introduction to politics. (2) When ethics is viewed as treating primarily of the moral distinctions, the connection with politics is equally close. For one of the most important functions of the state is the establishment of justice within its borders, that is to say, the enforcement of certain moral standards. And when it appears that the state is not adequately fulfilling this function, but that its laws are at various points in conflict with the ideal standards of justice, an ethical question arises, whether the duty of the individual citizen is not to obey the laws of the land, imperfect as they may be, while, if possible, laboring for their amendment. Besides, in the dealings of states with each other, many questions as to rights and duties arise, which a comprehensive treatment of moral distinctions cannot wholly ignore.

With Æsthetics and Economics. — In the second place, ethics is related to æsthetics and economics. These also treat of values; the one of beauty and such allied values as the sublime, the tragic, and the comic; the other of exchange-values. Some thinkers have pushed the connection between ethics and æsthetics so close, that moral goodness has been regarded as a mere species of beauty, correlative with the beauty of sounds and shapes and colors. Certain it is that moral goodness often strikes us as beautiful or sublime, and that vicious suggestions may be a serious blemish upon an otherwise beautiful work of art. However, many ethicists have regarded moral goodness as so widely different from all other values, that the analogy with beauty has been lightly esteemed or altogether denied. It may be added that some writers, to whom the conception of conformity to a fixed type has seemed all-important, have found a relationship between ethics and formal logic. For formal logic, too, deals with fixed standards. The canons of correct reasoning must be observed, or the demonstration is fallacious; and there is no middle ground between validity and invalidity. Here also the analogy has sometimes been pushed to extremes, and morality has been regarded as a species of truth. The connection of ethics with economics is seemingly not so close as with æsthetics, though many similar phenomena are to be observed in the two fields. Just, for example, as the increased scarcity of a needed article brings about a rise in its price, so the estimation in which a virtue is popularly held is affected by its rarity. Among a licentious people the chaste man is a saint. Among the deceitful Greeks the hero Achilles was admired for nothing more than for his absolute lack of guile.

With the Theory of Values. — Ethics, æsthetics, and economics may all be regarded as subordinate to a general science of values. Only in recent years has such a separate science been organized under the name of ' axiology,' or the ' theory of values.' But from the earliest times discussions of this nature have formed a part of the foundations of ethics. " What is good? " was one of the first questions to be asked when scientific attention began to turn to the problems of human life. The specifically ethical question, " What is happiness?" — that is to say: What is the sort of experience which is good in itself, and not simply as a necessary condition for some other experience? — only gradually distinguished itself from this more general inquiry.

With Sociology. — Since the origin (in the nineteenth century) of a distinct science of social institutions, called 'sociology,' its contact with ethics has been unbroken.[1] Moral sentiments are recognized as one of the great forces by which the customs and forms of organization of societies are shaped. Contrariwise, the customs and organizations are almost universally believed to be an essential factor in the maintenance and development of moral sentiments. Religious, political, commercial institutions all have their influence upon the moral life; none more than that oldest of institutions, which under various transformations has come down to us from the very beginnings of civilization, and has its roots in the instinctive traits of our prehuman ancestors, — the family. Consequently the study of social institutions, while it cannot for the purposes of ethics take the place of the study of the moral consciousness itself, is capable of illustrating it most admirably, and of casting light upon many of its most obscure problems.

With Psychology. — In common with all the other mental sciences, ethics is dependent upon the general science of mind, psychology. But the precise nature of this dependency is one of the most hotly debated questions of the present day. At one extreme are those who regard ethics as a branch of psychology, and particularly of social psychology. At the other extreme are those who declare that psychology is utterly incompetent to decide a single ethical question. The controversy is complicated by the fact that there exist two distinct types of psychological theory, the structural and the

---

[1] It should be observed that the sense in which this word is used still fluctuates widely. As we use it here it does not include social psychology, the importance of which for ethics is doubtless even greater.

functional; and the relation of ethics to each of these is matter for controversy. Meanwhile all are agreed that the ethicist must make constant use of psychological data and methods; and this is, after all, the most important point for us to note. When, as is often the case, the study of ethics is begun without a previous grounding in the elements of psychology, some attempt must be made to remedy the deficiency as occasion arises.

The ' is ' *versus* the ' ought to be.' — There is one phase of this controversy which we cannot pass over without notice. Psychology, it is said, treats simply of what is, and has no concern with what ought to be, and hence the distinctions between good and bad, right and wrong, do not fall within its province; while ethics is precisely the science of what ought to be, regardless of what is. Such a statement is open to criticism. For a peculiar form of ethical theory is suggested which in our day has few defenders. All admit, to be sure, that the mere fact that a condition of affairs exists, or that an act is commonly performed, does not prove it to be right. But that the standards of right and wrong are absolutely independent of circumstances of every sort — that under all possible conditions, in all ages and climes and in all stages of social development, the same laws of righteousness hold sway — is not so clear; and, if true, it is not to be lightly taken for granted. So weighty a doctrine ought not to be hidden away under cover of a verbal antithesis.

III. ETHICS AS A THEORETICAL SCIENCE AND AS THE PHILOSOPHY OF PRACTICE

Theoretical and Practical Sciences. — Sciences are sometimes classified as *theoretical sciences* and *practical sciences* (or *arts*). A theoretical science is the system of existing knowledge of a given subject-matter. The mathematical sciences, physics, chemistry, biology, and economics, are examples of such sciences. A practical science is a systematic body of knowledge bearing upon the accomplishment of *a given end.* The sciences of medicine and pedagogy are obviously of this kind.

Ethics belongs on both sides of the classification. It is a theoretical science having as its subject-matter the moral distinctions. But it is also a practical science, having as its object the assurance of happiness.

Philosophy and the Special Sciences. — There is another familiar division of the sciences, into *philosophy* and the *special sciences.* The difference is here one of comprehensiveness and generality. Here again ethics belongs on both sides. As the science of morality it is a special science, comprised, along with economics and æsthetics, under the general theory of values. But as a practical science it is not simply one among others. It is the art of life, having as its object the establishment of a universal policy. In this aspect, therefore, it is philosophical.

In this introductory study, we shall consider ethics primarily as a special theoretical science, paying only secondary attention to its significance as the philosophy of practice.

REFERENCES

HIBBEN, J. G., *The Problems of Philosophy*, Ch. VIII.
PALMER, G. H., *The Field of Ethics* (contains many further references).
DEWEY and TUFTS, *Ethics*, Ch. XI.
SIDGWICK, H., *History of Ethics*, Ch. I., and *Methods of Ethics*, Book I, Chs. I, II.
The opening chapters of the text-books of Mezes, Mackenzie, Muirhead, and Hyslop.

CHAPTER II

THE METHODS OF ETHICS

Empiricism *vs.* **Rationalism.** — The methods which have been used in ethical speculation have been to a varying extent affected by the views which philosophers have held with regard to the nature of scientific method generally. Of these views the two principal types are *empiricism* and *rationalism*. According to the former, all scientific truth is established by *induction*, that is to say, by deriving general rules from the comparison of particular instances, and by the gradual correction of one's theories through noting and taking account of the exceptions to them. Some empiricists — notably Socrates and Francis Bacon — have believed that absolutely certain truth could be obtained by such means; but for the most part it has been admitted that the best of theories is ever liable to correction in the light of some new observation. According to the rationalistic view, the first principles of science are all self-evident. They are either *definitions* or *intuitions of reason,* and in either case need no support from particular instances. Other laws can be regarded as properly established, only when they have been deduced from these first principles. Particular facts may suggest or illustrate the truth, but no number or variety of them can prove it. Geometry has always been the model science of the rationalist. Its axioms are his favorite examples of self-evident truths; and its consecutive demonstrations are to him the perfection of method. The geometrician uses particular figures in his work, but only for their suggestive value. He never imagines that by heaping up instances he can

14 INTRODUCTION TO THE SCIENCE OF ETHICS

strengthen the evidence in favor of any of his theorems. His proofs are strictly universal in their scope.

Between the extreme views various compromises have been made. Very generally it has been held that science has two distinct stages, the inductive and the deductive, and that the former is an indispensable prelude to the latter. Thus Aristotle believed that the first principles of science must first be brought to our attention by the devious and uncertain process of induction, but that when found they are perfectly evident in their own right. Experience, for example, has led us to notice that the straight line is the shortest between any two points; but once noticed it is in need of no experimental evidence. Many ancient and modern writers have adopted this view. It is a modification of Plato's, who believed that in order to pass from the imperfect truths of induction to the single supreme principle (for he thought that there was but one), no further induction, no further reference to particular instances, is necessary; but that by gradually removing the self-contradictions, which a rigorous analysis shows the inductive truths to contain, the perfect truth can ultimately be reached. This mode of procedure he called ' dialectic.'

Ethics as an Empirical Science. — Ethics is the oldest science to which inductive methods have been consciously and deliberately applied. Inductive reasoning has, of course, been employed since men were men. But so far as we know, Socrates (who was one of the founders of moral science) was the first to employ it with a distinct conception of its nature; and ethics (including political theory) was almost the sole field in which he was interested. According to him the object of scientific inquiry was to frame clear and consistent *definitions;* for example, definitions of justice, courage, piety, and the like. Taking any proposed definition as a starting-point, his practice was to question the one who had offered it, with regard to *border-line instances,* which would serve to show wherein the definition was too narrow or too broad — where it failed to include what the given term was obviously meant to cover, and where it actually included cases to which the term would never be applied. As each exception was pointed out, the interlocutor was invited to revise his definition accordingly, the hope being that a satisfactory form might thus ultimately be given to it. Ordinarily, however, this was not accomplished, and the interlocutor gave up the task in despair. The inquiry was then either dropped or continued in a *deductive* fashion — starting from commonly accepted premises which both parties were willing to admit as probably true, and leading up to the matter in hand. It is, however, to the first (inductive) part of the inquiry, with its generally negative conclusion, that the term 'Socratic method' is strictly applied; and it is obviously to this method of procedure that he mainly trusted for the improvement of his own insight as well as for the real instruction of his companions.

It might be supposed, therefore, that ethics would be regarded as the inductive science *par excellence*, and its later history throughout antiquity would tend to confirm this impression. Plato, indeed, looked forward to the construction of a purely deductive ethics as one of the great desiderata of philosophy. But his own speculation in this field was mainly inductive; and the literary expression of his results is in the form of Socratic dialogues. With his great pupil Aristotle, ethics is again confessedly an inductive science. "We must start," he says, "from the known. But this may mean either of two distinct things: 'what is *known to us*' [*i.e.* the data of experience], or, 'what is *certain*' [*i.e.* the truths of intuition]. It is clear that it is for us to start from what is known to us." Accordingly Aristotle is careful to call attention to the merely approximate truth and the 'practical' value of ethical principles. In fact, of all the ancient ethicists, the only ones to rely to any great extent upon mere deduction were the cynics and stoics; and, as we shall hereafter see, even in their case the most interesting part of the theory is largely inductive.

Rationalistic Ethics. — In modern times, however, a very strong tendency has shown itself, to distrust and avoid the use of induction in ethics, as if it were somehow unworthy of the subject. Especially among ethicists who give prominence to the impersonal standards of *duty*, it has been felt that the validity of moral standards must be absolutely certain and unconditional; and induction, it seemed, could never vindicate for them more than a merely relative force. So the attempt has repeatedly been made to give ethics a purely deductive form, and, especially, to find a body of self-evident truths from which the whole moral law could be clearly demonstrated. The *intuitionalist*, for example, looks upon the fundamental moral laws as so many axioms, precisely like the axioms of geometry, the absolute cogency of which cannot be doubted by any man who understands the terms in which they are expressed. Upon these axioms, a system of morals, like another geometry, must be built up; and the conclusions that are reached may be applied in common life with the same assurance as a demonstrated theorem of Euclid. It has not been uncommon for philosophers who exhibited in the main an empiricistic tendency, to insist that ethics, like mathematics, is (or can be made) a purely deductive science.[1]

The Genetic Method. — Since the middle of the eighteenth century a modification of the inductive method has been perfected, which during the last fifty years has become

[1] The so-called 'critical method' of Kant is not a distinct method of the same order as induction and deduction. It consists (so far as ethics is concerned) in a *deductive* analysis of *what is implied in the mere supposition that absolute moral laws exist.* Kant tries to show that the whole system of ethics can be derived from this one supposition, which (as he further believes) no rational being can avoid making. A dialectic method, similar to that advocated by Plato, has been attempted in modern times, notably by Hegel.

increasingly important for ethics. This is the *genetic method* of analysis. In general terms the method may be described as follows. The key to the structure and functions of any complex organic or social type is to be found in its past. What appears to be inextricably confused in the later form becomes simple and distinct in the earlier; and by following the development step by step the later confusion can be reduced to an orderly plan. The circumstances of each change, if these can be ascertained, are an indication of its meaning and importance. For every organism or organization stands in constant dependence upon its environment; and its whole development is subject to the necessity of readjustment to meet altered conditions in the environment.

Its Application to Ethics. — As applied to ethics, this means that the morality of the adult is to be explained by reference to the morality of the growing child; that the morality of civilized races is to be explained by reference to the customs and ideals of their ruder ancestors, as well as of other peoples by whom these were in any degree affected. Thus, if the problem were to explain the moral obligations of the modern European husband, most ethicists would not be content to ascribe them to the outcropping of an innate human sense for the requirements of the marriage relation. We should rather attempt to trace their development from the days when the wife was but a piece of property transferable at will — yes, further back, if it were possible, to the time when mutual affection and helpfulness and common attachment to the dependent offspring were the sole bonds between the ape-like human pair. Or, to take a narrower instance, if we were asked to account for the prohibition-sentiment in this country, we should not be apt to attribute it to the force of an innate human conviction that the use of intoxicating beverages is wrong. We should more probably attempt to trace its rise from the time when it was a mark of sobriety in a man to get drunk but half-a-dozen times a year, or even from the time when nightly drunkenness was looked forward to as one of the future rewards of the brave and just. The purpose in these inquiries would not be the learning of an interesting story. It would be *the more thorough analysis and understanding of the present moral consciousness itself*, — to perceive, for example, how much of it (if any) was instinctive, how much cultivated benevolence, how much respect for custom, how much prudential regard for economic conditions, how much religious feeling. For all these things and many more may be included in an apparently simple ' ought ' — or so the ethicists of to-day generally believe.[1]

Use of Ethnological Material. — The application of the genetic method to ethics would be a simpler matter, if our records of old moral standards and of the ways in which men viewed them were more complete. Not that we need a universal history of mankind; much less than that would make an ample basis for all our theorizing. But even in the case of the peoples of whom we know most, our information dwindles away rapidly as we go back of the period of the invention of writing. There are, to be sure, records of oral

[1] Attention must here be called to a serious and widespread error concerning the use of the genetic method. It is the supposition that by this method the developed form is explained in terms of its *origin*, in the sense of the *original simple form* from which it has sprung. Sometimes the assertion is even made, that since an absolute beginning can never be exhibited, the genetic method cannot really explain anything. Now the fact is, as we shall quickly show, that the use of the genetic method has nothing to do with the notion of an absolute beginning. Many of its ablest exponents would question whether any beginnings are ever absolute and would incline to the opinion that they are merely arbitrary and conventional assumptions of ours. It is true that the earlier stages of a development, as compared with the later stages, have a *peculiar* value for the method; but they have not a *greater* value. And if a choice were to be made, it is the later stages — those more closely resembling the form that is to be analyzed — that would have the preference.

Suppose, for example, it is the adult human brain that is to be analyzed. This is an organ of such extreme complexity, that, to a direct examination, it is utterly baffling. How does the anatomist proceed? In the first place, he arranges in an ordered series the brains of many other vertebrates, from

traditions which date from earlier centuries. But such traditions may become so seriously modified in the course of time, and so encrusted over with later material, as to be recognized only with great difficulty and uncertainty. Now the period before the invention of writing is of immense importance for genetic study. We are fortunate, therefore, in being able to supplement our records by a comparison with the savage and barbarous peoples that still exist — just as the paleontologist pieces out the geological record of the extinct forms of life upon the earth, by noting the survivals of the old types which still, in one place or another, have managed to persist. Much caution is of course necessary. It is not as if, while our race was steadily progressing, these simpler peoples were retaining unchanged the beliefs and practices of their ancestors — though at the same time it must not be supposed that social changes go on everywhere at anything like the same rate. But by a careful comparison it is possible in many cases to show important analogies between the morality of the backward peoples and our own

the lowest fishes to the anthropoid apes, which, on various grounds, he supposes may preserve the traits of man's ancestors. The brain of the chimpanzee is like a map of the human brain; the brain of the fish is like a schematic diagram. Starting from the latter, and running his eye along the series, he sees the baffling complexity of the human brain sort itself out before him. In the second place, he examines the brains of human embryos of every stage; and here again, as he passes from the simpler to the more complex, if he can but follow the dividing strands of the development, the problem of analysis is well advanced toward its solution. But the fish or the fish-like embryo, taken by itself, would be of very limited significance. The anatomist could learn something from it; but it would be of a very superficial and uncertain sort. It is the development that is instructive; and it is the more instructive, the fewer and slighter are the gaps in the record, and the farther back it can be extended. But, when they are taken by themselves, one chimpanzee is worth a thousand fishes.

Similarly, if it is the vocabulary of the English language that is studied, it is important to trace it to its Latin, Anglo-Saxon, and other sources. For a scientific knowledge of the English of to-day, a knowledge of Latin is indispensable. But, taken by itself, it is sufficient only to give one a superficial and dangerous conceit of knowledge.

primitive morality, and by more or less probable surmises to extend the historical record back far beyond the time when all direct evidences cease.

Survivals of Barbarism in Civilization. — Moreover, the survivals of old culture are not simply to be found among the backward peoples. They are present in ourselves. Consider, for example, the way in which the young girl is commonly taught to regard her chastity — as a precious possession which once lost can never be regained; as a kind of purity which, once contaminated, can never be restored to its former state. There is a certain amount of truth, no doubt, in these old conceptions; and yet at times they are brought into the most violent conflict with higher and better views. That a single slip on the part of an unprotected and sorely tempted girl may doom her, in her own eyes as well as in those of the whole community, to a lifelong degradation, is barbarism pure and simple. And it may help us to understand how our barbarian forbears felt about many other matters.

The Morality of Childhood. — Finally, the two genetic series, the development of the individual and the development of society, may be expected to illuminate each other at many points. Up to the present time, however, childish morality has been very inadequately studied. The practical problems of moral education have, indeed, received the attention of many of the greatest and noblest thinkers. But the more fundamental theoretical problem of distinguishing the characteristic childish ways of thinking and feeling about moral distinctions is still in a very unsatisfactory condition. Less help, therefore, can be derived from this source than the ethicist would wish.

Value of the Genetic Method. — The genetic study of morality has not made the older direct methods superfluous — if only because it is always in terms of the inner life of to-day that the records of the past must be interpreted. This fact has been used by thinkers of conservative tendencies to discredit the value of genetic studies. If the study of our own morality must give us the terms in which to understand that of primitive man, how can the knowledge of the latter help us to interpret the former? Is not the whole genetic procedure a vicious circle? But, after all, the case is much the same as with our understanding of one another. No one of us can see directly into another's heart. We must interpret one another's words, actions, gestures, in terms of what we ourselves have thought and felt. Nevertheless we know that a richer self-knowledge is thus gained. The wise saying of Schiller applies without modification to the study of primitive man:

"Wouldst thou thyself discern, then see how the others are living. Wouldst thou the others know — look into thine own heart."

Moral Dynamics. — One result of the genetic study of morality has been to bring into prominence a new set of ethical problems, concerned with the discovery of the *factors of moral evolution* and the laws of their operation. These problems bring our attention forcibly back to the direct analysis of our own moral consciousness. Historical records at the best are disconnected. It is hard to catch in the act the most important changes. Their significance was not fully felt at the time, and their gradual stages passed unnoticed. *Moral dynamics* can be studied to the greatest advantage in the present or in the very recent past. Our own day is one of rapid moral changes. The social and economic transformations brought about by the varied utilization of steam and electricity and by the rise of the corporation of limited liabilities are having their inevitable effect upon traditional standards of right and wrong. Never was there a time when the ethicist could study to better advantage the phenomena of moral progress. The civilized world has become a veritable laboratory for his use.

REFERENCES

ARISTOTLE, *Nichomachean Ethics*, Book I, Chs. I–IV.
WUNDT, W., *Ethics*, Introduction.
SETH, J., *A Study of Ethical Principles*, Introduction, Ch. I.
TAYLOR, A. E., *The Problem of Conduct*, Ch. I.
LEVY-BRUHL, L., *Ethics and Moral Science*.
STEPHEN, L., *Science of Ethics*, Ch. I.
HOBHOUSE, L. T., *Morals in Evolution*, Part I, Ch. I.
DEWEY, J., *The Evolutionary Method as applied to Morality*, Philosophical Review, 1902, pp. 107–124, 353–371.

CHAPTER III

THE FIELD OF MORAL JUDGMENTS

I. Character and Conduct

Order of Procedure. — When one attempts a systematic account of so complex a matter as morality, it is not easy to find a natural order of procedure. On every page one finds oneself taking for granted positions which are justified only on some later page; and when the attempt is made to reverse the order of exposition, no improvement is effected. In the case of ethics a partial remedy for this difficulty lies in the fact that the reader knows a good deal about morality already, if only in an uncritical, common-sense fashion; so that except where our own conclusions fly in the face of common sense, we can presume upon this prior knowledge. The difficulty is greatest where we touch on questions upon which a wide difference of opinion exists. Here we must (until we have had time to discuss these questions on our own account) adopt a middle-of-the-road policy, expressing ourselves in ways that will not be grossly inconsistent with any of the more important theories. And we shall be the more justified in this course, because, as a matter of fact, there is reason to think that in none of the great ethical controversies has any side been wholly right or wholly wrong.

The Study of Moral Judgments. — One of the oldest and most persistent grounds of difference has been the question whether morality is essentially (or predominantly) a matter of *feeling* or a matter of *judgment*. In the following chapters we shall take for granted that both feeling and judgment are essential, and easily and quickly pass into each other, though at any given time either may operate without the other.

Because the moral judgment is, in general, clearer and steadier than the feeling, and hence more readily referred to, we shall for the most part (where it does not matter otherwise) speak in terms of the judgment.

The Question before Us. — The study of moral judgments involves two main questions: first, What is the *field* within which we employ them, or to what kinds of things do they apply? and, secondly, What is their *significance*, or how do we intend to characterize the things to which we apply them? In logical terms, we need an account of the *subjects* and the *predicates* of these judgments. The present chapter will try to furnish an answer to the first question, so far as it can be done without anticipating our answer to the second — or, at least, without anticipating it any farther than common sense will authorize us in doing.

General Answer. — In a general way the answer which we seek is obvious enough. Moral judgments apply to character and to conduct. We may, perhaps, go farther and say that they apply to *character as it shows itself in conduct*, and to *conduct as it springs from the agent's character;* but this will need some justification.

Objections: (1) In the first place, it may be objected that character may be good or bad without showing itself in conduct; just as a talent may slumber in obscurity and be none the less real for that. Suppose a brave man dwelling in the midst of perfect security, or a man with the heart of a tyrant born to the life of a slave. Opportunity may give him the chance to exhibit his true self in action; but, if not, is not the one still brave and the other still tyrannical?

Suppose we admit this — though we shall soon find that the admission means less than at first sight appears. Nevertheless it remains true, that if we are to judge of a man's character, his conduct must ever be our surest evidence; and this holds, even of ourselves. There are secondary indications, to be sure: features and tones of voice, and (in our own case) feelings and opinions in plenty. But, after all, "the tree is known by its fruits." Experience has shown us only too well that a benevolent countenance may be the mask of cruelty, and that nothing is more deceptive than the fine feelings in which we luxuriate without putting them into effect. If there is actionless virtue, it is an unknown quantity — what the philosopher calls a 'thing-in-itself.' However, we must beware of taking the term 'conduct' too narrowly. The crouch must be counted as well as the spring. A good part of conduct consists in preparing ourselves for future contingencies, in assuming *attitudes* upon various issues; and this sort of conduct is observable both in ourselves and in others. "Thou shalt not covet" may be kept or broken as clearly as "Thou shalt not steal."

(2) In the second place, it may be said that conduct may be right or wrong in itself, wholly apart from the character that prompts it. A gift of money to the poor may spring from charity or from hypocrisy; but in either case is not the act itself right? Would you feel warranted in advising the giver to withhold his gift? Again, if the act were a theft, would you stop to inquire what the agent's motives were before pronouncing it wrong? What if it were an act of sacrilege or treason?

There are at least two distinct misunderstandings involved in this objection. It should be remembered that it is through men's conduct that we judge of their character; and this has to be done, more or less, by *general rules*. Now there are some deeds that we commonly condemn on sight, without reflection. In such cases we need not stop to inquire about motives, because the conduct itself is warrant for attributing an evil character to the agent. But so far from its being true that we judge the act and not the man, we are very apt to judge the man *too harshly*. We dub the man who has committed a single theft a 'thief,' and that may be a cruel exaggeration.

But the other misunderstanding is more serious. It consists in picking out a single act from the course of conduct of which it is a part, and insisting that there is nothing wrong with it, in itself. As well pick a single phrase out of an incorrect sentence, and say: "Is there anything intrinsically wrong in this?" The hypocritical gift does not stand by itself. It belongs to a general policy. To say that it is right as far as it goes means only that the wrongness lies elsewhere; and it is far from justifying the inference, that conduct may be judged one way and character the other.

Restatement. — What we suggested may, therefore, be affirmed with some confidence; namely, that moral judgments apply to character and conduct simultaneously, though with varying emphasis upon the one or the other. Men are such as their deeds declare them; and to judge a deed is to judge the character of him who would commit it.

II. THE MORAL AGENT

Capacity for Deliberation and Self-judgment. — But who are the men, and what are the deeds, that we judge? The men are obviously those whom we regard as capable of some *deliberation.* The baby, who acts from sheer impulse, upon the latest suggestion that has entered his head, we do not think of judging morally. We call it a 'good' or a 'bad' baby, but that means no more than 'comfortable' or 'troublesome.' Similarly with the grossly imbecile and the insane: we do not count them as moral agents. But a capacity for deliberation is not enough. The good or bad man must be capable of *passing a moral judgment upon his own acts.* This is probably why we do not regard as moral agents even the highest of the lower animals. For though scientists believe that they are almost entirely incapable of deliberation, this is not the popular opinion; but few men have been willing to accredit them with a moral faculty. The utmost that even their good friend Darwin could say was that "dogs have something very like a conscience." On the other hand, as we are very apt to attribute to little children thoughts and feelings like our own, we are inclined to pass moral judgments on them from a very early age.

Moral Judgments on Animals and Things among Savages. — Here it may be objected, that while we may limit our moral judgments in this way, all men are not in accord with us. Many peoples have pronounced moral judgments freely upon animals and even upon inanimate objects. The savage is righteously indignant at the cocoanut which falls upon his head and thinks it treachery in the spear that it fails to strike the game; and he *punishes* them accordingly. If a tiger has killed his near kinsman, he seeks it out and compasses its death with as strong a sense of duty as if it were a human criminal. But this is because the savage does not draw the line between rational and irrational or unconscious beings, as we do. He thinks of the offending cocoanut either as alive and spiteful, or, at least, as harboring a malicious sprite, whom he tries to reach; while the animals are regarded as being in all essential respects like men. Properly viewed, therefore, there is here rather a confirmation than a contradiction of the view expressed above.

Similar Phenomena among More Advanced Peoples. — It may still, however, be said that among many peoples far removed from primitive savagery the legal punishment of animals and inanimate things for murder has been kept up for a long time. Athens had a special court for such cases; and the great Plato in his model code of laws gave it his indorsement (*Laws*, 873 E–874 A). The man-slaying animal was killed, and either animal or thing was thrown outside the borders. By the early Hebrew law, "If an ox gore a man or woman to death, the ox shall be surely stoned [like a man that had committed a foul crime] and its flesh shall not be eaten." (*Exodus* xxi. 28.) Similar practices were found in Europe in the middle ages, and vestiges of them remained down to the nineteenth century.

Explanation. — But here there are evidently several factors involved. In the first place, legal forms are wonderfully tenacious, and are often preserved when they lead to consequences that are generally acknowledged to be foolish or positively harmful. Our own legal procedure is notoriously full of instances. In the second place, the 'punishment' may be a precautionary measure. It may prevent the repetition of a real danger. And where there is no real danger (as in the case of a knife that has fallen on a man), superstition readily imagines one. Bad magic or ill luck may attach to it. The shedding of human blood is especially thought of as causing a *pollution* that must be removed. That is why the Athenians 'banished' the fatal thing or the carcass of the fatal animal; and that is why the Hebrews were forbidden to eat the murderous ox. Or an accidental death may be supposed to indicate some divine displeasure. So the English law of the *deodand* (repealed only in 1846) directed that a thing which had caused a man's death should be confiscated and sold for charity, in order that God's wrath might be appeased — though the innocent owner might thereby suffer a ruinous loss. Here again the legal practice long outlived the superstition. In the third place, though we may no longer judge animals or things as we should moral beings, we are quite capable of being *angry* with them, and even of hating them. And so, unless we are unusually enlightened, we like to vent our ill feeling on the thing that has deeply hurt us. Finally, even though we may cherish no ill feeling, we like to have a thing to which evil associations cling put out of the way.

We have, therefore, no reason to infer that any moral judgment is involved in the matter, or to suppose that such a judgment is ever passed except upon agents who are conceived to possess the power of deliberation and moral judgment.

III. Extent of Moral Conduct

Moral Conduct is Voluntary. — The conduct that we judge must, if it springs from the agent's character, be *voluntary* — at least in the sense that his body must not be the helpless tool of a superior power. Ordinarily, we may add that the agent must not be coerced by intense pain or fear; for except under special mental conditions — say the enthusiasm of an heroic purpose — pain or fear may move our limbs as irresistibly as any external force, and so we do not blame a man for what he does under such circumstances.

Deliberate and Unreflecting Acts. — From what has been said above we may infer that the conduct that is open to moral judgment consists *primarily* of deliberate acts, and especially of acts which the agents themselves are thought to have judged; for except for these we should not regard the agents as moral beings at all. But we do not stop here. If the man is *capable* of deliberation and moral judgment, he need not show his capacity in each and every case. We freely approve or disapprove his most unreflecting acts. The very fact that a man did *not* stop to reflect may exhibit him to us all the more vividly as a hero or as a villain. How is this to be accounted for? The explanation comes to us from Aristotle. Our unreflective actions are (generally speaking) the result of *habit*. But our habits are formed by acts which in the first instance are more or less deliberate, — as the trite example of learning to play a piece of music sufficiently illustrates. Our habitual conduct is thus, to a large extent, what our deliberate conduct has made it. Consequently, habitual conduct is *indirectly* subject to moral judgment as being an evidence of what deliberate conduct has been, and hence of what the agent's character was and is.

Conduct preceded by a Moral Judgment. — We may add to this that conduct which is preceded by a moral judgment as to the rightness or wrongness of the contemplated course of action has an especially important part in the shaping of character and of future conduct, and may well be considered as the moral conduct *par excellence*. Many ethicists, ancient and modern, have even held that no act is morally good, if it is done for any other reason than that it is the right thing to do; and in modern times Immanuel Kant insisted that if there is the least *admixture* of any other motive, — say love for one's friend or country, — the act loses all its moral worth. This last view may be set aside as an exaggeration; and, indeed, Kant himself admitted that on his theory we should have no logical ground for believing that an act with any degree of goodness at all had ever been committed.

Summary. — If we reflect how our conduct upon one occasion helps to determine how we shall behave upon another occasion, we shall have no difficulty in seeing that *almost all* our voluntary conduct is, directly or indirectly, *open* to praise or blame: first, acts that are accompanied by a moral judgment; next, deliberate acts in general; and finally, habitual acts. If there are any exceptions, they must spring from original instincts that have been unreached by conscious control; and in the well-grown child, not to speak of the adult man, such acts are of very slight importance.

The Correction of Habits. — There is another side of the matter, of which we must also take account. We frequently judge habitual acts in this sense, that we hold that the habits which they exhibit *ought to be corrected*. (Less important are the favorable judgments, that the habits need no correction.) The habits are wrong, we say; and this means, not so much that they have been wrongly incurred, as that the agent would do wrong *to continue to indulge them*. The judgment thus looks forward, rather than back. But it equally involves an indirect moral judgment upon deliberate, morally controlled acts; namely, the acts by which the habits in question are conceived to be corrected or tolerated. This sort of judgment is particularly important, as it is a means by which we call men's attention to their evil habits and thus, perhaps, bring about their correction. When we have declared to a man that one of his habits is wrong, it is no longer a *mere* habit, but a habit which has been brought before his own moral judgment; and his later persistence in such conduct must be judged accordingly.

Morally Indifferent Conduct. — It should be observed that the fact that almost all our conduct is open to moral judgment does not imply that if any given act were judged, it would necessarily be found to be appreciably good or bad. The vast majority of our acts are, so far as we know, indifferent. Of course we never stop to judge more than a petty fraction of them; and we should quickly defeat our own ends if we should attempt to do so.

IV. CONTENT OF THE MORAL ACT

1. *The Problem*

Complexity of Deliberate Conduct. — The question may be raised, how much the act, as a subject of moral judgment, comprehends. For a deliberate act is a fairly complicated phenomenon. Let us take an example. A cowboy, who has lost his money at gambling, is weary of the hard life of the ranch and longs for a debauch in town. *He tampers with a railroad switch.* The train, he thinks, will certainly be derailed; all on board will be more or less shaken up; and some may be seriously injured or even killed. The thought makes him wince, though he has seen bloodshed more than once; but he is unwilling to go back to the ranch, and he must have his fling. In the confusion, he counts upon being able to surprise and overawe the passengers and crew, kill any one who attempts resistance, and make off with the valuable contents of the express car. What actu-

32 INTRODUCTION TO THE SCIENCE OF ETHICS

ally happens is, that while the train is partly derailed, no serious injury results, and the man himself is wounded and taken prisoner.

Analysis. — Here we may easily distinguish between the *external* side of the act, as it might have been seen by a favorably situated spectator, and the *internal* side, or *volition*, of which only the agent himself could be directly aware. The former, we may say, contains the *physical act* itself — the voluntary movements made in tampering with the switch — and the *actual consequences* which followed from it. These consequences were in part *foreseen*, but for the most part *unforeseen*, by the agent. Again, the volition contains two parts or factors — we need not now ask which term is more appropriate. In the first place, there is the emotional factor, the combination of *motives* which urge the man to persist in, or refrain from, his act: discontent, greed, lust, etc., on the one hand, and pity and fear, on the other. (The stronger emotions, which dominate the act, are often called simply ' the motive.') In the second place, there is the intellectual factor, or *intention;* that is to say, the act and its consequences *as foreseen by the agent*. The particular consequences for the sake of which the act is performed, and to which (as we say) the dominant motives attach, are the *end,* or *purpose* — in our example, the escape from drudgery, and the debauch in town. From the end we distinguish the *means* devised to accomplish it: the tampering with the switch, the display of force, and, if necessary, murder. And we similarly distinguish any *other consequences* which the agent perceives to be involved in his act, but in which he takes no effectual interest — *e.g.* the risk of injury to the train and its occupants.

For a second example, we may consider the act of a woman who drops a ten-dollår bill into the hat of a professional beggar. Her *motive* is pity; her *end* is to relieve misery; and the gift is intended as a *means* to effect this end. *Actu-*

THE FIELD OF MORAL JUDGMENTS 33

ally, let us say, the beggar spends the money in a debauch from which he never recovers.

The whole division may be set forth thus:

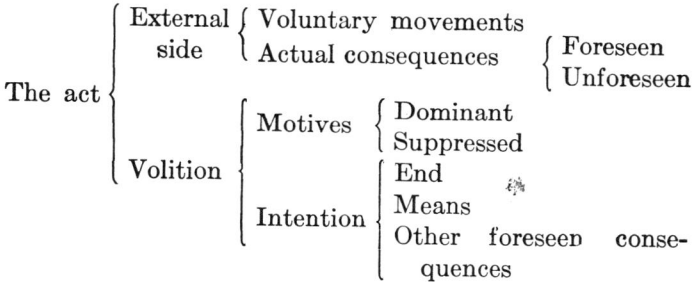

How Much does the Moral Act Comprehend? — Now almost every fraction of the whole act as thus analyzed has been regarded as the proper subject of moral judgments. No thinker of any consequence has thus singled out the physical side to the neglect of the psychological side; but there has been a good deal of difference of opinion as to whether the psychological side alone constitutes the moral act. Again, some have held that only the motive counts, while others have said the same of the intention. Though no one has seriously held that the *end* alone is of consequence (apart from the means and from other anticipated consequences of the act), men have sometimes imputed this view to their adversaries, and it goes by the name of *jesuitry*. This makes at least four important views as to the constitution of the moral act: (1) that it is the act and its consequences as a whole; (2) that it is the volition; (3) that it is the motive; and (4) that it is the intention; while (5) the view that it is the end may be dismissed from consideration.

2. *Status of Unforeseen Consequences*

The Problem. — From what was said in an earlier part of this chapter, we may be led to infer that so far as the consequences of the act are not foreseen by the agent, they do not express his character and hence form no part of *his* act. It is not due to the robber, we may say, that the train holds the track and that hundreds of men and women escape injury; and it is not the woman's fault that the beggar does not make better use of his opportunity. But when we reflect upon our judgments in such cases, do we find that they confirm this view? Is not our condemnation of the former far less severe and uncompromising than it would be if the horrors of an actual wreck were before our mind? And would we not admire the latter far more if there were a reconstructed life to show for her charity?

Indirect Approach. — These questions are not so simply answered as a hasty inspection might lead us to suppose. No excuse is commoner than, " I didn't mean to "; but it is by no means always accepted. It will be well for us to approach the consideration of the problem indirectly, and, before attempting to determine the moral significance of unforeseen consequences, to try to see clearly just what the *foreseen* consequences contemplated by the moral judgment include.

(1) Meaning of ' Foreseen.' — ' Foreseen ' is a very much broader term than ' definitely expected.' We foresee not only certainties but probabilities and possibilities of every degree. The maid who empties a pitcher of water out of a window may see the man standing on the sidewalk below; or, without glancing out, she may be well aware that men are constantly passing by; or the hour may be such that she thinks there is very little chance of any one's being in that locality. Now it is obvious that even slight possibilities may affect the moral value of an act. It is commendable to take into account a chance of doing good, even though a strong probability of a different result is perceived; and it is blameworthy to take chances of doing harm, even though the chances are not great. The good physician does not spare his pains upon the desperate case; and the good soldier holds the fort against overwhelming odds. And, on the other hand, the chauffeur who disregards the warning signals at a sharp turn in a narrow road is condemned as rash, even though there may be very little chance that another vehicle is approaching just at that moment.

Some Possibilities are Negligible. — And yet this must not be pushed too far. For if we attempt to allow for all the possibilities in every situation we shall never be able to act at all. We must omit chances of doing good, and we must take chances of doing harm. Probability must to a large extent be the guide of life. We may, then, fairly say that possibilities of a very low grade do not fall within the scope of the moral act; and such possibilities are regarded as ' unforeseen,' or ' unintended,' even though we have had them distinctly in mind.

Negligibility is Matter of Opinion. — But just how slight must the possibility be to warrant our ignoring it? There is no general answer. The degree varies greatly. Large interests, of course, lessen the attention that we can spare to small ones; and the necessity for prompt action excuses what might otherwise be pure rashness. But beyond such vague principles as these, all is matter of opinion — either one's own peculiar personal opinion, drawn from one's own experience, or the public opinion which grows out of the general experience and is more or less shared by all the members of the community.

The Common Opinion as Standard. — What happens when the spectator and the man whom he is judging differ in opinion as to the possibilities that may be disregarded? The former may say that the latter is committing a mere *error of judgment,* and acquit him of evil-doing. For an error of judgment is not an immoral act or even an act at all; and no goodness of heart can take away a man's liability to error. It may, however, lessen it. The good man who sincerely tries to do what is right, takes his failures and his almost-failures to heart and corrects his judgment by them; and besides he is ready to take note of, if not to accept, the criticisms of others; whereas the bad man, who is less anxious to avoid evil consequences, goes on his way unreflecting. It thus often happens that an error of judgment may be taken as an indication of an immoral character. The chauffeur who cares very much whether he causes serious injury is very likely to form a tolerably sound judgment as to what he can safely do. We therefore take the common opinion as a rough standard, and regard any man who is distinctly less careful than it calls for as in this respect a bad man.

(2) **Unforeseen Possibilities.** — Now, is not the case perfectly similar with the possible consequences which are not simply disregarded but are not borne in mind at all, or which the agent may be too ignorant to anticipate? A man cannot bear everything in mind; still less can he know everything. Accordingly, when we see any one acting in entire unmindfulness of possibilities which we ourselves think of as important, we often excuse him on the ground of forgetfulness or ignorance. And yet these are not always an excuse. The man who is anxious to do right is, generally speaking, less prone to forget and more ready to learn. There are some things which every good man may be expected to know and to remember. There are others which lack of experience may easily cause him to overlook. If the woman, who, without investigation, gave ten dollars to a professional beggar, were very young or had lived a very circumscribed life, we should not think ill of her for her impulsiveness. But when a man wastes his strength in dissipation; when he spreads slanderous reports; when he neglects the training of his children — in such cases we are not apt to admit the plea that he did not think of the possible consequences. For that is one of the characteristics of a bad man: not to think of consequences. As a general rule, the careless man is a man who does not care.

THE FIELD OF MORAL JUDGMENTS 37

The moral judgment which we pass upon an act because of its unconsidered possibilities is thus, like the judgment upon a wholly unreflective act (see above, p. 29), *indirect*. A man who was incapable of learning from experience how to weigh chances, and whose attention was so weak that it wandered constantly from the things that concerned him most, would be an idiot and not a moral agent at all. Of men in general we may safely say that what they now fail to consider is determined by what they have in the past considered.

(3) **Effect of Actual Consequences.** — In all this, let it be observed, it is mere possibilities that we have been discussing. We condemn the man who neglects his children, though there have been many cases in which neglected children have grown up into strong and useful citizens. So much is clear. But now let us ask what particular effect the *actual consequences* have upon our moral judgment.

Exaggeration of Moral Value. — It is easy to see that, as a rule, they affect us more strongly than mere possibilities do, and that consequently the good or evil quality of the act is greatly intensified in our eyes. When a man tries to do us a service, we perceive his kindness; but when he succeeds, the more vivid sense of the benefit makes the kindness seem far greater. This effect, however, is one which reflection tends to weaken, and consequently is regarded as an *illusion*. In our cool moments of afterthought we do not hesitate to say that, where the endeavor is the same, success and failure do not affect the moral value of the act.

Prima Facie **Evidence of Possibility.** — At the same time the fact that a consequence occurs is *prima facie* evidence to us that it was reasonably possible; that is to say, that it was possible enough to call for forethought. That is the position which we naturally assume; and evidence (or prejudice) to the contrary is necessary to make us take any other. When an automobile runs down a child, our tendency is to charge the chauffeur with criminal carelessness, unless a strong personal regard for him, or the obvious impossibility of his avoiding the accident, produces a contrary effect. Now this is by no means a fallacious tendency, but is fully in accord with the logic of probabilities. Other things being equal, the fact that a thing does happen is presumptive proof that it was likely to happen.

Evidence of Intention and Purpose. — Furthermore, the actual consequence is *prima facie* evidence to us (though somewhat weaker than before), that it was *intended* by the agent, and even (with still weaker force) that it was his distinct *purpose* in acting. What we see coming from a man we ascribe to him, unless further evidence or passion makes us think otherwise. This, of course, does not apply to our own acts, for we are well aware in advance what our intentions and purposes are — in so far as we really have them. But we have to judge of the other man's intentions mainly by his overt acts; and, in assuming that he means to do what he actually does, our judgment follows the natural path of least resistance.

It must not be forgotten, however, that this assumption is capable of being removed by reflection; and the more given to reflection we are, and the less apt to be carried away by the impression of the moment, the more likely we are to correct our moral judgment by attentively discriminating between what the agent did or did not intend to do, as well as between what he might or might not reasonably have foreseen.

Summary and Conclusion. — We may, therefore, say, by way of summary, that it is only as the actual consequences of the act are assumed, or reflectively believed, to be due to the character of the agent, that they are regarded as belonging to the act. Unforeseen consequences are in themselves indifferent. They may, however, be indirectly judged, in so far as they are felt to be indications of the way in which the agent intentionally acts.

The theory, that the psychological side of an act alone constitutes the act as morally judged, thus turns out to be substantially correct. Man is not a bodiless spirit, and his actions are not mere thoughts or feelings. And for the most part it is only as thoughts and feelings are incarnate in actual deeds that we are able to perceive and judge them. Still, as our account has shown, it is the psychological side of the act that, so far as it appears, is of determining significance for the moral judgment.

These conclusions are exactly confirmed by the study of the development of *punishment*. Among peoples of a low grade of culture, little or no distinction is made between the *reparation* exacted for intentional or unintentional injury, and the *penalty* incurred by intentional injury. But as civil and criminal law have become differentiated from each other, the latter gradually gives up the cognizance of unintentional acts. Thus to the savage it is all one whether I kill his brother accidentally or of malice aforethought. He will get satisfaction if he can, either by killing me or by killing some near relative of mine. In a civilized country the state will punish for a criminal act, if it was intentional, but only exceptionally otherwise. But if I infringe upon legally protected rights, the law will compel me to make restitution, whether I intended the act or not.

3. *Motive* vs. *Intention*

The Motive as Object of Judgment. — It has been said that moralists have been seriously divided upon the question, whether the motive or the intention is the proper and ultimate object of moral judgment. On the one side, it is urged that it is the motives that make up the character of the man, of which his intentions are but an after-effect. It is love and hate, charity and greed, pride and humility, and the like that make different objects appeal to us and set us a-following after them. And the only way in which the objects are of importance for the moral judgment is that they serve to indicate the inner springs of feeling. In two actions, if the intention is alike but the motive is different, the moral value differs with the motive. When one man enlists as a soldier from patriotism and another from ennui; when one man refuses to fight from religious scruples and another from cowardice; we admire the former and have contempt for the latter. When the objection is made, that the same feeling may be rightly indulged on one occasion, while it would be wrong to give way to it on another, the reply is, that all depends upon the *other* motives which are active upon the two occasions. Motives are higher and lower; and, in the good man, when they clash the higher prevail. Parental love, for example, is noble as compared with love of money; it is petty as compared with patriotism.

The Intention as Object of Judgment. — But, on the other hand, it may be urged, that while in a general way one motive may be regarded as higher than another, yet one cannot from that infer that the one ought always to take precedence over the other. In the familiar conflict between love of country and love of wife and children, the issue has not always to be decided in the same way. The urgency of the needs upon both sides, the consequences reasonably to be expected from the choice of each alternative, must be weighed. It is the *intention* alone that provides a sufficient basis for the decision. Motives are good, when they give rise to good intentions. As for the examples cited, where change of motive alone is supposed to bring about a change in the moral judgment, the evident fact is that the intention also changes. The coward, for example, does not see the same consequences impending upon his proposed enlistment that occur to the sturdy Quaker. Most of the terms used to denote emotions imply some particular sort of an object, and the intentions with respect to this object are taken for granted when the motive is said to be good or evil in itself.

THE FIELD OF MORAL JUDGMENTS 41

'Parental love' implies the intention to care for one's children; 'greed' implies the intention to grasp after all the good things in sight; and so forth.

Criticism and Conclusion. — As between the two opposed theories, the latter (making the intention the ultimate object of moral judgment) appears to have the best of the argument. But a simple reflection serves to show that this theory also is defective. In forming an estimate of the moral value of a man's intention, it is far from being an irrelevant circumstance, *to what part of the intention the motive attaches* — which of the anticipated consequences constitutes the end, or purpose, of the act, and which are aimed at simply as a means to this end, or anticipated in a (wholly or relatively) indifferent way. Suppose that a legislator, voting for an anti-gambling bill, believes that the measure will be of great advantage to the state, and also believes that his own part in passing it will increase his chances of reëlection. Each of these anticipated results forms a part of his intention, and would be considered in forming an estimate of the act, but the estimate would vary greatly according as we believed the one or the other to be the sole or principal end in view. But it is the feeling that determines this.

We thus reach the result, that the true object of the moral judgment is the complex whole which motive and intention make up together; that is to say, the *volition*. It is *thoughts colored by feelings* that we judge — not gray outlines of thought, nor vague splashes of feeling.

APPENDIX TO CHAPTER III

THE INTENTION TO DO RIGHT

The Question Stated. — There is another question, intimately related to those discussed in the foregoing pages, which may be conveniently discussed in this place. We have seen that the moral conduct *par excellence*, aside from which no other conduct would be regarded as open to moral judgment, is the conduct which the agent himself judges at the time of action. Now when such a judgment accompanies the act, how is the judgment of the spectator (or of the agent himself at some later time) affected by it? Does the intention to do right always make an act right? In more general terms, must we always say that an act is right or wrong according as the agent at the time believed it to be right or wrong?

The Affirmative Answer. — This is a question which a survey of our actual judgments in such cases seems to answer decisively — in each of two contradictory ways. The story of Philip the Second and the Spanish Inquisition occurs as a fair test case. What are we to think of the part that he played in that memorable persecution, in the course of which thousands of innocent men and women were put to death with the most horrible tortures? So far as we know, he was perfectly assured of his own righteousness in the matter. He was but doing his manifest duty. Now what more could he do, and what more can any man be expected to do? To be sure, he had a strong natural vein of cruelty, and his *purpose* seems to have been mainly selfish — he was morbidly anxious to secure the salvation of his own soul. But what of that? One must not judge a man as one would a god; and if a man lives up to the dictates of his conscience, he is virtuous in the only way a man can be.

The Negative Answer. — This sounds reasonable; but somehow it is hard to accept it. It seems as if, on the same grounds, one would have to pardon the very worst acts of the worst men. For (as Aristotle pointed out) one of the essential characteristics of wickedness is the perversion of moral standards. How, then, shall we regard the very viciousness of a man's character as an excuse for the viciousness of his conduct? If Philip thought that duty required him to destroy heresy with fire, so much the worse for his own miserable self.

Compromise. — As usual, where there is a strong conflict of opinion, there is a popular compromise view. We are asked to distinguish between *formal* rightness and *material* rightness. Conduct which agrees with the agent's own moral standard is formally right, while conduct which agrees with the true standard is materially right. But, even supposing the person judging is possessed of the true standard, this distinction does not help much. For the question remains, What is formal rightness worth? Is it a shadowy delusion, or is it something real and precious? Perhaps the fact that the terms of the compromise are capable of being interpreted to suit either extreme has helped to make it popular.

We must try to go a little deeper and see what the fundamental points at issue are, and how the truth on both sides can be satisfactorily accounted for.

The Case for the Affirmative. — On one side there is the conviction that *no man is ever compelled to do wrong*. Where no freedom of choice is left, there is no scope for moral valuation. Now, for a man to do what he believes to be wrong is certainly wrong, even though, apart from this belief, it would be precisely the right thing for him to do. To go against one's conscience is wrong from every point of view. Suppose that Philip, believing as he did that heresy was a deadly sin, and that the men whom he consigned to the flames were in any case doomed to eternal torments and might easily lead others into their awful condition; thinking, too, that perhaps the torture of the flames might lead the dying sinner to repentance and salvation in the very hour of death — suppose he had allowed a natural aversion to the thought of suffering to withhold him from his duty. Would not this have been vastly worse than what he actually did? If so, then, if the course he took was wrong, how was it possible for him to act rightly? It is not a question of what would have been right for one of us to do in Philip's place, but of what it was right for Philip to do, being the man he was. If it is never right to disobey one's conscience, it can never be wrong to obey it.[1]

Here we must obviate some possible misunderstanding. The view which we are now presenting does not imply that a man's moral standards cannot change — that as he reviews a former act, committed in the full belief in its rightness, he may not conclude that on a similar occasion it would be well to do otherwise, or that he may not deeply regret the lack of insight which he then displayed. It does mean that the act was nevertheless morally right, and that the contrary course, inasmuch as it was condemned by the best judgment the man then possessed, would have been distinctly wrong. Again, it does not mean that a man ought to have unlimited confidence in his own judgment, but simply that, in the last resort, it is in his own judgment that he *must* trust. For the respect paid to a commonly received opinion or to the advice of a respected friend is, after all, the man's own judgment. Finally, it does not mean that one ought to desire nothing

---

[1] As thus stated, the argument applies only to conduct which is believed by the agent to be not only right (*i.e.* permissible) but obligatory. But it may be extended to cases where the given alternatives seem to him to be equally innocent. If in such a case we say that the course which he pursues is wrong, are we not taking his moral character out of his power and making it the sport of chance? But that is to deny him all true liberty and responsibility.

except to do what is right, and to regard everything else with the indifference of a cynic; but simply that one ought not to desire to do anything that does *not* seem right. Why should there not be plenty of good things in the world, which a man may innocently seek after and enjoy?

The Case for the Negative. — On the other side there is the persistent conviction that men like Philip are wicked men, and that to condone their wickedness is to be false to our most precious ideals, to deliver ourselves over to a moral anarchy. If we make an idol of well-intentioned ignorance, every motive for self-enlightenment is taken away. Whether or not virtue is identical with knowledge, or with some sort of knowledge, it is outrageous to pretend that no knowledge is involved in it. Human virtue may not be the virtue of a god; but it is the virtue of a man, not of a beast.

How far are these last considerations valid? Let us see.

Examination of the Negative Arguments. — In the first place, it is an error to suppose that when a man resolves to follow the best judgment that he possesses, he will not try to better his judgment. Rather will he have a new and powerful motive for doing so. And if he sees another well-intentioned man doing what seems to him to be ill-advised, there is no reason why he should not wish to enlighten him in the matter. Nay, the very fact that the other man is doing his best gives an additional incentive to advise him; for there is the greater chance that the advice, if sensible, will be acted on. We do not "make an idol of well-intentioned ignorance" when we say that in all grades of ignorance or enlightenment to be well-intentioned is right and to be evilly intentioned is wrong.

Motives for Improvement not Affected. — But is not a man with a good conscience content with himself, and does not a man who is content with himself cease to try to improve? This is a plea that is often heard; but it only needs to be set down in black and white for us to see how groundless it is. A man with a good conscience is content with himself — on the whole. But he may be profoundly discontented with himself in many particular respects. In fact, as ordinary self-observation suffices to show, an earnest effort at self-improvement is one of the things that conscience most commonly demands of us. Quite as obviously false is the supposition that if we regard a man as morally justified in his foolish conduct, we can have no reason to wish him to be wise enough to act differently. If we have any affection or sympathy for him, we will wish to save him the many pangs which the consequences of his folly may bring upon him — to say nothing of desiring for him the joy which expanding knowledge itself brings. And if we are selfish we will still wish to avoid ill consequences to ourselves. For men live together in so intimate a union that they are deeply concerned with one another's mode of life. The conditions of their happiness are most complexly interwoven. Now, doubtless the morality of our neighbors is much the most important factor in their usefulness to us. But it is not the only factor. We would rather have them ignorant and good than well-informed and malignant. But surely we would like best to have them good and wise to boot.

General Agreement of Moral Standards. — In the second place, what of the fear of moral anarchy? Is this well founded? Let us note, first, that the consciences of well-intentioned men in any society show a strong mutual resemblance. Individuals are peculiar, but they are not altogether peculiar. The approval of certain modes of conduct as right, and of certain other modes as wrong, runs pretty uniformly through all classes of men and women. The differences that are observable are mainly with respect to the degree of importance of the various moral requirements, or with respect to the validity of the excuses that may be urged for various deviations from the usual requirements. Thus some will regard adultery as the deadliest of sins, and some others will regard it as of much less consequence than commercial dishonesty; but all will agree that it is wrong. Thus, again, one merchant may hold himself to strict truthfulness in his advertisements, while another may feel that trade customs are such that customers expect some degree of exaggeration and make allowance for it; but both agree that to receive money on false pretenses is wrong — as a general rule. The *actual* difference in men's moral standards is thus far from being anarchical. To judge them by their own standards is, in general, not very different from judging them by our own or by the standard of public opinion. In fact, in most cases there is no practical difference. We cannot see into other men's consciences; and unless there is special reason for thinking them (or ourselves) peculiar, we are compelled to take for granted that they think as we do, and as men in general have been found to do.

The Remaining Question. — Still, there are many evident exceptions, and the question remains, how are they to be judged? What of the genial captain of finance, who, in the firm conviction that all is right that is not criminal, waters the stock of a railroad system to several times the physical value of the property? What of the courtly libertine, who thinks himself a man of honor, and regards the systematic corruption of young women as mere pleasantry? Because these men do not condemn themselves, must we forever acquit them? And if we acquit them, is not this anarchy?

The Social Environment as an Excuse. — The answer is not perfectly simple. Sometimes we do acquit them, or at least palliate the offense. There are reckless libertines, for example, who are among the most admired characters of history. Obviously, in such cases we take account, in some way, of the social conditions under which the men developed, and we regard them as in some measure excused by their environment. At the same time, it must be admitted, we often refuse to acquit them; and even when the conditions of their upbringing have been unfortunate, we make scant allowance on that account. No doubt we are not wholly fair in this. Factors of personal charm or repulsiveness, including even personal beauty or ugliness, move our feelings and give a bias to our judgment. But all the discrepancy is not thus to be explained. Even in our calmest reflective moments the fact remains that while we admit environmental conditions as some excuse for ill conduct, we seldom accept them as a complete excuse, and sometimes allow them almost no weight at all. The question, therefore, recurs with undiminished force: If it is right for a man to do as he thinks right, how are we justified in judging him by any other standard than his own? Or is our reflective moral consciousness involved in a hopeless self-contradiction?

Final Considerations. — The solution of the difficulty lies along lines with which a previous discussion (cf. p. 29) has made us familiar. In so far as a man appears to us to be the passive product of forces among which his own will counted for naught, we do not regard him as morally responsible. But common observation shows that a man's character and opinions are largely formed through his own voluntary acts. Generally speaking, it is not the environment as such, but our own voluntary reactions upon it, that make us what we are.[1] What effect external forces have upon us depends upon what we are already. More particularly, the way in which we obey or disobey our consciences has a good deal to do in determining the whole development of our consciences. It is by doing what we believe to be right that we become aware of the defects of our conceptions of right and wrong, and they are enlarged and corrected and refined. And by persisting in doing what we believe to be wrong, we confuse

---

[1] It may be urged, to be sure, that ultimately these voluntary acts must be traced back to involuntary beginnings in the shape of inherited instincts. But, however that may be, the question here is, not where the will comes from, but, having arisen, what part it plays in the determination of conduct.

and distort our conceptions. Thus our moral judgment upon an act may have a *double bearing*. An act in conformity with conscience, which, considered by itself, is perfectly right, may be a most significant index of the stunting of conscience by habitual disobedience to it in the past. As we have already had occasion to remark, there are things which a man may be expected to know, and among these a goodly body of moral distinctions have their place; and while ignorance of them may be regarded as a sufficient excuse for a particular course of conduct, it is none the less convincing evidence of general moral worthlessness.

Conclusion. — The truth, then, is that both parties to the controversy are fundamentally correct in their views, and no compromise is necessary. The apparent contradiction arises from the attempt to limit the moral judgment to a single item of conduct; as, indeed, the use of the terms 'right' and 'wrong' constantly tempts us to do. If, instead of asking whether an act is always right when the agent thinks it right, we asked whether an act is always just *as good* (or bad) as the agent thinks it; or, better still, whether a man is always just as good (or bad) as he takes himself to be; every one would without hesitation reply in the negative.

REFERENCES

ARISTOTLE, *Nichomachean Ethics*, Book III, Chs. I–V.
WUNDT, W., *Ethics*, Part III, Ch. I, Sect. I.
STOUT, G. F., *The Groundwork of Psychology*, Ch. XVIII.
WESTERMARCK, E., *The Origin and Development of the Moral Ideas*, Chs. VIII–XIII.
MEZES, S., *Ethics, Descriptive and Explanatory*, Ch. II.
DEWEY and TUFTS, *Ethics*, Chs. X, XIII.
HYSLOP, J. H., *Elements of Ethics*, Ch. III.
MUIRHEAD, J. H., *Elements of Ethics*, Book II, Ch. I.
WRIGHT, H. W., *Self-realization*, Part I, Ch. I.

CHAPTER IV

RESPONSIBILITY AND FREEDOM

I. Responsibility

Definition. — By *responsibility*, we mean the relation of a man to his conduct, by virtue of which it makes him the subject of moral approval or disapproval, especially the latter. As thus defined, it is closely connected with the notion of legal responsibility, in the sense of *liability to punishment*. The two notions, however, are clearly distinct. There are many immoral acts for which society has no punishment; and, on the other hand, punishment is often inflicted for reasons far removed from moral guilt. Moral responsibility is *liability to censure*. Of course, to be liable to censure implies that one is equally liable to a favorable judgment, if one's conduct appears to deserve it. But (for reasons which need not here concern us) the possibility of unfavorable judgment is emphasized.

The feeling of responsibility, especially in the form of *remorse*, has been thought by many writers to be the most distinctive feature of the moral life. When, for example, Darwin attempted to show how a social animal, such as man's ape-like ancestor, was bound to develop a conscience as soon as his intelligence was sufficiently advanced, it was the sense of remorse for a cruelly heedless act that he had especially in mind. This, no doubt, was one-sided; but certainly no experience is better fitted than that of remorse, to impress the importance of moral values upon us.

Lapse of Responsibility. — Responsibility has temporal limits, though these are very indefinite. The misdeeds of childhood and youth sometimes awake in us a sense of shame. Nevertheless we do not usually regard ourselves as still responsible for acts committed so long ago. We have left them behind us. And there are frequent illustrations of a lapse of responsibility for acts committed even in manhood. A few years ago, a convict, who had escaped from a federal prison, and later had married and settled down to a respectable life, was betrayed through the malice of a former associate. There was a very strong public feeling of sympathy for him. The police officer who made the arrest, and who under the circumstances could have claimed a substantial reward, scorned to take it. Appeal was made to the President of the United States for a pardon; and though he regarded it against public policy to grant a full pardon he did commute the sentence to a short term.

Its Cause. — What is it that causes responsibility to cease? Evidently a change of character — such a change that the character can no longer be regarded as expressed in the act in question; or, in other words, such a change as to warrant the expectation of different conduct in the future. The change may take place gradually, or it may be accomplished by a sudden acute repentance. Mere regret or even remorse, however, is not enough. These may be *sentimental, i.e.* may not represent the character as actual temptation reveals it. Nothing is commoner than ineffectual regrets that leave the man as they find him. If responsibility is to fall from a man, there must be a decided change of heart, showing itself in consistent conduct.

II. THE RELATION BETWEEN FREEDOM AND RESPONSIBILITY

Indeterminism. — We have elsewhere remarked that a man is not held responsible for what he does under physical compulsion or (generally speaking) under the influence of overmastering pain or fear. Such things reduce him to the level of the unconscious mechanism, or, at least, to the level of the irrational animal; and it becomes out of place to apply moral predicates to him. A certain class of moral theorists have extended this principle. They have held that a man cannot be held responsible for his acts, except in so far as he is their *first cause;* that is to say, except in so far as his will is undetermined in its choice by any previous condition whatsoever. In a word, the will must be *free.*

This is one of many senses in which the expression 'freedom of the will' has been used. (1) Sometimes it stands for *knowledge* both of the particular circumstances of the action and of the various values that are at stake. (2) Sometimes it means the *power of deliberation,* the suspension of action while various motives are being weighed. (3) It may denote the control of lower motives by higher motives. Where the former have the upper hand a man is often said to be the 'slave of his appetites.' (4) It may mean the control of conduct by one's own judgments of value, be these correct or incorrect. But we are now to consider it in a sense very different from all these: (5) *the exemption of volition from the principle of cause and effect.* It is conceived that the will is not determined by the conditions at the time. Given the same conditions, external and internal, in the minutest detail — character, habits, knowledge, ideals, momentary feelings and desires — the act *might* be different. The will is indeed *attracted* or *repelled* by different motives, but not *controlled* by them. It must freely yield to a motive before volition takes place. The will sits as a judge over the different impulses, and decides between them as between different claimants. The fact that a man is good leaves him equally free to do evil things; and if he be evil, that fact leaves him at all times free to do the very noblest things. This theory is called 'indeterminism,' or 'libertarianism.' The contrary theory is called 'determinism.'

Alleged Dependence of Responsibility upon Freedom. — As has been said, some moralists have held that unless the will is, in this last sense, free, all moral judgment is invalid, for the agent is not responsible. Determinism, it is urged, makes of a man a mere machine, and, indeed, a mere part of the world-machine. What he does he does not of himself, but as the universe acts through him. Some thinkers, admitting the force of this contention, have proceeded to deny the existence of any responsibility. Blame not the man, they have said, but blame his parents and teachers who have made him what he is. And yet, why them? The calm conclusion of science, we are told, is this : *Judge not at all.* For the most part, however, men have been unwilling to accept this conclusion. If they believed that there could be no responsibility unless indeterminism were true, they have regarded this as a proof of indeterminism. And if they were convinced that the universality of the law of cause and effect could admit of no exception, then they have denied that responsibility was for that reason at all impaired.

Let us consider this alleged dependence of responsibility upon freedom.

The Dependence Unreal. — A little consideration should show us that there is a serious misunderstanding here. We judge a man's acts in so far as they are conceived to express his character. That means that they must be free in the sense of being *his* acts, due to his being the sort of man he is, not forced upon him *despite* his character. But it does not mean that they must be free in the sense of being independent of his character. For in so far as the acts are not caused by his character, they do not express that character, and hence are not open to moral judgment.

But, it may be urged, if a man's character is the product of previous influences, are not those influences responsible for his acts? Most assuredly (we may reply), in so far as those previous influences consist of other moral beings — his parents and teachers and associates. But, much as the gun upon a rider's shoulder is carried both by the man and by the horse, so an evil deed that is directly due to the agent's character may (at least in part) be indirectly due to his father's character, and thus be a valid reason for our passing an unfavorable judgment upon both.[1]

The indeterminist argument is sometimes given a special point by being applied to the infliction of punishment. Can it be right to inflict pain upon a man for his misdeeds, when he is considered to be the inevitable product of a combination of previous conditions? Is not punishment on such a basis simply adding one evil to another? Certainly, if punishment is an evil. If we are to think of punishment as a mere act of vengeance, it will be difficult indeed to find any adequate excuse for it. But if punishment is intended as a good to all concerned, and especially to the evil-doer himself, the only excuse it needs is its *efficacy*. Why, because circumstances have joined together to make a wicked man, shall we not try to make him a better man?

Dependence of Responsibility upon Determinism. — If the argument for the dependence of responsibility on indeterminism is thus unconvincing, there are, on the other hand, reasons for holding that responsibility is dependent on determinism. For responsibility, as we have seen, depends on the continuity of character; and this can only be observed in so far as conduct is uniform and hence predictable. A good man must be more likely to do right than a bad man; and if the latter has this probability against him,

[1] The argument is often connected with the religious belief in a personal God and in everlasting punishment. If God, who is himself a moral agent, is the ultimate cause of all that we are, is not he, rather than ourselves, responsible for our sins? And how, then, shall he be justified in damning us? The only answer to the former question is that he certainly *is* responsible, though the possibility lies open that the creation of sinful man may be part of a larger purpose (not wholly comprehensible to us) which fully justifies it. To the second question it must be replied that everlasting punishment, if it be a truth, is one which no one has succeeded in justifying upon *any* grounds whatsoever. The dogma is based, of course, upon a retributive conception of punishment.

it is hard to see how his act can be regarded as a fresh creation, undetermined by previous circumstances. Moreover, we can say that indeterminism, by making conduct unpredictable, makes moral praise and blame ineffectual and moral education impossible. In particular, the practice of punishment is made ridiculous — for what else can the infliction of pain be expected to accomplish, if it cannot help to determine the culprit's future conduct?

If it is suggested that perhaps volition is partly determined and partly undetermined, we may reply that in that case it remains true that it is only by reason of *the degree of determination that exists* that responsibility or moral education is possible, or that punishment is justifiable.

The Kantian Theory. — In this connection we may mention Kant's famous argument to prove that to acknowledge a moral *obligation* implies the assumption that man must be absolutely free *to do what is right*. Moral obligation (he said) is conceived to be absolute and unconditional; it means that we ought to act in a certain way, in obedience to a moral law, *regardless of circumstances*. But we are never under obligation to do the impossible. Now all our natural motives (*i.e.* those that are causally determined) vary with circumstances; hence if all our motives are causally determined, there may be circumstances under which we cannot do right, and hence are without moral obligation; which is absurd. Therefore there must be a distinctive moral motive which is wholly supernatural and undetermined; and this Kant identifies as *reverence* for the moral law. The weakness of the argument lies in the initial assumption that moral obligation is to follow certain rules regardless of circumstances. Kant himself reduced this to an absurdity when he declared, "that to tell a falsehood to a murderer who asked us whether our friend, of whom he was in pursuit, had not taken refuge in our house, would be a crime." The question is too far-reaching for us to discuss here; but we shall elsewhere give reasons for holding that moral laws are by no means so rigid and invariable as Kant supposed.

III. Further Arguments for Indeterminism

We may now be interested in examining some other considerations that have been urged in favor of indeterminism or of determinism.

1. The Intuition of Freedom. — Beginning with the former, we have first to note, not an argument, but an assertion, that we have a direct (intuitive) consciousness of our freedom. It is safe to say that the main basis for this assertion is (1) our *not* being fully conscious of the causes of our acts. It is an appeal to ignorance. Mental phenomena are very complicated, if not in themselves, at any rate in their preconditions, conscious and unconscious; and it is easy for a man to overlook even important factors in the forming of his decisions. Add to this (2) our consciousness, based upon experience, that we can do a great many things *when we so desire* and are not forcibly restrained. We are very chary nowadays of trusting in alleged intuitive knowledge, for it is fatally easy to claim and (when it is disputed) fatally hard to validate; and the intuition of indeterminism has the least claim to respect of any.

2. Change of Choice. — In popular discussion it is sometimes urged that a man can prove his freedom by "doing it over again the other way." A certain choice has been taken; the conditions are repeated; and now, to prove his point, the man does differently. The reply is, of course, that the similarity of external conditions does not necessarily imply that the motives are the same; and in this case we can even lay our finger upon one important new motive: *the man's desire to prove his point.*

3. The Destruction of Effort — Fatalism. — If determinism were accepted as true, would it not destroy all effort? And

RESPONSIBILITY AND FREEDOM 57

if, as a matter of fact, determinists have not been especially inert beings, does not this prove that they did not really believe in their doctrine? If we believe that everything in the universe is completely predetermined, how can we intelligently try to accomplish anything? And if, on the contrary, we do constantly frame ends and endeavor to accomplish them, does not this prove that in our hearts we believe in our own freedom?

Before directly replying to these questions, it will be well for us to note the difference between determinism and *fatalism*. Fatalism is the belief that certain events — especially death — are bound to occur in a certain way (or to occur at a certain time) no matter what the previous conditions are. Thus a woman believed that she was fated to be drowned at sea; and when a steamer in which she had taken passage was wrecked, she refused to enter a life-boat, because, as she said, she would only bring disaster to the others in the boat. A Filipino quack doctor made the most extravagant claims with regard to his healing powers. When a number of his patients died, he was not in the least disconcerted. He had been perfectly able to cure them, he said, but *their time had come* — as, indeed, the fact of their death proved. And when a man's time has come to die, nothing can prevent it!

It is not difficult to see that fatalism is more closely allied to indeterminism than to determinism. It is a belief in the *discontinuity* of events. Determinism is a belief in their complete continuity: that nothing ever happens except as an outgrowth of previous conditions.

Now fatalism does sometimes produce a sort of apathy. When a man believes that all the important issues of life are fixed in advance, in such a fashion that nothing that he can do can have the least influence upon the result, it is only natural that he should not feel very energetic. Sometimes, we may add, fatalism produces an opposite effect, especially when it attaches only to the issue of life and death. The Turkish soldier, for example, who believes that the day of his death is appointed, fights with an extraordinary abandon. If his time has come, no cowardice will save him; and if it has not come, no danger can be fatal to him.

But there is nothing in determinism to produce either the one effect or the other — either indifference or desperation. The determinist believes that his impulses are efficient causes by which the future course of events must in part be shaped. Why, then, should he cease to feel? He believes that his efforts count for something in determining his happiness or unhappiness. Why, then, should he cease to struggle? There is no reason; just as there is no reason why he should feel more passionately or struggle more desperately than the given conditions warrant.

To be sure, a belief in determinism will not of itself awaken any sources of feeling in man's nature; but, then, nobody has ever pretended that it did. If a man is without love or ambition or loyalty, determinism will not inspire them in him. But neither if he has them will it take them away.

IV. FURTHER ARGUMENTS FOR DETERMINISM

Let us now turn to the evidences that are offered in favor of determinism.

1. The Intuition of Determinism. — Just as indeterminism has been based on an alleged intuition, so has determinism. It has been held that the law of cause and effect is an axiom self-evident to human reason. But apart from our growing unwillingness to rely on intuitions, there are particular reasons why the law of cause and effect should not be put upon such a basis.

The distinguishing marks of an intuition are supposed to be its clearness and distinctness and its universal application. But few maxims of science or philosophy have been more shifting and uncertain in their meaning than this;

and none have been more in dispute. "Nothing happens by chance, but all things follow from necessity," is an old formulation, which might be more intelligible if we were first told what chance is; and yet how can chance be defined except as absence of causal necessity? — a vicious circle. "Every event presupposes a previous event upon which it follows according to a universal rule," is another famous version, the only fault with which is that it is obviously untrue. One event, taken by itself, does not cause another, regardless of all other attendant circumstances. There are no separate and distinct chains of causation, but a constant interference. Shall we then say that the true causes and effects are not events but *tendencies* — tendencies which may thwart or conceal one another, but which are real none the less? But what is a tendency? Some men have held that it is nothing else than the momentum of a body moving in space, and that causality is simply the communication of motion from one body to another by impact. The discovery of the law of gravitation, which seems to imply ' action at a distance,' made this theory impracticable. In our own time many men declare that all causality is transformation of energy, and that the law of cause and effect, when properly stated, is nothing more or less than the law of the conservation of energy. But when we try to apply this law to the explanation of mental phenomena — *e.g.* the association of ideas — it becomes meaningless, at least so far as we can now see. Besides, there are men who hold that all causation is psychical — that the very conception of a cause comes to us from the operation of our own wills, and that the action of bodies upon each other must be interpreted after the analogy of our own conscious behavior.

The plain truth of the matter is that ' cause ' and ' effect ' have no single intuitively clear and distinct meanings, but a variety of meanings, some very clear and some very hazy, all held together by the fact that they are conceptions according to which we explain the conditions of one time by the conditions that have gone before. " All conditions prevailing at any one moment can *somehow* be completely explained from the conditions that prevailed at any previous moment : " such is the law of causality.

In saying this we must not be understood to imply that the law of cause and effect is meaningless or useless. On the contrary, there is much virtue in a ' somehow.' The point upon which we are insisting is that the presumption is all against the theory that we have an *intuitive knowledge* of such a law.

2. Determinism as a Presupposition of Science. — It is sometimes said that determinism is an unavoidable assumption in all scientific work. For the business of science is to explain; and any condition that was inexplicable would lie outside the limits of science. To study anything is to assume that it can be explained and hence is subject to the law of cause and effect. Furthermore, science can never recognize any occasion for the opposite assumption. No matter how long a phenomenon has seemed to contradict all known principles, we can still take for granted that it is to be explained on principles yet unknown.

This argument has its force, but it does not prove all that it is sometimes supposed to prove. The fact that I try to explain a phenomenon does imply that I take for granted that the phenomenon is explicable : if I believed otherwise, I should not try. And the universal program of science, to explain anything and everything that may interest the human intellect, similarly rests upon the presumption that all things are explicable : in so far as this presumption is false, science is foredoomed to failure. It is an essential *postulate* of the science which acknowledges no bounds. But that hardly warrants us in saying that any endeavor to explain anything can only be justified on the basis of a complete determinism.

3. The Progress of Science. — How far does the actual progress of science prove the truth of determinism? It is easy to reply that it does not prove it at all: that however far men may have succeeded in laying bare the causal connections of things they can never be warranted in a leap to the conclusion that causal connection is universal. But this is not wholly just.

Determinism as a Regulative Principle. — A formally correct and sufficient proof of the principle of determinism cannot be derived from any evidence whatsoever. The world is too vast and too complicated for that. But neither can the principle ever be disproved by any evidence whatsoever. On each side there is always the refuge of infinite ignorance. But just because it can never be proved or disproved, its significance is that of a *regulative principle*. It is not so much a matter of objective fact as of *intellectual policy*. What it declares is that we shall *look for* causal explanation everywhere and in all things, and never remit our search on the plea that this or that phenomenon may possibly lie outside the realm of law.

Now when determinism is thus viewed as a regulative principle, the sort of proof that is necessary to establish it is precisely what is afforded by the progress of science. In ancient times the wisest men felt themselves justified in rejecting it. Plato and Aristotle believed in the existence of universal causal laws; but they thought that in no individual case were these laws more than approximately realized. In each thing or event, as they thought, there was an element of blind, irrational *chance*, which could never be accounted for in any way. So far as physical events are concerned, this notion (though disputed by the stoics) persisted down to modern times; until it was dispelled by the early triumphs of inductive science, culminating in the discovery of the law of universal gravitation. It was not that the scientist was now ready with a complete explanation of anything and everything; but that the disposition of his mind was now to look for uniformity in all things, and to regard apparent chance as the manifestation of unknown causes.

It is true that in relation to mental phenomena the notion of the uncaused still lingered. But it is almost within a generation that the wide and successful application of experimental, comparative, and genetic methods to psychology gave it its present secure place among the natural sciences. So that although the determinist position had its earnest advocates from the time of Hobbes onward, the spirit of the times was not definitely against indeterminism. The popular consciousness was almost unanimous in its belief in the freedom of the will, and the scientific consciousness was far from being unitedly opposed to it. The case of Descartes (one of the fathers of modern thought) is typical. For the material universe he accepted the principle of determinism as intuitively certain. But the will he believed to be absolutely free. How both these propositions could be true together was, he confessed, an insuperable mystery.

But in our own time we have become far more familiar with the uniformities of psychological phenomena. The discovery of Weber's law (of the relation between the intensity of the stimulus and the intensity of the sensation) marked an epoch here. The science is still young, to be sure; and in certain fields, such as sensation, perception, attention, and memory, far more has been accomplished than in some others, such as emotion and will. But the same is or has recently been true of the sciences of external nature. Of the vast and all-important subject of heredity, for example, both in the plant and in the animal world, what is known is but a scanty fringe upon the vast unknown. And as the deficiencies in our knowledge of the external world count to us as no argument against the universality of its causal laws, even so there is no reason to regard the actual limitations of psychology as pointing to the existence of any transcendent, incomprehensible factor in mental phenomena.

V. Physical and Quasi-physical Determinism

Let determinism remain altogether vague, and it has little difficulty in maintaining its position against all the assaults of indeterminism. But when it begins *to specify the mode of determination*, then the advantage is all on the side of indeterminism. This has been the real strength and *animus* of the free-will theory: not in its opposition to the conception of a universal causal necessity, but in its resistance to certain specific theories as to the way in which men's voluntary acts are determined. Two of these must be noted here.

Physical Determinism. — In the first place, there has been the theory, that men's thoughts and feelings are not causes of events, but helpless accompaniments of them; that the only true causes are physical forces operating between material bodies. This is not simply determinism, but a *physical determinism*. Against such a view we may fairly urge (1) that the causal value of thoughts and feelings is as obvious and familiar to us as any other whatsoever. To deny this value is to sacrifice plain fact to a far-stretched theory that is founded at best upon facts that are no plainer. And, furthermore, (2) when we try to apply the theory to mental and social phenomena it vanishes into thin air. It is not meant to be so applied.

The Mechanical Analogy. — In the second place, there is the far more important theory, which looks upon human motives as causes, but interprets their action *after the analogy of mechanical causes*. The favorite illustration is the ' parallelogram of forces.' If a force a, acting alone for a given time upon the object M, would move it to P; and if the force b, acting alone for the same time, would move it to

Q; then the two forces, acting together, would move it to R, the point which with M, P, and Q marks out a parallelogram. In the special case where the two forces have the same direction or opposite directions, they simply add themselves to each other in algebraic fashion. If they have the same direction, they reënforce each other; if they are opposed, the stronger triumphs, but with diminished strength. Even so, it is said, a man's motives push him in one direction and another, and his actual conduct is but the resultant of their united forces. In every conflict the strongest motive prevails. If the motives diverge, but are not absolutely opposed, the agent takes a middle course.

This way of thinking is a fair example of the danger of carrying an abstraction too far. In the principle of the parallelogram of forces the object appears only as a *point* upon which forces external to it act. Its own nature counts for nothing in the supposed result. Now even in the mechanical realm this is not strictly true. The object is not a point but has its shape, size, consistency, mass, etc. Put a differently formed object in its place and the result would be different. Moreover, the forces which act upon it are not so external to its nature as might be supposed. Substitute lead for iron in a magnetic field, and the difference is easily seen.

But if the abstraction is not wholly valid in its applicaton to the physical world, it is much more strikingly invalid in its application to human conduct. A man is as far as possible from being a mere point; and the motives which actuate him are as far as possible from being external to his nature. To use a well-worn example, the glass of wine which upon one man exerts an almost irresistible attraction, is hateful to a second, and is taken or left by a third with cool indifference. It is a man's character that determines what things attract and what repel him; and to leave that character out of account and think of the motives as a set of external mechanical forces is the very extreme of falsification.

Conclusion. — It is in its opposition to theories like these that the main significance of indeterminism has lain. Indeed, it is not hard to see that, *at bottom, determinism and indeterminism have stood for very much the same thing.* The one in opposing the superstition of chance, the other in insisting that man is not the helpless sport of external forces — both have pointed to the truth, that man's character is the essential cause of his acts, and that upon this causal relation his moral responsibility depends.

REFERENCES

GIZYCKI, G. VON, *Introduction to the Study of Ethics*, Ch. VII.
LOCKE, J., *Essay concerning Human Understanding*, Book II, Ch. XXI.
HUME, D., *Enquiry concerning Human Understanding*, Sect. VIII.
GREEN, T. H., *Prolegomena to Ethics*, Book II, Ch. I.
WUNDT, W., *Ethics*, Part III, Ch. I, Sect. III.
FISKE, J., *Outlines of Cosmic Philosophy*, Part II, Ch. XVII.
STEPHEN, L., *Science of Ethics*, Ch. VII, ii.
ALEXANDER, S., *Moral Order and Progress*, Book III, Ch. III, ii.
HYSLOP, J. H., *Elements of Ethics*, Ch. IV.
PAULSEN, F., *System of Ethics*, Book II, Ch. IX.
SIDGWICK, H., *Methods of Ethics*, Book I, Ch. V.
SETH, J., *Ethical Principles*, Part III, Ch. I.
RASHDALL, H., *Theory of Good and Evil*, Book III, Ch. III.
BERGSON, H., *Time and Free Will*, especially Ch. III.

CHAPTER V

GENERAL SURVEY OF MORAL STANDARDS

Classification. — Before undertaking a systematic study of the theories of morality, it will be well for us to take a brief survey of its principal varieties and phases. In the introductory chapter we noted the existence of two sets of predicates, ' right ' and ' wrong,' and ' good ' and ' bad,' and called attention to the distinction between impersonal and personal morality which they suggest. For our present purpose it will be convenient to make use of a somewhat different classification.

In the first place, moral values may be thought of as belonging (1) first to the act and secondly to the character of the man who would commit such an act; or (2) first to the character, and secondly to the ways of acting in which such a character shows itself. For example, it is wrong to steal, and the man who does so is a thief; and it is good to relieve the needy, and he who does so is charitable. And, on the other hand, it is good to be brave and to be master of one's passions, and the deeds by which one evinces these traits are in so far praiseworthy. The distinction is largely a matter of emphasis, and the two sides shade into each other; but the extremes are well marked.

In the second place, where the moral value belongs primarily to the act, the standard by which it is judged may be (*a*) a definite set of external requirements, to which, it is thought, men ought simply to conform, regardless of aught else; or the standard may be (*b*) the happiness of one's fellow-men.

GENERAL SURVEY OF MORAL STANDARDS 67

We have, then, a threefold division of moral standards.

Moral Standards
- I. Standards applying primarily to the Act
  - a. Standards of Duty
  - b. Standards of Benevolence
- II. Standards applying primarily to the Agent
  - Standards of Virtue

Here I a corresponds to the impersonal morality mentioned above; and I b and II correspond to the personal morality.

It is probable that all three kinds of standards have a place in the morality of every people, civilized or uncivilized. But among some peoples one kind predominates; among others, another. Thus the morality of the ancient Jews was clearly a morality of duty, and that of the Greeks was quite as clearly a morality of virtue; while Christianity ushered in a morality in which the standards of benevolence have a much larger part.

I a. STANDARDS OF DUTY

1. *Instinctive and Customary Standards*

(1) Instinctive Standards. — Among the standards of duty, we may first consider certain standards which appear to have a direct *instinctive source*. There are some kinds of conduct, such as cannibalism and incest, which arouse in most men an instinctive loathing or even horror; and this is attended with a feeling of intense moral disapproval.

George Sand tells a story of a company of wandering actors shipwrecked on a barren rock in the Adriatic Sea. They are without food, and death by starvation is imminent. The captain of the vessel dies, and one of the actors throws himself upon the corpse with the intention of devouring it. But the leader of the company grapples with him, and, after a desperate struggle, succeeds in throwing the body into the sea. The subordinate actor is a man who throughout the narrative is everywhere represented as thoroughly contemptible; while the leader is pictured as a noble and even heroic figure; and their acts upon this occasion are evidently regarded by the writer as eminently in character. It might well be argued (from the standpoint of benevolence) that the one man was doing exactly what the occasion required — supporting his life without injury to anyone else — while the other was wickedly wasting a most valuable food-supply; but that is not the way that George Sand expected the incident to be regarded by her public.

Religious and Magical Sanctions. — If we ask ourselves why we regard such acts as these as wrong, the answer most obvious to the psychologist is that the feeling that they are wrong has sprung from the sense of their loathesomeness.[1] Other reasons, however, are more often given; and certain of these are interesting, as showing the close connection between duty and benevolence. These reasons mostly fall under the two heads of *bad magic* and *offended deities*. Incestuous love, for example, is often regarded as bringing a pollution upon the culprits, and through them upon their family and kindred, or even upon all who are in any way connected with them. For magical pollutions are *catching* (like infectious diseases) and a whole city or tribe may suffer from them. Or, as we have suggested, some deity may be particularly averse to incest; and he, like the infectious pollution, is apt to wreak his baleful spite, not only upon the guilty ones, but upon all their kith and kin. (Both of

---

[1] The reader should be on his guard against supposing that because the feeling of disgust or loathing is instinctive, the moral judgment or sentiment is likewise instinctive. The latter very probably develops out of the former, and in its earlier stages cannot be clearly distinguished from it. But the very fact that the moral nature of the feeling is the product of a psychological development means that it is something higher than mere instinct.

these modes of explanation become more and more refined as culture advances; but they then take on forms which belong elsewhere in our account.) In either case it will generally be said that the loathing for the sin is due to the universal fear of the pollution or of the divine displeasure which it causes. The psychologist, however, can scarcely doubt that the true explanation runs the other way — that the supposed pernicious consequences of the sin are imaginative products of the loathing which is naturally excites. This distinguishes standards of this sort from those which are primarily standards of benevolence.

Crudeness of Such Morality. — Conformity to standards such as these is the crudest form of morality with which we have to deal. It shows its crudeness in many ways. Emotionally, the sense of moral condemnation is closely fused with the feeling of loathing or horror. Perhaps as a consequence of this, little distinction is made between intentional and unintentional wrong-doing. The man who unknowingly has eaten human flesh is like a leper even in his own eyes. According to the Greek story, Œdipus in all ignorance kills his father in self-defense, and soon after, in equal ignorance, marries his mother, who bears four children to him. When many years later the facts come to light, his horror of himself is such that he puts out his own eyes. It may be added that the infectious pollution follows upon the involuntary offense just as upon the voluntary; and that the offended deity looks only to the external act, and cares nothing for the motive. On the other hand, the infection may be removed by magical devices in which repentance plays no part; and the deity likewise may be bribed, by sacrificial offerings, to forego his vengeance.

(2) **Customary Standards.** — Divided from the foregoing by a very uncertain line are the standards set by long-established custom. The commission of adultery offends against no human instinct. But many men feel toward it

an aversion which is weaker, but hardly different in kind, from that which they feel toward incest; and their moral condemnation of it is very similar. So of sacrilege, of obscenity, and, among many peoples, of breaches of hospitality; and so also of a host of other offenses, not against instinct, but against custom that has become well-nigh as strong as instinct. Other customary standards are regarded less seriously; so that a whole scale of offenses may be devised, ranging from the most abominable to the most trivial.

Relation to Instinctive Standards. — We have said that the line between instinct and custom is uncertain. All customs are, of course, in the last resort outgrowths of instinct, just as all languages are outgrowths of the instinctive *ga* and *boo* of infancy. But because we cannot point to a precise time when, for example, *mamma* changes from a mere babbling to a true word, we do not therefore deny the reality of the change. At the same time it must be confessed that, as applied to the adult man, the distinction between instinct and custom (or habit) is merely one of degree, for the simple reason that scarcely any original instinct remains unmodified in the adult man. Thus the instinctive aversion to cannibalism is fostered by all manner of social influences — or may, on the contrary, be altogether rooted out. So also, while incest appears to be naturally horrible to us, there is nothing natural about the long lists of 'prohibited degrees' which are to be found in the marriage laws of many peoples. As far as ethics is concerned, the sole point of importance here is this: that our feelings toward 'unnatural' sins are apt to contain so powerful an element of sheer disgust, that any definitely moral sentiment is apt to be submerged, or at least seriously restrained in its development. For most purposes the standards derived from instinct and those derived from custom may be regarded as alike customary.

Not All Customs are Moral Standards. — It is obvious that among civilized men not all customs are viewed as having

GENERAL SURVEY OF MORAL STANDARDS 71

moral significance.[1] A man who thoughtlessly wanders downtown without his hat is perhaps the most uncomfortable creature in existence; but his conscience does not prick him. An eccentric young college professor, whose health was delicate, tried the experiment of going barefoot during one of his summer vacations. Walking into the village post-office one day, he met an old lady friend, and accosted her. "Get out of my sight," cried the old lady, horrified. Yet, as she told the story, she expressed no moral condemnation of the young man's conduct. It was, to her, simply disgusting.

But it should be observed, in the first place, that the line of separation is not clearly marked. Bad taste passes easily into indecency and immodesty. And, in the second place, among savages the line practically disappears, and it may be roughly said that "every custom constitutes a moral law." Their sense of right and wrong is in all things guided by the modes of conduct which have come down to them from their ancestors.

Sanctions. — The iniquity of offenses against custom is usually conceived in much the same fashion that we have already noted: they bring pollution or the displeasure of supernatural beings. To rob or murder the unsuspecting guest is an infamy. It is enough to put a curse upon the dwelling where it was committed, from which the inhabitants would suffer as long as the house stood. Better, then, let the man depart in peace and intercept him at the first turning of the road. He may then be seized, brought back, and held for ransom, or even murdered in cold blood, and no such evil be incurred. Petty moral offenses, of course, bring ill-luck or divine ill-favor in a roughly proportionate measure.

---

[1] Sometimes, it is true, the term 'custom' is used in a narrow sense, so as to include only such traditional modes of behavior as are felt to be morally required. (The German *Sitte* and the French *mœurs* are regularly so used.) In that case 'customary morality' is tautologous: 'custom' alone expresses the whole idea.

Separation of Moral Guilt from its Consequences. — As men become more reflective, the distinction between moral guilt and its supernatural consequences is drawn and becomes increasingly clear. We have observed that these consequences may fall upon innocent and guilty alike. Œdipus in the depth of his misery was still self-assured that he was innocent of any moral wrong; and his sons and daughters, who in various ways suffered with him, were even more evidently guiltless of the crimes of parricide and incest. So Orestes would have been held a craven if he had failed to avenge his father's death; but because one of the murderers on whom he took vengeance was his own mother, the furies pursued him none the less relentlessly. 'Wrong' is therefore not the same as 'accursed.' It denotes a peculiar quality which belongs *naturally* to certain kinds of voluntary conduct. And it is senseless to ask *why* such conduct is wrong. It is wrong *just because it is wrong*. Moreover, what is wrong is always and everywhere wrong. It cannot be right, any more than black can be white or bitter can be sweet.

Reduction of Morality to Convention. — The development may, however, take a further turn. We are all to a great extent the slaves of custom; but the uncivilized man is bound by it far more closely than we can easily imagine. His whole course of life is minutely prescribed and hedged about with innumerable taboos. Civilization, though it introduces many new notions of propriety, dispels many more; and of those that remain an increasing part are viewed with little seriousness. We conform, say, because nonconformity attracts attention, and that is disagreeable; or because of mere inertia, since it is a saving of energy to do as others do without tormenting our brains to think of novelties. But to the savage, and, to a surprising degree, even to the comparatively advanced barbarian, every innovation is bad, and, if not positively immoral, is perilously near it.

It is inevitable, then, that the reflection should occur that right and wrong, just and unjust, honorable and dishonorable, are only other names for *customary* and *contrary to custom;* the custom itself being explained as due to a more or less arbitrary convention. What tends especially to the formation of this conception is the knowledge of other men with other customs and likewise other moral standards. As commerce increases, and diplomatic intercourse likewise extends, the most diverse traditions are brought into sudden and striking contrast. The first result is a mutual contempt; the next a species of external toleration — as when a people are willing to admit that polygamy may be all very well for their neighbors, but would condemn to death or exile the man who attempted it among themselves. It is at this stage of affairs that the custom-conception is most apt to become prominent; and it may help to bring on a further stage, the breakdown of morality. For *the convention might have been otherwise.* One custom, when you are used to it, is, it is felt, as good as another. The distinction between right and wrong is thus *illusory;* it has no real basis in permanent facts; and the man of sense will disregard it as often as his convenience requires.

2. *Personal Authority*

Distinction between Personal Authority and Law. — Among uncivilized men there is no one who is looked upon as authorized to change a custom or modify a moral requirement. There is no legislative power. The mightiest chief holds his authority subject to time-honored traditions. When, in exceptional instances, social reforms are carried through, the leaders usually claim that they are simply restoring an ancient custom which has fallen into disuse, or that they are acting as the mouthpiece of an interested deity.

There are, however, persons who have the right to direct

their fellows in matters which custom has left undetermined. They have, we repeat, no legislative power; but they can issue commands and injunctions which it is the duty of the others to obey. Why are these not laws? In the first place, because, as a rule, they are not general in their application, as laws are, but are addressed to particular men on a particular occasion. And, in the second place, because, even when they reach beyond the particular occasion, they express merely the ruler's will; and when he is dead or deprived of power they lapse at once.

Analogous to the commands of the chieftain are the commands of the parent, the husband, the master. It is the recognized duty of the child, the wife, the slave, to obey — not because the things commanded were in themselves obligatory, or because the things forbidden were in themselves wrong, but simply because he who is in authority has so ordered. The child, for example, who has been forbidden by his mother to eat a certain kind of fruit, begs for permission to do so; and if the permission is granted, he eats the fruit without a twinge of conscience.

Relation to Custom. — There is no clear line of distinction between this morality of obedience to authority, and the morality (above treated) of compliance with custom. The persons who are obeyed are *those to whom customary morality gives the right to command.* Sometimes on the surface this does not appear to be the case. The chief, let us say, has won his place by killing his predecessor. The husband has tamed his wife with a club. And the slaves and children know what to expect if they are caught in any disobedience. But it will generally be found that the force of custom is the real determining factor in the matter. Men may submit to a usurping chief out of mere fear, without feeling that he has any rightful claim upon them, and while eagerly awaiting the opportunity of casting off his yoke. And the like may be true of the other relations which we have mentioned.

But such a state of affairs does not constitute the *recognition of authority*, of a right to rule and a duty to obey. And this, we say, is what force alone does not produce. Again, there is such a thing as personal ascendancy, by which one man, without the use or display of force, imposes his will upon those about him. But this is far from constituting authority. It frequently happens that those who obey most slavishly are in a state of constant resentment against the personal influence which they cannot throw off. They are as far as possible from recognizing obedience as a duty. And even where there is no resentment, the sense of duty may be entirely absent. The personal ascendancy of the wife, for example, may keep her husband in complete subjection, without either of them having the least notion that it is his duty to obey her.

The force of custom, we repeat, is a necessary factor in the constitution of authority. Where, for example, the chief has won his place by force, it will be found, perhaps, that the traditional sentiment of the people is that the strongest men should rule. By this we do not mean simply that as a matter of fact the strongest man generally *does* rule, but that custom requires that he *shall* rule and makes it wrong to resist him. Where the custom is different — where, for example, the oldest men are the rightful rulers — the strong man who laid hands upon his honored chief would be an object of universal detestation, and his rule would in all probability be short. Or, again, the usurper may establish himself in power by seizing the traditional *symbols* of authority, the chief's club or ring or robe or scepter; or he may be initiated into his office by the rites and ceremonies which tradition requires.

Again, when the husband beats his young wife into submission, why does she not kill him as he sleeps and make her escape to her own people? Because she and they alike believe that he has the right to beat her. She *expects* to be beaten; and having been beaten, she loves him none the less for it. And he too feels that he has a right to command and to require obedience. The use of force is simply a means by which the tradition is maintained.

Much the same may be said of the part which personal ascendancy plays. It is almost indispensable to the successful ruler. And, on the other hand, the possession of traditional authority is in itself an important source of personal ascendancy. The office gives weight to the man. He feels his own dignity; and the added self-importance makes itself felt in his bearing, and that tends to induce a suitable attitude in others. In any case, as we have said, personal ascendancy does not amount to authority. But it is one of the most potent means by which such authority as tradition sanctions is acquired and maintained.

Divine Authority. — An especially interesting and significant example of authority is that of a god. It illustrates in striking fashion the principles which we have just considered. The primitive gods have no legislative function. They do not alter customary standards — even where they are regarded as the protectors of those standards. A god, for example, is angered by inhospitality, and vents his anger upon the offender and his household. But no one imagines that he might have bidden men be inhospitable, and then have been angered by hospitality. However, the gods do issue commands, and it is (generally speaking) the duty of men to obey.[1] Why? The answer is analogous to the answer in the case of human authority. They are wiser than we, and stronger, and the wise and strong ought to

[1] The boundary-line between mere authority and legislative power is, of course, much more tenuous in the case of a god than in that of a human chief or assembly. For he is immortal and exceedingly wise and powerful; so that there is no set term to his commands, such as death or infirmity sets to those of human chiefs. It is because of this fact that early law-makers so often claim to be speaking for a deity. The divine authority serves as a bridge between human authority and legislation.

GENERAL SURVEY OF MORAL STANDARDS 77

rule. We are their property, and the masters ought to rule. We are their creatures, and the makers (like parents) ought to rule. Or, again, we are their creatures; and, as a man, personifying the work of his hands, expects it to serve his purposes, so the gods have a right to expect us to serve their purposes. *Aside from the analogy of human authority, a man owes a god no obedience;* though he may, indeed, stand in awe of him and obey his behests for that reason, just as he might be cowed into obedience to a man whose authority he did not acknowledge.

3. *The Authority of Law*

Logically, then, the duty of obedience to personal authority is simply a particular case of the duty of conformity to a customary standard.[1] And yet it was necessary to give a distinct account of it, for the reason that the particular case sometimes develops so as to cover the whole field.

The Legislature. — As we have said, authority is at first limited, as well as supported, by custom. There is no authority to change a customary standard. With the rise of *states* this limitation begins to disappear, or at least to recede. For a state possesses a *legislature;*[2] and though this legislature, too, in the last resort, owes its authority to custom, yet it comes to have in a larger and larger measure the power to change customs — even those customs to which

---

[1] The question may be asked, whether, in the case of obedience to parents, the authority may not be due to instinct rather than to custom. The answer very decisively is that there is no instinct of obedience. Little children have to learn to obey. It is true that they have a very high degree of suggestibility; and this is of good service in teaching them obedience. But unfortunately their suggestibility is often largely *negative.* Telling a child, or even hinting to a child, to do one thing is very apt to make it wish to do just the opposite.

[2] It should be observed that, as the term is here used, the legislature may consist of one man, or of a limited assembly, or of the whole body of citizens. The legislature is that man or body of men which can make laws.

in earlier times the strongest moral sentiments have attached. Thus laws are passed affecting the marriage-relation and the avenging of family wrongs.[1] To be sure, there are always limits to this power, in customary standards which are too strongly intrenched for any legislature to dare attack. But, especially where the legislature consists of the whole body of citizens, this limitation is for the most part unfelt, for the simple reason that no large part of the assembly is likely to *wish* to legislate against their deepest moral convictions. To act wrongly under great temptation is human, and states as well as individuals do so. But deliberately to authorize what is universally felt to be wrong-doing, or deliberately to forbid what the common moral sentiment requires, is another and far more serious thing; and legislatures seldom desire to do it. Thus, we repeat, the limit to the legislative power is unfelt; and more and more in the mind of the people the distinction between right and wrong comes to be merged with the distinction between what the law of the land permits and what it forbids.

Natural and Divine Law. — But the two distinctions never entirely coalesce. In the first place, there are moral standards of which the state takes no account — often by reason of their pettiness. And, besides, there are moral standards by which the legislator, in the very act of changing the law of the land, feels himself bound. Men in general are 'just' or 'unjust' according as they obey or disobey the laws. But the laws themselves are appraised as 'just' or 'unjust' laws — evidently with reference to some higher standard. Again, the laws of the land, much as they may

---

[1] The state of New York permits the marriage of uncle and niece, or aunt and nephew. Not many such marriages are performed — custom is too strongly against it. But where they are performed, public indignation against the act is very slight. The provision of the law is accepted as a moral justification.

GENERAL SURVEY OF MORAL STANDARDS

change, preserve a certain likeness. Never, for example, is murder, theft, or adultery freely permitted. And, similarly, as the laws of different states are compared and their specific differences are noted, their larger similarities also come into view; and in a more or less vague way it is recognized that some things are unlawful the whole world over, while others are lawful in one place and unlawful in another. In these ways arises the notion of a *natural law*, universal and changeless; and because there can be no law without a legislator, and the natural laws have the support of the most ancient religious sanctions, they are inevitably regarded as *divine laws*.

The divine law easily embraces the whole of morality — if one leaves out of account the general duty to obey the divine law itself, which must, of course, rest upon some other basis. But this exception is easily overlooked; and it is not at all uncommon for men to regard all morality as consisting in obedience to the arbitrary will of the gods. (By 'arbitrary' I mean that it is supposed, not that the gods forbid murder because it is wrong, but that murder is wrong simply and solely because they forbid it.) Mere custom is not thought of as establishing a moral standard. Where the custom has not been divinely ordained, it is at best indifferent, and is only too apt to be a serious corruption of the right and proper manner of life.

The Moral Law Hypostatized. — In conclusion, we must note that sometimes the notion of a legislator falls into abeyance, and the moral law is looked upon as having, so to speak, an existence in itself. It is *hypostatized* — an eternal law without a law-giver. God himself is subject to it, although, since he is absolutely good, it is no constraint upon him. To say that God is just would have no meaning, if conformity to the eternal law were not his duty as it is ours.

I b. The Standards of Benevolence

1. *Ideality of Benevolence and Virtue*

Benevolence and Virtue set no Definite Exactions. — The moral values which we have yet to consider differ from the foregoing in one most striking respect. Their standards are *ideal*. An imperative of duty must be fairly clear and explicit — as doubt increases, duty fades away — and it must not be impossible of complete fulfillment. But the standards of benevolence, and still more the standards of virtue, or self-development (which we are to take up last), are not capable of exact statement. Their *spirit* may be set forth in words, and has in fact found its expression in proverbs that are among the most precious heritages of the race; such, for example, as the old priestly maxim, which Jesus regarded as almost the finest in the Mosaic writings: " Thou shalt love thy neighbor as thyself." But you must not ask for definitions of terms. If you do, the only answer is a *story*. That is because the morality of benevolence (for example) does not exact any definite course of conduct. It does not *exact* anything. Whatever is felt as an exaction is duty. But, on the other hand, it sets no bounds to the gift of love — except an absolute self-surrender. So also the morality of virtue exacts nothing; but it sets no bounds to human aspiration — except the perfection of the all-wise and all-powerful God. Accordingly, the question of possibility does not arise. Moral valuation is here the measuring of the actual by the ideal.

Measurement by an Ideal need not be Condemnation. — It must not be supposed that the valuation is necessarily negative, as if in the light of the ideal all things were to be condemned. That is a position which is sometimes taken by men of a juristic frame of mind, who have become conscious of the infinitude of the standards of love and perfection. Such men interpret these as *infinite duties;* and since they find no one who fulfills such duties, they pronounce all men (themselves, of course, included) to be utterly and altogether vile. But this is to mistake the nature of the ideal; just as it would be mistaking the nature of ideal beauty to declare that every flower that blows is utterly and altogether ugly. Ideals are realized in things; realized, to be sure, in varying degrees, but not less truly realized for that. Just as there is beauty in the common flower, so there is kindness in the common man. So far from implying universal condemnation, the judgment by an ideal standard tends rather to lead to an enlargement of sympathetic appreciation. The best judge is he who sees what good there is in everything. Not that disapproval is done away with. But the more it is reflective, the more it is *qualified*, just as approval is qualified.

Doing More than One's Duty. — The ideal standards of benevolence and virtue stand in a peculiar relation to certain of the standards of duty; and it is this that has given rise to the old dispute, whether a man can do more than his duty. There are certain degrees of kindness and loyalty, courage and good sense, which we *expect* from men; and there are common manifestations of these qualities that we regard as a normal and reasonable requirement. They are distinctly duties. This is the case, for example, in the relations of father and child. It is the recognized duty of the father to provide for the support of the child; and the latter has his reciprocal duties. So long as the conduct remains at this level the ideal standards of benevolence are not applied; or, if they are applied, the judgment is one of indifference, or of very mild approval. To earn money with which to buy bread and shoes for one's children is 'simply doing one's duty.' But beyond the limits of all such duty there is an unmeasured scope for loving care that cannot be reduced to duty, and does not need to be. It is not *felt* as duty by the man himself. It is not looked upon as duty by others. The morality is of another, freer type. On the other hand, the neglect of parental duties is a form of cruelty. Thus arises the peculiar relation to which reference has been made. *The performance of duty* (as thus conceived) *coincides with the indifference-point between kindness and cruelty.* The like might be said of the relation of duty to courage and cowardice, or to wisdom and folly. To do merely one's duty — to do merely what any set of external standards require — is to fail to interest the idealizing conscience at all.

In answer, then, to the old query, whether a man can do more than his duty, we may say: No, so long as it is a question of duty. A man can do more than his duty, only when the question behind his conduct is such as this: What is best for my child, my friend, my country? or, How shall I be true to my manhood?

2. *Benevolence in General*

Grades of Benevolence. — Happiness, or unhappiness, the value of a condition of life considered as a whole, contains many factors of varying complexity. To try to make a man happy may be to devote oneself to his amusement, to assist him in his business, to improve his taste, to convert him to the true religion, or — any one of a thousand things. Whatever goods there are in human life, it is morally right and good to help our fellow-men acquire them. The morality, therefore, is of many grades, according to the kind of good which is in question. We need not attempt a classification here. Perhaps a satisfactory classification would be beyond our powers. Lowest of all, no doubt, is the imparting of an idle pleasure. Highest of all we would surely rank the endeavor to make men morally better.

Flexibility of the Standards of Benevolence. — Whereas the standards of duty are hard and fast prescriptions, changing, to be sure, but always resisting change, the standards of benevolence are adaptability itself. Duty looks above and beyond the particular case; benevolence is immersed in it. It is for this reason that they supplement each other so admirably. But they sometimes conflict. The shoemaker-saint, who stole leather that he might make shoes for the poor, is a familiar illustration; and our experience is filled with similar temptations. "To do a great right do a little wrong," is the constant plea. Many excellent men have held that on such an occasion duty ought always to have the preference. Formally they are right, of course; for it is mere tautology to say that a man 'ought always to do his duty.' But when it comes to actual practice the common sense of humanity is against them. *Summum jus, summa injuria.* The particular circumstances cannot be utterly ignored. Why this is true, and how far it is true, we shall try to determine hereafter.

The Direction of Benevolence set by Duty. — One important relation between duty and benevolence is this: that, for the most part, duty fixes the general limits within which benevolence is exerted. A man seldom or never stands in a perfectly uniform relation to all those by whom he is surrounded. There are some whose happiness is of especial concern to him; and this is wholly proper. If he treats his own son and his neighbor's son alike, he is probably not treating either rightly. In other words, there are *duties of benevolence.* These do not exhaust the life of kindness, but they do give it its general direction. If dutifulness without benevolence is hard, benevolence divorced from a sense of duty is weak and unmanly. It does not even command gratitude from those who receive its benefits, much less the approval of disinterested observers.

3. *The Objects of Benevolence*

(1) Benevolence to Individuals

Benevolence is extended primarily to individuals, and in normal characters it never wholly loses this primitive personal touch. It shows itself in acts of kindness in which the happiness of particular persons is the only object in view.

Biological Significance. — Man is a social animal; and there is a strong tendency in him to sympathetic feelings of joy and sorrow; and with these sympathetic feelings are connected the impulse to relieve distress and impart pleasure. But man's life, even among the lowest savages, is almost everywhere far *more* social than that for which organic evolution has fitted him — as we may infer from the study of his nearest relatives among the apes — and the course of civilization has generally tended to bring him into larger and more complex relations with his fellows. This has involved a constantly increasing exercise of sympathy. There is no reason to think that in this development man's inborn sympathetic tendency has become stronger, any more than his eyesight or his hearing. How, then, has its operation been so greatly increased? In the first place, the establishment of any sort of lasting relation between man and man helps them to imagine each other's case, and is thus a favorable condition for sympathetic emotion. In the second place, an important factor in the result has been morality. Moral approval and disapproval have reënforced natural sympathy and helped it to subdue opposing influences. Some ethicists would say that this is the chief function of morality; it is at any rate a very important function.

Relation of Benevolence to Love. — It has just been said that any sort of lasting relation between men tends to facilitate sympathy. This is seen in the members of the family, the community, the state, and all manner of voluntary associations. Especially favorable to sympathy is the very complex group of sentiments to which the name 'love,' in one of its uses, is attached. All this is recognized in our moral standards. Love makes sacrifices praiseworthy, which without it would be folly; and it makes reservations ignoble, which without it would be most proper. Love is not morality. It may even be markedly vicious. But love and morality are close coadjutors; and one of the best fruits of morality is the capacity for strong and enduring love.

(2) Devotion to an Institution

Benevolence Universalized. — Though benevolence begins with the individual, it does not stop there. It *universalizes* itself in two ways: first, as devotion to an institution; and, secondly, as devotion to a cause. These two forms of benevolence are not always easily distinguishable from each other; as when an institution stands for a single definite cause. There is a difference, however. Vassar and Wellesley colleges are both institutions for the higher education of women; yet one may love the one and despise the other. Often, too, an institution has many aims, and yet keeps its individuality in the prosecution of them all. A family and a community are institutions of this kind; and so also is that supreme institution, a nation-state. To love one's country includes an interest in a thousand causes.

Preference of the Wider Institution. — It is generally felt that as institutions increase in magnitude, devotion to them increases in moral value. The community, for example, is more than the family, and the state is more than the community, and they should be preferred one to another accordingly. Some moralists have exalted this into a universal moral rule; but in that form it will not hold. The narrower institution has its claims upon our goodwill even as against the broader, as our common moral standards recognize. The well-known French law, which exempts from military service a widow's only son, may serve to illustrate this point.

So also the individual has his claims upon us, as against institutions of every grade. Sometimes devotion to an institution hardens a man's heart against particular individuals. A patriot may be led by his patriotism to be a ruthless oppressor of the poor. But though such men may be pardonable we certainly have no great admiration for them.

Devotion to Humanity. — There is an institution in the making which is wider than the state: humanity. By 'humanity' we do not mean simply all men, but all men as organized in some fashion into a real whole which can claim our allegiance. In many ways this organization is going forward: through the improvement of the means of communication, the extension of travel and commerce and diplomatic intercourse, the growth of unions, the universal news-service, the international circulation of the masterpieces of literature, music, and painting. It means much, when, for example, funds can be raised in America for educational institutions in Turkey or India. In some minds, at least, the conception of a common good of the human race is growing up, and is inspiring a benevolence of the noblest order.

(3) Devotion to a Cause

Very similar remarks may be made with reference to the other form of universalized benevolence: devotion to a cause. There are causes which affect the welfare of great numbers of men: civil liberty, popular education, the equalization of wealth or opportunity, prohibition, etc. Such a cause may very largely absorb a man's benevolence. Instead of feeling for the separate individuals as such, he masses them under general conceptions. When the individuals' own private joys and sorrows do come into the account, it is as significant illustrations of widespread conditions.

As compared with the more primitive personal benevolence, the devotion to a cause has both its advantages and its disadvantages, and both are sufficiently obvious. It is, so to speak, longer and narrower in its scope. Ordinarily we regard it as the higher, nobler form; but when, as sometimes happens, it results in a hardening of the heart to immediate influences, we attribute much less merit to it. Nay, in extreme cases, it may even be regarded as a vice. The physician who, in the cause of human health, experiments upon the bodies of his helpless and confiding patients, is looked upon rather as a monster than as a benefactor of the race. If we are to be fair, however, we must remember that in a very similar way an absorbing love for a few persons may make one insensible to the needs of others. "None so selfish as the father of a family." And ordinarily it is well that this is so. If men did not love narrowly and intensely, and did not become absorbed in single, definite aims, the world would be much the poorer in consequence.

(4) Devotion to a Representative

Personal Loyalty. — There is a peculiar type of benevolence which unites in itself the characteristics of individual and collective benevolence, and which historically has often marked the development of the latter from the former. It is devotion to the representative of an institution or a cause. In the person of the representative, the values of the complex institution or abstract cause are embodied in the most vivid and moving form. For illustration we need think only of the power which loyalty to a king or chief has been in the world.

The Love of a God. — The place which the love of a god has had in the moral life is similar. A god may be loved as the god of one's fathers, the god of one's country, the god of one's salvation, the god of humanity — generally speaking, the institution which seems to be of supreme value in life. He is not loved from personal acquaintance. To be sure, a certain notion of his character is spread abroad among the people — much like the legendary character which a monarch is given in the popular consciousness — and this awakens an enthusiasm of loyalty. But this notion itself obviously arises from the cause or institution for which the god stands.

The God of Humanity. — By Christians the love of God has generally been regarded as the supreme form of benevolence. Among free-thinking moralists the love of humanity is generally accorded the highest place. The difference is not without its importance; but this is less than might be supposed. For the God of Christianity is a God of humanity. He represents all of the highest interests of mankind, as the believers understand them. For them, to love God and to love humanity are inseparable.

We have again to observe here what we have observed before: that the higher without the lower is held of little account, or its genuineness is denied. "How shall ye love God whom ye have not seen, if ye love not your brother whom ye have seen?" The higher benevolence is an outgrowth from the lower; and when the lower dies, the higher cannot maintain its vigor and purity.

II. THE STANDARDS OF VIRTUE

1. *The Kinds of Virtue*

We have considered morality as conformity to a given external standard, and as devotion to another's welfare. We have now to consider the immediate value of moral character in itself, or *virtue*.

Further Classification. — Virtue is of two kinds. The first kind, comprising *justice* and *love* (or *charity*), simply *repeats the standards of duty and benevolence*, looked at, however, from a different point of view. The fulfillment of duty, for example, is no longer regarded as the mere satisfaction of a foreign demand. It is a pride and a pleasure. "His *delight* is in the law of the Lord." And similarly of the fulfillment of specific duties. Honesty, veracity, chastity, are viewed as treasures of the soul, of incalculable value to the possessor, and beautiful in the eyes of the beholder. So, too, of the various forms of benevolence. These are not a mere robbing of the self to make others rich; they are riches in themselves.

The other kind of virtue (with which we shall here be more particularly concerned) consists of certain qualities of mind which, in some degree, are necessary to *all* morality — qualities without which one cannot be consistently honest or chaste or obedient, or kind or loyal. Thus they present, as it were, a *cross-division* of morality. These qualities are comprised under the general heads of *courage, temperance,* and *wisdom.*

(1) Courage

Definition. — By 'courage,' as the term is here used, is not meant fearlessness, whether due to impassivity, ignorance of danger, confidence in one's own strength or skill, or natural buoyancy of spirits. The brave man may be fearless, but he may also be nervous, cautious, self-distrustful, and pessimistic. The more fear a man feels, the more need he has for courage. Courage is the *strength of determination that cannot be moved from its course by pain or fear.*

Kinds of Courage. — Courage is said to be of various kinds according to the sort of pain or danger which it resists. Some men will face physical injury without hesitation, who cannot bear the thought of disgrace. Some, whom no threats against themselves can move, are made cowards when wife or child is concerned. There are limits, no doubt, to every man's endurance; and the nearer limits are in different directions for different men.

But of far greater importance for ethics is the difference in the quality of courage due to difference in the *motives* by which the resistance to pain or danger is inspired. Lowest in the scale are the instincts of self-preservation. A cornered rat will fight; and a human coward in a corner may look very much like a hero. A man may also be brave for gain or glory; the latter motive being considered much the nobler. But the moral courage, which alone is essentially good, is inspired by the sense of duty, or by benevolence, or by an ideal of character.

In What Sense Courage is a Virtue. — The difficulty has often been raised, that courage cannot be a virtue, because it can be displayed by the worst of men in the most vicious pursuits. But the objection is unsound. For courage is a virtue, not in the sense that whoever has it is morally good, or that whatever is done with it is morally right, but in the sense that it is a *necessary* quality of the good man, and that on countless occasions a man cannot, unless he is brave, do what is just or kind. Not every villain is a coward, — not by any means, — but every coward is a villain. Without moral courage, no high degree of justice or benevolence is possible.

Is Moral Courage Sufficient? — The question may be asked, whether a man who possessed moral courage and was a coward in all other respects could be called a brave and good man. At first sight the question appears to be a fair one; but as a matter of fact it is of a kind to which a direct answer cannot be given. It is much as if one should ask whether, if a man's moral nature were separated bodily from the rest of his character and given to another man, it would still retain its old significance and value. We could only answer yes and no at once. For this condition is an inconceivable one. Character is not divided into distinct sections; and in particular the moral character (as we shall hereafter see) is most intimately connected with all the other sides of man's complex nature. A man is not *born* morally good; he becomes so only through a process of educational development. And it is not to be thought that up to a certain point in that development he shows no power of self-control in the presence of danger, and then instantly exhibits such power in a high degree. No, a man who is distinguished by courage of the moral type is bound to be a brave man generally — not in all things, for we all have our weaknesses, but for the most part. This is why, although only moral courage is essentially good, no one in his ideal of virtue fails to include non-moral courage also.

The Primitive Conception of Courage. — In fact, among peoples of a low degree of culture, no distinction between moral courage and the lower grades of courage is formed. Courage with them means, of course, preëminently courage in war, where a man exposes his life for the safety or glory of his clan; and no effort is made to distinguish whether this is due, say, to self-confidence in superior strength or skill, to an overmastering desire for glory, or to patriotic devotion. And so what appears to be the same quality, when exhibited in a private quarrel or even in an act of treason, is still virtue and is admired as such. Furthermore, even the physical qualities of bulk and strength are not definitely set off from the mental quality of courage, as if the latter were a moral excellence and the former not. The physical and moral qualities are ranked together. Strength and courage make a valuable man, just as (we may add) beauty and industry make a valuable woman. The case is thus much the same as we found with respect to certain customary standards of duty. The moral sentiment is not clearly differentiated from feelings and sentiments of a lower order.

(2) Temperance

Definition. — As courage is strength of determination in the face of threatening pains, so temperance is strength of determination in the face of inviting pleasures. It does not mean insensibility to pleasure or self-denial for the denial's sake. It means that a man cannot be swayed by the nearness and accessibility of a lesser good to give up a greater good for it.

Relation to Courage. — Temperance is the same quality of mind as courage, seen from a different point of view. This seems hard to realize, when we see a man who has shown himself brave yielding to temptation. But in just the same way a man who has shown himself brave before one danger may flee from another; and so also a man who has conquered one temptation may surrender to another. Courage is no more different from temperance than courage is from courage, or temperance from temperance. Each means the control of temporary and superficial, but, for the time being, intense feelings, by the relatively permanent and deeper lying forces of character.

Corollaries. — It follows that all that we have said above with regard to courage may be directly applied to temperance. Men are temperate, as they are brave, from a variety of motives, among which is ambition for wealth or power or glory. But the noblest temperance is that which has its springs in respect for the standards of justice, in devotion to others' welfare, or in a sense of the beauty of the temperate character itself. Temperance of the lower kinds may be displayed by evil men in the prosecution of evil enterprises. It is accordingly not sufficient to constitute moral goodness. But without temperance, and, in particular, without some degree of 'moral temperance' (if we may so call it), a good character is unthinkable.

Persistence of Primitive Conceptions. — Temperance is like courage also in the fact that peoples of a low degree of moral culture do not distinguish it sharply from mere insensibility, on the one hand, or from physical endurance, on the other. And it may be added here, that the same often remains obstinately true of men of a higher culture. Plato, in the *Banquet*, depicts his ideal philosopher drinking all night, till his companions are under the table, and the reader is expected to admire the hero for his prowess. The excuse is, first, that wine is no temptation to him, and, secondly, that it does not visibly affect him. I am afraid that even to-day we are more than half inclined to admire the performance. The same tendency is shown in the confusion of chastity with physical virginity. A 'virtue' preserved only by bolts and bars or by constant espionage may be preferred to a real chastity that has been a prey to guile or even to physical force. The author of *Tom Jones* assumes that by committing a rape upon a young woman a man can force her either to marry him or to give up all hopes of happiness. In the *Vicar of Wakefield*, the heroine, who is supposed to have been betrayed by a mock-marriage, is regarded as utterly ruined — until the marriage turns out to have been a real one.

(3) Wisdom

Courage and temperance together constitute what is called 'strength of character.' But character does not need strength alone; it needs judgment. The intellectual side of morality is *wisdom*. A good man cannot be a weakling; so also he cannot be a fool.

Definition. — 'Wisdom,' in the widest sense of the term (as it is now used),[1] means *knowledge of the relative values of things*. Of course, in order to know values one must know many other particular facts and general truths; but this is subsidiary. The main thing is to know how to choose; and if one has an immense amount of other knowledge and is deficient in this, he is not wise.

Kinds of Wisdom. — There are as many different orders of wisdom as there are orders of values among which to choose, or, again, as there are diverging lines of human interest and activity. Good judgment in business may or may not go with judgment in art or in the social world. There is common ground, to be sure; but also there is in each department of life something which requires a special experience for its appreciation.

The highest type of wisdom is the knowledge of the moral

[1] Elsewhere in this volume it is used as the conventional translation of σοφία, which in Aristotle denotes knowledge of pure science. In that connection the word 'prudence' is used just as we here use 'wisdom.'

values themselves, as measured by the various kinds of standards which we have been discussing. We shall hereafter try to make clear — though, in a way, it is obvious enough to common sense — that moral values stand in a very close relation to values of the lower kinds. It may not be quite accurate to say (with Leslie Stephen) that to show that drunkenness is injurious is the same as to show that it is morally wrong; but it is certain that it is the injurious effects of drunkenness that have caused men to pronounce it morally wrong. The higher values of life are not to be resolved into the lower; but men's experience of the lower values has given at least a general direction to the evolution of the higher values. And so moral wisdom, the knowledge of the supreme values, cannot exist by itself. A man cannot be a general imbecile and a moral sage.

Relation of Wisdom to Courage and Temperance. — We have seen above that courage and temperance are the same quality of character seen in different relations. With some reservations the same remark may be applied to wisdom also. This is hard for us to understand, because so often we see men display great heroism and self-restraint in the support of a sadly misguided cause, — the uprising of the Scotch Highlanders in favor of the Young Pretender, for example — or, again, weakly deserting a cause of which they rightly approve. But in cases of the one sort we perceive, on reflection, that the folly displayed is, in reality, a high degree of wisdom that has failed because of its application to new and untried conditions. The whole social existence of the Highlander was based upon his fidelity to his hereditary chief. This was his best wisdom, approved by the experience of his clan for centuries. The support which he gave to his 'rightful sovereign' was simply an extension of the wisdom of the clan. Now of course this does not warrant us in saying that a mistake is not a mistake; but it should serve to warn us against associating the courage of the High-

GENERAL SURVEY OF MORAL STANDARDS 95

lander with this particular mistake, and forgetting that it had grown up in connection with convictions which within their own limits were eminently wise. And in cases of the other sort, where wisdom seems to be coupled with cowardice and weak indulgence, examination may be counted on to show that the supposed wisdom is in reality of a very shallow nature. Men do not always act according to their convictions. Any man, no doubt, may be unmanned under sufficient stress of danger or temptation. But deeply settled convictions are not lightly discarded. It requires powerful motives to suppress them. So that when we see a man easily led to act against his better judgment, we may rest assured that the judgment itself was little more than a form of words, with little genuine appreciation behind it.

The close mutual relation between strength and wisdom is to some extent recognized in common speech. Courage (or what would otherwise be courage) without wisdom is not courage but rashness; temperance without wisdom is not temperance but miserliness. And, on the other hand, a general knowledge of values, without the 'courage of one's convictions,' would by no one be called wisdom.

Why, then, is the distinction between strength and wisdom preserved? If the two are inseparable, if neither is itself without the other, why are they not simply identified? There would be some advantage in identifying them, and some moralists have done so; but the greater advantage is on the other side. It is often by no means a useless procedure to separate in our minds various aspects of one thing or event which in reality belong together, especially if they vary in degree or extent independently of one another, or seem to do so to common observation. This last is the case with wisdom and strength. They are related together as the fullness and accuracy of knowledge to the efficacy of its control of conduct. And though in a general way we may say that probably no change in the one can occur without some corresponding change in the other, nevertheless in our actual observation of men we estimate the two qualities in great part separately. This is largely because we judge a man's wisdom not only from his deeds but from his expressed opinions; whereas we are much less inclined to judge courage and temperance from words alone, except under circumstances where the words amount to deeds.

The Cardinal Virtues. — Courage, temperance, and wisdom, together with justice, are the four so-called *cardinal virtues*. The virtue of benevolence, or charity, is not included, because the Greek moralists, to whom the list is due, treated benevolence either as a form of justice or else as included in *friendship*. And friendship obviously is not a virtue of a single man, though the forming and maintaining of friendships is one of the most notable ways in which his virtue can manifest itself — a truth which the Greeks were fond of pointing out.

2. *Virtue without Effort*

When we compare the morality of virtue with that of duty and benevolence, one very important difference soon appears. From the point of view of duty or of benevolence we attach little importance to conduct which, though right and good, calls for little effort on the agent's part. If I pay my rent promptly when next it falls due, no one will praise the deed. If I tell my children a story to-night at bedtime, neither they nor any one else will pay any attention to the moral quality of the act. It is only when I persist in my duty under strong temptation to the contrary, it is only when the benefit which I confer costs me dearly, that any approval is aroused. There must be the keen sense of obligation or of personal loss. But from the point of view of virtue, common acts, performed without effort, are exceedingly important. To be *such a man* as always to meet my petty obligations promptly, is to be a very worthy sort of man. To be the sort of father that is ready to put down his book to tell the children their bedtime story is to be a very good sort of father. The separate acts are little or nothing; but the trait of character, which underlies and includes them all, is much.

Not only is this true, but, furthermore, from the point of view of virtue the conduct which only a keen sense of obligation can force through, the benevolence which costs a pang, does not appear to be especially admirable. As Aristotle puts it, he only is virtuous who takes pleasure in acting virtuously. The reason for this difference is simple. From the point of view of duty, the essential thing is that the obligation has been performed, and the act appears admirable in comparison with the breach of duty that under such circumstances would not have been surprising. From the point of view of benevolence, the essential thing is that the impulses of selfishness were as a matter of fact overcome; and the act appears admirable in contrast to the easy-going acquiescence in another's ill, into which many men, under the circumstances, would have slipped. But from the point of view of virtue we note the weakness and hesitancy displayed, and contrast them with the strength and decision that would not for a moment have left the issue in doubt.

3. *The Imitation of the Ideal*

The Hero. — The values of virtue are very commonly represented in our consciousness in the concrete form of the ideal personality, or *hero;* and in that case our morality becomes in a peculiar sense an *imitation* — not an indiscriminate imitation of the traits of character of the men and women about us, but a *selective* imitation of what is regarded as best. Primarily the heroes are real individuals, perhaps parents or friends — " Can't any boy be as good as Ma " — perhaps famous men of the present or of the past. The imitation of one's ancestors long exerted a powerful influence upon men, because of the way in which it allied itself with devotion to the family as a permanent institution. The heroes may also be imaginary; but if they are known to be such, their influence is, in general, greatly diminished.

The Divine Model. — Most notable of all objects of moral imitation is the superhuman or *divine* hero; Hercules, Buddha, or the incarnate God of Christianity. The imitation of Christ has been the supreme formative and guiding influence in the lives of many of the noblest of men.

Influence of Religion upon Morality. — This is the third principal mode that we have found, in which religion has set its impress upon morality. The gods are guardians of justice; or chiefs; or legislators. They are friends of men; or (changing to the singular) the loving Savior of us all, whom we love in turn with an unquenchable love. Or they are the archetypes of every human perfection, toward which our aspirations are set. Needless to say, in actual life all these conceptions unite together, reënforcing one another in varying degrees, according to the character of the moral agent.

REFERENCES

WUNDT, W., *Ethics*, Book III, Ch. IV.
MEZES, S., *Ethics, Descriptive and Explanatory*, Chs. IX–XIV.
DEWEY and TUFTS, *Ethics*, Part I, Chs. III–V, IX, XIX.
MACKENZIE, J. S., *Manual of Ethics*, Book III, Chs. III–V.
SORLEY, W. R., *The Moral Life*.
ALEXANDER, S., *Moral Order and Progress*, Book II, Ch. VI.
TAYLOR, A. E., *The Problem of Conduct*, Ch. IV.
HOBHOUSE, L. T., *Morals in Evolution*, Part II, Chs. I, II.
READ, C., *Natural and Social Morals*, Book II, Ch. VI.

PART II

THE CLASSICAL SCHOOLS

INTRODUCTORY NOTE

Object of Part II. — Ethics is a science that has grown up through centuries of controversy; and, what is more, all the old controversies are still alive, or may at any moment be reborn. What the science is to-day cannot, therefore, be satisfactorily understood without some knowledge of the age-long disputations. In the following chapters we shall attempt, not a history of ethics — for that would exceed our space — but a critical account of some of the more important and typical ethical theories. In general we shall follow the historical order, but not strictly. The ethicist is often at least as closely connected with the kindred thinkers of a previous century as with the rival thinkers of his own.

In this account we shall limit ourselves for the most part to the ethical thought of Greece in the fifth and fourth centuries B.C. and to that of England in the seventeenth, eighteenth, and nineteenth centuries A.D. In Germany, in the half-century that centers at the year 1800, ethical speculation of the greatest importance was carried on; but it will suit our convenience to give it only a secondary place.

Preliminary Classification. — It will be helpful to have before us, for purposes of reference, a classification of problems and theories, which will serve to map out this part of our study.

As the student will recall, the theories of ethics have had as their starting-point the consideration either of *happiness* or of the *moral values*. During ancient times the theory of happiness was generally the point of departure. In modern times it has generally been the theory of moral values.

Ancient Ethics: Its First Problems. — Curiously enough, however, in the beginnings of the science it was the moral values that first attracted attention. In the latter half of the fifth century B.C. we find the following questions discussed: (1) *How far are the moral distinctions natural, and how far merely conventional?* (2) *Is morality always profitable?* (3) *Is morality a matter of feeling and habit, or of intellectual discernment?*

The Three Great Schools. — At the beginning of the fourth century these questions are all still prominent. But behind them looms up the other question: *What is goodness in general, and what is human happiness?* And this soon becomes the primary issue between ethical thinkers. It divides them into three well-marked schools, holding the following distinctive theories:

I. *Hedonism,* according to which happiness consists in *pleasure,* and unhappiness in *pain,* and things in general are good or bad according as they tend to produce pleasure or pain.

II. *Rigorism,* according to which happiness is identical with *virtue,* and unhappiness with *vice,* and nothing else is good or evil.

III. *Energism* (or the *self-realization theory*), according to which happiness consists in the *normal exercise of man's faculties,* and *especially of his highest faculty* (supposed to be pure reason); and things in general are good or evil according as they produce favorable or unfavorable conditions for such exercise.[1]

In these formulæ, and quite generally in ethical literature, the term ' happiness ' is the conventional translation of the Greek εὐδαμονία, which was used by thinkers of all schools to

---

[1] In his classification of ethical theories, Aristotle also mentions, as requiring critical notice, Plato's theory, that the goodness of anything is due to the active presence in it of the eternal *idea of the good.* As he suggests, the theory is really of far more importance for metaphysics than for ethics; but we can hardly avoid giving some account of it.

denote the highest human good, however great their disagreement as to the nature of this good. A less misleading translation would be 'well-being'; and this might be defined as 'a condition of mind that is intrinsically desirable.' It is well, however, to follow convention in such matters. It is necessary to make this explanation because sometimes the term 'happiness' is used as an equivalent for 'pleasure and the absence of pain.' Of course, in hedonistic literature the two meanings coincide.

The three views thus defined persisted side by side, with various compromises and harmonizations, throughout the whole history of the ancient science of ethics. Energism had decidedly the least influence in ancient times, but it has had an immense influence upon modern thought, especially in the nineteenth century.

The Beginnings of Modern Ethics. — Modern ethics arose in the seventeenth century in the endeavor to answer the question: (1) *What is the significance of the moral law, and how can its authority be demonstrated?* Involved in this was the further question: (2) *What is the nature of man, and for what manner of life is he naturally fit?*

The Classical English Schools. — But in the eighteenth century (which is the classical period in English ethics) the first place was taken by the psychological question: *How do we perceive the distinctions between right and wrong, good and bad?* The principal writers were divided into three schools, according as they professed:

I. *Intuitionalism,* or the view that the moral quality of conduct is its agreement or disagreement with an intuitively perceived body of law.

II. *Sentimentalism,* according to which the moral quality of conduct or character is its capacity for stimulating a certain class of sensations or feelings.

III. *Utilitarianism* (or the *derivative theory*), according to which the moral quality of conduct is its tendency to increase or decrease the general sum of pleasure; and the appreciation of this quality is not an innate faculty, but is developed in each man's experience from an original desire for pleasure.

The Hedonistic Controversy. — The nineteenth century is marked by a *revival of the ancient controversy between hedonism and energism,* with regard to the nature of happiness. (In the eighteenth century the principal adherents of all schools had been more or less definitely hedonists, with only an occasional imperfect expression of the energistic view.) The hedonistic side was championed by descendants of the old utilitarians. The cause of energism was supported by men who were strongly influenced by the German idealistic philosophy that had its rise in the speculations of Immanuel Kant.

REFERENCES ON THE HISTORY OF ETHICS

SIDGWICK, H., *History of Ethics.*
MARTINEAU, J., *Types of Ethical Theory.*
WUNDT, W., *Ethics,* Part II.
PAULSEN, F., *System of Ethics,* Book I.
HYSLOP, J. H., *Elements of Ethics,* Ch. II.
ROGERS, R. A., *Brief History of Ethics.*
HOBHOUSE, L. T., *Morals in Evolution,* Part II, Chs. VI, VII.
WATSON, J., *Hedonistic Thinkers from Aristippus to Spencer.*

CHAPTER VI

THE BEGINNINGS OF ETHICS

I. THE SOPHISTS

Their Occupation. — The beginnings of ethics were a consequence of the rise of democracy among the states of Greece, which took place during the fifth century before Christ. Hitherto, under an aristocratic régime, inherited wealth was the chief requisite for political power. Now birth and money lost a part of their influence. The humblest origin need not prevent any citizen of talent from becoming a leader in the state. Above all things else, the art of the orator was in those times essential to the politician. In the public assembly, as well as in the law courts where his enemies might at any time bring him, the power to hold and sway an audience was the chief element of success. Consequently, the ambitious young men of wealth were ardently desirous of training along this line, as well as in other branches of the art of governing men; and a number of enterprising teachers soon appeared in response to this demand. These were the *sophists*. In the absence of organized schools, they traveled from city to city, giving their instruction at the homes of wealthy patrons, and arousing the most intense enthusiasm. In addition to oratory and politics, most of them taught other subjects belonging to a polite education, such as literature, history, geography, and mathematics; all of which, indeed, were felt to have a real value in preparing a young man for civic usefulness.

Their Philosophical Interests. — The sophists were practical men, training their pupils for practical ends. But incidentally they were led to do some acute thinking upon the theory that lay behind the practice; and in so doing they made an epoch in the history of human thought. The earlier philosophical thinking of the Greeks had been almost entirely limited to 'physical' problems, that is, to the explanation of external nature. In a hundred years, a long succession of ingenious theories of the constitution of things had been originated, involving many scientific conceptions which have since proved wonderfully fruitful; but very little had been securely established. The sophists were well acquainted with the old physical theories, and some used them for purposes of display. But their originality lay elsewhere — in reflections upon man and society; upon language, science, and religion; upon the nature and origin of law, civil and moral. Each sophist was independent of the others, and their teachings, though showing some common tendencies, were widely divergent.

Prejudice against the Sophists. — The sophists were the first Greeks to be professionally engaged in higher education; and consequently men of conservative tendencies were intensely prejudiced against them. They were doing for money what had always been the work of friendship, to be paid for only with respect and affection. The young man who wished for higher culture had simply attached himself to some accomplished friend of the family, and informal companionship had done the rest.[1] The leisure-loving Greeks had a certain contempt for professionalism in any form, even for their great artists and successful athletes.

---

[1] "Gorgias of Leontini, Prodicus of Ceos, and Hippias of Elis . . . each of them, my friends, can go into any city, and persuade the young men to leave the society of their fellow citizens, with any of whom they might associate for nothing, and to be only too glad to be allowed to pay money for the privilege of associating with themselves." (Plato, *Apol. Soc.*, 20 A, Church tr.) These, with Protagoras of Abdera, who died earlier, are the greater sophists. Thrasymachus of Chalcedon, who is also important for ethics, belonged to a younger group.

THE BEGINNINGS OF ETHICS 107

Added to this, they did not like to have the faith of the young men upset by an impious prying into the religion and morality of their fathers. Besides, the actual teaching of certain of the sophists had (as we shall see) a decidedly skeptical tendency, which increased as time went on.[1] In this respect they went no farther than the hardened men of the world about them. They gave scientific expression to a widespread spirit of unbelief. But for this very reason they were feared and hated the more.

Their Real Character. — It is not to be thought that the sophists were men of evil character. Certain of them may have been so; but the great leaders of the movement certainly were not. They are uniformly represented as honorable and worthy men. With the exception of Gorgias, who was more exclusively a rhetorician, they all gave formal instruction in morality. *The Choice of Hercules*, an allegory of Prodicus, in which the greater value of virtue as compared with self-indulgence is set forth, has been preserved by Xenophon (*Mem. Soc.* II, 1) in a rough transcript, and is a fine piece of moral eloquence; and though Prodicus used to recite the piece as a specimen of his rhetorical ability, its tone is far removed from insincerity.

The Weakening of Popular Morals. — There are two beliefs with regard to moral laws that may be said to constitute the common-sense view of the matter: first, that these laws are universal and unchangeable; and secondly, that obedience to them is profitable. Not that common sense is unwavering in either belief; for, indeed, common sense has a habit of being upon both sides of every question. One

---

[1] Thus, as to religion, Protagoras declared: "Whether the gods exist or not, I have no means of knowing. For there are many difficulties in the way — the obscurity of the problem and the shortness of human life." Others were still more outspoken. It was perceived that the religions, like the laws, of different peoples are very dissimilar; and this led to their being regarded as mere superstitions, or as a clever device of politicians for preventing secret crimes.

finds a widespread assumption, that whatever is not forbidden by the law of the land is right enough; and an even more widespread suspicion, that the rascals have an advantage in the struggle for the good things of life, or, at any rate, that it is not well to push one's probity too far. The other views, however, are the dominant ones. Now at this time the widening of the civil and commercial relations of the Greek states with each other and with the outer world was leading to a serious questioning of the old convictions. The moral standards of different communities were too unlike for all to be eternally authoritative; and men of sense could not forever keep saying that their own ways were right and those of all other men wrong. Even among the Greeks themselves, it was found that there was scarcely any course of conduct, however abhorred in one community, that was not in some other community regarded as eminently right and proper. Thus the Thebans condemned the exposure of infants; Athenian fathers practiced it without shame; while in Sparta the government decided which of the newborn infants were to be preserved, and which put out of the way.

Nature *vs.* Convention: Hippias. — Among the sophists the question was definitely raised: *What is the natural basis, the permanent element* (φύσις), *of morality, as distinguished from what is mere artifice and convention* (θέσις)? That there was such a permanent element seems to have been at first unquestioned. Tyrants and free assemblies might make and unmake statutes as they pleased; but since the very act of legislation might be just or unjust, there must be something higher by which to judge it. This, thought Hippias, could only be discovered by setting aside in thought all that legislative caprice had ordered in one place and another, and looking to the underlying principles of justice which are everywhere tacitly acknowledged, and which are the spontaneous dictates of human nature. " Law is a tyrant over men, and forces them to many things contrary to nature." As to just what the natural standard was supposed by him to contain we know almost nothing. " Like is by nature akin to like," was one of his maxims — an early expression of *cosmopolitanism*. Governments he evidently believed to have been established by the voluntary agreement of men as a device to secure an impartial arbitration of disputes between individuals, and thus preserve the balance of justice amid the extremes of personal feeling.[1]

Protagoras: the Moral Feelings. — Protagoras, the greatest of the sophists, maintained that there is, indeed, a *universal* element in morality, but one which, as he says, is " not of natural or spontaneous growth." That is to say, it consists of certain feelings, the capacity for which is not inherited, but is passed on from generation to generation by means of social tradition, or *education* — much as the ability to speak Greek is not inherited, but is transmitted by social influences. These moral feelings are those of *shame* and *justice*.

Importance of Morality. — The importance of these feelings, which insures their universal perpetuation, is that without them organized society, and even the race of mankind, could not be maintained. For, in the first place, government is not a mere convenient device. Only in civil society can man, feeble creature that he is, be saved by united action from his natural enemies. And, in the second place, government is not possible by means of any mere wisdom or technical skill; for these could never restrain human selfishness. It must have a foundation in feeling. Hence the necessity for morality. Without shame and justice a man is essentially an outlaw.

The Moral Tradition. — The social influences by which morality is perpetuated are active from infancy to age. First there is the family with its precepts and punishments; next the schools of letters, music, and gymnastics, the main

[1] Such a theory is satirized by Plato in *Protagoras*, 337 E–338 B.

object of which is the formation of character; and finally the state, which by the promulgation and enforcement of its laws continues to guide and control the individual until death. Virtue is a branch in which all men are willing teachers; for each stands to profit by the improvement of every other; and as a result the worst of civilized men is immeasurably better than the savage. The opportunities for improvement being approximately equal, the moral differences between individuals are to be ascribed mainly to differences in the congenital endowment which make them more or less apt pupils. The sophist is simply a little wiser in moral matters than the majority, and much more skilled in the art of instruction. Hence he can promise to his pupils a steady improvement in virtue, and his services are admittedly worth all he charges.

Conventionality of Moral Standards. — What, now, are we to say with respect to the external standards — the laws and ordinances, in accordance with which the moral feelings are trained? Whence are they derived? Protagoras, in the extant account, answers only that those of the state are the "inventions of good and ancient law-givers," and he leaves us to infer a similar origin for those inculcated in the family and the schools. Their whole content is thus to an undefined extent *conventional*. All men must have *some* laws; but one people has one code, and another has perhaps a radically different code, to each of which, equally and indifferently, the moral feelings are caused by training to attach themselves. What *seems* right to any people *is* right so far as that people is concerned.

Ethical Skepticism: Thrasymachus. — Now this is very plausible as far as it goes. But there is one relevant circumstance which it passes over; namely, that not all laws have the sanctity of age, but new ones are made by every popular assembly. What reverence will a citizen feel for laws that he has seen in the making, especially when he realizes the pressure of selfish interests that has forced their passage? Brushing aside all sentimentality, Thrasymachus of Chalcedon boldly defined justice as "the interest of the stronger." In every state the rules of just and unjust are made by the dominant party to suit their own selfish ends. It is the part of prudence for the weaker to obey (or conceal his disobedience) and thus escape punishment. But if a man can be unjust enough — if he has the power to overthrow the dominant party and substitute his interests for theirs — that is of course much to be preferred. Justice is thus a prudent *middle ground* between the weak, unfortunate injustice that is followed by punishment, and the victorious injustice that goes scot-free. All talk of justice as having a value in itself is nonsense. To be restrained by moral scruples is " charming simplicity," " egregious good-nature " — letting oneself be victimized.

"**Callicles.**" — In the *Gorgias* of Plato, Callicles, a freethinking man of the world who has enjoyed a sophistic education, expresses a similar but somewhat subtler view. The rules of morality, he declares, are a conventional device of the great mass of human weaklings to hold in restraint the men of exceptional ability who would otherwise oppress them. According to nature they ought to do this; for might is the only natural right — as every foreign conquest well illustrates. But it is dinned into them from infancy that they must be content to have no more than their neighbors, that equality is honorable and just — for equality is as much as the consciously inferior man dares hope for. Thus the superior men are cheated by empty words. But one who had sufficient force of character would break loose from this mystification and trample our unnatural laws under foot. Instead of being a slave he would be a tyrant, and show the world what natural justice is.

II. Socrates

His Historical Position. — The position of Socrates with reference to this whole movement of thought is peculiar. He was an intense patriot and temperamentally conservative. Although a poor man, he shared to the full the aristocratic prejudice against receiving pay for the imparting of liberal culture, and this in itself marked him out from the ranks of the sophists. But he also felt deeply the dangerous tendencies toward selfish individualism which the sophistic theories were evincing, and he feared their effect upon the civic ideals of the state's most promising young men. At the same time, he saw that to go back to a blind traditionalism would never do. The principle of free inquiry was right. But he believed that a sufficiently careful examination would show that the traditional morality and the institutions of government contained a core of eternal worth; and moreover that this core consisted of no mere blind feelings, but of distinct *conceptions*, that could be expressed in universally applicable definitions.[1] To the finding of this permanent core, and the separation from it of all that was arbitrary and nonessential, he devoted his life. This would make righteousness no longer a matter of ingrained prejudice, but of scientific knowledge; and the threatened ruin of the state through the undermining of the morality of its citizens would be effectually prevented. As a *constructive critic*, Socrates thus

---

[1] The reader who has some acquaintance with the history of philosophy will recognize that this difference between Socrates and Protagoras is symptomatic of a much larger difference, which runs through their whole thought. Protagoras believed that knowledge consisted of perceptions, or of images derived from perception. Between knowledge and mere opinion he saw no radical difference: when our opinions do not get us into trouble we call them knowledge. Socrates, on the other hand, considered the distinction between knowledge and opinion an absolute one, and made it the foundation of all his thinking. According to him, knowledge, in the proper sense of the term, is not made up of perceptions, which vary from moment to moment and from man to man, but of *conceptions*, which are constant and alike for all men, and hence are capable of exact definition. (Cf. p. 14.)

came between two fires. On the one hand he was very generally classed with the sophists as one who was impiously tampering with the moral convictions of the young men; and on the other hand the sophists and their friends looked upon him as a malicious enemy of free thought.

1. *Fundamental Assumptions*

(1) Theory of Desire. — There are two mainsprings of Socrates's ethical theory. The first is the assumption (almost as a self-evident truth), that *no man ever willingly chooses for himself the worse of two given alternatives;* and hence that if a man knows what is best he will be sure to act accordingly.

We are all aware of experiences that seem to contradict this. As Aristotle says, Socrates speaks as if incontinence, or weakness of will, did not exist. In a later age Ovid gave us the classical expression of the common view of the matter: " I see the better things and recognize their worth — I follow after the worse." But according to Socrates the so-called knowledge that does not control conduct is no knowledge at all, but mere opinion. It lacks the clearness, definiteness, and certainty of real knowledge. And that is why, under the influence of passion, it fluctuates and changes into its opposite. For that is what occurs when one acts, as the phrase is, ' contrary to one's judgment.' At the moment one has simply lost faith in it.

To be sure, most of the so-called knowledge upon which men pride themselves is couched in terms which they cannot define. But that simply means that it is all mere opinion. Now on many topics a probable opinion is perhaps all that is needed; at any rate it seems to be all that we are capable of devising. But in the field of moral conduct we need knowledge, we need an absolute assurance — if the Greek states are not to go to ruin. And since in this case we are dealing with facts of our own nature, open to our direct inspection, there is no reason why knowledge should not here be possible.

Accordingly, it was natural that Protagoras should make justice and honor matters of feeling, determined by tradition, while Socrates made them a matter of science, to whose final criticism all traditions must submit.

I

(2) **Theory of Value.** — The second mainspring is his theory of value; namely, that the good is the useful; or, since it is the good of humanity that alone concerns the serious thinker, that *the good is what is useful to man.* This surprises us; for we are apt to think of a kind of goodness, or value, which is more than mere utility; beauty, for example, not to speak of moral values. But Socrates held of beauty, too, that it is nothing more or less than fitness for some purpose. " ' Then is a dung-basket beautiful ? ' ' Yes, by Jove, and a golden shield is ugly, if the one is beautifully made and the other badly made, each for its own purposes.' " Hence the beautiful thing becomes ugly when applied to a purpose not its own. Goodness and beauty are at bottom the same. The one is *usefulness to somebody;* the other is *adaptation to some use.* All things are good and beautiful, or bad and ugly, in precisely the same respects; as, indeed, the common idiom, by which the expression 'beautiful-and-good' (καλοκἀγαθόν) was used almost as a single word, made it easy for the Greek to believe.[1]

It would probably not be fair to Socrates to say that he denied the existence of an ultimate good, which had its value in itself, apart from any application; though language is ascribed to him which seems to mean this. " If you ask me whether I know anything that is good *for nothing,* I neither know it nor care to." The truth seems to be that he did not distinctly put such a question to himself. He looked at life from a point of view to which the conception of a good-in-itself did not obviously belong. Life presented itself to him, not as a series of alternate strivings and achievements, but as a chain of activities each of which led on to others, and was not to be considered apart from its consequences. Even death did not end the chain. For, not to speak of the possi-

---

[1] It should be noticed that καλόν (beautiful) includes what we should call 'honorable,' and must often be so translated; just as αἰσχρόν (ugly) includes what is dishonorable, or shameful.

bility of an after-life (concerning which he would not dogmatize), there is the lingering good or evil fame to be considered, to which one's conduct in this life gives rise.

Public and Private Good. — For each man the good is what is useful to himself; but this must not be understood too narrowly. Here again we must note that a question which in later days has become most important is not distinctly raised. Socrates never, so far as we know, asked himself whether a man's private good might not conflict with the good of the society in which he lived. He simply takes for granted, as the intensely social life of the Greeks made it natural to assume, that public and private good are the same. A man's advantage may extend as far as his interests. The good of each includes the good of all with whom his life is bound up — family, friends, fellow-citizens — even foreigners, perhaps, though Socrates admits that the nearer of kin make the stronger appeal.

2. *Theory of Virtue*

The Central Thesis. — Putting together the two fundamental doctrines, we speedily arrive at the most famous of Socrates's teachings: that *all virtue is knowledge.* Speaking generally, no matter how good anything ordinarily is, it may on occasion prove to be an evil. So it is with beauty, health, riches, fame, technical skill. Likewise what is good for one man may be evil for another. But goods are of two sorts, those of the soul and those of the body. And among the goods of the soul there is one that is unconditionally good; namely, *wisdom* (σοφία), or *the knowledge of what is good and evil.* From this no evil can flow. For let it be recalled that, according to Socrates, such knowledge always brings about the choice of the good. Now the so-called 'virtues' are merely wisdom in various relations, and the 'vices' are different aspects of folly. This is obvious in the case of temperance (σωφροσύνη). "Wisdom and temperance he did not distinguish. But by a man's using what he knew to be honorable and good, and avoiding what he knew to be shameful, he judged a man to be both wise and temperate. When he was further asked whether he regarded as wise and continent those who knew what they ought to do but did the opposite, — 'No more that,' said he, 'than foolish and incontinent. For I think that all men do whatever (among the given possibilities) they prefer as most advantageous to themselves. So I believe that those who do not act rightly are neither wise nor temperate.'" But the same is true of all the other virtues. "He said that justice and all other virtue was wisdom. For just acts and all things that are done virtuously are honorable and good.[1] And those who know them prefer nothing else to them; while those who do not know cannot do them, but, even when they try, miss the mark."

Courage. — But the most striking illustration of Socrates's theory of virtue is to be found in courage. For this too is wisdom. Mere fearlessness is not courage, for that may be due to ignorance or madness. The brave man in every situation is the man who knows how to face it. Thus the Spartans stand firm in the battle line, because they know how to use their shields and spears. Give them the light arms of the Thracians or the bows of the Scythians, and they would be no longer brave. But the worst evils are moral evils. Hence the highest courage — that is to say, the greatest wisdom — is to be shown in preferring every other evil, even death itself, to these.

The Utility of Virtue. — It is clear, then, that while Socrates conceives of no ultimate good, he does believe in an *absolute good* — unmixed with evil and more precious than any other. But its value is that of a *supreme usefulness*. "Not from wealth does virtue come; but from virtue come

---

[1] They are clearly honorable; and, as we have seen, Socrates believes that the honorable and the good are identical.

wealth and all other human goods, both public and private." So he was continually crying in the ears of his fellow-citizens. "When some one asked him what he thought to be the best pursuit for a man, he answered: 'Happiness.' (εὐπραξία; etymologically, 'doing well.') Asked further if he thought that good fortune could be a pursuit, he said: 'I regard fortune and happiness (or unhappiness) as altogether different. To chance upon something that one wants, without looking for it, is, I think, good fortune. To perform well what one has learned and thought about, I consider to be happiness, and those who pursue this course seem to me to be happy.'"

According to Socrates the virtuous life is a very pleasant one; in fact, the most pleasant possible. Even the lower pleasures are advanced in value. Temperance in diet gives every morsel a relish. Temperance in all things takes away the annoyance of petty deprivations, leaves a man free to act for himself and his friends, and by winning general confidence puts him in the way of all manner of advantages. If the good man thinks little of bodily gratifications, that is because he has other and sweeter sources of pleasure, which not only give delight for the moment but promise a permanent benefit. The feeling of present success is always pleasant. But most pleasant of all is it to feel that one is becoming better and is gaining better friends.

Self-knowledge. — As virtue is the knowledge of good and evil, so the supreme virtue is the knowledge of the good and evil in oneself, that is to say, of the extent of one's own knowledge and ignorance. This is the significance which Socrates found in the famous inscription at Delphi: "Know thyself." This is the motive of that constant self-examination and revelation of others to themselves, in which he was engaged. To have a virtue is to know the class of good and evil things with which it is concerned; and to know is to have in one's mind a *conception*, such as can be expressed in an exact definition. The object of ethical inquiry is to bring forward these conceptions and separate them out from the mass of opinion with which they are confused. Without this one can have no proper assurance that one is doing right, but may, perhaps, perform the worst iniquities in the belief that they are pure and holy. It is only through the knowledge of one's limitations that one can rationally strive to remove them.

Moral Education. — From this point of view we can understand Socrates's paradoxical theory of moral education. Virtue, he said, could not be taught, and he ridiculed the claims of the sophists that they were able to teach it. " 'Callias,' said I, ' if your two sons were colts or calves, we could hire an overseer for them, to perfect them in their own proper excellence; and he would be a groom or a farmer. Now since they are men, whom do you intend to get for an overseer? Who understands their sort of excellence — that of the man and the citizen? I suppose you have inquired, since you have sons. Is there anyone,' said I, ' or not.' ' Why, certainly,' said he. ' Who,' said I, ' and from where, and for what fee? ' ' Evenos, the Parian, Socrates,' said he, ' for five minæ.' And I congratulated Evenos, if he really knows this art and teaches so properly. And I should be proud myself and take on airs, if I knew it; but I do not, fellow Athenians." True moral education is more than a process of admonition and punishment. No *overseer* can train a man. Yet Socrates was confident that his followers had been greatly benefited by their association with him. The key to the apparent contradiction lies in his belief that moral advancement involves for each man an active process of self-analysis, which no other can take upon himself, and which no teacher can guarantee. The teacher and the pupil must be *companions*, engaged in a coöperative search. The teacher too is a learner, ever submitting his own convictions to new tests, and correcting them day by day. And with the best of intentions success must ultimately depend upon the blessing of God.

Did Socrates allow no place to *habituation* in the formation of character? In principle he did not; but as a matter of fact he did. His whole philosophy was based upon the distinction between knowledge (as the term is applied to exact science) and opinion; and, as we have seen, he holds that all virtue is knowledge. But when examples of such knowledge are to be cited, he is represented as using the art of the carpenter, the musician, or the physician, or even the practiced skill of the diver or the soldier. He seems to have taken for granted that in the acquiring of knowledge the training of the body has its essential place. And so, in the cultivation of every virtue, study and exercise ($\mu\acute{\alpha}\theta\eta\sigma\iota\varsigma$ καὶ $\mu\epsilon\lambda\acute{\epsilon}\tau\eta\varsigma$) go hand in hand. Perhaps it was by reason of this loose conception of knowledge that Socrates was able to assume the possibility of knowing without knowing that you know — the knowledge acquired in practice being afterwards brought to clear attention by a searching induction.

The Standards of Justice. — There is one important feature of Socrates's ethics which we have not yet considered, though it is involved in the conception of virtue as knowledge. Knowledge is distinguished from opinion by its perfect definiteness and certitude. This implies that the *objects* of knowledge are similarly definite and immovable — that they cannot be arbitrary fictions that change with the changes of fashion or of personal whim. When, therefore, Socrates says that justice is knowledge of what is just and unjust, he implies that the distinction between just and unjust is an absolute one. Now justice means conformity to law; and the question arises, how, when laws change as they do, an eternal justice is possible. Socrates's answer is twofold. In the first place, even though laws be temporary, it may be eternally obligatory on us to obey whatever laws are in force. (Even so a state of war is temporary; yet it is not for that reason any the less the citizens' duty to fight for their country manfully while the war lasts.) But if that be true, as he believes, then it must be an eternal law that men should obey the temporary laws. (As Xenophon puts it, it is the pleasure of the gods that just and lawful should be the same.) In the second place, however, this is not the only eternal law. There are others too, which are universally in force, even though they are not always recognized or obeyed; for when they are disobeyed, the penalty naturally and inevitably follows. Such are the laws, that men should worship the gods, honor their parents, be grateful to their benefactors. But the most important law of all is that men should seek knowledge and especially self-knowledge; for the penalty is ignorance and folly. It was upon this ground that Socrates, at the trial which resulted in his condemnation and death, refused to purchase any indulgence by promising to discontinue his investigations. " Fellow Athenians, I love you and embrace you, but I will obey the god rather than you." But what, then, becomes of the broken human law? Are its claims to respect undone? Not by any means. It is no law of God that we should break even an unjust law for our own temporal profit; and though adhering to the higher standard, Socrates was ready and willing to lay down his life in obedience to the lower standard.

Religious Notions. — Of Socrates's religion a few words may be said. The indications are that he accepted in the main the traditional religion of the people, regarding it as a state institution to which the obedient citizen was bound to give his allegiance, and which, moreover, was substantially confirmed by the fulfillment of oracles, dreams, and other indications of the future; but that he imposed upon it, so to speak, a monotheism. The old gods — the sun and moon, for example — were thus recognized as finite beings, like men, though vastly superior to men in intelligence and worth. But above them was one who was god in a different

THE BEGINNINGS OF ETHICS 121

sense,[1] a being of infinite knowledge and goodness, the author and ruler of the world, and, above all else, the eternal legislator and judge. The evidence for this Socrates found in the beauty and order of the universe; in the adaptation of man's surroundings, and especially of his bodily structure to his needs; and in the inevitable necessity by which, as he believed, happiness attended upon virtue and misery upon vice. His notion of prayer was characteristic. He would pray for nothing in particular, but only for 'the good.' For any good fortune which he might specify might prove to be an evil to him. And the chief good was not to be had by good fortune, but to be attained by persevering effort. Of immortality he seems to have thought as a precious hope, suggested by ancient and traditional lore. The idea of a future judgment was reasonable enough; though he believed that divine judgment was perfectly executed in this world.

The Issues. — Is the basis of morality to be found in feeling or in intelligence? Are its values perceived by the excitation of certain peculiar sentiments, or are they objects of rational knowledge? Are the laws of morality, like the laws of particular states, useful conventions, which might well have been otherwise, but which, as matters stand, serve their turn very well; or are they eternal laws, so bound up with the nature of things that whether men recognize them or not their authority is undisturbed?

REFERENCES

XENOPHON, *Memorabilia of Socrates*.
PLATO, *Apology of Socrates*, *Protagoras*, and *Hippias Minor*.
GROTE, G., *History of Greece*, Chs. LXVII, LXVIII.
ZELLER. E., *Pre-Socratic Philosophy*, Section III, and *Socrates and the Socratic Schools*, Part II, Ch. VII, Ch. IX, C.

[1] At the same time, Socrates seems to have identified him with Zeus and Apollo — especially with the god of Delphi. Even so Heraclitus of Ephesus had said of the supreme being: "He is willing and unwilling to be called by the name of Zeus."

GOMPERZ, T., *Greek Thinkers*, Book III, Chs. IV–VI; Book IV, Ch. IV.
CAIRD, E., *Evolution of Theology in the Greek Philosophers*, Lecture III.
BLACKIE, J. S., *Four Phases of Morals*, Ch. I.
FORBES, E. T., *Socrates*.
BENN, A. W., *The Philosophy of Greece*, Chs. I, IV, V.
WATSON, J., *Hedonistic Theories*, Ch. I.

CHAPTER VII

HEDONISM

The Socratic Schools. — The many-sidedness of Socrates's moral philosophy is such that it is no wonder that after his death his disciples at once separated into at least three different schools, each emphasizing a different aspect of the master's doctrine. The leaders of these schools were, at first, naturally enough, certain of his older pupils: *Euclid* of Megara, *Antisthenes* of Athens, and *Aristippus* of Cyrene. Euclid was of a speculative turn of mind, and set himself to drawing the conclusions that followed from asserting that virtue is one; that it is knowledge of the good; that the only absolute good is virtue itself; and that what can be truly known must be eternal. And he emerged with the beautiful doctrine, that all that exists is one perfect being; all variety and change, and especially all evil, being an illusion. Antisthenes was an ardent reformer; and what struck him as important was the fact that virtue was in itself sufficient to make life worth living, and that, as the only unconditionally good thing, all else was to be despised in comparison with it. To the genial Aristippus the significant point was that the virtuous life was full of pleasure. After a few years, a much younger pupil of Socrates rose to a prominence in which he overshadowed all his elders. This was *Plato* of Athens. At the outset he stood closest to Euclid; but he developed all sides of Socrates's doctrine in a remarkable way. Euclid's theories were not very fruitful for ethics, and we shall therefore omit them from consideration here. Those of the other men have profoundly affected the later history of the science.

In the present and the following two chapters, we shall study the three lines of speculation thus initiated.

I. Aristippus

Conception of an Ultimate Good.—We have remarked that in Socrates's thought the happy life appears as an indefinitely prolonged chain of activities, each of which leads on to others, without a definite goal being anywhere reached. To the generation which followed him this seemed an impossible position to maintain. Unless there is something which is good in itself, without reference to anything that may come after, how can anything be good at all? If the means is to have value, the end must have value; and though this end may itself be only a means to a further end, the series of means and ends must have a final stopping-place; else all value is illusory.

The Pleasure-theory.—According to Aristippus [1] this stopping place is reached in each feeling of pleasure. This, whatever else may happen, is good. There is no need of refinements or vague speculations about the matter. What makes the happy life worth living is the pleasure in it. It is not as if such a life had any peculiar higher value in itself for which it should be pursued. Its value is that of its particular pleasant moments — offset, to be sure, by whatever painful moments it contains. For pain, too, is a stopping place in the chain of consequences. Every feeling of pain is bad in itself. If any proof is wanted for these assertions, we have only to observe that all men, nay, all animate beings, from the very moment of birth, pursue pleasure and avoid pain — except, perhaps, where some abnormality interferes with the ordinary course of nature.

---

[1] Aristippus of Cyrene (in Africa) was a typical sophist, wandering from city to city and teaching for pay. His wit and courtliness made him a favorite among men of the highest rank. How long he studied with Socrates we do not know; but he evidently met him in a spirit of considerable independence. It is probable that he had previously been a pupil of Protagoras, of whose principles (not only in ethics but in the theory of knowledge) we are frequently reminded. Late in life he established a school in Cyrene, the members of which were called *Cyrenaics*.

All pleasures are alike, all pains are alike, except in quantity. All that is pleasant is good, in so far as it is pleasant, no matter how shameful it may be or how productive of painful after-effects. Similarly, all that is painful is evil, in so far as it is painful. Between pleasure and pain lies the apathy of indifference.

Aristippus and his earlier followers held that the greatest pleasures and pains are those of the body, *i.e.* those that arise from a present stimulus acting upon the senses of touch, taste, or smell. (Sight and hearing, they thought, affect us mainly by exciting sympathy.) The pleasures and pains of the mind, *i.e.* æsthetic feelings, those arising from memory or expectation, and those arising from sympathy with others, were therefore regarded as of less importance. However, this point was not of fundamental importance, and some later members of the school modified it considerably.[1]

Application to Moral Values. — And now, what is virtue? Virtue consists in whatever qualities of mind enable the possessor to get pleasure and avoid pain; and in this use alone their value consists. Of these qualities wisdom is the chief, — so far Socrates was right, — but it is not the only one. There are virtues which even the fool may possess, such as a cheerful and confident disposition. Wisdom is not in itself sufficient to insure an unbroken succession of pleasures. But the wise man is for the most part happy, and the foolish man is generally unhappy. Wisdom brings with it release from three of the main sources of pain: *envy, passionate desire,* and *superstition;* for all these arise from vain opinions. Aristippus gave special warning against the second of these. That we should master pleasures and not be mastered by

---

[1] *Anniceris* is especially mentioned as laying emphasis upon the pleasures of sympathy. *Theodorus* even declared that physical pleasures and pains were indifferent — that the only real good and evil were the joy and grief that spring from wisdom and folly. But this was going far toward rigorism.

them [1] is his best-known maxim. To be too fond of one pleasure is to be blind to others. We should make the most of what is at hand, without longing for what is absent.

As for the just and the honorable, they are merely what law and custom make them. But they are not for that reason unimportant. The good man does nothing unseemly, for he has a wise regard for punishment and social opprobrium. Friendship is an excellent thing. The friend is useful much as an arm or leg is, and should be prized accordingly.

II. OTHER HEDONISTS

Plato and Eudoxos. — The system, it will be seen, is beautifully simple, and for that reason it has been attractive to many men. Outside of the Cyrenaic school the pleasure-theory found important advocates. Plato, in an early work (the *Protagoras*), adopted in a tentative way the main principles of the school, but tried to show that wisdom ought still to be considered as the sum of all virtue. We always choose, he says, the greatest apparent pleasure, but we do not always compare pleasures correctly. The art of life is a sort of *calculus*, by which pleasures, present and future, are measured against each other. To be 'mastered by pleasure' is really to be mastered by ignorance of its relative smallness. It seems probable that this criticism had a deep effect upon the development of the theory. However, in later works he rejects the whole theory decisively. One of his pupils, the astronomer Eudoxos, reverted to it, and added to the older arguments in its support the curious new one, that pleasure must be the supreme good because it is *above praise*.

Epicurus. — But the most important of the ancient advocates of pleasure is *Epicurus* (341–270 B.C.); not for the originality of his work, indeed, but for its extraordinary

---

[1] This is the purport of the ancient anecdote, which relates that when Aristippus was reproached for being a lover of Lais, the Corinthian courtesan, he replied: "I am not her lover. She is mine."

success. After a very superficial education, he established (in 306 B.C.) a school in Athens, which maintained his teachings without essential change for over six hundred years, and during the greater part of this time exerted a powerful world-wide influence. This success was no doubt due in part to personal qualities in Epicurus, for he was a man who inspired both love and admiration. (His followers to the latest days called themselves after his name, *Epicureans*.) But it was mainly due to the fact that he worked out a scheme of life, by following which the wise man might assure himself of happiness. For it is one thing to tell men of what happiness consists, and leave them, perhaps, to despair of securing it for themselves;[1] and it is another thing to promise it.

General Resemblance to Aristippus. — With this definite promise of happiness all that is original in Epicurus's teachings is closely connected. Meanwhile the general structure of his ethical system is precisely the same as with Aristippus. That pleasure is good and pain evil needs no proof. All animals from birth naturally seek the one and avoid the other; and so do we. Pleasure *feels* good, just as fire feels warm, snow looks white, or honey tastes sweet. No man willingly gives up a sum of pleasure except to avoid pain; no man accepts an unnecessary amount of pain except in order to secure pleasure. The virtues — wisdom, temperance, courage, and justice — are the necessary and (as Epicurus adds) sufficient means of securing happiness, and in this consists their value. Wisdom is the architect of the happy life and frees us from the turbulence of the passions; temperance makes the most of things; courage dispels imaginary evils; and justice wins the good will of the public.

[1] Certain of the later Cyrenaics, led by *Hegesias*, the "persuader unto death," even held that the happy life was an impossible ideal — that escape from labor and pain was the most that could be looked for. As was pointed out in ancient times, Epicurus's position is not without its likeness to that of Hegesias; the great difference being that Epicurus frankly identifies absence of pain with the ideal itself.

Friendship, too, is precious as a fountainhead of pleasure and a bulwark against misfortune. Superstition is recognized as a prime cause of unnecessary suffering; and Epicurus by teaching that death ends all (so that there is nothing in it to fear), and that the gods in their eternal bliss are too far above us to think of interfering in human affairs,[1] believed that he was bestowing a great blessing upon men.

Absence of Pain the Greatest Pleasure. — Of the distinctive features in his view, the most important is the doctrine, that between pain and pleasure there is no middle ground of indifference, but that with the total removal of pain one already enjoys the most intense pleasure. To us this is apt to seem ridiculous; but the Greeks had a great love for calm (γαλήνη), and such an exaltation of it appealed to many as perfectly just.

Higher and Lower Pleasures. — A second feature is the express recognition of the distinction between *higher* and *lower* pleasures, though these are not understood as ultimate qualitative terms. The lower pleasures are those which are mixed with pain or followed by painful consequences. The higher pleasures are free from evil admixture or after-effect: they are literally *purer*. This distinction led to the exaltation of social and intellectual pleasures over the indulgence of physical appetites, and the mode of life of the genuine Epicurean became a very sober affair.

The Storehouse of Memory. Suicide. — Closely connected is the cult of *pleasant memories*. With these, thought Epicurus, one could so store one's mind that even amid the worst tortures one could preserve a balance of pleasure.[2]

---

[1] Supposed cases of divine interference were all to be explained mechanically, according to an atomic theory of matter, modeled after that of Democritus of Abdera. Epicurus's physics, however, is an exceedingly childish affair. Like Aristippus, he was ignorant of mathematics.

[2] He himself, while dying in great pain, wrote to a friend: "All these sufferings are counterbalanced by the joy in the memory of our past discussions."

HEDONISM

Pain " when severe is short and when long is moderate " ; and if we will but banish it from our memories it is more than half conquered. Still, if pains persist in returning and nagging at us, and life has lost its charm, it is always possible to leave it as one would a tasteless comedy ; and this thought must always be a comfort.

NOTE

With all its simplicity, the pleasure-theory contains several distinct elements which we shall do well to distinguish.

I. There is the *general theory of values*: that for each man his own pleasure and pain are alone good and evil (desirable and objectionable) in themselves ; and that everything else is good or evil to him, in so far as it brings him pleasure or pain. This is called simply *hedonism* (from ἡδονή, pleasure).

II*a*. In ancient times the foregoing theory is generally based upon a certain *theory as to the objects of desire and aversion*: that no animal desires anything except pleasure for its own sake, or avoids anything except pain for its own sake ; all things else being desired or avoided on account of the pleasure or pain expected from them. This is called *psychological hedonism*, or the *selfish theory*. It is easily seen that the hedonistic theory of values might be held, while this support was rejected ; for could one not naïvely desire things for their own sake, even though upon reflection one were compelled to admit that their real value consisted in their pleasure-producing properties ?

b. Some Epicureans held that as a result of *habit* one could come to desire the happiness of a friend for its own sake ; and modern hedonists have applied this theory much more widely.

III. There is a *theory of moral values*. It is held that the goodness of virtue and the evilness of vice consist in their tendency to produce pleasure and pain respectively. This is called *ethical hedonism*. It is, of course, only the application to moral values of the general theory of values. It is found in two varieties, the one characteristic of ancient ethics, the other of modern ethics :

a. Only the individual's own pleasure or pain (and hence only the value of his virtue or vice to *himself*) is counted. This is called *egoistic hedonism*.

b. Virtue (or vice) in conduct or character consists in its tendency to increase (or decrease) the *general sum of pleasure* in society at large. This is called *universalistic hedonism*, or *utilitarianism*.

The terminology is somewhat confusing, and the student is especially in danger of failing to distinguish between the selfish theory and egoistic hedonism. This error must be avoided. The selfish theory has, in fact, often been entertained by utilitarians.

REFERENCES

PLATO, *Protagoras.*
DIOGENES LAERTIUS, *Lives of the Philosophers,* Books IX, X.
CICERO, *De Finibus Bonorum et Malorum,* Books I, II.
GROTE, G., *Plato and the Other Companions of Socrates,* Ch. XXXVIII.
ZELLER, E., *Socrates and the Socratic Schools,* Ch. XIV; *Stoics, Epicureans, and Sceptics,* Chs. XIX, XX.
GOMPERZ, T., *Greek Thinkers,* Book IV, Ch. IX.
WATSON, J., *Hedonistic Theories,* Chs. II, III.
WALLACE, W., *Epicureanism,* Ch. VII.
TAYLOR, A. E., *Epicurus.*
HICKS, R. D., *Stoic and Epicurean,* Ch. V.
MUIRHEAD, J. H. *Elements of Ethics,* Book III, Ch. I.
THILLY, F., *Introduction to Ethics,* Ch. VI.
WRIGHT, H. W., *Self-Realization,* Part II, Ch. II.

CHAPTER VIII

ENERGISM

I. GENERAL FEATURES OF ANCIENT ENERGISM

The Appeal of Energism. — If hedonism is attractive to many minds by reason of its simplicity, it is repulsive to many others by reason of its prosaic bareness. To reduce all the values of human experience to a dead level — to measure poetry and morality, or even athletic sport, as one measures the pleasures of the table — will always seem to some minds a grossly mistaken project.

The theory of energism, or self-realization, avoids this dead-leveling. It starts from man in the fullness of his many-sided nature; and it conceives of happiness as the symmetrically rounded life of such a man. Instead of attempting to eliminate variety, it admits it on principle. Happiness is pleasant, but that is only the beginning of its characteristics. As different human faculties come into play, different kinds of pleasure are experienced; and to eliminate from the description of the happy life the differences of kind, is to falsify the description through and through.

Self-realization is an aim that appeals to honorable pride and ambition. The very notion that there is in oneself an immanent ideal to be realized is to many men inspiring. To one who has once felt this inspiration the proposal to look for happiness in uniform bits of pleasure such as any beast might feel will always seem ignoble. It is not a mere matter of argument. It is a temperamental reaction. One feels that hedonism may have truth in it, but that it does not do justice to the dignity of man.

Plato and Aristotle: their Common Features. — In the present chapter we have to consider two ancient theories of self-realization, those of Plato and Aristotle. Both are comprehensively designed and minutely developed theories; and they cannot be satisfactorily understood without much attention to detail. But there are certain general characteristics of the two theories that may easily be lost sight of in a detailed treatment, and that ought to be understood throughout.

1. The capacities of human nature are supposed to be *fixed in advance*. The soul has a certain set of faculties to be exercised. Life consists in exercising them. Neither Plato nor Aristotle contemplates the possibility (which is very real to us) that the higher faculties of man are products of social culture. They realize, indeed, that among civilized men certain faculties are exercised which their barbaric ancestors could not exercise; for example, the intuition of abstract truths. But the reason, as they see it, is merely that those ancestors lacked the necessary security and leisure. The advance of civilization simply makes possible the realization of inner potentialities that have all along been latent.

2. Moreover, the capacities of the individual, as well as of the race, are fixed in advance. Most men are defective. One or more of the faculties is feeble or even completely wanting in them. For most men, therefore, happiness in the full sense of the term is impossible.

3. The set of human faculties is an ordered system, in which each has a definite rank. And men are of different rank according to the faculties which they manifest.

4. The lowest of men's faculties (such as hunger) they have in common with the beasts. On the other hand, the highest faculty, and the rarest, is more than human, for it is common to the human and the divine nature. This is *pure reason*. Simply to know truth, with no further end in view — that is the utmost of which man is capable. All lower activities

may rightly be regarded as only the external conditions of this one. And the great bulk of mankind, who are incapable of pure reason, serve no higher purpose in the economy of nature than to give peace and leisure to the favored few.

5. Plato and Aristotle thought of the individual as, primarily, the *citizen.* Life meant for them, first and foremost, civic life. Plato's principal ethical work is the *Republic;* and Aristotle expressly treats ethics as a branch of politics. But it is noteworthy that both conceived of the life of reason as ultimately an *individual* life. The state must establish the conditions under which leisure to think is possible; and it is in the contact of friend with friend that the stimulus and direction of scientific inquiry are found. But, in the last resort, what a man knows, it is he that knows. The supreme happiness of contemplation each must enjoy for himself alone.

Thus the ancient energism, as represented by these preëminent thinkers, is *anti-evolutionary, aristocratic, intellectualistic,* and, in the last resort, *individualistic.*

II. PLATO

Comprehensiveness of his Thought. — The great significance of Plato's ethics (as of all his thought) lies in its synthetic character. It is the result of a large-minded attempt to do justice to all the various one-sided views which others had assumed. His chief inspiration came from Socrates; but in the working out of his system Protagoras's conception of specific moral feelings, trained to their part by habituation, has a subordinate, but very important place. By the rigorist Antisthenes he was probably not affected; difference of character, as well as of social position, put a chasm between them. But that virtue is a good in itself, and not simply as a means to pleasure, was a doctrine that early appealed to his own generous nature. Aristippus, on the other hand, he regarded as an able thinker, with whom his account had to be made; and he returns to the discussion of the pleasure theory repeatedly in the course of his long literary career.

Life. — Plato, better than any other man, represents the spirit of aristocracy in ethical thought. Born in a noble and wealthy family (of which he was intensely proud) he had an unmixed contempt for the masses of mankind. Under the influence of Socrates, however, he came to believe in an aristocracy of intellect rather than of mere birth, though always believing that the lowly born and the hopelessly stupid were generally the same. From his youth he moved in literary and philosophical circles. With Socrates he was associated from his twentieth year. After the death of Socrates, he traveled widely, visiting Egypt, Cyrene, southern Italy, and Sicily, pursuing the study of mathematics, and thus becoming intimately acquainted with members of the Pythagorean religious society, in which mathematics had been extensively cultivated. The influence of this study upon his ethical theory will call for our attention. On his return to Athens, he founded a philosophical institute, which was called (from the neighboring ' gymnasium ' or public park) the *Academy*. Here, except for two later visits to Syracuse (where he unsuccessfully attempted to influence the younger Dionysius in favor of his advanced political ideas) he spent the remainder of his life, and here his great work was done : oral teaching, varied by literary production in which the highest talents of the poet, the systematic thinker, and the religious enthusiast are combined.

Ethical Writings. — Plato recognized that his own philosophy was an outgrowth of that of Socrates ; and his earliest dialogues (such as the *Hippias Minor, Protagoras, Laches, Charmides,* and *Euthyphro*) are largely devoted to the exposition and defense of Socrates's views. But the Socrates of these dialogues is most keenly interested in bringing to light certain of the difficulties involved in the historical Socrates's position; in part self-contradictions, in part disagreements with common moral experience. The ethical doctrines contained in the dialogues of his middle and later years (the *Gorgias, Meno, Phaedo,* and *Republic,* and the *Philebus* and *Laws*) may be regarded as the result of an attempt to solve these difficulties in the master's own spirit.

1. *The Virtues in General*

Goodness in General. — If we examine into the conditions under which anything is called 'good,' we always find a definiteness of proportion in the relation of its various parts. Any artist or artisan in his work chooses, in the first place, materials that he can shape in a certain way, and then fits them together in an orderly and systematic fashion. So also the physical trainer does not try to make any one muscle as strong as possible, but to develop the whole body symmetrically. Carry the induction as far as we may, we find that goodness is always marked by orderliness and regularity, badness by disorder.

The Virtues. — The soul is no exception. Its proper condition, or excellence, is marked by order. And this is what we call *temperance, courage, justice,* and *piety;* and the insight by which the order is established we call *wisdom.* This insight is either *knowledge* (which it must be if the virtue is to be permanent and thoroughly trustworthy) or *right opinion,* which is all that most men possess. (In this recognition of common-sense morality as possessing a certain value despite the absence of exact knowledge, Plato successfully tones down one of Socrates's extreme views.)

Distinction Between the Virtues: Earlier Theory. — If now we proceed to ask how these virtues are distinguished and interrelated, Plato's first answer (in the *Gorgias*) is that temperance, courage, justice, and piety are all the same quality of orderliness seen in different relations. Temperance is orderliness as such. Piety and justice are orderliness as it manifests itself in conduct toward gods and men respectively. Courage is orderliness as manifested in the pursuit or avoidance of anticipated goods and evils. The essential condition of all is wisdom; for we must follow Socrates in asserting that a man always acts as seems best to him at the time.

Mature Theory: the Problem. — But in his most important ethical work, the *Republic*, Plato's theory has very materially developed. In the first place, he is no longer content to define the virtues in terms of *relations* to various objects or situations. He insists upon knowing what they are *in themselves*, as qualities of the soul itself. In the second place, he has given up Socrates's extreme intellectualism, which, indeed, had been more apparent than real, and had shown its inadequacy the more clearly to Plato, as he learned from the example of geometry what an exact science really is.

Analysis of the Soul. — He now finds that the soul consists of several distinct and partly independent parts, or faculties. First, there is *reason*, by which we have knowledge and opinion. Secondly, there are the *appetites*, which are due to the soul's union with a body that is subject to constant wants. Reason and appetite have nothing in common. But there is a third faculty which has something of the nature of both. The ' *spirited element* ' it is called; by which is meant susceptibility to the emotions that hold a man up to a standard of personal dignity: honor, shame, indignation. This is like reason in the fact that it has standards; and, indeed, these standards are given it by reason, though it has to be *trained* to recognize them. It is like appetite in the way in which it impels men to action. Now reason has no direct control over appetite, on account of their utter dissimilarity. There is no argument against hunger. It is only through the spirited element, by means of the standards of self-respect which are set up, that reason is able to hold appetite in check. The Socratic axiom, that every man chooses what seems to him best, holds good, then, only in so far as the spirited element has been brought by training into conformity with reason.

Analogy of the Man and the State. — Upon this analysis of the soul, Plato now bases his classification of the virtues. In order to guide his procedure, he calls into play an elaborate analogy between the individual and the state. The state contains three kinds of citizens, distinguished by the predominance in them of one or the other of the mental faculties: the philosophers, or men of intelligence; the warriors, or men of honor; and the artisans and merchants, or men of greed. In an ideally ordered state the first would direct the whole administration of war and peace, for they alone can *know* what is best. But because the men of greed are unamenable to reason the only way in which they can be governed is through the men of honor. The warriors must be trained to act in accordance with the standards which the philosophers impose upon them, and they must then forcibly keep the industrial and commercial class in order.

The Virtues in the State. — What are the peculiar excellences of which these several classes are capable? The *wisdom* of the state is, of course, lodged in the philosopher-rulers; it is their insight into the common welfare. The *courage* of the state belongs to the warriors; it is their fidelity to the standards of honor, to which they have been trained. The industrial class, base creatures, are capable of no virtue except as the warriors, directed by the philosophers, impose it on them. They may be forced to put such a limit to their cupidity as the welfare of the whole state demands, *i.e.* to be *temperate*. As for *justice*, that belongs to no class, but to the state as a whole. It is simply the division of labor between the classes, by which each performs its own function without loss of efficiency through friction or misapplied effort.

138 INTRODUCTION TO THE SCIENCE OF ETHICS

The Virtues in the Individual. — As applied to the individual, wisdom, the knowledge of the good, is the virtue of reason. Courage is the virtue of the rationally trained spirited element. Temperance is the virtue imposed by reason, through the spirited element, upon the cowed appetites. And justice is the harmonious functioning of all the faculties.[1]

Plato was a restless thinker, and there are indications that he continued to remodel his ethical doctrine, as well as other parts of his philosophy. But this is his latest systematic account of the virtues, and there is at least one feature in it that remained undisturbed to the end. It is the conception of the soul as a complex unity, containing a rational and an irrational[2] element, the latter requiring training under the direction of the former in order to acquire its proper virtue. All virtue is not knowledge, but knowledge is essential to a high development of virtue — though, as we have seen, the knowledge may belong, not to the individual in question, but to those by whom he is trained and governed.

The question arises, how wisdom itself is acquired. The answer involves the whole of Plato's metaphysics. We must be content with a mere sketch of the leading notions.

2. *Wisdom*

The Theory of Eternal Forms. — Whenever we attempt a scientific definition (Plato observed), it is always of something assumed to be perfect, a standard of its kind. We define

---

[1] This seems far-fetched, and except for the analogy of the state it would lack all plausibility. But the student must remember that Plato's problem is to define justice as it exists in the just man, considered entirely apart from his relations to other men. So also the justice of the state is defined entirely without reference to its relations with other states. Plato's conception is that if the inner harmony exists, the external harmony will follow as a matter of course.

[2] We group together under this term the spirited element and the appetites.

types, not the particular things of ordinary sense-experience, with their multitude of peculiarities and imperfections. The straight line of science is not the edge of a ruler, or the path of a swift projectile, or even the line of vision. It is *absolutely* straight, as these are not.

Now it was a widely accepted maxim of philosophy that *the knowable is the real;* that whereas what appears to the senses and impresses itself upon our unscientific opinion is either flitting *phenomenon,* passing from non-existence to existence and back again with the course of time, or else a mere *illusion* of ignorance, what is manifest to reason is eternal. Plato boldly drew the conclusion that the true reality is not the world of space and time, but a system of eternal typical forms (ἔιδη, or ἰδέαι; the latter term is often anglicized as 'ideas,' which is sadly confusing). And since, in the last resort, the apparent can only be explained in terms of the real, he concluded that the form-world is the true cause of the sensible world — that all the definable character of the latter is due to the active presence in it of the forms. Thus a ruler is straight *because* the form of straightness inheres in it; the wheel is round because roundness is in it; Socrates is temperate because temperance is in him, and just because justice is in him. That they are imperfect is due to *matter*, which all phenomena contain, and which is the source of all those individual irregularities of which science takes no account.

The Hierarchy of Forms. — A similar relation exists among the forms themselves. For they are of different degrees; and the higher ones inhere in the lower and give them character, just as the forms in general do to sensible things. Thus the circle is a line because of linearity; justice and temperance are good because of goodness. Goodness is the supreme form, for it inheres in all the others. (They are all good, and every sensible thing is good in so far as it exemplifies its type. That is why goodness in anything is always marked by regularity.) Hence goodness is the ultimate cause of all things; and since things are explained by revealing their causes, the conception of goodness is the ultimate explanation of everything, temporal or eternal.

The Conceptions of the Forms — Suggested by Particular Things. — The question, how wisdom is acquired, resolves itself, therefore, into the question, how the conceptions of the several virtues, and finally of goodness itself, are brought to mind. There is a curious difficulty here. All the temperance, justice, etc., which we have ever seen in men, is imperfect; and yet it is evidently from the observation of such examples that we arrive at the conception of the perfect forms. How is this possible? A similar question arises in connection with the conceptions of geometry. No one of us has ever seen a perfect square or circle. The physical objects to which we apply these terms, even the diagrams which we draw to exemplify them, are far from geometrical exactness. Yet it is clear that without having perceived these imperfect instances, the exact conceptions would never have occurred to us. Obviously the physical objects *suggest* the perfect types — let us say, by reason of their resemblance to them.[1] The same is, of course, true of virtuous men and deeds. They suggest to us the conceptions of the virtues in their purity.

The Spontaneity of Reason. — But when one thing brings another to mind by reason of the resemblance between them, the latter thing cannot be something that is altogether strange to us. If the sight of a man calls up his brother's face, the image of the brother must have been lingering in our memory; we must have seen him at some time. Then if the geometrical diagram or the good man's conduct suggests to us the perfect square or circle or the perfect virtues, must we not have had some previous intuition of these

[1] This is the view presented in the *Phædo*, and will suffice for our purpose here.

ENERGISM

absolute types? Plato was at first inclined to answer this question in the affirmative, and concluded that we must have had an existence before this present life, when the intuition of the perfect types was enjoyed. Later, however, he dropped this fantastical theory — perhaps he never seriously committed himself to it — in favor of the simpler conclusion, that the conceptions of geometrical and ethical types *belong to the structure of our minds.* We are built in such a fashion, that when the appropriate suggestions come we *spontaneously* think these thoughts. So it is, he thinks, with all possible science.

The Development of Wisdom. — Now this implies that the virtue of wisdon belongs *naturally* to all men that are capable of it.[1] It needs no training by means of habit and exercise, as other virtues do, but simply an awakening through appropriate suggestions. This is the significance of the Socratic method, by which a mere series of questions suffices to lead us from ignorance to knowledge. All knowledge sets out from the things of sense-experience, passing from these to the lowest forms (those of mathematics), and gradually mounting higher and higher till it reaches the private and public virtues, and, last of all, goodness itself.

Supreme Value of Wisdom. — So much for the nature and origin of wisdom. A word must be added as to the relation between wisdom and the other virtues. Let us consider first the classes in the ideal state. It is the ruler's knowledge of the eternal forms that is the source of all the other public virtues. But this is not its only value. To the rulers themselves it is its *least* value. They realize that it is only in a well-ordered community that men like themselves could ever develop. They realize, too, that the service of the state calls for the exercise of all the faculties of the mind, from the lowest to the highest. And yet they regard the work of

[1] Plato thinks that as a matter of fact only a very few men are capable of wisdom — ἀνθρώπων γένος βραχύ τι.

government, not as a supreme self-realization, but as an unavoidable distraction from their highest calling — the contemplation of eternal reality. It is the same in the individual. The highest function of reason is not the guidance of conduct, but *pure theory*. As Plato expressed it, in language which has been much admired, the whole life of the philosopher is a preparation for death, *i.e.* a withdrawal as far as possible from the body and its impressions and impulses.[1] He is a man, to be sure, and not a god, and the wants of the body are ever with him; and so he controls them as best he may. But *so far as he can* he puts himself in a sphere where courage, temperance, and even justice have no place — the realm of pure theory.

This is the feature of Plato's philosophy that called forth the tremendous protest of *stoicism*.

3. *Pleasure*

Insufficiency of Hedonism. — We must now turn to an aspect of Plato's theory which has had the strongest influence upon later thought — his treatment of pleasure. It has been said that he was early inclined to accept a hedonism in which all virtue was reduced to wisdom in the calculation of pleasures and pains. But with the development of his views an identification of pleasure and goodness became impossible for him. For goodness meant for him an eternal objective reality; and pleasure is only too obviously an evanescent feeling. Besides, to seek the greatest possible amount of pleasure seemed to imply that one let one's desires of all sorts grow to the full extent of one's power to satisfy them; and this clearly left out of account the character of regularity and symmetry which a good state of the soul ought to have.

[1] It should be observed that according to Plato's theory of immortality it is the bodiless reason alone — not the appetites or even the half-congenial emotions of honor — that lives on.

ENERGISM

Classification of Goods. — Nevertheless he was ready to admit that unmixed pleasure is a good, and unmixed pain an evil; and he saw also that the experience of any good is indirectly or directly pleasant. Thus he recognizes three classes of goods: (1) those that are good in themselves, but not otherwise; (2) those that are good as means to ulterior ends; and (3) those that are good both as means and as ends. These are (1) the *pleasant* (*i.e.*, unmixed pleasures, from which no painful consequences proceed; (2) the *useful;* and (3) the *both pleasant and useful.* The odor of a violet is an example of the first; uncongenial work, of the second; and vigorous health, of the third.

Beauty is the same as goodness: it is *goodness as it appeals to man's spirited element.* It is this which makes the well-trained youth *love* goodness before he is able to distinguish it rationally. Beauty has, of course, the same divisions as goodness as such. The beauty of a bell-tone, that of a spear, and that of a ship may serve as examples.

Virtue is placed by Plato in the third class of goods: those that are good both as means and as ends. That virtue is generally useful, is conceded; and a due examination of the conditions of social pleasures, and of the peace and security which are necessary for the full enjoyment of even physical pleasures, shows that the usefulness of virtue is great beyond all comparison. But, apart from its usefulness, it has a value in itself which exceeds every other known to men. For nothing can be so essential to a man's happiness as the proper state of his soul.

Qualitative Differences Between Pleasures. — Why is not this to all practical intents a hedonism? Let goodness-in-itself be what you please; if goodness as we experience it is always pleasant, what more could Aristippus ask for? Admit that it is goodness, not pleasantness that makes anything good; if the two are inseparable, what is the difference? Plato's answer is that hedonism fails to take account of two essential considerations: first, that the good (as has been shown) everywhere exhibits order and symmetry; secondly, that *pleasures differ in kind,* and this difference in kind affects their value, so that a lesser amount of pleasure may often be better than a greater amount of another kind. The description of the good simply as pleasant is, therefore, one-sided and misleading.[1]

More explicitly, he believes that pleasures differ *according to the faculty* whose exercise gives rise to them. There are pleasures of satisfied appetite, pleasures of glory, and pleasures of knowledge. It is idle to compare these quantitatively. How, then, are we to determine their order of worth? The industrial class, the warriors, and the philosophers each maintain that their own kind of pleasure is the best. But it is to be observed that the artisans and merchants have felt only the pleasures of appetite; the warriors have felt these and glory too; the philosophers alone have felt them all. Their testimony, therefore, is the only competent one; and we may conclude that *to know* is the highest pleasure of which man is capable.

III. Aristotle

Relation to Plato. — The ethics of Aristotle differs from that of Plato's riper years less in its contents than in its metaphysical basis. There is a similar distinction between *intellectual* and *moral* virtue (to use Aristotle's terms), the former developed by instruction, the latter by training. There is a similar interpretation of moral virtue as consist-

[1] Plato's direct arguments against hedonism are for the most part of only historical interest. (1) Good and evil are logical contraries, *i.e.* as anything increases in goodness it decreases in badness, and *vice versa*. But in the satisfaction of desire, the desire itself is painful, and the appeasing of it is pleasant; and yet as the desire diminishes the pleasure of appeasing it diminishes also, and they finally cease together. Hence pleasure and pain are *not* logical contraries, and cannot be identical with good and evil. (2) The good in anything makes it good, and the evil in it makes it evil. But

ing in measured symmetry. There is the same exaltation of truth for truth's sake above all other human interests, and of the intellectual few above the masses. There is the same treatment of pleasure, as belonging to all happiness, but as differing in quality according to the faculty that is active in experiencing it; and consequently the same rejection of hedonism as a very one-sided account of the nature of the happy life. We find, however, a great advance in precision of statement, due in part to controversy with other pupils of Plato.

Life. — Aristotle of Stagira belonged to a family of physicians; and his philosophy is largely due to a revision of Plato's mathematically minded theories in the light of biological evidences. He was a member of the Academy, as pupil and as teacher, from his nineteenth to his thirty-eighth year, when Plato died. Later he was for three years the tutor of the young prince Alexander of Macedon. In 335 B.C. he returned to Athens and established a new philosophical school near the gymnasium called the *Lyceum*. (His followers were known as *peripatetics, i.e.* strollers, from their conversations in the shady walks of the gymnasium.) Here he labored until the death of Alexander, when his unpopularity with the masses made it dangerous for him to remain in Athens. He died in Chalcis in the following year.

1. *Metaphysical Basis*

Form and Matter. — Aristotle's most striking divergence from Plato's philosophy is seen in his doctrine that reality is not mere *form*, but the *concrete individual,* to which both

pleasure in a man makes him not good but *pleased;* and pain in him makes him not evil but *pained*. Both of these arguments obviously confuse the *presence of a quality in consciousness*, with the *inherence of a quality in an object*. Here, as so often in the history of human thought, the man's hostile criticisms are of far less moment than his positive suggestions. It is because Plato feels that energism is true that he casts about for arguments to prove that hedonism is false.

L

form and matter belong. With one exception (to be noted shortly) the forms have no existence except as they are exemplified in material things. If all the particular horses in the world were destroyed, the form of the horse would never be able to impress itself upon matter again. Aristotle admits, however, that all the definable character of things is due to the forms; that the forms are unchangeable; and that they alone are strictly knowable. Matter means, in fact, only the *potentiality* of receiving form; while form is what anything *actually* and definitely is. There is *no unformed matter*, for that would be mere indefiniteness. But a *pure form* must be the most real thing in the world; for it is actual through and through, eternal, and changeless. By arguments which we cannot here reproduce, Aristotle identifies this pure form with a Mind, whose only activity is the contemplation of the eternal truths which its own nature contains; which Aristotle regards as a truly divine bliss.

The Functions of the Soul. — Again, with Aristotle, the relation of higher to lower forms is not simply that the higher inhere in the lower and thus give them character. It is that the higher form *supervenes* upon the lower form, carrying the development of the individual to a higher stage. Thus inorganic matter has a certain form, or character. But the plant has all this *and more;* for in the plant a higher form, namely, the vegetable ' soul ' (or vital principle), has supervened upon the inorganic form; so that the merely physical properties of the plant are subordinate to the functions of nutrition and reproduction. So the animal is all that the plant is and more ; for its vegetable functions are subordinate to the functions of sense-perception (including memory and imagination), pleasure and pain, desire, and locomotion, which are the functions of the animal soul. So also man is an animal and more. The distinctively human faculty, *i.e.* reason, has no direct connection with the body ; but it acts upon the animal faculties in man, developing perception into inductive knowledge, and desire into intelligent will. And in addition reason has two functions of its own, in which it is like the divine mind: intuition of first principles, and deduction of other truths from these.

Goodness. — As for the form of the good, Aristotle denies that there is any. Goodness is not a single attribute which all good things have in common. There is no common quality belonging to a good grape, a good reputation, a good judgment, and a good action. Goodness includes any number of qualities, held together only by their similar *relation* to our happiness, *i.e.* as parts of it or as somehow contributing to it. Moreover, if there were a form of the good, it would be of no importance for ethics. For ethics has nothing to do with a good apart from us, but only with the good of human experience; namely, happiness.

2. *Happiness*

Various Theories of Happiness. — When we ask what it is that is good, not as a means to further ends, but as an end in itself for which all else is valued, men are well agreed in answering: *Happiness*. But as to what happiness is, they differ greatly. Is it something such as health or wealth or honor, as most men think? Or is it pleasure or knowledge or virtue generally, or a combination of these, as philosophers have thought? Grant that these things (or most of them) are sometimes desired for their own sakes; by 'happiness' we mean something that is *always* desired for its own sake, and never for the sake of anything else. This at once clearly rules out all the above except pleasure; for even knowledge and virtue are desired for the sake of happiness. It must be added, that happiness is thought of as *all-sufficient*, so that no addition of anything else could make a more desirable sum. It is the most desirable of all things. This excludes pleasure, too. For who would be willing to be a lifelong imbecile, though he was to enjoy the most intense childish pleasures all the time? Moreover, things like sight, memory, and the various virtues, are pleasant, indeed; but we should desire them even if they were not. We thus require not simply pleasure, but pleasure of a certain quality, and, more than that, the various kinds of concrete experience with which pleasure comes.

The Best Life. — What, then, is happiness? Surely a kind of *life*, that is to say, the best life. But life is the activity of the soul. If we wish to find the best life, we must see what the soul's faculties are, and especially what faculties are peculiar to man; for we do not think of plants or even animals as being ' happy ' in the same sense in which man may be. Passing over, therefore, the functions of nutrition and reproduction, and those of mere sensation and impulse, we may say that the happiness of man is to be found in the life of his rational nature — including, of course, that of his senses and appetites in so far as they are controlled by reason, as well as the activities of pure reason itself. Within these limits, if it should appear that any one function (say pure thought) was the real end of the others, happiness would lie in it.

Relation of Happiness to Virtue. — But a faculty may function well or ill, as is evident in such cases as digestion and sight and hearing; and this is true also of the rational nature. By happiness, or the best life, we mean, of course, *right* functioning. But if that is to be possible, the faculty must be in a certain normal condition; and this we call its excellence, or *virtue*. Happiness may therefore be defined as " the activity of the soul in accordance with virtue, or (if there be several) the best and most perfect virtue "; to which Aristotle adds that one needs, of course, a normal term of years to lead such a life in.

Partial Truth of Earlier Theories. — This conclusion is confirmed by the fact that it curiously combines and harmonizes the older views. It does not identify happiness with virtue, but it declares that it must be *according to virtue*. A distinction is here drawn between virtue and happiness, to which Aristotle attributes great importance. Virtue he regards as a mere condition into which the soul may be brought. The virtuous man is no less virtuous when he is asleep or in any other way hindered from manifesting his virtue. But happiness is the manifestation of virtue in action. Again, according to this view, happiness is not pleasure; but *pleasure always attends upon happiness*. For it must be noted that the performance of any function, when we are in the right state for it, is pleasant; the quality of the pleasure varying according to the function concerned. A life according to virtue is thus necessarily a pleasant life; and, on the other hand, no one can be said to have a virtue until the conduct which it calls for is pleasant to him. Finally, even the external goods are included after a fashion — namely, either as necessary conditions of the happy life or as instruments with which its various activities are carried on. For to live at all the means of food and warmth are necessary; and to live in a desirable way much more is necessary, freedom and leisure especially; and it is not very easy to be happy without some degree of personal comeliness and family rank, or without the comfort of friends and children. So also one cannot act liberally without something to give, or courageously without physical strength.[1] Good fortune is thus necessary for complete living; still it is the life itself that constitutes happiness.

3. *Virtue*

Classification of Virtues. — Human activities are of two kinds: pure theory and practice. The former is the func-

---

[1] In the same spirit, Plato insists that the virtuous life is impossible to the chronic invalid — "such a person is of no use either to himself or to the state."

tion of reason alone; first in the *intuition* of fundamental truths, and secondly in the *deduction* of other necessary truths. In practical activity, while reason (in the sense in which it acts upon the lower nature) is the guide, the motives are given by the appetites. Three divisions of virtue may therefore be distinguished: *wisdom* (pertaining to pure reason); *prudence* (pertaining to practical reason); and *good character;* or, grouping the first two together, we may speak of the *intellectual* and the *moral* virtues.

The Acquirement of the Virtues. — No sort of virtue belongs to man naturally — except as a potentiality of his being. Nature gives him only aptitudes which may be developed into virtue or vice. None of the appetites is, as such, good or bad; nor is natural cleverness. Virtue is a *form*, for which the natural man is the appropriate matter. The intellectual virtues are acquired by *instruction*. More explicitly, prudence is acquired by the forming of correct inductions; while when induction has been carried far enough the faculties of pure reason are awakened into activity, and these never err when they act at all. The moral virtues are acquired by *habituation* to correct conduct. Mere theorizing will no more secure a good disposition than it will a sound body.

Moral Virtue: the Golden Mean. — As Plato pointed out, moral virtue always shows a certain symmetry; and this is seen in the fact that every such virtue is a *mean* between two extremes of excess and defect, which are vices. Thus courage lies between rashness and cowardice, temperance between self-indulgence and insensibility, modesty between bashfulness and shamelessness. Not that the mean is a mathematical average, for it often lies nearer one extreme than the other (as courage lies nearer to rashness than to cowardice); and, besides, the tendencies in each direction vary greatly from man to man. It is a point which *prudence* must determine as well as may be, though it can never do so with absolute accuracy. For conduct consists of individual acts, and the individual is never susceptible of exact scientific determination. With all the good principles which experience can suggest, there is always necessary a certain *sense* of what is right and wrong in the particular case.

Justice. — All this applies equally to justice — which, however, is an ambiguous term. Sometimes it means simply ' obedience to law '; and as laws are made for the enforcement of all sorts of virtues so far as the community is affected by them, the term is then equivalent to good character in general. Generally, however, it is taken to include only the virtue displayed in the transfer of ' external ' goods and ills. So taken, it may mean either (1), in the distribution of goods, to give to each man in proportion to his desert, or (2), in the requital of benefit or injury, to avoid imposing upon another or being imposed upon oneself. In either sense, it is clearly a mean between extremes. In the precise application of the term, justice applies only to dealings between free and equal citizens, living under subjection to law. Only in a modified sense does it apply to the relations between master and slave, or father and children, or even husband and wife.

Laws are partly natural, partly conventional. The former are valid whether we recognize them or not; the latter are the work of the legislative body. Even the natural laws are capable of some modification — in all forms of life some variation from the type is to be expected. But the type none the less remains fixed eternally, and is no harder to distinguish than other natural types. The whole purpose of the state is the common interest of the citizens; and what makes for this is fundamentally just. *Equity* is the correction of the general rules of justice where they fail to fit the particular case — just as in the case of other virtues the general principles need supplementation by a native sense of right and wrong.

Relation between Prudence and Moral Virtue. — If prudence is necessary for moral virtue, it is equally true that moral virtue is necessary for the development of prudence. The basis of prudence is the natural sense of right and wrong in particular cases, since from the particular feelings all general principles must be derived, even including the conception of happiness itself from which all other practical principles depend. But experience shows that in men of evil character the sense of right and wrong is perverted, and the general principles are wrongly formed.[1] Good character and prudence are thus inseparable, neither being possible without the other. How then can one get either? Only by being trained by men who are already good. By being made to perform acts that are ' externally ' right — we cannot call them ' essentially ' right or good until they express the agent's own character — the disposition to perform such acts is acquired, and with it the consciousness of the moral principles that are involved.

Friendship and Citizenship. — In the systems of Plato and Aristotle, as in Greek ethics generally, no special virtue of love or benevolence is recognized. The place is taken by the notions of *friendship* and *citizenship*. Love is not a virtue, if only that it is a natural instinct — parental, filial, fraternal, sexual, or even for man as such; " for man is

---

[1] Hence Aristotle is careful to distinguish between vice, which is marked by wrong moral principles, and *incontinence*, which is marked by the inefficacy of correct moral principles to control conduct. The incontinent man, under the stress of emotion, either does not call to mind his moral principles, or if he does recall them he fails to realize their significance — they are like verses recited by an intoxicated man. (This is what Socrates failed to observe.) Furthermore, in order to apply general principles to particular cases, particular observations are always necessary; and these the incontinent man fails to make impartially. He knows (after a fashion) that *sweet things are to be tasted* and that *hurtful things are not to be tasted:* but he observes only that *this thing is sweet* (which may be true), while he overlooks the fact *that this thing is hurtful.* Incontinence may therefore be said to be a physiological condition analogous to sleep or madness or intoxication.

ENERGISM

always akin to and dear to man." The chief ' forms ' which this natural endowment takes are, on the one hand, friendship, and on the other hand the institutions comprised in the complex organism of the state. Friendship is not, strictly speaking, a virtue, though it is only possible at its best between good men who love each other for their goodness; and the friendship of the good is a great help to increase in virtue. Besides, the true friend is a second self; and being with him directly intensifies the good man's consciousness of life — that is, increases his happiness. So also we find no special virtue of patriotism; but this is because devotion to the state comprehends all the moral virtues. The state is absolutely necessary for man's moral development; indeed its true end is the virtue of its citizens.

4. *The Supremacy of Pure Reason*

Of the two kinds of activity, practical and theoretical, which is the best? The latter, to be sure; for it is the exercise of man's supreme faculty — the ruling element which is most truly himself. Strictly speaking, therefore, we should say that happiness is simply *contemplation of truth*. This conclusion may be confirmed upon various grounds. Contemplation of truth is the most pleasant of all activities. Even the search for truth is admittedly very pleasant — how much more so must be the actual possession of it? Contemplation depends less upon external conditions than the moral life; for (aside from material conditions) the latter absolutely requires men toward whom to act morally, while the former can to some extent go on in isolation. Contemplation is desired absolutely for its own sake; it is the very essence of the *leisure* for which all toil is spent. But even the noblest practical activities — war and politics — look to ends beyond themselves, and are the opposite of leisurely. And if a life of pure contemplation would be rather divine than human (for though reason is the highest and most essential element in man's nature, he has a lower element as well), nevertheless it behooves man to put off his mortality as far as possible and live in the exercise of his highest faculty, in which the divine life solely consists. As a man among men, the sage will choose to live morally; but his highest life is an absolute selfishness — the love of what is best in himself. It is, after all, *as an animal*—by virtue of his lower nature — that man is social; and even the state is the sphere of prudence, not of wisdom. The highest end which the state can accomplish is to secure to a few highly endowed individuals the leisure for private contemplation.

IV. Concluding Comments

Intellectual Aristocracy. — Thus the ancient energism, despite its endeavor to take a broad view of life and its activities — or perhaps even on account of its attempted breadth of view — tends to emphasize the importance of those activities which are (or were) the exclusive privilege of an aristocracy.[1] To be sure, it is an intellectual aristoc-

[1] One of the most interesting differences in the social ideals of the two philosophers is seen in their treatment of women and the family. Plato regards the family as an institution that is of no significance for the upper classes of his ideal state. It would simply tend to weaken their civil allegiance. Temporary unions, designed for the procreation of healthy children, are all that is desirable. It is even better if parents do not know their own children; for then all men and women (of the same generation) will have their children in common; and all children will be brothers and sisters. The women of these classes, like the men, are chosen for their special ability as warriors or as thinkers; and, aside from childbearing, their lives are devoted to their specialties — their infants being cared for by lower-class women. For, though women are on the average inferior to men in every respect, they vary greatly, and even a woman philosopher is not impossible; and they ought, like men, to be classified according to their ability. Aristotle has a lower estimate of women and a higher estimate of the family. (It is amusing to note that Aristotle was a married man, whereas Plato was not.) The institution of the family, he thinks, is necessary for all classes of citizens; and instead of weakening civil allegiance, it is its most important source. Moreover, to spread out the relations of parents and children and

racy — for the professional philosopher it could hardly be otherwise. But none the less it is held that the vast majority of men are *born* incapable of true happiness and must forever remain so. Men belong naturally to different social levels. Some men (as Aristotle frankly declared) are born masters, and some are born slaves. Greeks, who are a superior people, ought never to be enslaved, but only barbarians. Full citizenship, in the sense of membership in the sovereign body, is a privilege that belongs by right only to men of culture. But most men are incapable of culture. The ultimate object of a liberal education is to fit men for a life of leisure; its nearer object is to fit men for the occupations of war and government without which leisure is impossible. Thus, in Plato's ideal state, only the rulers and the warriors are supposed to receive any education. The masses have only their apprenticeship in their various callings. Such a low happiness as they are capable of enjoying is provided for them by their rulers' care. They are *irresponsible*.

Can Ethics be made an Exact Science? — If now we compare the Platonic and Aristotelian systems of ethics, the most important difference that emerges lies in Aristotle's insistence that moral virtue can *never* be a subject of exact knowledge, but must ever remain in the domain of individual perception, or tact. Plato's more direct followers in the Academy refused to follow this lead. They still hoped for an ethics of the mathematical pattern — a system of ideal forms of character and conduct by which the life of the individual and the state might be guided. However, the difference was not so great as might be supposed, as the Academics (like Plato himself) were perfectly ready to admit that in the practical application of the ideal forms they must

of brothers and sisters, as Plato suggests, would simply destroy their value. But women are radically inferior to men, and none are capable of any high degree of culture.

always be adapted to the particular circumstances which perception disclosed.

Academic Skepticism. — It is somewhat surprising to find that while Aristotle's school suffered very little change save a gradual decline, Plato's school underwent a series of striking revolutions. Some seventy years after Plato's death, *Arcesilas* introduced a thorough-going *skepticism* into the Academy; and this held sway there for two hundred years. The skeptics, of whom the greatest was *Carneades* (B.C. 213–129), denied the possibility of exact knowledge altogether. We never get beyond the possibility of error, they declared; though when our opinions are repeatedly confirmed they become more and more probable, and may reach a *practical* certainty. In ethics they were unwilling to commit themselves to any theory of the chief good. Pleasure, absence of pain, the satisfaction of natural appetites, virtue — all these are plausible ends for human endeavor, and there is no need to reject any of them. Probability is our only guide; and, looking to it, we shall not be carried away by foolish passions. Not to expect too much from nature or man or ourselves, and to be content (so long as is possible) with what befalls — that is the way to enjoy a philosophic calm.

Eclecticism. — In the first century B.C., this skepticism gradually gave way to a dogmatic *eclecticism*, which professed to harmonize the ethical teachings of Plato, Aristotle, and the older stoics, and presented the strange mixture that resulted, as a perfect science.

REFERENCES

PLATO, *Gorgias, Crito, Phædo, Symposium, Republic.*
ARISTOTLE, *Nichomachean Ethics*, especially Books I, II, X.
BURNET, J., *Aristotle on Education.*
GREEN, T. H., *Prolegomena to Ethics*, Book II, Ch. IV.
ZELLER, E., *Plato and the Older Academy*, Chs. X, XI; *Aristotle and the Earlier Peripatetics*, Ch. XII.

GOMPERZ, T., *Greek Thinkers*, Book V.
CAIRD, E., *Evolution of Theology in the Greek Philosophers*, Lectures IV–VI, XI.
RITCHIE, D. G., *Plato*, Ch. VIII.
TAYLOR, A. E., *Plato;* and *Aristotle*.
SETH, J., *Study of Ethical Principles*, Part I, Ch. III, xiv.
THILLY, F., *Introduction to Ethics*, Ch. VII.
BENN, A. W., *The Philosophy of Greece*, Chs. VII, VIII.
DICKINSON, G. L., *The Greek View of Life*, especially Ch. III.

CHAPTER IX

RIGORISM

Democracy in Ethics. — As the ancient energism was essentially aristocratic, so the democratic spirit is represented by the rigorism of the cynics and stoics. Happiness, they declared, is open in its fullness to every man. All classes are artificial. The virtue of master and slave, of the highborn and the lowly, of man and woman, are the same; and where virtue is present all inequalities are leveled. There are no conditions of fortune, to which virtue is subject in expressing itself in conduct; and the life according to virtue is the supreme good.

I. THE CYNICS

History of the School. — Antisthenes was the illegitimate son of an Athenian citizen and a Thracian woman, and consequently had not himself the rights of citizenship; and he was, besides, a man of little property. No doubt these circumstances had their effect upon his philosophy. He managed to obtain a good education — he was a pupil of the sophist Gorgias — and became a teacher of rhetoric. When he was already in advanced middle life, he fell under the influence of Socrates, and gave up his profession in order to follow him. After the death of Socrates he commenced teaching in the gymnasium Cynosarges (which was used by the half-Athenians); from which he and his disciples were called *cynics*. The word also carried the connotation of *dog-like* (as if from κύων, dog), on account of their contempt for the luxuries and even the decencies of life; and they welcomed this interpretation as an unintended honor. It was a chief aim of the members of the school to exhibit in their own persons how independent human nature really was of all artificialities, virtue alone being sufficient at all times. A good part of their success was due to the fact, that in spite of their hard manner of life they kept themselves constantly in the best of physical condition. Among the disciples of Antisthenes was the famous *Diogenes of Sinope* (who sought ' a man ' in the daytime with a lantern, and made himself at home in a tub). Diogenes and the later cynics (perhaps Antisthenes also) lived and dressed as common beggars. *Crates* of Thebes gave away considerable wealth on joining them, and influenced his betrothed wife Hipparchia to do the same. At the end of the fourth century the school became merged in *stoicism*.

The Nature of Virtue. — Antisthenes follows his master in holding that virtue is essentially one, and entirely comprised in wisdom, or prudence. He even declares that *every act* of the wise man is in accordance with all virtue. It is impossible to be wise without being temperate, to be temperate without being just, to be just without being brave. And as Socrates held that knowledge was unshakable by passion, so Antisthenes holds that, once acquired, it can never be taken away. Wisdom, however, is by no means so abstractly intellectual a matter as the mathematician Plato supposes. To acquire it the exercise of the body is necessary as well as the education of the soul. Moreover, the amount of knowledge that is necessary is not great. Virtue is a thing of deeds, not of wordy erudition. A so-called ' liberal ' education is of no real use. It is simply a temptation to turn one's attention to non-essentials.

The Cynic Paradoxes. — According to Socrates, virtue is the one unconditional good. But since the right use of all other things depends upon virtue, Antisthenes prefers to say that it is the *only* good. So also, vice is the only evil. All else is in itself indifferent, becoming good or evil only as it is virtuously or viciously incurred. Antisthenes loved to startle his hearers by paradoxical expressions of this principle. Labor (πόνος), he said, was good; and the saying gained point from the fact that the Greeks used this word, as we use 'pain,' to include all kinds of trouble and suffering, making it the direct opposite of pleasure (ἡδονή). And he equally declared that pleasure was an evil. "I would rather be mad than pleased," is one of the sayings attributed to him. But he illustrated his praise of labor by the story of the great Hercules (the bastard-god, whom he delighted to honor), which he interpreted as an heroic perseverance in duty, in defiance of all obstacles. Even so, every good man must labor to withstand temptation and subdue passion. So with pleasure. The pleasures that follow labor are worth pursuing, but not those that precede labor — or, as it is elsewhere put, those that call for regret. Pleasure as such is valueless, not worth stretching out a finger for. The same sort of judgment is passed upon the other things that men ordinarily most desire or fear. Ill-report is a good thing — as good as labor. Praise does not call for thanks. Enemies serve one purpose of the truest friends, for they detect and reveal our faults. Wealth without virtue gives no pleasure, and no good man can love it. Death is the crowning moment of a happy life.[1]

The Sufficiency of Virtue. — Virtue, then, is sufficient for happiness;[2] in fact happiness is nothing else than to live according to virtue. The wise man is absolutely superior to fortune. He regards all evils as not affecting him. If he is the son of a slave, he is still well-born; he has untold riches in his mind; he is lovable, and all the good are his friends; nothing is strange or difficult to him; and he has a weapon

[1] We are told that Antisthenes regarded immortality, not as the universal possession of men, but as the privilege of the just and holy.

[2] One of the ancient accounts adds: "It needs nothing additional except the strength of Socrates." This is inexact, for strength is an essential aspect of virtue itself.

of defense of which nothing can deprive him. All that others have is his; for he is without envy. He is the true king, for he is his own ruler and stands in fear of no man.

The Moral Standard. — But just what is virtue? It is prudence, the knowledge of good and evil. But now, if we content ourselves with saying that the good is that which is according to virtue, we are wandering in a circle. That refined dialectician, Euclid of Megara, fell into just this difficulty. Some sort of standard is necessary, if one is to escape. Antisthenes has a standard, though it is a peculiarly negative one. It is the *absolute independence of the virtuous man.* For since virtue is sufficient for happiness, the virtuous man must be self-sufficient. He must feel no need that must be satisfied from without, except those that are inseparable from the support of life and health; and when these are unsupplied he keeps his independence by simply dying without a struggle or regret. So long as he lives, he stands in his own might, " setting nothing above liberty " (Diogenes).

The Cynic Conception of Nature. — Here was involved the old sophistic antithesis of nature and convention. But Antisthenes (and still more his successors) applied it in a way of which the sophists never dreamed. For what was natural was now interpreted to mean, what the health of the individual and the preservation of the race demanded. And they found that man was a remarkably tough animal. A single rough garment was enough protection; the simplest fare maintained his vigor; he needed no house (though Antisthenes had one); and he could lie down anywhere. Antisthenes and Diogenes made studies of the habits of savages, and even of the lower animals, in order to determine with exactness what primitive man was like. Once started on this line, the cynics found no stopping-place. Diogenes went so far as to justify cannibalism and incest. Antisthenes believed in marriage (for the sake of offspring) and in connubial love — "for the wise man knows who ought to be loved." But Diogenes found marriage superfluous — a community of wives and children was much simpler. Again, Antisthenes believed in patriotism, and even in an active participation in politics; and several of the maxims attributed to him are political counsels. "The safest city wall is prudence; for it cannot fall or be betrayed." "Cities are destroyed when they cannot distinguish wicked from good men." But the later cynics found patriotism irrational; they were citizens of the world. It is to their lasting credit that they were among the first Greeks to denounce slavery as an unnatural institution.

Shamelessness. — The wise man, as we have seen, is sufficient to himself; and in following nature he counts as nothing the opinions of other men. He is utterly *shameless*. "It is for a king to do well and be ill spoken of." Here again the disciples went far beyond the master. Antisthenes seems to have set no store by wantonly offending the susceptibilities of others. But the later cynics prided themselves upon their disregard of all the rules of decency.

'Apathy.' — Finally, in being true to nature, the wise man is free from all violence of passion; for this is entirely due to groundless opinions. And how can a man be swayed by passion, when he has in his own power all that is necessary for his welfare? He enjoys the equanimity ($ἀπαθία$) of the consciously strong. Not that the cynic was a stock or a stone. He knew, for instance, how to love his friends. But whatever emotion he might feel, he did not propose to stake his happiness upon anything outside himself.

Religion. — It is noteworthy that the notion of a god plays no part in the cynic system of morals. A god is not necessary as a lawgiver (except as the creator is necessarily in some sort a lawgiver), for man's own nature is the supreme law. And he is not needed to reward the good, for the very essence of their goodness is absolute self-sufficiency. Antisthenes

RIGORISM

did believe in a single supreme God, who was unlike any created thing and was not to be represented by any image. He went further than Socrates, in declaring that the gods of the popular religion were mere ' convention.' But nothing positive in his conception of God is recorded; and it seems to have played a very small part in his philosophy.

II. THE STOICS

Relation to Cynicism. — The last of the great ethical systems of the pagan era, and (until the rise of Christianity) the strongest positive moral influence in the world, was stoicism, founded by Zeno of Citium about the end of the fourth century. Its founder had been a pupil of Crates the cynic, and in his teaching most of the characteristic notions of the cynics were incorporated — except, indeed, their athleticism, which was a natural omission, as Zeno was a lifelong invalid. The cynics had taught that the only good is virtue, the only evil vice; that happiness is life according to virtue, and any other life is misery; that pleasure and pain and all things else are indifferent; that virtue is freedom from all that is external to one's nature, *i.e.* from habits and opinions and the needs and passions thence arising. All this is good stoic doctrine. What is new in the ethics of Zeno and his successors is, first, a *half metaphysical, half religious background;* and secondly, a *genetic theory of the relation of morality to instinct.* Beyond this we have only elaborations of cynicism.

1. *The Background*

The Universal Nature. — The first of these, though important in other connections, can receive only brief consideration here. The stoics were *materialistic pantheists*. They believed that mind and matter are not two kinds of substance, but that mind is a kind of matter, an omnipresent *ether*, or *fire*.[1] It is active matter as distinguished from the passive matter with which it is everywhere united; in other words, God, the soul of the universe. All the processes of nature are his life, the self-expression of his nature; wherefore the universe, with all that it contains, is absolutely perfect. And as his nature is eternal and rational, all that takes place is in accordance with invariable law.

Human Nature. — Human reason is, as it were, a spark of the universal fire. Our nature is the same as the cosmic nature. We are free beings; not, indeed, as if we were able to change the course of things, for this we cannot do; but free to assent to, or to dissent from, what is necessary. To assent is to agree with the universal nature, and hence also with our own nature. To dissent is to be at odds with the world and with ourselves.

2. *The Relation of Morality to Instinct*

The Primitive Instincts and their Objects. — The first actions of every sentient creature are impelled, not (as the hedonists thought) by the love of pleasure, but by the instincts of self-preservation. The newborn animal feels its own existence and clings to life and health; and it is impelled toward things that are necessary or wholesome, while it shrinks from death and from all that seems to threaten death. By examination we can make out for each species a list of the objects of its natural affection. The body and its parts, and appropriate food and protection, will be universally included; and in the case of man we must add truth, whether gained through direct perception or through correct reasoning.

Value and its Gradations. — Now the general process by which new objects of choice are added to that which instinct dictates, is simply this: that we choose the things

---

[1] The latter term is from the old cosmologist, Heraclitus of Ephesus, whose enigmatic sayings the stoics were fond of interpreting as anticipations of their own doctrine.

which, we perceive, tend to secure the objects of instinctive (or previously developed) choice. Such things, like the primary objects themselves, are said to be *in harmony with nature*, and to have *value;* while things of a contrary tendency are said to be *contrary to nature*, and to have *negative value*. As the power of reflection begins, it is seen that the *choice* of valuable things (*fitting* conduct) is itself of value, being preferable to heedless choice; and, further, that the *habitual* fitting choice is valuable as compared with the merely occasional. And, finally, as the faculty of abstract thought matures, there arises a perception of *fitness* itself; and the complete ordering of life by this principle, making a life *according to reason*, is seen to be in the highest degree fitting and valuable. But this is what we mean by virtue.

Goodness. — At once, however, it is clear, that such a life is more than merely valuable. To be absolutely governed in one's conduct by the rational perception of fitness is *good*. This word ' good ' has been loosely used by the would-be catholic Plato and his successors. To speak of ' external goods ' and ' goods of the body ' is outrageous. The objects of natural affection, all things in harmony with nature, and even fitting acts and habits, are simply valuable. The fitting act that is committed simply because it is fitting — in other words, the *right* act — is not only valuable but good.

Is this to quarrel about terms? Yes; but terms are important when they express differences in kind. The difference between goodness and other values is such a difference.

Some Distinctions of Terms. — The good is man's wellbeing, or happiness, and thus is worthy of being *desired;* while the merely valuable forms no part of true happiness, and is not worthy of being desired. The merely valuable is more or less *acceptable;* that is to say, when it is a matter of choice, it is fitting to choose the more valuable in preference to the less valuable. Similarly, what is contrary to nature, and thus has negative value, is more or less *unacceptable*, though not necessarily *evil*. *Wrong* conduct is indeed evil; by which is meant the unfit conduct of a rational agent, as indicating the blindness of reason to its unfitness. What is neither good nor evil is *indifferent*. What has no value at all, either positive or negative, is *utterly indifferent*, or *neutral*.[1]

Let us illustrate some of these distinctions. Wealth is acceptable, and poverty is unacceptable. Wealth has a positive value, because it enables the possessor to provide the things that are necessary for the satisfaction of his natural impulses; while poverty has a negative value. If we have to choose between them, the former is to be preferred; to choose it is the fitting thing to do. But the virtuous man does not desire wealth. He does not think of it as something essential to his well-being. He does not, so to speak, set his heart upon it. The loss of wealth leaves him as happy as before. But he does desire to live rationally by being diligent in his business and administering his property economically. For such (rational) conduct is right and good. So also he does not desire health, nor is he unhappy in sickness; but he does desire to live rationally by obeying all hygienic laws.

Summary. — The essential points to be noted are these: Moral value, or goodness, is late in the order of temporal development, but is not for that reason inferior. On the contrary, it is a distinctly higher product. It arises as an

---

[1] The following table of contrasted terms may be of service:

In harmony with (contrary to) nature:	In harmony with (contrary to) reason:
valuable — having negative value — neutral	good — evil — indifferent
fitting (duty) — unfitting	right — wrong
acceptable — unacceptable	desirable — objectionable
convenience — inconvenience	benefit — injury

indirect means to the securing of the objects of natural preference. But, having thus arisen, it is of a radically different nature from these objects. In a sense it continues to be dependent upon them; that is to say, it is dependent upon the distinction between things acceptable and unacceptable. For if there were no such distinction there would be no possibility of rational choice. But as soon as virtue exists, it is absolutely independent of the *actual presence* of anything whatsoever — even of the continuance of life itself. For death is not an evil; and when it is fitting for the virtuous man to die, his acceptance of death is the last act of a happy life.

3. *The Stoic Paradoxes*

Verbal Paradoxes. — The conclusions which the stoics immediately proceed to draw from these doctrines are among the most notorious of paradoxes. Some of them, to be sure, are only verbal. When it is said that physical pain is not an evil, it must be understood that it is nevertheless exceedingly unacceptable, and that a very strong revulsion is naturally caused by it. When it is said that the wise man is as happy in sickness, poverty, and ill-repute as in health, riches, and honor, the meaning is that he is as virtuous, and hence, as we may phrase it, as worthy of emulation. But others of the paradoxes are more than verbal. In general these may be described as attempts to give precision to the various distinctions set forth above. Several of the most important are *restatements of qualitative distinctions in quantitative terms*.

No Mixture of Virtue and Vice. — In the first place, it is maintained that the division of men into virtuous and vicious admits of no middle ground. There are no partly virtuous and partly vicious men. When reason controls conduct it does so absolutely and at all times. Men are either virtuous or vicious; and whereas every act of the virtuous man is right, every act of the vicious man is either indifferent (in case it happens to be fitting) or wrong.

No Gradations of Virtue or Vice. — In the second place it is said that all virtue is equally great; that is to say, in the sphere of the good there is no better or worse. All good men are equally estimable, and all their acts are perfect. The like is said of vice. To steal a penny is as evil as to betray one's country. This is one of the quantitative restatements above referred to. All virtue is equally (*i.e.* with equal truth) virtuous; and hence it is equally (*i.e.* in an equal degree) virtuous. All vice is equally vicious (in the same two senses).

Corollaries. — (1) It follows that there is no gradual improvement in morals. There is only the total transformation from consummate vice to consummate virtue. It is true that as time goes on a larger and larger proportion of the vicious man's acts may be fitting, and hence merely indifferent; and as this happens the man may be said to be *approaching* virtue. But he is as vicious as ever all the while. It is like the opening of the newborn puppy's eyes. He is blind, and is gradually approaching the possession of sight. But he is as blind just before his eyes open as at any previous time.

(2) It also follows that the longer of two happy lives is not a whit more desirable than the shorter. For the desirability of the happy life consists, not in the merely 'acceptable,' which it may contain in greater or less amount, but in its virtuousness, which does not increase with time. A happy life would be no happier if it endured a thousand years; just as a musical note would be no higher if it were similarly prolonged. Duration has no more to do with happiness than with musical pitch.

Infinite Superiority of Virtue. — In the third place, virtue is infinitely more valuable than anything else whatsoever. This is another translation from the qualitative to the quantitative. If the virtuous life possesses a value of an essentially new and higher type, then no quantity of mere 'acceptables' can ever be equivalent to it. Hence, as compared with any merely acceptable thing, the value of virtue is infinite, *i.e.* is incapable of being increased by the addition of any finite value. The stoics were never tired of setting this forth in striking illustrations. In the happy life the addition or subtraction of all the gifts of fortune makes not so much difference as the addition or subtraction of a single penny would make to the wealth of Crœsus, or as a drop of water more or less would make to the great sea.

Suicide. — The stoic doctrine of suicide is an unimportant detail; but it should be noticed for the light it throws upon these paradoxes. Like the Epicureans, the stoics regarded suicide as sometimes justifiable. But whereas the Epicurean could defend his position by saying that when life is no longer worth living it ought to be left, the stoic had no such excuse; for to him the life of the vicious man was always absolutely wretched and that of the virtuous absolutely happy, and neither the wretchedness of the one nor the happiness of the other could be increased or diminished by a longer or shorter term of life. He therefore has recourse to the following argument. The fitness of conduct consists in the choice of the more acceptable in preference to the less. When life is filled with a preponderance of things contrary to nature — such as sickness, poverty, and pain — the cessation of life becomes more acceptable than its continuance; and under these circumstances suicide is fitting. Hence, as the wise man always does what is fitting, he will in such a case unhesitatingly commit suicide, altogether regardless of the fact that he is as happy as can be!

4. *The Virtuous Life*

Unity of Virtue. — More precisely, now, what is virtue? Is it an attribute of character, or of conduct? Of both. There is no good character that does not constantly express itself in right conduct; and there is no right conduct except that which arises from good character. Plato and Aristotle were radically wrong when they imagined that reason had a function of its own — pure thought — separate from, and superior to, its control of conduct. Except as theory contributes to practical ends, it is a vicious frittering away of life. The supposed distinction between wisdom (as the virtue of pure thought) and prudence is illusory. Wisdom and prudence are the same. Socrates was right: to know is to act accordingly. All the virtues are but various aspects of a single reality. Every right act (that is to say, every act of a good man) exhibits every possible virtue. Wisdom, temperance, courage, and justice mutually imply each other.

Passions and Rational Feelings. — Since reason, late as is its appearance in the development of the individual, is certainly a part of man's nature, virtue (or the proper functioning of reason) may well be described as a state of health; and vice is as truly a state of disease. The various forms which this disease takes are the *passions* ($\pi\acute{a}\theta\eta$), perturbations of the soul by which reason is blinded and paralyzed. These are many in number, but may be comprised under four heads: *grief* ($\lambda\acute{v}\pi\eta$), *passionate desire* ($\dot{\epsilon}\pi\iota\theta\upsilon\mu\acute{\iota}a$ — lust, in the widest sense of the term), *fear* ($\phi\acute{o}\beta\text{os}$), and *pleasure* ($\dot{\eta}\delta\text{ov}\acute{\eta}$) — by which last term the stoic means, not mere agreeable feeling, but, as in the case of the other passions, a state of absorption in the feeling, a surrender of the rational nature. This distinction is of great importance. The stoic wise man is said to be free from passion; but this does not mean that he is devoid of feeling. For feelings may be perfectly natural and healthy, both in quality and in intensity; and in such case, unless other considerations interfere, reason dictates that we obey our feelings, for that is following nature. We should eat as we have appetite, exercise as we find it exhilarating, and enjoy the beauties of nature and art. Once more: if we had no natural inclinations toward or away from things, there would be nothing for reason to work upon. Passion is the subjection of reason to the feelings which it is its function to control. Moreover there are certain *rational feelings* (εὐπαθείαι) which are peculiar to the virtuous life. These are comprised under the three heads of *determination* (βούλησις, contrasted with lust), *caution* (εὐλάβεια, contrasted with fear), and *joy* (χάρα, contrasted with pleasure). The sage's existence, far from being an idle and cheerless one, is vigorous and delightful.

Social Character of Virtue: how Explained. — (1) There is one impression which one is very apt to get from a first survey of the stoic theory of virtue, but which is as far from truth as possible. That is, that the stoic idea of the life ordered by the rational perception of harmony is a selfish, or, at least, an individualistic, ideal — like the supreme happiness of contemplation, in the systems of Plato and Aristotle. The stoic view is that *all good is intrinsically social.* The explanation they find partly in a peculiar characteristic of man's natural instincts: *all of the objects of natural affection and dislike are social in their scope.* The impulse to ward off a blow from oneself is no more natural than the impulse to ward off a blow from another man; the impulse to recoil from pain is no more natural than the impulse to relieve another's pain; the impulse to learn is no more natural than the impulse to teach; and in each case the latter impulse may easily be far stronger than the former. In fact, so thoroughly social a creature is man, that the prospect of utter loneliness takes away the attractiveness from every object whatsoever. Man is a member of human society, as assuredly as his own arm is a member of his body. And so bound together is he with his fellows, that every acceptable or unacceptable experience of any one affects in a like manner every other in some degree, however slight.

Now since this is true of man's instinctive constitution, fitness (or harmony with nature) means consistency with the interests, not only of the individual, but of society as a whole. Nay, since the whole is more than the part, fitness requires that the interests of society be paramount. And not simply the existing generation must be counted (for society lives on from generation to generation), but the remotest posterity as well. It is *natural* for man to live, not for himself, but for his family and neighbors, and above all for the state. The stoic sage did not propose to secure happiness by avoiding annoyances in a selfish isolation. The cares of the parent and the citizen are a proper part of human life. A man *can be happy* if cut off from them; but to live in the midst of them is clearly preferable.

(2) But such an explanation is only partial. For though the fitting act is in accordance with the common interests, still, as rightly performed by any one good man, it is *his* act, and the virtue which it displays is *his* virtue. Why, then, is it not a private good? Here the stoic falls back upon his metaphysical religion for the answer. All reason is one. All rational beings, both gods (*i.e.* superhuman personalities) and men, are members of a single universal organism. Each one, by living in accordance with his own nature, is put in touch with the universal harmony and enjoys it to the full — nay, becomes a factor in that harmony. Every good man, therefore, in each of his acts, is directly benefiting every rational being that is capable of receiving benefit — namely, the virtuous. And the like is true of vice. Every wrong act (*i.e.* every unfitting act of a vicious man) is an injury to all who are capable of receiving injury — namely, the vicious. Not only, therefore, through their social instincts, but still more through their rational nature, all men are bound together in unity.

Friendship. — This unity, however, is one which only the good actually experience. In them it is called 'friendship.' The good, and the good alone, are friends; for they alone can confer real benefit upon each other. Friendship is therefore said to be a good; not as if it were a good in addition to virtue, but because its goodness is one of the essential characteristics of virtue itself. Virtue is good, not only to its possessor, but to all other good men.

The Equality of Benefits. — Here follows one of the most remarkable of the stoic paradoxes. To benefit can only mean to incite or restrain according to virtue (just as to injure can mean only to incite or restrain according to vice). But if this influence fell upon different men unequally, that would make it easier for some men to be good than for others; and hence virtue would not be wholly voluntary — which seemed a monstrous conclusion. Hence it was laid down that all benefits (and all injuries) are equal. All the virtuous are equal sharers in one another's virtue. And, similarly, all the vicious, no matter how close in their approximation to virtue, are equal sharers in one another's vice.

The Laws of Nature. — The universal society of gods and men has its laws, obedience to which is justice, and disobedience to which is injustice. In contrast to the varied and changing statutes of men, these laws are eternal and everywhere in force. These *laws of nature* are simply a description of the natural life, expressed in the form of commands. They bid us do what is fitting and abstain from what is unfitting. Consequently, obedience to the law does not constitute virtue (for that is merely fitting conduct), though disobedience to it, on the part of a rational being, is always vice. Virtue is the obedience to law, that springs from the rational perception of harmony.

Thus, as the system finally works out, stoicism may be regarded as equally an ethics of *virtue* and an ethics of *duty*. The notion of the personal value of morality is kept prominent; but the ultimate standard is an eternal *code*, which is absolutely authoritative on its own account. It is interesting to observe that it was this legal aspect of stoicism that most appealed to the Roman world. This was notably the case with the great popularizer of Greek philosophy, *Cicero*. And in the consolidation of the empire, amid the difficulties arising from the differences of law in its many provinces, the Roman jurists found the conception of a universal law of nature a most useful means of harmonization. The law of nature was viewed as the rational norm, from which the laws of the particular states were conventional variations. And thus there arose the conception of a *state of nature,* in which men had not yet formed particular states and were governed by the laws of nature alone — a conception which, as we shall see, was of great importance in the early development of modern ethics.

REFERENCES

CICERO, *De Finibus Bonorum et Malorum,* Books III, IV.
EPICTETUS, *Discourses.*
DIOGENES LAERTIUS, *Lives of the Philosophers,* Books VI, VII.
GROTE, G., *Plato and the Other Companions of Socrates,* Ch. XXXVIII.
ZELLER, E., *Socrates and the Socratic Schools,* Ch. XIII; *Stoics, Epicureans, and Sceptics,* Part II, Chs. X–XII.
CAIRD, E., *Evolution of Theology in the Greek Philosophers,* Lectures XVIII, XIX.
GOMPERZ, T., *Greek Thinkers,* Book IV, Ch. VII.
ARNOLD, E. V., *Roman Stoicism,* Ch. III.
DAVIDSON, W. L., *The Stoic Creed,* Chs. VII–X.
HICKS, R. D., *Stoics and Epicureans,* Ch. III.

CHAPTER X

THE BEGINNINGS OF MODERN ETHICS

I. THE POINT OF DEPARTURE

The Omitted Centuries. — If this part of our work pretended to be a history, there are many matters of which we should have to take account, which for our present purposes must be passed over. From the beginning of the Christian era philosophy was intensely religious. This was true of all the chief thought movements: the Jewish-Alexandrian philosophy, neo-Platonism, and the philosophy of the Greek and Latin fathers of the Christian church. Much as might be learned from a study of their ethical doctrines, as well as from those of the scholasticism and mysticism of the middle ages, we prefer to pass directly to the re-birth of the science of ethics which took place in England, in the seventeenth century. In the modern development of the science, and especially in the controversies of the great English schools, we shall find ample material for our instruction.

The Inherited Theory. — Modern ethics, like ancient ethics, had as its first problem the determination of the *natural basis of morality*. But it differed from the ancient science in taking its rise, not from the simple notions of common sense, but from a learned theory inherited from stoicism. This theory was that of the existence of a universal and eternal code of *laws of nature*, under which alone man originally lived, and from which all the peculiarities of civil laws are local and transient variations. These laws command men to do what it is *fitting* for them to do, in view of their social and rational nature, and of their consequent relations to each other and to God.

God as Sovereign. — In one striking way this traditional theory had departed from the ancient form. The religious pantheism had been given up; and in its stead was the Christian belief in individual immortality and a personal God. Consequently the laws of nature were conceived to be *his commands*, and might reasonably be expected to be enforced by rewards and penalties, especially in the hereafter. They were thus literally *laws* in the sense of *statutes issued by an omnipotent sovereign*. Some theologians (under the influence of the great English schoolmen, Duns Scotus and William of Occam) even went so far as to declare that it is only because God has commanded obedience to the laws of nature, that they are at all obligatory upon us, and that ' fitting ' means simply what is pleasing to him. He might conceivably, they said, have commanded otherwise; and then what is now right would be wrong, and *vice versa.* But the more orthodox view (as it had been held by Thomas Aquinas) was that there is an eternal distinction between fitting and unfitting, and that God's commands simply give the force of law to this distinction. He commands the fitting because it *is* fitting. He might, to be sure, have created us differently, and then different conduct would be in accordance with our nature. But we being such as we are, the law of nature follows necessarily from our given constitution; and even in the absence of any revelation from God we can to a considerable extent make out, from the study of this constitution, what our natural obligations are.

Grotius. — The classic modern exposition of this view is contained in the treatise on international law (*De Jure Belli et Pacis*, 1625) of Hugo Grotius. This work is based upon the interesting conception, that since *sovereign states* in their dealings with each other are controlled by no man-made laws, they are *subject to the laws of nature alone*. Thus they furnish a vivid illustration of the relations between individual men in the original state of nature.

II. HOBBES

The New Impulse. — The study of the ancient ethical classics produced more or less important revivals of all the ancient philosophical schools. In the seventeenth century the most important of these was the *Platonism* that flourished in Cambridge University. But the impulse that gave birth to modern ethics came from a body of original and daring speculations that set all tradition at naught, and, rejecting all previous moral science as utterly fallacious, essayed to build up the true science from its foundations. The publication of these speculations in the *De Cive* (1641) and *Leviathan* (1651) of Thomas Hobbes of Malmesbury won for him, it is true, not a single disciple of importance, but it excited opposition and awakened thought as scarcely any other event in English literary history has done.

Political Attitude. — Hobbes, the most hard-headed and opinionated of men, worked out his ethical theories during the time of the Puritan agitation against Charles I. It appeared to him that such agitation was exceedingly foolish and threatened the very foundations of social security. But, at the same time, he had no faith in the Cavalier dogma of the divine right of kings. Accordingly, his theories are prompted by the desire to prove the necessity of an undivided sovereign power, from facts that would be apparent to all men of sense and sobriety.

1. *Fundamental Principles*

Method. — Hobbes got his ideal of scientific method from the study, in middle age, of a copy of Euclid's *Elements;* which, however, he imperfectly understood. He believed that all true science begins with arbitrary definitions of the terms to be used, and that its whole procedure consists in drawing deductions from these definitions. (The axioms of Euclid, he thought, could all be proved from mere definitions.) Hobbes's ethics, therefore, is professedly a *deductive science*.[1] In its actual mode of presentation, however, it is not carried back to the primary definitions, for these belong to natural philosophy, or physics, which Hobbes regards as fundamental; and though Hobbes believed that natural philosophy could be developed to a point where moral philosophy would follow directly from it, he never attempted to work out the full connection. As matters stand, his ethics is grounded on an *inductive study of human nature*, and especially of the *passions*, though its procedure thereafter is rigidly deductive. Against the Platonists he maintains that there are no intuitively known truths from which deductions can be drawn.

Psychology. — Hobbes's account of human nature is based on a *materialistic psychology*. He believed that the only substances that exist are *material bodies*; and also (as the mechanical discoveries of Galileo had suggested) that all the qualities and changes of matter are reducible to *rest* and *motion*. (God, the first cause of all things, no doubt exists; but his nature is utterly unknowable to us, and so it would be an idle use of terms to call him a substance.) *Consciousness* is only a form of motion in which certain bodies may be put. Of course that is not what it appears to be; and hence Hobbes is led to distinguish between the conscious process as it *appears* (which he calls 'fancy') and as it really *is*. *Sensation*, for example, is really the elastic rebound of the central nervous organ after it has momentarily yielded to some pressure from without; but the 'fancy' of sensation is some particular color, taste, smell, sound, or feeling.

---

[1] In reading his works, the student must bear in mind that whenever a word or phrase has been defined it must always be understood *exactly as defined* (except, of course, where there is reason to think that a real confusion exists); for Hobbes uses many common terms in uncommon senses. For example, according to him, independent states are always at *war* with each other; but the proposition is not nearly so alarming as might be supposed.

THE BEGINNINGS OF MODERN ETHICS

So *imagination* (or memory, which is the same thing) really is the gradually subsiding vibration that lingers after sensation; while the ' fancy ' is a less vivid likeness of the ' fancy ' of sensation. So also *endeavor* is the faint beginning of a voluntary motion toward, or away from, some object, being in the one case *desire* and in the other case *aversion;* but the ' fancy ' of desire is *pleasure,* and the ' fancy ' of aversion is *displeasure,* or pain. To desire a thing and to be pleased with it are thus, for Hobbes, but two sides of the same fact;. and so also are to be averse to a thing and to be displeased with it. All the *passions* of men are simply desire and aversion for different sorts of objects and under different sorts of circumstances; as, for example, hope is desire with the expectation of getting the object; despair is desire without any such expectation; charity is desire that some one else shall obtain what he desires. Desires and aversions are either *instinctive* or *acquired.* The origin of the latter is that we desire whatever experience shows is apt to be followed by pleasant effects, and are averse to what is apt to be followed by unpleasant effects — or even what we are not sure will be harmless.

Theory of Values. — We are now prepared for Hobbes's definition of ' good ' and ' evil.' " Whatever is the object of any man's appetite or desire, that is it which he for his part calleth ' good ': and the object of his hate and aversion, 'evil '. . . . For these words . . . are ever used with relation to the person that useth them, there being nothing simply and absolutely so." In other words, we do not desire things because they are good; but their being good *means* the fact that we desire them. If A desires a thing and B does not, the thing is good for A and not good for B. If a dispute arises between them as to whether the thing is good or not (as, for example, when a money payment has to be made in case the thing is good), the only way to settle it is to lay it before an *arbitrator* — either some one agreed upon by the disputants or some one legally appointed to judge such cases — whose decision is accepted as authoritative. There is nothing in the thing itself upon which a universally valid judgment of good or evil can be based.

Hobbes not a Hedonist. — We should note very carefully that Hobbes is not, strictly speaking, a hedonist. According to him pleasure is not good, for it is not desired; it is the 'fancy'-side of the process of desire itself. One might then as well say that desire is good. Of course he does hold that *pleasures* (in the plural, meaning pleasant experiences) are good; for their being pleasant *means* that they are desired, which is as much as to say that they are good. This distinction is one which Hobbes's contemporaries, and indeed most of his successors, failed to appreciate; and accordingly he has been generally known as an Epicurean. Perhaps he was not perfectly clear about the matter himself.

In what Sense an Egoist. — If Hobbes is not a hedonist, there is nevertheless some reason to class him with Epicurus as being an *egoist*. From his definition of 'good,' he at once infers that no man ever desires anything save his own good. This in itself is insignificant enough, for it means no more than that every man desires what he desires. But Hobbes puts his egoism in more definite terms. Pleasures, he says, are either *of sense* (that is, arising directly from the perception of a present object) or *of the mind* (that is, arising from expectation of consequences); and the latter are all reducible to *glory*, or the pleasure arising from the imagination of one's own *power* (or means of accomplishing his desires). Thus the pleasure that men often take in giving pleasure to others, even without hope of any return, arises from the imagination of the power so employed. "There can be no greater argument to a man of his own power, than to find himself able not only to accomplish his own desires, but also to assist other men in theirs." Parental affection is of this sort. Similarly, pains are either of the body or of

THE BEGINNINGS OF MODERN ETHICS

the mind; and the latter are all reducible to *dejection* from the imagination of *weakness*. For example, pity, or sympathy for another's misfortune, arises from the imagination of a like misfortune as occurring to oneself; and that is why, in so far as men think themselves exempt from misfortune, they cease to have pity for others.

The student should note, however, that Hobbes's theory does not imply that we are charitable and sympathetic only *for the sake of* some future good to ourselves, or *in order to avoid* some future evil. The father does not care for his children in order that he may have the sense of power; but he desires to do so *because* the thought of caring for them suggests to him the sense of power. The good Samaritan does not pity the wounded traveler in order to ward off a similar evil from himself; but he pities him *because* the sight of his distress suggests to him the thought of a similar evil to himself. The relation is one of cause and effect, not of means and end. Thus, if egoism is defined as the doctrine that men desire the good (and are averse to the evil) of others, only for the sake of securing some further good (or of avoiding some further evil) to themselves, Hobbes is not an egoist.[1] He does, however, believe that, as a matter of fact, the vast majority of mankind are exceedingly selfish.

The Laws of Nature. — Such being Hobbes's theory of good and evil, his account of moral laws, or laws of nature, need not surprise us. They are *general rules*, discovered by reason, *for self-preservation*. They direct one not to do what endangers his life, and not to omit what best preserves it. Thus, since intemperance leads to sickness and death, it is a moral law to *be temperate;* and, similarly, it is a moral

[1] Hobbes defines 'cruelty' as "*contempt, or little sense*, of the calamity of others," not as pleasure in it. And he adds: "For that any man should take pleasure in other men's great harm, without other end of his own, I do not conceive it possible." But the pleasure which we take in small mishaps to others (at which we *laugh*), and the grief which we feel at their greater misfortunes, are indeed without ulterior ends of our own.

law to *be brave,* *i.e.* to face dangers unhesitatingly when they cannot without greater danger be avoided. Every man is instinctively averse to death, as the greatest of evils; and though sometimes other evils (such as infamy) appear to be still greater, so that men choose death in preference, yet, as a general rule, the fear of death is the strongest of all passions. Hence, breaches of the moral law may generally be regarded as due to ignorance.

The laws of nature in which Hobbes is especially interested are those which relate to the *maintenance of social security*. For a proper understanding of his ethics some knowledge of his theory of society is therefore necessary.

2. *The State of Nature*

Society is Artificial. — Here we are at once startled by a proposition which Hobbes declared to be demonstrable from the preceding account of human desires and aversions — namely, that *man is not naturally a social animal,* or is not naturally adapted to social life. He thus demolishes at one stroke the whole basis of the orthodox theory of the laws of nature. Let us see how he proves his case.

The Persistence of Desire. — Since pleasure is but one side of the process of desire, there is no such thing as the " repose of a mind satisfied." To enjoy is to desire to continue to possess. Human happiness, at any rate in this world, is a progress of desire from one object to another; each end attained being only a stepping stone to some further end. There is no *summum bonum* in the possession of which desire can rest. Desire, like sensation and imagination, ceases only with life itself. Hence all men seek not only to obtain, but also to secure to themselves, the means of happiness. For the most part the means of happiness are limited. One man's possession means another's deprivation. Hence, human power is *relative;* that is to say, to be strong means to be stronger than one's competitors. Accordingly, there

THE BEGINNINGS OF MODERN ETHICS 183

is in all men " a perpetual and restless desire of power after power"; not for the sake of more intense pleasures, or because they would not be content with a moderate power; but because more power is always necessary to protect what they already have and others already covet.[1]

The Causes of Quarrel. — Now, as we see men about us, their powers are very unequal. But this inequality is due to civil institutions. Naturally (*i.e.* before the establishment of states) all men are practically equal; for the strongest cannot save himself from sudden death at the hands of the weakest, and the intellectual differences between them are even less than the physical. Hence, where there is no fear of a supreme power, there must be unrestrained competition, and from this constant quarrels must arise; for there is no way to secure possession of goods like killing or driving off the competitor. Even though a man is not naturally contentious, fear will make him strike when opportunity offers, in order to forestall an ambitious neighbor. Add to this the fact that man's natural love of *glory* is enough to make him fight in order to secure respect from others. For the sense of one's own power is chiefly fed by the acknowledgments of it by others; and hence every man wishes that others should value his powers (of whatever kind) as highly as he himself does.

Universal War. — Greed, fear, and pride — these three passions are enough to keep the natural man in constant strife. Hence the state of nature is not society, but *a war of every man with every man.* Not that fighting must be always going on; for *war means not simply battle but insecurity from attack;* just as peace means security.

If it be objected that security is to be found in the love which all men naturally bear one another, Hobbes denies that there is any such universal love. We love some men, hate some others, and are indifferent to the rest. Those who

[1] As in the case of a state which 'rectifies' its boundaries.

love each other may join together for protection; but, aside from the fact that love is perishable, their numbers must be too small to give real security. The hope of booty may always raise a temporarily greater force against them. If it be said that the fear of divine punishment may restrain men from mutual hurt, Hobbes admits that it has such a tendency, but denies that the tendency is strong enough to produce security; for the fear of distant evils is of small effect.

The State of Nature not Necessarily an Historical Fact. — This conception of the state of nature is, of course, a *logical construct*, deduced from a description of human passions, by considering to what they would lead if not kept in restraint by the civil power. In other words, it is an *abstraction*. Hobbes is not committed to the view that such a state ever existed in the world. In fact, if the terms be taken strictly enough, he does not believe that there ever did. For the mated pair are in general held together by love; and the child is necessarily subject to the authority of the father or mother, on whom he depends for his sustenance. Within the limits of the family, therefore, the state of nature is impossible. Even allowing for this exception, Hobbes does not believe that the state of nature was ever universal among mankind; but he thinks that the life of many savages illustrates it very well. And if that be not enough, he points to the attitude of independent states toward each other, even in time of so-called peace — "in continual jealousies, and in the state and posture of gladiators; having their weapons pointing and their eyes fixed on one another . . . which is a posture of war"; though by preserving peace within their borders they maintain the prosperity of their subjects. Nay, even within the protection of the law, every man shows, by the ordinary care which he takes to protect his person and property, what the fundamental tendencies of human nature are.

THE BEGINNINGS OF MODERN ETHICS

Misery of the State of Nature. — That man is by nature unfit for society, does not mean that he has not every reason to *desire* it. Indeed, he has. The state of nature being one of utter insecurity, there is in it no place for industry or commerce, for history, science, or art; and the life of man is " solitary, poor, nasty, brutish, and short." There is no established authority, no law, no justice or injustice, no property rights. Man's natural need of society is great enough. The question is, how is society possible for such a creature?

3. *The Conditions of Peace*

The First Law of Nature. — The rules which reason shows must be followed for the establishment of peace are the most important of the *laws of nature*. The first and fundamental rule is *to seek peace, whenever there is hope of obtaining it*. Of course, when peace cannot be had, a man has no motive not to secure himself by any other means which are in his power; which Hobbes calls the *right of nature*. In the war of every man against every man, each is governed by his own reason alone; and since anything that he can use may help in the struggle, he has a *natural right to all things* — even to another's life.

The Limitation of Rights. — The establishment of peace involves a general surrender of this unlimited liberty. Hence, where peace requires it, each man must be content with so much liberty toward other men as he is willing that others shall use toward him; which is the second law of nature. In place of the natural right of all men to all things, there thus arise *exclusive rights* to person and property — rights in the proper sense of the term.

Here a new problem emerges, which is of prime importance in the sequel. A right of nature (like an exclusive right) can be surrendered only by expressing one's intention not to continue to exercise it. How, then, can the surrender be made effectual? What can keep a man from changing his intention and reasserting his right? Only the fear of some inevitable evil consequence. Hence if peace is to be established, a power must be created which is capable of inspiring such fear.

Inalienable Rights. — The surrender of a right is a voluntary act; and hence its object must be some good to the agent. Rights, therefore, for the loss of which no compensation can be made, cannot be surrendered. Thus the right of self-protection is inalienable, for self-protection is the ultimate purpose for which all rights are surrendered; and so also is the right not to accuse oneself or any one, " by whose condemnation a man falls into misery," of crime.

The Performance of Contracts. — The third law of nature is that which is the basis of the distinction between *justice* and *injustice*. It is that men carry out their contracts; that is to say, deliver at the appointed time any goods to which, for a consideration, they have given another the right. That this is necessary to peace, and so truly a law of nature, is evident from the fact that if contracts were not generally fulfilled, they would not be made; and hence men would be constantly led into violence in order to supply their needs. Not to perform contracts is *unjust;* all other acts or omissions are *just.* (Why disobedience to law is unjust appears in the sequel.) Here again it is to be observed that in the state of nature, where there can be no assurance that a man will do as he has contracted, no effective contract can be made — unless both parties act together under each other's eyes. For the one who should act first would be simply subjecting himself to the other's caprice. A power that can compel the performance of contracts is therefore necessary before there can be justice or injustice.

The Universal Formula. — The remaining laws of nature — Hobbes enumerates nineteen — may be passed over here. They call for gratitude, mercy, modesty, impartiality — in short the type of conduct which makes it practicable for men to live together in society. All, as Hobbes says, may be comprehended in the single formula: " Do not that to another which thou wouldst not have done to thyself."

4. *The Function of the State*

The Laws of Nature Eternal. — There are two important comments which Hobbes makes upon the laws of nature as thus set forth. The first is that they are *eternal* and *unalterable*. For they are *deduced* from perfectly general characteristics of human nature. So long as men exist, they cannot be secure of life and limb except where *peace* prevails; and the laws of nature which we have discussed are the necessary conditions of peace.

But Not Universally Applicable. — The second comment is that a good part of moral conduct is *practicable* only where one has good reason to expect similar conduct from others, *i.e.* in a state of peace. " Force and fraud are in war the cardinal virtues." To be alone in keeping faith is mere self-destruction, and hence is contrary to the end of all morality, which is self-preservation. In the state of nature, therefore, all that the laws of nature unconditionally dictate is a *willingness* to follow them whenever circumstances seem to make it practicable. The first law states this explicitly: *Seek peace, whenever there is hope of obtaining it;* and all the succeeding laws are dependent upon this. Nevertheless, certain of the laws are always practicable — for example, the law of mercy (that revenge should be indulged in only for the sake of future security). This is true, of course, of the precepts of individual life, such as *Be temperate*, and *Be brave*. But these are not sufficient to make life secure.

The Civil Power. — The question therefore arises in an acute form: How can morality be made generally practicable? Hobbes answers: Only by the establishment of *civil government*. A power must be set up which is able to punish all serious breaches of the law of nature within its domain, whether committed by one man or by any combination of men. Such a power can be created only by a general submission of all the men to one man or assembly of men; that is to say, by an express or implied contract of every man with every other, not to resist the will [1] of a certain man or assembly of men, which thus becomes possessed of the joint power of them all. This man or assembly is the *sovereign;* those submitting are the *subjects*. If the sovereign be one man, he is called a *monarch;* if it be an assembly, it may be *aristocratic* or *democratic, i.e.* contain either some or all of the subjects. In any case the powers and functions of the sovereign are the same: to enact laws, appoint subordinates, judge controversies, punish crime, reward public service, and carry on war. These powers are theoretically *inseparable;* that is to say, in so far as they *are* separated the state is not a true state; and to that extent insecurity, or civil war, prevails.

Relation between the Civil Laws and the Laws of Nature. — *The object of the state is to make morality practicable.* Hence the moral laws are an essential part of the civil laws of every true state. If the sovereign issues a command that contradicts the moral law, it strikes at public security, and in so far makes the state not a state, and thus assails its own supremacy. To a certain extent the moral law leaves matters open which the civil law must determine in one way or another. Thus if morality is to be established, the distinction between mine and thine must be enforced. But how it shall be determined what is mine and what is thine, the sovereign must declare. So also indiscriminate homicide can never be permitted; but just what constitutes unjustifiable homicide is for the sovereign to say.

On the other hand, the moral law enjoins obedience to

---

[1] Except, of course, for direct self-preservation or its equivalent, the natural right to which is inalienable.

the civil laws, because it is only by such obedience that the state can be preserved and peace maintained. Thus the moral law and the civil law *contain each other*.

III. CUDWORTH

Misinterpretation of Hobbes. — Such, in outline, is the system of ethical speculation which so profoundly shocked the honest folk of England. Calmly considered and clearly understood, there is nothing very extraordinary in its teachings. But it was not calmly considered, and it was scarcely understood at all. The Cambridge Platonists were especially indignant at what they considered to be an attack upon the eternal validity of moral laws (which Hobbes sturdily maintained), making them dependent upon the arbitrary will of the sovereign — not observing that for Hobbes a sovereign *is* a sovereign only in so far as it maintains the moral laws.

Moral Distinctions Independent of the Will. — Ralph Cudworth's *Treatise concerning Eternal and Immutable Morality* was not published until 1731, when the Hobbian controversy had long given way to other issues, and its direct influence was therefore very slight. But it contains in brief compass (in its first two chapters) the best statement of the Platonist position which we possess. No real distinctions (says Cudworth) can depend upon mere will, whether it be man's will or God's. White things can be made black, and round things can be made triangular; but the difference between white and black, round and triangular, belongs to the eternal ' nature of things,' which God himself cannot alter. So long as a thing is round it *is* round and not triangular, and it has all the properties that distinguish round things from triangular things. Merely willing it to be triangular affects it not at all. So it is with the distinction between moral good and evil. That, too, is eternal. Mere will cannot make anything right or wrong — cannot, that is, impose or remove a moral obligation. To be sure, when a legitimate ruler issues a command (which does not exceed his authority), his subjects ought to obey him; and thus certain acts which were formerly permissible to them become wrong. But that is only because, prior to this command, it was *already obligatory* upon the subjects to render him a certain measure of obedience. The authority of statutes thus rests upon the absolute authority of the eternal laws of natural justice. How effective this is as a reply to Hobbes the reader can easily estimate.

IV. CUMBERLAND

Intellectual Character. — It remains for us to speak of the great Bishop of Peterborough, Richard Cumberland. While Cumberland's fame is far inferior to Hobbes's, his positive influence upon the future of English ethics was probably much more extensive. Hobbes, with all his genius, was an exceedingly narrow-minded man. One clear view of a subject satisfied him. He never tried to see it from a second angle. As we read his pages we find much that is true, much that is instructive, but little that is satisfactory. Cumberland was of a very different type — preëminently broad-minded, tireless in his endeavor to see his subject from every point of view. The consequence is that though much that he wrote is weak, his work as a whole is of great importance.

Problems. — Cumberland wrote his treatise (*De Legibus Naturae*, 1672) in reply to Hobbes; but, as he himself felt, its main importance is not critical but constructive. He states and discusses four main problems of ethics: (1) *What is the nature of good and evil in general?* (2) *What is the nature of moral good and evil?* or, as it is otherwise put, *What is the content of the laws of nature?* (3) *What is the psychological origin of the laws of nature?* (4) *What is the nature of man, and for what manner of life* (social or solitary) *is he*

THE BEGINNINGS OF MODERN ETHICS 191

accordingly best fitted? But before taking these questions up there is a preliminary point to be made clear.

The Laws of Nature as Conditions of Happiness. — It will be recalled that according to Hobbes the laws of nature are not *laws* until they have entered into the civil laws of some state. They are merely the logically demonstrable conditions for the attainment of a certain universally desired end — self-preservation. It is one of Cumberland's primary objects to show that even prior to the establishment of states the laws of nature were indeed laws; that is to say, *laws of God*, clearly promulgated by him, and enforced by promises of reward and threats of punishment.

But the difference between the two men is not fairly put in this way. Cumberland is, to all intents, what was later called a *deist;* in fact his ethical treatise is one of the principal sources of English deism. He thinks of God as the *intelligent first cause* of all things. Aside from the interference of man's free will, all that goes on in the universe, whether physical or mental, takes place according to universal uniformities established by God at the creation; so that everything that happens is a necessary consequence of the original arrangement which he, in his omniscience, gave to things then.[1] The consequence is that his proof that God has promulgated the laws of nature amounts only to showing that these laws are so obvious as to arise inevitably in men's minds, without the necessity of voluntary attention. The proof that God has annexed to these laws both

[1] Cumberland does not, indeed, deny the possibility of miracles and special providences. As an orthodox churchman, he devoutly believes in both. But they play no essential part in the scheme of things, as he views it, and he generally ignores them. He believes, too, in a future judgment, by which the good shall be consigned to heaven, and the wicked to hell. But this also is a consideration which he is content for the most part to ignore. Moreover, he wishes his work to be *scientific;* he wishes it to make a universal appeal to thinking men, independently of all religious dogma; and again this helps to make his position essentially that of a deist.

promises and threats consists only in showing that obedience to them is obviously the most important means of securing happiness. Practically speaking, one may drop God, who has done his part, out of the argument altogether, and consider the laws of nature as the *obvious and essential conditions of happiness.* And, as a matter of fact, Cumberland, instead of stating the laws in the form : *Do thus and so, or I, the Lord God, will diminish thy happiness,* prefers the simple declarative form : *To do thus and so constitutes the greatest happiness of the agent.* The real difference, then, between him and Hobbes is not that he includes in his scheme a divine sovereign whom Hobbes omits, but that he views morality in its relation to happiness, whereas Hobbes views it in relation to the preservation of life as such.

(1) **Energistic Theory of Values.** — In his general theory of values Cumberland follows the Aristotelian tradition. Happiness is, for him, a *mode of life,* the full and free activity of the healthy organism. Things in general are good, according as they preserve or enlarge the powers of the mind or body, and thus contribute to make the happy life possible.

But Cumberland regards the difference between this view and hedonism as unimportant. Since pleasure is an invariable accompaniment of the happy life, he sees no objection to identifying happiness with pleasure rather than with the life itself. He does, however, object decidedly to Hobbes's theory, that the good is for any man that which he desires. We desire, he says, *what we conceive to be good;* and in this we may be, and often are, mistaken. Whether a thing is good or evil to a man is not determined by its relation to his passing inclinations, but by its actual influence upon his happiness. And while some things are good for one man, bad for another, there are also things which are good for whole multitudes at once — such as peace — and so may properly be called *common goods.* Peace does not cease to be a common good because some fool desires to disturb it.

THE BEGINNINGS OF MODERN ETHICS 193

(2) **All Morality reduced to Benevolence.** — Cumberland believes that all the laws of nature are contained in one fundamental law: *Be as benevolent as possible to all rational beings:* or, as he states it (with its sanction): " The greatest benevolence of every rational agent toward all the rest constitutes the happiest state of each and all of the benevolent, so far as it is in their own power; and it is necessarily requisite to the happiest state which they can attain; and therefore: The common good is the supreme law." [1]

Property Rights. — That all morality is reducible to benevolence Cumberland regards as fairly evident, except in the case of justice. The absoluteness of property rights often seems to result in much misery — as when a single wealthy reprobate wastes resources that might support many poor and honest folk in comfort. Cumberland's treatment of this point left a deep impress upon English thought. Some goods, he said, to be enjoyed must be divided; and, that they may be fully enjoyed, their possession must be secure. Grant that the present division of property is not ideal. It is very tolerable, since under it we do enjoy the happiness which we actually enjoy. And when the dangers of anarchy, from the unsettling of established rights, are considered, no man or assembly of men is competent to devise a new division so much better than the present, as to warrant us in risking the attempt to change.[2] Hence, benevolence dictates that we leave to every man his own.

(3) **The Laws of Nature learned from Experience.** — The question as to the origin of the laws of nature is a particular form of the question which the philosopher Locke later asked with regard to human ideas in general; and it is answered in much the same fashion. We have no reason to suppose that any of our ideas or principles are *innate*. We can account for the origin of all of them *in experience*. Cumberland is, in fact, a much more thorough-going empiricist

[1] *De Legibus Naturae*, Ch. I, Sect. IV.   [2] *Op. cit.*, Ch. VII, Sect. IX.

than Locke. For while Locke thinks that all our ideas are derived from experience, he further thinks that, when once the ideas have been acquired, we can compare them together in the mind, and thus obtain an intuitive knowledge of certain fundamental truths. Cumberland, on the contrary, believes that the fundamental truths, too, are learned from experience. And the type of certain knowledge is for him, not the mathematical axioms that men generally regard as self-evident independently of experience, but such propositions as *All men are mortal*, which are obviously learned from experience.

How they are Learned. — It is incumbent upon him, therefore, to show (*a*) how the ideas contained in the law of universal benevolence, and especially the notion of a common good, inevitably arise in the mind; and (*b*) how the connection between them, which the proposition asserts, is impressed upon the mind with such evidence, that no sane and unprejudiced man can doubt it.

(*a*) **Origin of the Constituent Ideas.** — The notion of *good* we all derive from the food, clothing, and shelter, and the mutual aid, by which our lives are supported and cheered. The human affection by which aid is prompted we thus conceive as a good will, or *benevolence*. It is obvious that through counsel as well as by physical aid our benevolence may help great numbers of men. From the close resemblance between us we see that the helper can be repaid, and that by mutual aid men may be supplied with many things; whereas, if hostility took its place, the utmost want and imminent danger of death would ensue. Hence the notion of a *common good;* which, by reason of our likeness to each other, may easily embrace all whom we may ever know.

(*b*) **Their Necessary Connection.** — We see that the individual can have no greater defense and no greater positive source of happiness than the sincere benevolence of all toward all — in the general effects of which he shares —

THE BEGINNINGS OF MODERN ETHICS 195

together with the more particular benevolence, or friendship, of some few chosen individuals toward himself. And we see in ourselves, as well as in the behavior of others, that there is no way to encourage either general benevolence or friendship to be compared with the manifestation of the same affection in one's own acts. (Cumberland adds that if it is the favor of the first cause that is to be won, we surely cannot please him better than by our good will toward him and toward his human children.) Hence the obvious proof of the proposition to be proved.

Cumberland regards these simple considerations as in themselves fairly convincing. But he supplements them by another line of thought, in which account is taken, not of the consequences of benevolence, but of the intrinsic character of the benevolent life.

(4) **The Social Nature of Man.** — Is man by nature fitted for society? Hobbes pointed out certain characteristics of men that tend to make him unfit for society, and concluded that, beyond the limits of small families, he is not naturally social. In reply, Cumberland undertakes a detailed examination of man's physical and mental traits with a view to determining the truth of the matter; and he emerges with the conclusion that man is certainly adapted to a social life. Much of the discussion is antiquated, and at some points it is fantastic or trivial; but it is on the whole convincing. The power of forming conceptions and universal propositions; the faculty of speech; the power of deliberation; the emotions of love, pity, and gratitude; the persistency of parental affection; the variety and delicacy of the means of the expression of the emotions — these are quite sufficient to refute Hobbes's extreme contention.[1]

[1] The possibility remains, to be sure, that our present mode of existence is vastly *more* social than that to which man's organically inherited traits are adapted; and that an important part, if not the whole, of the significance of morality consists in the fact, that by means of it man is made over in such a fashion that he becomes capable of a complexly and intensely social life. The truth would thus lie between Hobbes and Cumberland.

Social Service Essential to Happiness. — And now, since man is a social animal, it follows that his natural powers can be exerted in their due degree, only in the service of society. A life confined to selfish ends falls far short of man's capacities. That he may truly live, that he may adequately realize his own potentialities, he must devote himself to the common good. Not only is benevolence of supreme utility, but the benevolent life is in itself the supremely happy life.

It is interesting to note that the word 'constitutes' (*constituit*) in Cumberland's formation of the law of benevolence is intentionally ambiguous, just in order to cover these two points. Benevolence 'constitutes' happiness both as a contributing *cause* and as a *part;* or, as Cumberland puts it: " Benevolence is both the intrinsic cause of present happiness and the efficient cause of future happiness, and is necessarily requisite in respect of both."

REFERENCES ON THE HISTORY OF MODERN ETHICS

See references on the history of ethics, p. 104.
ALBEE, E., *History of English Utilitarianism.*
STEPHEN, L., *The Utilitarians.*
WHEWELL, W., *Lectures on the History of Moral Philosophy in England.*
HALL, T. C., *History of Ethics within Organized Christianity*, pp. 438–467.
MACKINTOSH, J., *On the Progress of Ethical Philosophy, chiefly during the Seventeenth and Eighteenth Centuries.*

REFERENCES ON THE BEGINNINGS OF MODERN ETHICS

HOBBES, T., *Leviathan.*
STEPHEN, L., *Hobbes.*
TAYLOR, A. E., *Hobbes.*
CUDWORTH, R., *Treatise concerning Eternal and Immutable Morality.*

CUMBERLAND, R., *On the Laws of Nature* (Maxwell's translation), especially Chs. I, II.

Locke, J., Essay concerning Human Understanding, Book I, Chs. III, IV, 7, 8; Book II, Chs. VII, XX, XXI, XXII, 2, 9, XXVII, 18–20, XXVIII, XXX, 4, XXXI, 3–5; Book III, Chs. V, esp. 3, 15, IX, 6–9, XI, 15, 16; Book IV, Chs. III, 18–20, IV, 3–10, XII, X, 8, 11, XIV, 4; and *Miscellaneous Papers* (in Lord King's *Life of John Locke*, Vol. II), pp. 120–133.

CHAPTER XI

THE CLASSICAL SCHOOLS OF THE EIGHTEENTH CENTURY

I. Preliminary Remarks

Mode of Treatment. — In the present chapter we must briefly consider three important types of ethical theory. Partly for brevity's sake, but more for the sake of clearness, we shall limit ourselves to a schematic account of the views generally held by members of each school, without taking account of individual variations of opinion, except in a few instances where these are of unusual interest and importance.

Hedonistic Theory of Values. — It will make matters easier for us, if we note at the outset (and bear in mind throughout) that *all* the thinkers with whom we shall have to deal were *hedonists in their general theory of values*. All are agreed that pleasure is the sole ultimate good and pain the sole ultimate evil. I say this in spite of the fact that Shaftesbury (the founder of the moral-sense school) expressly rejects hedonism, and declares for the Aristotelian view; for in the details of his argument it is on the hedonistic theory that he constantly relies. The general acceptance of hedonism is largely due to the influence of John Locke, who gave forcible expression to it in his celebrated *Essay concerning Human Understanding* (1690), — a work which formed the background of English thought in the eighteenth century, and by which almost all the ethical writers were directly affected.

Nativistic and Empiristic Theories of Moral Distinctions: Utilitarianism. — It was, then, not about values in general,

CLASSICAL SCHOOLS OF EIGHTEENTH CENTURY 199

but about *moral values* in particular, that men disagreed, and especially about *the mode in which these values are perceived*. Two of the schools differ from the third in holding to a *nativistic* theory of the moral consciousness: they believe that the capacity for moral approval and disapproval is an original endowment of human nature, not to be reduced to or derived from any other. The other school holds to an *empiristic*[1] view, maintaining that this capacity grows up in each man from the inborn tendency to desire pleasure and avoid pain. Hence it has been appropriately called the 'derivative school,' though a more common name for the theory is 'utilitarianism.'

Intuitionalism and Sentimentalism. — The two nativistic schools differ essentially in this: that according to one school approval and disapproval are functions of *reason*, while according to the other they are *feelings* to which men (by virtue of their peculiar mental constitution) are subject. According to the one school, right and wrong are *relations* between different sorts of acts and different sorts of situations, relations which exist independently of our perception of them. According to the other school, an act's being right or wrong means simply its capacity to stimulate in us a certain peculiar feeling. The term 'intuitionalists' is sometimes loosely used to include both nativistic schools,

[1] The reader should not confuse the psychological term 'empiristic' and the logical term 'empiricistic' (from 'empiricism'). An empiristic theory is a theory that some mental function, which is in question, is not innate in us, but is acquired by each individual — say through the process of association. Thus whereas nobody would think of entertaining an empiristic theory of color sensation, most psychologists hold to an empiristic theory of the visual perception of distance. Empiricism is a theory according to which all knowledge of general truths is derived by induction from particular facts. As we shall see, the English sentimentalists (mentioned in the next paragraph) are empiricists; but their theory of the perception of moral good and evil is not empiristic but nativistic. On the other hand, the utilitarians of the eighteenth century, while their theory of moral perception is empiristic, are rather rationalists than empiricists in their notions of scientific method.

which are then distinguished as ' rational ' and ' perceptional.' We shall distinguish them as *intuitionalists* and *sentimentalists*.[1]

The Typical Writers. — The student should realize that the differences between particular writers are not always so sharp as the main lines of cleavage between the three schools would lead us to expect. John Locke (whom we mentioned above) is a curious mixture of intuitionalism and the derivative theory. Joseph Butler (*Sermons upon Human Nature*, 1726), who partly on account of his position as a bishop of the English church, but far more on account of the simplicity, earnestness, and winning common sense of his writings, has had a lasting influence upon English ethics, shows affiliations with both of the nativistic schools. In the account which follows, we shall have to neglect men of this sort, and fix our attention upon the more sharply defined types. Of the intuitionalists we shall bear particularly in mind Samuel Clarke (1706) and Richard Price (1758); of the sentimentalists, Francis Hutcheson (1725 and 1755) and David Hume (1740 and 1751); of the utilitarians, John Gay (1731), William Paley (1785), and Jeremy Bentham (1789).

Let us begin with the intuitionalists.

II. Intuitionalism

1. *The Mathematical Analogy*

Mathematical Conception of Reason. — The key to the understanding of these men's views is that when they speak of ' reason ' they always have in mind the example of the employment of reason in *mathematics*. In order to make clear what they think about morals, the first essential is to

[1] The term 'moral-sense theorists' is widely used instead of 'sentimentalists'; but it strictly applies only to the earlier members of the school, who regarded the moral sense, or conscience, as analogous to the external senses, such as sight and smell. See below, p. 211.

explain what they think about geometry and algebra and their applications.

(1) **The Axioms.** — The mathematical sciences take their rise from certain propositions (the ' axioms ') that need no proof, being self-evident. The knowledge of these truths is an innate capacity of human nature. Not that all men know them ; for very little children certainly do not, having never thought of them. But as soon as the ideas which such a proposition contains have been formed in the mind, and have been compared together in the way the proposition calls for — in other words, as soon as the proposition is *understood* — its truth is at once seen to be unquestionable. For we perceive an eternal relation between the ideas, and the perception of this relation is the knowledge of the axiom. Thus not every one knows that a straight line is the shortest line between two points. But as soon as any one has acquired the ideas of straight line and shortest line, and has compared them together in his mind, the relation of necessary coexistence between them is manifest.

Now the intuitionalists hold that the like is true of our knowledge of right and wrong: that this knowledge too takes its rise from the perception of self-evident relations. A new-born child has no idea of himself or of his conduct, and it will be long before he has any idea of God. But as soon as he acquires these ideas and compares them together, he will see that a certain sort of conduct is *fitting* toward God, namely, love, worship, and obedience. In other words, that sort of conduct is *right* toward God, and a man *ought* so to act. Again, as soon as he compares himself and his fellow men together, he sees that they ought to treat each other justly and kindly. And when he compares his own present condition with his possible future life of happiness or misery, he sees that he ought to be prudent. All these relations are as certain and obvious as the fundamental mathematical relations; and like these they are no mere subjective impression of ours, but a part of the eternal nature of things.

(2) **Deductive Procedure.** — From its axioms mathematics deduces other propositions of narrower and narrower scope. The whole course of the argument is from the more general to the less general. And, finally, there is the application of the truths of the science to particular concrete circumstances. The application is always a *deduction*. For example: All triangles of sixty and thirty degrees have the hypothenuse double the shorter side; this grass plot is a triangle of sixty and thirty degrees; therefore, etc.

The like is true of the case of morals. From the axioms we deduce a great variety of special duties under different conditions. And the application to the particular case in hand is in the same deductive way. For example: It is fitting that a man should show gratitude for kindnesses received; this man shows gratitude for kindnesses received; therefore his conduct is fitting. Or, negatively: This man does not show gratitude for kindnesses received; therefore his conduct is unfitting, or wrong.

The rules according to which conduct is fitting or unfitting are called 'moral laws.' If one does not know a moral law, one has no means of knowing whether the conduct that falls under it is right or wrong.

(3) **Truths Independent of the Will.** — Mathematical truths do not depend upon any one's will, not even God's. It is only particular things — their existence, qualities, states, and relations — that can be affected by a will. The universal relations of which mathematics treats are necessary and eternal. God did not make two and two equal to four, and he could not make them equal to five. He need not have created anything at all, and he can, if he will, annihilate all that he has created; but whenever and wherever two things and two other things exist, there will be four things.

CLASSICAL SCHOOLS OF EIGHTEENTH CENTURY

So also of the universal relations of fitness and unfitness. It is not due to any command of God's that certain modes of conduct should be fitting under certain conditions — that love and equity, for instance, should be fitting in the intercourse of man and man.[1] God need not have created man if he had not pleased, and he could have made him a very different sort of creature if he had so desired. But having made man, and having made him what he is, he does not in addition make man's moral relations. No, these flow inevitably from man's nature.

(4) **Absurdity.** — To think that two and two are five is to think absurdly. To act with unkindness towards one's fellow men — to act as if all men were not truly in need of one another's love and coöperation — is to act absurdly. And, speaking generally, wickedness is the same thing in act that falsity is in thought. It is setting oneself in opposition to the eternal ' nature of things,' than which nothing could be more absurd.

Here let us take our leave of the mathematical analogy, which from this point can give us little detailed help.

2. *Obligation. Reward and Punishment*

The Righteousness of God. — It is inconceivable that God should commit any absurdity. Hence we must suppose that in his own acts he always directs himself according to the moral law. All his doings are absolutely right.

Moral Obligation. — In so far as man, too, is a rational being, it may be said to be his nature to act rationally, *i.e.* morally. And, as a matter of fact, we find in man a weak but fairly constant impulse to do the right. We do the right *unless* there is something in particular to be gained by doing

---

[1] Still less can such a relation depend upon the will of an earthly sovereign. (This is urged as a crushing criticism of Hobbes.) To be sure, when the sovereign bids me do a thing which was before indifferent, I ought to do it; but that is because previous to his command I owed him obedience.

wrong — or unless our nature has been perverted by habitual wrong conduct in the past. The idea of right conduct is, to a rational being as such, pleasant, and the idea of wrong conduct unpleasant; and we are always impelled toward what is pleasant in idea and away from what is unpleasant. The pity is that we are not purely rational, but also sensitive beings, constantly impelled by sensual inclinations to commit rational absurdities. And, indeed, if our sensual impulses did not to a great extent oppose one another and thus cancel out one another's force, our impulse to do right would have little sway over our conduct. This weak but constant tendency of our rational nature is called the *feeling of moral obligation*. It is a feeling, which, unlike all other feelings, is entirely independent of our sensations, having its source in reason alone.

God's Commands. — Since God invariably directs his actions by the moral law, it cannot be but that he wishes us to act thus also; for he cannot have created us with the intention that we should act against himself. But since his wish is thus manifest it amounts to a command. Right is not right merely because God commands it; but he assuredly commands it because it is right.

The Certainty of Reward and Punishment. — There is no real command without authority; and there is no real authority without the ability and the intention to reward obedience or punish disobedience. (Of course, to miss a reward is in some sense to be punished, and to escape punishment is in some sense to be rewarded.) Now we cannot elude God's observation, nor can we resist his might. It is, therefore, certain, that the good must on the whole be happy, and the wicked miserable.

The Future Life. — This is a conclusion that our observation in this life does not verify. It is not true that in human affairs 'honesty is the best policy.' The best policy includes an occasional dishonesty when detection or punishment is

CLASSICAL SCHOOLS OF EIGHTEENTH CENTURY 205

improbable. And, aside from the matter of general policy, we note that accidents are constantly happening. We need little experience of the world to see that the righteous are often oppressed with suffering, while the unrighteous indulge in all manner of unrestricted pleasure. But this only proves that there must be a life beyond the present, in which the justice of God shall be made manifest, and the righteous and the unrighteous shall alike meet with their deserts.

Summary. — Thus, while moral relations are independent of future reward and punishment, future reward and punishment are a necessary consequence of moral relations in such a world as ours. As it was sometimes expressed, right and wrong are *logically prior* to reward and punishment. It is *because* right is right and wrong is wrong that reward and punishment are themselves *right* and may be confidently expected from God.

Reënforcement of Moral Obligation. — The expectation of a future reward and punishment is necessary in order to make it possible for the ordinary man to act rightly when such a course appears to be contrary to his temporal interests. There are men — heroes, we call them — in whom the feeling of moral obligation is so strong that even the utmost danger or pain cannot make them swerve from the course of righteousness. But the vast majority of mankind are not so constituted. This was the great mistake of the high-sounding morality of the stoics, the mistake that made their teaching so ineffectual. The ordinary man *cannot* act rightly unless he believes that so doing will promote his own happiness, or, at least, not oppose it, and it would be unreasonable to expect him to do so. And therefore God has made the evidence of his existence and of his purposes toward man so clear and obvious, that if men were not the slaves of sensual lusts, none of them could possibly remain ignorant of these truths.

3. *The Universality of Moral Laws*

Such is the system of intuitionalism. To us of the twentieth century it seems hard and bare. To its advocates of the eighteenth century — and these were numerous — it seemed to possess certain strong recommendations.

(1) **Moral Laws are Objective.** — It raised morality above the level of conflicting individual impressions, and gave it the status of objective truth. No man could set up a standard of his own and declare that by following his private conscience he was acting rightly. If his conscience was not in accord with the eternal moral law, so much the worse for him; he was condemned already. He might as well claim that an addition, in which he had set down 8 and 5 as making 14, was right, because that was the way it had seemed to him.

(2) **The Fundamental Laws are without Exceptions.** — Moreover, according to this system, the fundamental principles of morals were seen to be *universal*, admitting of no particular exceptions. If injustice is wrong, nothing can make it right. The more special laws, being due to the application of the more general laws to changeable human circumstances, may indeed break down. The law, *Thou shalt not kill*, breaks down when we try to extend it to the soldier in battle or to the officer of the law, or even to the private citizen who acts in self-defense. That is because the law is thereby carried beyond the limits within which it is a valid application of first principles. But the first principles and all direct deductions from them are absolute. (The distinction is analogous to that between pure and applied mathematics.)

Why was the universality of the fundamental laws felt to be important? Because moral practice was thus given a regularity, and social institutions a stability, that seemed to be otherwise impossible. In the eighteenth century, men were especially concerned to maintain the inviolability of property rights. Ethicists of all schools vied with each other in proclaiming their loyalty to this doctrine; but the intuitionalists were no doubt in the best position to defend it. If the principle of justice is an axiomatic truth, there seems to be little room for any excuse for depriving a man of his own.

(3) **Moral Laws are Valid for All Men.** — It belongs to the universality of the moral laws that they are valid everywhere, and for all men. What is wrong for Peter is not right for Paul; and what is wrong for the Greek is not right for the barbarian. Just so, there is but one geometry for all the nations. If differences in men's moral standards are reported to us by both ancient and modern writers, it may be said, first, that most of these reports are doubtless superficial and inaccurate. Secondly, men who are addicted to evil practices often profess to consider them innocent, though in their hearts they know them to be wrong. Thirdly, though the moral axioms are self-evident to one who attends to the significance, men who are led away by selfish desires may easily fail to attend; just as, from lack of due consideration, it might never occur to a man that two intersecting straight lines cannot both be parallel to a third straight line. Lastly, such genuine differences in moral standards as do occur must be regarded as being due to the application of the same fundamental principles to varying social conditions.

(4) **They are Changeless.** — It goes without saying that moral principles are not only universal spatially, but temporally also. All apparent changes are explained away like the apparent differences between the morals of different climes.

III. Sentimentalism

1. *Empirical Standpoint*

The Question of Fact. — But with all the advantages which the intuitionalistic theory can claim, the question remains: Does it square with the *facts?* And, in particular, when we see men committing noble or contemptible acts, is our approval or disapproval brought about by a piece of deductive reasoning — by an application of a general rule to the given case? And here let us not try to dodge the issue by saying that we reason, but reason unconsciously. Reasoning is a conscious process; and unconscious reasoning is a preposterous contradiction in terms. If our approbation or disapprobation is the logical conclusion of a deductive inference, we should have no difficulty in attesting the fact. Can we?

Perceptions before Rules. — This was the question raised by the leaders of the sentimental school, and answered by them in the negative. These men were *empiricists*. To their mind the advancement of human knowledge is not so much deductive as *inductive*. The particular comes before the universal, the fact before the reason for the fact. And this attitude of theirs they show in the domain of morals as elsewhere. Their whole mental disposition inclines them to think that we first perceive the goodness or badness displayed on particular occasions, and only later (if at all) learn to bring our perceptions under general rules.

2. *The Analogy of Beauty*

But the sentimentalists, too, are influenced by a pervasive analogy. As the example of mathematical relations was determinative for intuitionalism, so the example of *beauty* is determinative for the present theory.

(1) The Immediacy of Perception. — When we look at a thing and find it beautiful, we do not — ordinarily, at any rate — reason out its beauty. We do not say, for example: Everything with such and such proportions is beautiful; this object has those proportions; therefore it is beautiful. Sometimes we may approach such a procedure, as when we note the conventional ' points ' of a fashionable breed of horses or dogs, or count the lines of an alleged sonnet to see if there are just fourteen. But ordinarily our impressions of beauty are gained in a much more simple and direct fashion. We look, and are impressed. That is why we can speak appropriately of a *sense* of beauty. To see that a woman is beautiful requires no more reasoning than to see the color of her hair.

Now, according to the ethicists of the sentimental school, the case is plainly the same in the perception of the moral qualities displayed in conduct. When we see a man beating a little child, we do not have to reason thus : To torment one who is helpless is cruel ; this man is tormenting one who is helpless ; therefore he is cruel. No ; as we look a sensation of moral indignation arises spontaneously within us. And, similarly, if the child's mother, at the risk of serious injury to herself, should try to stop the beating, we should feel, far more quickly than we could reason, a glow of admiration for her courage and self-sacrifice.

(2) **Approval and Disapproval are Unanalyzable and Involuntary.** — The moral sense and the sense of beauty are like the external senses of sight, hearing, taste, etc., in the fact that they give rise to simple, unanalyzable sensations, that can be gained in no other way. The sensations derived from the moral sense are of two kinds : those of approval and those of disapproval ; either of which may occur in a great many different intensities and in all sorts of mixtures and fusions with other feelings. The moral sense and the sense of beauty are like the external senses in this too : that however much in the way of reflection and volition may *precede* the sensation, the sensation itself contains no reflection or volition. I may reflect whether I shall look out of the window at the lawn, and I may finally will to do so. But in the sensation of green, as I then become conscious of it, there is nothing but the green itself. And so long as the same stimulus continues to act upon my visual organs, I shall continue to see that same green. So it is with the sense of beauty or

ugliness, of virtue or vice. My detestation of this man's cruelty, or my admiration for that woman's kindness, is perfectly spontaneous and involuntary.

(3) **The Idea-stimulus.** — The moral sense and the sense of beauty differ, however, from the external senses in one all-important respect. The exciting cause of the external sensation is *physical* — a change of some sort in the nervous mechanism. The stimulus of the moral sense or the sense of beauty is an *idea* either of perception or of imagination. When, for example, I contemplate a fine painting, the sensations of color, with their various shades and intensities, are externally excited. The sensations combine with fainter images that are revived by association, to form an idea (or percept) of the object. This idea, now, is the direct stimulus of the sense of beauty. So the idea of an act of kindness may be the direct stimulus of the sensation of approval.

The formation of the idea may be a very simple matter of direct perception; or it may be a very complicated matter, involving much reflection and reasoning. Suppose, to take an extreme instance, that the object to be appreciated as beautiful or ugly is Shakespeare's *King Lear*. To form an adequate idea of the play as a whole may well test a man's utmost mental capacity. Or suppose that the act to be appreciated as good or bad is Henry the Eighth's declaration of the independence of the Church of England. Here again, in the formation of the idea of the moral action, the utmost critical ability of the historian may be called into play. The idea of the moral act of another person can never be quite so simply formed as the idea of an æsthetic object often is, because the moral act is essentially psychical in its nature — an unseen determination of the will, which the observer must imaginatively reconstruct from the evidences afforded by the external aspect of the act. It is only in one's own case that a direct perception of the inner motives of conduct is possible.

But, whether the formation of the idea be simple or complicated, the stimulation of the æsthetic or moral sense takes place always in the same way; and the æsthetic or moral sensation that results is equally a peculiar and ultimate experience.

The Sentiments. — This difference, which we have remarked, between the sense of beauty and the moral sense, on the one hand, and the external senses on the other hand, came in time to affect the terminology of the school. The former were called *sentiments*. Nor was it a matter of terminology alone; for the sentiments were treated as a class of *emotions*, differing from another class, the *passions*, in that sentiments are seldom very intense, while passions (such as love, fear, and envy) are usually much more intense than the sentiments and sometimes reach a very high degree of intensity indeed. It was believed, too, that the sentiments were like other emotions in this: that no idea is capable of exciting them unless it is accompanied by a sensation (or idea) of pleasure or pain (Hume). All this, however, did not change the fundamental feature of the theory. Moral and æsthetic approval and disapproval are elementary contents of the mind, spontaneously called up by their peculiar stimuli — not modes of rational judgment.

(4) Relativity of Beauty and Virtue. — Nothing is beautiful or ugly, virtuous or vicious, in itself. To say that a thing is beautiful *means* simply that the contemplation of it arouses in us the feeling of æsthetic approval; and to say that an act is bad *means* simply that the thought of this act arouses in us the feeling of moral disapproval. It is just as it is with the external senses. If there were no sense of sight, there would be no colors; if there were no sense of hearing, there would be no noises or tones. If a man is without a moral sense, he is, in so far, like one born blind. There is no way of making up to him his defect; and the world must ever remain for him devoid of virtue and vice.

This is the feature of the moral-sense theory which called forth the most severe criticism: that it gave the moral distinctions between right and wrong, good and bad, the same *relativity* as the distinction between red and yellow or hot and cold. (According to the intuitionalists, it will be remembered, these distinctions are strictly objective, belonging eternally to the ' nature of things,' like the distinction between equal and unequal or straight and curved.) For if morality is relative to feeling, then we must bear in mind that all feelings are individual. What is bright to one man's eyes may be dark to another's, and what is cold to one man's skin may be hot to another's. That may all be very well so far as beauty and ugliness are concerned — " There is no disputing about tastes." But as applied to moral good and evil it is abominable, for it resolves the whole order of society into anarchy.

Uniformity of the Moral Sense. — The answer of the sentimentalists to this criticism is that it is a gross exaggeration. Among normal, sound-minded men, the moral sense varies scarcely at all. Superficial critics often exclaim upon the prodigious differences between our moral standards and those of the ancient Hebrews, Greeks, and Romans, or even those of the French people of our own day. But these differences, great as they are, touch only the externals of conduct, and are for the most part to be justified by the very different conditions under which men in different times and places live. The appreciation of the underlying qualities of character remains practically constant. Thus the early Hebrews sanctioned polygamy, and we condemn it; and they regarded all plastic art as sinful, while we find it innocent. But in all times and places kindness, courage, loyalty, justice, and wisdom have been admired, and cruelty, cowardice, treachery, injustice, and folly have been despised. The economic and social conditions which made polygamy justifiable have disappeared; and the temptation to idolatry, which made the representation of human and animal forms dangerous, is no longer prevalent. But the good heart and the evil heart are what they have always been.

Moral Defectives. — The moral sense, it has been said, is uniform in its operation among all mankind. There are individuals whose moral sense has deteriorated, just as there are individuals whose sense of sight or hearing or taste has decayed; but these are readily recognized as abnormal. And, practically, these men no more disturb the values of morality than the blind or the deaf affect the greens or browns of the landscape or the shrill twittering of the birds.

Infallibility of the Moral Sense. —The moral sense may from two different points of view be regarded as infallible. In the first place, since, as we have said, right *means* only what the moral sense approves and wrong what the moral sense disapproves, it follows at once that whatever the moral sense approves is right, and that whatever it disapproves is wrong. It is the same, of course, with the sense of beauty, as it is also with the external senses. What feels hot *is* hot; what tastes sour is sour; what seems beautiful is beautiful; for, in respect to sense-qualities, to-seem and to be are the same. The moral sense is infallible just because there is no standard outside itself by which it might be judged.

In the second place, the moral sense (except in case of abnormality) is infallible because of its uniformity among all mankind. That is to say, if we judge one man's moral sentiments by comparing them with the sentiments which other men receive from like objects, we find them to be in entire agreement.

Error in the Idea-stimulus. — Here again we must bear in mind that the object which directly stimulates the moral sense is not an external fact but an idea; and that in the formulation of this idea an indefinite amount of reflection and even abstruse reasoning may enter. Now any part of this reflective process may be seriously in error. Thus it may happen that a man of perfectly sound moral sense may appear to approve of the most dastardly crime. But that is because he has not formed a correct idea of it. His approval is of the act *as he conceives it to have been;* and if he explains this conception of his to any other morally sound man, the latter will certainly agree with him.

This is the way in which the moral-sense writers explain most of the variations in men's moral standards that are not to be ascribed to changed external conditions. As men learn to form clearer and fuller conceptions of conduct, their standards of righteousness naturally become more adequate. Not because the moral-sense has changed its action in the slightest, but because the intellectual stimulus to its action has changed. So much can be explained in this way that the later moral-sense writers gave up the notion of a defective moral sense. In cases where the earlier writers would have said that a man's misjudgments were certainly due to some intrinsic defect, the later writers blame all on ignorance, inattention, or faulty reasoning.

(5) **Utility of Rules.** — Since the moral sense (like the æsthetic sense) acts spontaneously when its peculiar stimuli are present, what is the significance or utility of moral rules? We do not need these rules in order to judge conduct, any more than we need æsthetic rules in order to see that a picture or a poem is beautiful. Why, then, do we have them at all? In the first place, the rules satisfy a certain intellectual curiosity. We are interested to determine what sort of objects stimulate our approbation or disapprobation; and the rules sum up the results of our observation. Sometimes the rules are based on insufficient observation, and hence do not always hold. Just as the study of the ancient drama led critics to certain rules of the unity of time and place, which the modern romantic dramatists showed to be entirely without cogency; so in the field of morals

men have jumped to such conclusions as, *All dancing is wrong*, which a wider experience fails to confirm.

In the second place, our moral generalizations have an important effect *upon the formation of the idea of the particular conduct* that is to be appreciated. The like is true, again, of æsthetic generalizations. If I am thoroughly convinced that the unities of time and place are sacred, I may sit through a performance of *A Winter's Tale* without being able to take in half the beauty of the drama. My previous expectations are so perverse that I cannot form other than a distorted notion of the whole; and the play, *as I see it*, is really as poor as I take it to be. When a moral rule has become firmly fixed in a man's mind, it has a powerful influence in directing his attention and in determining just what he shall notice. If I believe that all who dance are wicked, that fact may be sufficient to blind me to the utmost generosity and courage. But it must not be supposed that this effect of moral rules is wholly bad. On the contrary, they fulfill a very important function. They give a stability to our moral reactions toward our fellows, that would otherwise be impossible. Our ideas are never a bare reproduction or a full reproduction of the external reality. We cannot but add from our imagination; and we cannot but neglect what does not appeal to our interests. The influence of moral rules may mislead us on occasion; but in the absence of all rules we might, for want of any proper direction of our attention, go even farther astray.

3. *Obligation*

Relation between Virtue and Happiness. — In our account of intuitionalism we gave due place to the doctrine that the good must ultimately be happy and the wicked miserable. There the proof turned upon the will of God, and verification was looked for in another world. The sentimentalists have a similar doctrine; but, moved as they are by the spirit of empirical science, they try to find evidence for their view in the common experience of mankind, maintaining that even here and now virtue is the good and vice the evil of every man. They try to show that the virtuous character is that which is in itself the source of the most enduring satisfaction and best predisposes one to the full enjoyment of all pleasures and to the calm endurance of all pains; and furthermore that it is only in so far as men are virtuous that they can hope for that loving companionship and coöperation of their fellows upon which human happiness largely depends. They try to show that vice is in itself a condition of uneasiness and turmoil, in which the higher pleasures are for the most part impossible and the lower pleasures quickly lose their savor; and that even when the chances of fortune set the wicked man in a position of power and affluence, and visit the good man with poverty and affliction, the real advantage in all probability lies with the latter. They cannot claim (apart from the religious faith which they may have) that every good man is bound to be happier than every bad man; but they do maintain that under any circumstances the chances that a man can increase his happiness by wrongdoing are practically *nil*. In other words, according to the sentimentalists, *it is never good policy to do wrong*, even when this life only is considered.[1]

The Two ' Obligations.' — The term ' obligation ' is used by these writers in two senses. On the one hand, it is used to denote the fact that a certain course of conduct is the only right course under the given circumstances. To be ' obliged ' to pay one's debts means, then, that not to pay them would necessarily be wrong. On the other hand, it may denote the fact that a given course of conduct can be counted on to bring the agent greater happiness than any alternative, so that to act otherwise would involve a sacrifice.

[1] The reader of the *Republic* cannot fail to observe that this is substantially the Platonic view.

In this sense, to be 'obliged' to pay one's debts means that if one does not pay them one will have to suffer for it. The first interpretation gives us 'moral obligation,' or the 'obligation of conscience'; the second, the 'obligation of self-love.' And the doctrine of the school is that these two obligations, although logically distinct, are practically coincident.

Feelings of Obligation. — It goes without saying that a man's moral obligation may diverge widely from what he *feels* to be for his best interests. But in that case his feeling as to his interests is mistaken; whereas the feeling of moral obligation is infallible. To feel an obligation of self-love and actually to lie under such an obligation are not at all the same thing; to feel a moral obligation *is* to lie under it.

In thus maintaining the distinction between moral obligation and the obligation of self-love, the moral sense theorists are in accord with the intuitionalists. It will shortly be seen that this is a point upon which both of the nativistic schools differ from the utilitarians, according to whom moral obligation is simply the highest self-interest.

4. *The Stimuli*

The Further Question. — In the preceding pages it has been our aim to give an account of the sentimental theory, which, while not absolutely faithful to any one of the writers, fairly represents the common thought of the principal men. But there remains to be treated a question of maximum importance, concerning which their disagreement is too great to be reconciled.

This question concerns the *stimuli* of the moral sense. What is their nature? Just as we might ask with regard to the stimuli of sound: What is the nature of auditory stimuli generally, and how do those which produce tone differ from those which produce noise? — so we have to ask concerning the stimuli of the moral sense: What is their nature generally, and how do those which produce approval differ from those that produce disapproval?

Extent of Agreement. — On the general question all the writers are still so far in agreement as to hold that the stimulus is always the idea of a trait of character as it expresses itself in conduct. The moral-sense ethics is thus preëminently an *ethics of virtue* (in contrast to the intuitionalistic *ethics of duty*).

Shaftesbury: Harmonious Character. — But immediately disagreement sets in. According to Shaftesbury, approval is stimulated by any indication of an harmonious character, disapproval by any indication of an ill-balanced character; and an harmonious character is one which is so organized as to be for the good of society (or of the human species) as a whole. To show more clearly what this amounts to, he divides all human propensities into three kinds: the natural (or benevolent) affections, the self-affections, and the unnatural (or malevolent) affections. And he finds that in the harmonious character the natural affections are very strong, the self-affections are moderate, and the unnatural affections are altogether absent.

Hutcheson: Benevolence. — This theory soon led to one much simpler. According to Hutcheson, the one stimulus of approbation is benevolence, and the one stimulus of disapprobation is the yielding of benevolence to some stronger motive. Hutcheson attempts to show that all other virtues, such as courage, prudence, or justice, are reducible to benevolence. Justice, for example, while it may involve an apparent disregard of certain personal interests, is always directed to the furtherance of more extensive interests. And courage, when not prompted by benevolent motives, is either morally indifferent or positively wrong.

Butler's Criticism. — The question whether all virtue is reducible to benevolence was actively discussed by moral-

CLASSICAL SCHOOLS OF EIGHTEENTH CENTURY 219

sense theorists. Bishop Butler urged that while for God this might well be true, for man it could not be true; for the simple reason that we have not sufficient intelligence and foresight to guide our conduct by a calculation of the interests involved. To try to live according to the dictates of pure benevolence would result most disastrously. We should soon be drifting into the most abominable crimes — all for the sake of the general happiness. For us, therefore, justice must always be a second virtue, irreducible to benevolence. It was generally felt that Butler's position was the more sound.

Hume: Sympathy. — According to Hume, the stimulus of approbation is any trait of character which is *sympathetically felt* to be useful or immediately pleasant either to the possessor or (more importantly) to others who may be affected by his conduct. Disapprobation is aroused by any trait which is sympathetically felt to be harmful or immediately unpleasant to the possessor or others. The list of virtues and vices is thus greatly increased. Justice is valued wholly by reason of our sympathy for those who may generally be expected to benefit by it. Benevolence is mainly valued for a similar reason, but also because we sympathize with the immediate pleasure which the benevolent man feels in the practice of his virtue. Discretion, enterprise, industry, frugality, sobriety, and perseverance are examples of virtues that are such because they are useful to their possessor. Courtesy, modesty, decency, and wit are immediately pleasant to others. Cheerfulness and self-respect are immediately pleasant to oneself.[1]

Adam Smith: Propriety and Merit. — Adam Smith's theory, in which the moral-sense school reached the limit of

---

[1] It may be recalled that Plato has a somewhat similar theory. According to him all goodness and beauty is either useful or pleasant or both. The novelty in Hume's view lies in his recognition of the part played by sympathetic feeling.

its development,[1] is of extraordinary importance, in spite of the fact that its psychological basis is slight. For Smith was a great observer of human nature in the large, even though his knowledge of its inner workings was defective. According to him, our sentiments of approbation and of disapprobation are of two kinds: those of *propriety* (and *impropriety*) and those of *merit* (and *demerit*). (1) The sentiment of propriety arises in us, in the first instance, from a feeling of sympathy with the motives that actuate the agent whom we are observing. It is, so to speak, a *sense of the accord of feeling between us;* and though the sympathetic feeling itself may be painful, this sense of accord is pleasant. Thus a man shows indignation at a gross insult, and we feel a kindred indignation. This indignation itself is unpleasant. But at the same time we feel a pleasant sense of being able to sympathize with his indignation; and this is as much as to say that we feel the propriety of his indignation. However, it is to be observed, an actual sympathetic feeling is

---

[1] *Theory of the Moral Sentiments* (1759). It should be observed that Smith considered his theory radically different from that of the moral-sense school, though he recognized a certain kinship with Hume, in that Hume too had used sympathy as the basis of his explanation. The point is that Smith denies that there is any *peculiar elementary sentiment* of approbation or disapprobation. "If we attend to what we really feel when upon different occasions we either approve or disapprove, we shall find that our emotion in the one case is often totally different from that in another, and that no common features can possibly be discovered between them. Thus the approbation with which we view a tender, delicate, and humane sentiment, is quite different from that with which we are struck by one that appears great, daring, and magnanimous. . . . As the emotions of the person whom we approve of are, in those two cases, quite opposite to one another, and as our approbation arises from sympathy with those opposite emotions, what we feel upon the one occasion can have no sort of resemblance to what we feel upon the other." Smith's remarks here are, however, based upon any unfortunate confusion between the *sympathetic emotion* (which, of course, resembles the other man's emotion) and the *sentiment of approbation*, which, according to his theory, must be quite distinct; for even though the sympathetic emotion be unpleasant, the sentiment of approbation is pleasant. Smith is really much closer to his predecessors than he supposed.

not necessary as a stimulus to the sentiment of propriety. We may not be in the mood to sympathize; or the lack of sympathy may even be due to permanent limitations which we recognize in our own character. It is enough if the conditions appear to us to be such *that a normal observer* (the "ideal spectator") *would sympathize.* This normal observer is, of course, for each man an idealization of himself. Thus we all regard fortitude, the suppression of the signs of grief, as a virtue; because we are easily led to sympathize when the signs of emotion are slight, but are repelled when they are excessive. Our sense of the propriety of our own conduct is throughout dependent upon our conception of the attitude of the ideal spectator.

Similarly, the sentiment of impropriety is the feeling that we, or the ideal spectator, cannot sympathize. It is an unpleasant sentiment, as that of propriety is pleasant.

(2) Our sentiments of merit and demerit are aroused under conditions where we (or the ideal spectator) can sympathize *with the gratitude or resentment* which the agent's conduct may excite in those affected by it; not their actual gratitude or resentment necessarily, but their gratitude or resentment *if they should feel any.* In other words, a sentiment of merit or demerit is a feeling of *the propriety of gratitude or resentment.* All of the more important virtues and vices fall under this head. When, for example, we see one man assisted in his need by another, we put ourselves in imagination in the place of him who has been assisted, and thus see his benefactor in the most favorable light; and even if the recipient of the favor does not respond in any way, we as it were respond in his place.

Adam Smith's theory is thus, like Hume's, based upon sympathy. But there are two great differences. According to Hume, the sympathy is for the pleasant or unpleasant consequences of conduct. According to Adam Smith it is sympathy either for the motives of the agent himself, or for the gratitude or resentment that may be aroused. Again, according to Hume, the sympathy is the actual sympathy of the person judging. According to Adam Smith, it may be only the probable sympathy of the ideal spectator.

The Weakness of Sentimentalism. — We have given these details, because they serve to exhibit in striking fashion the weakness in the sentimental school that led to its ultimate overthrow. In their descriptive analysis of the moral life, these men had no rivals in their time. But their explanations took too much for granted; and as time went on the assumptions were increased. The underivable moral sense was a good deal to manage at the outset; but the more and more complex psychological mechanism imagined for its stimulation was too much for the theory to carry. It is therefore not surprising that even within the lifetime of Hume and Adam Smith the drift of opinion set in strongly in favor of utilitarianism.

An Intuitionalist Criticism. — Utilitarianism we shall shortly have to consider. Here we must note an objection of the intuitionalists. The advocates of the moral sense have appealed to experience to show that the approval and disapproval are not a process of reasoning — not the application of a general rule to the particular case. The consciousness of a rule, they say, is superfluous. But, as a matter of fact, is it not rather the feelings that are superfluous? Or, if they be not superfluous, is it not true, at any rate, that they can vary widely in quality and intensity without affecting the moral judgment? For let us admit that we have such feelings: that either accompanying our moral judgments or, perhaps, even preceding them, there arises in us a spontaneous sense of the charm of virtue and of the repulsiveness of vice. Let us admit, too, that these feelings have a real function in our mental economy. They reënforce the rational consciousness of moral obligation, which, indeed, in most of us is none too powerful. Still the fact remains that moral judgment is one thing and the accompanying feelings another; and that it is by the judgment that the distinction between right and wrong is ultimately decided. The mistake that the moral-sense theorists have made is in confusing the moral judgment, which is rational, with its emotional accompaniments. And as for the analogy of beauty upon which they lay so much stress, that is indeed more than an analogy; for the so-called moral feelings are really (at least in part) *æsthetic feelings* — they are *feelings of the beauty or ugliness of human conduct and character*. Now it is true that virtue is beautiful and that vice is ugly; but that does not justify us in confusing virtue with the beauty of virtue, or vice with the ugliness of vice.[1]

IV. UTILITARIANISM

1. *The Utilitarian Program*

Products, not Elements. — It will be recalled that utilitarianism differs from the two theories which we have been examining, in holding that the perception of moral values is not a simple and original quality of human nature, but grows up in each man from psychological elements of a non-moral character. Conduct is morally good or bad, according as it tends to increase or decrease the happiness of all concerned. But we have no native impulse that forces us into good conduct, as thus defined; and we have no native admiration or contempt for the good or bad conduct that falls under our observation. The feeling of *obligation*, the feeling of *approbation* or *disapprobation*, are products, not elements, of our experience.

Much the same thing is to be said of the feeling of benevolence, which, aside from any sense of obligation, makes

[1] For Hume's discussion of a similar objection see *Treatise of Human Nature*, Book III, Part III, Sect. 1.

the good man desire the happiness of his fellow men independently of any consideration of his own happiness, even when a certain degree of self-sacrifice is called for. Benevolence is not by any means a fiction. It is a real characteristic of human nature. But it is not natural in the sense of being original and elementary.

Utilitarianism vs. Sentimentalism. — The moral-sense theorists are substantially correct — the utilitarians say — in their account of the moral experience of the man of developed character. The recognition of moral good and evil is in such a man a matter of spontaneous feeling. The possibility of performing a benevolent act is at once an imperative claim upon him; and the perception of such an act is sufficient to arouse his approbation. And it may be well enough to label this fact of his nature a ' moral sense.' But the moral sense, like the benevolence of which it so warmly approves, and indeed all the higher human affections and impulses, is *derived from the mere desire for pleasure and avoidance of pain.*

How does the Moral Being Arise? — Thus is determined the scientific program of the utilitarian school. Instead of contenting themselves with a mere description of moral experience, these men start from certain very simple and general psychological principles (which they regard as sufficiently established) and try to account for all the facts in terms of these principles. They try to show how from the infant, who is not yet a moral being, such a being arises.

Rationalistic Method. — But, it is to be observed, they do not go about this by a study of the actual development of morality in children. Child psychology, founded by J. J. Rousseau in his *Émile* (1762), has no influence upon them. Nor do they take any systematic account of the historical development of morality in the race. Their theory is an ingenious logical construction, a reasoning out

CLASSICAL SCHOOLS OF EIGHTEENTH CENTURY 225

how, on the accepted principles, the origin of the moral being *must* take place.

The Assumptions. — Let us, therefore, set down in systematic order the principles which utilitarianism takes as its starting point.

I. Pleasure is the only original object of desire, and pain is the only original object of aversion.[1]

II. The intensity of the desire or aversion is determined by the *intensity* and *duration* of the conceived pleasure or pain, together with its degree of *probability or certainty*, and perhaps also its *nearness or remoteness* in time.

III. When we desire any circumstance A, and perceive that a second circumstance B is an efficient means of bringing about A, we are *in so far* led to desire B. We say, " in so far," because there may be other causes that tend to make us averse to B; and in that case our resultant attitude will be the joint effect of all the causes acting together. Similarly of aversion : if we are averse to A, and perceive that B tends to produce A, we are in so far led to be averse to B.

It follows that if we think of any future circumstance as directly or indirectly causing in us pleasure or pain, we desire, or are averse to, this circumstance proportionately.

IV. When we have come to desire a circumstance as a means to some further end, this further end tends to drop out of our attention, and eventually out of consciousness; so that we then desire the means ' for its own sake,' as we say. The like is again true of aversion. The stock illustration of this principle is the *miser*, who has once loved

[1] As regards the nature of desire or aversion, the utilitarians generally hold that it is *a present feeling of pleasure or pain attaching to the idea of a future condition or event*. Thus to desire the defeat of the French forces is to take a present pleasure in the thought of their defeat as occurring. And the statement, that we naturally desire our own pleasure, *means* that we are so constituted that the idea of a future pleasure is even now pleasant to us. However, this theory has been widely held outside the utilitarian school; and we therefore do not set it down among their peculiar doctrines.

Q

his gold for what it will buy, but now loves it so ardently for its own sake that he is unwilling to part with it for anything.

Thus, while pleasure is the only thing which we originally desire for its own sake, we are capable of learning to love for their own sakes an indefinite number of sources of pleasure. It is thus that we learn to desire, among other things, the happiness of our fellow men, or of particular men whom we love. It is in this way, also, that we develop our love of virtue and our detestation of vice — in other words, our moral sense.

We are now ready to consider the utilitarian account of morality, which falls into two parts, treating respectively of *obligation* and of *approbation and disapprobation*.

2. *Obligation*

Two Problems. — It is to be explained how it is that men come to *feel obliged* to act in such a way as to promote the general happiness. Also, it is to be shown that they are, as a matter of fact, so *obliged;* and this latter point may conveniently be taken up first.

(1) Actual Obligation: Definition. — " Obligation is the necessity of doing or omitting any action in order to be happy " (Gay). To say that a man is *obliged* to act in a given way, is to say that if he acts otherwise he must necessarily lose in the amount of pleasure he experiences, as compared with the amount of pain. If we regard pleasures as positive quantities, and pains as negative, we may say that when a man acts contrary to his obligation, the *algebraic sum* of his pleasures and pains is diminished.

Classification of Sanctions. — The pleasures and pains upon which obligations depend are called *sanctions*. These may be classified as follows:

I. *Natural,* depending upon the causal connections of natural events (as distinguished from the behavior of personal beings). In this way we are obliged to take sufficient food and avoid poisonous substances.

II. *Social,* arising from the approval and disapproval, gratitude and resentment of our fellow men. In this way we are obliged to defer to public opinion.

III. *Civil,* resting upon the system of rewards and punishments established by the state. It is thus that we are obliged to be law-abiding citizens.

IV. *Divine,* resting upon the will of God — the rewards and punishments which he will bestow upon men in the hereafter.

To these may be added the *internal* sanction of conscience itself, our satisfaction or regret as we survey our own conduct in retrospect. But this, as we shall see, is not in origin independent of the others.

Supremacy of the Divine Sanctions. — When we examine the four kinds of sanctions, we note at once that the social and the civil sanctions are not certain. Men often deceive each other successfully, and sometimes even outwit the law. These sanctions, therefore, do not suffice to establish an indubitable obligation. And the natural sanctions, though they are certain as far as they go, are altogether insufficient to determine how we shall direct our conduct. The rascal and the saint may equally observe the force of gravity and the boiling point of water.

Furthermore, in comparison with the divine sanctions, the other three classes are really negligible. For the divine sanctions are absolutely certain; and since God is omnipotent, we may be well assured that the rewards and punishments proceeding from his hand will far outweigh any earthly pain or pleasure. The divine sanctions, therefore, are in themselves sufficient to impose absolute obligations. In all things we are obliged to do as God wills.

The Will of God. — Now theologians have proved from natural evidences (altogether apart from any supernatural revelation) that God is infinitely benevolent, and that he has created men with no other purpose than to make them as happy as possible.[1] He must therefore prefer that men should be well disposed toward each other, acting harmoniously for the greatest good of all, rather than that each should work only for his own interest, to the neglect or detriment of the interests of all others. That is to say, it is God's will that we should in all things seek the greatest happiness of the greatest number concerned; and hence we ought so to act. And because we are all created equal in God's sight, each man should count for one, and no man for more than one.

(2) **The Feeling of Obligation.** — So much for the proof of our *actual obligation*. When we turn to consider how it is that men *feel* this obligation, the argument takes a somewhat different course. It is to be admitted that the vast majority of men, by reason of their ignorance or unreflectiveness, are, to a large extent, unaffected by the divine sanctions. Either they have not learned to expect a future judgment, or they do not consistently bear in mind the awful alternative that awaits them. They are often far more strongly moved by their immediate hopes and fears than by all that heaven or hell can hold in store for them. And yet they are not without feelings of moral obligation. Hence, in explaining these feelings, we must take into account the operation of all four classes of sanctions.

General Agreement of the Sanctions. — We note, then, that all four classes are in general agreement. We cannot do much for our fellow men by disregarding the natural laws upon which our health and efficiency rest. And, though men are often deceived as to their interests, and though they are also often deceived as to one another's intentions, still, in the long run, the man who is devoted to their welfare is

---

[1] Thus, while the utilitarians deny the existence of an original benevolence in man, they are ready to admit it in God. This part of their theory is obviously a mere logical *tour de force*.

loved, and the man who disregards it is treated with hatred or indifference. Similarly, though the laws of the land sometimes constrain men to immoral conduct, this is by no means the general rule. What is forbidden as crime is generally wrong, though not all that is wrong is forbidden. A state in which the laws were to any considerable extent opposed to the practice of morality could not long escape dissolution.

Value of the Lower Sanctions. — Thus the divine sanctions may be in great measure replaced by the lower sanctions in the formation of our feelings of obligation; although without the divine sanctions these feelings must naturally be less powerful and less trustworthy. The corrective experiences of our common earthly life suffice to impress us pretty forcibly with the consciousness, that if we wish to be happy, we must seek our happiness in connection with the happiness of our fellows. In producing this effect, the constant pressure of the social sanctions is doubtless the principal factor. The fear of the law does not, in itself, go far toward making a man good, though it is a valuable auxiliary.

Obligation without Sanctions. — But the objection will be raised: How does this account for the fact that men may still be controlled by feelings of moral obligation, when, to all appearances, they are in no danger from any human resentment? The fact is that under such circumstances their feelings of obligation are often greatly weakened — especially if they have no vivid sense of the reality and power of God — and consequently they often succumb to the temptation to seek only their own selfish ends. When this weakening does not occur, it is because, *through habituation, the feelings of obligation have become independent of their original sanctions.* The compelling impulse to do what is right because it is necessary for happiness has become an impulse to do right without regard to any further consequences. The end has dropped out of mind, while the means remains as potently attractive as ever.

Always, however, the divine sanctions remain as the complete rational justification of morality to the reflective inquirer who asks why, after all, he ought to consider the welfare of his fellow men, whenever he finds himself so strong or so clever as to be independent of their wishes.

3. *Approbation and Disapprobation*

The theory of approbation and disapprobation is quite as simple.

The Obligation to Encourage Morality. — Even if action for the good of the greatest number were not profitable to the agent himself, it would still be most desirable from the standpoint of his fellows. To be sure, any particular fellow might prefer to be especially favored by everybody all the time; but that everybody should be willing to do this is so exceedingly improbable as to be out of the question. All things considered, the happiness of each is best assured by the morality of all the rest. By encouraging morality in each of his fellows, therefore, each man is promoting the happiness of all. He is *obliged*, therefore (according to the foregoing account of obligation), to encourage morality in every man.

The Obligation to Praise or Blame. — Now how can he do this? The only means by which a man's conduct is controlled is the expectation of pleasure or pain — until, through association, other ends have become directly attractive. To influence a man to act rightly, one must, therefore, cause him to expect pleasure as a consequence of right action, and pain as a consequence of wrong action. This may be done to some extent by instructing him with regard to the consequences of his acts, especially with regard to their everlasting consequences. The most efficient means, however, is at once to reward the right act and to punish the wrong — not necessarily in the formal ways provided by the state, for these are not always practicable, but at least by expressions of *praise* and *blame*. For praise is grateful to men, by reason

CLASSICAL SCHOOLS OF EIGHTEENTH CENTURY 231

of the pleasant direction which it gives to the imagination; and blame is for a similar reason unwelcome. We ought, therefore, to praise any conspicuous right conduct, and we ought to blame wrong conduct. Now to recognize that any conduct *ought to be praised* or *blamed*, is to *approve* or *disapprove* of it.

Importance of the Intention. — With this explanation, various characteristics of moral approbation and disapprobation are easily understood. Since the object of praise is to encourage, and of blame to discourage, conduct similar to that which is praised or blamed, it is seldom advantageous to praise or blame *unintentional* acts. We therefore — if we are reflective men — do not feel that such acts ought to be praised or blamed; that is to say, we do not approve or disapprove of them. It is the intention that we judge. On the other hand, the feelings which prompt men to action (the *motive*) matters not at all, provided the intention is the same. All motives, from reverence to loathing, are natural; and all have their place, large or small, in the economy of human life. In themselves they are neither good nor bad. But any motive becomes good or bad according as it gives force to a good or evil intention.[1]

Particular Selfish Interests Irrelevant. — We see, too, why our approval or disapproval is unaffected by the way in which the particular acts benefit or injure ourselves. For though (say) a particular right act may hurt me, it is still to my advantage to encourage that *sort* of conduct in the community.

Self-approval and Disapproval. — We approve and disapprove of our own acts, as well as of those of other men. For when we act rightly, we can see that other men ought to praise our conduct, and when we act wrongly, we can see that they ought to blame our conduct — even though, as a matter of fact, they do not do so.

[1] Cf. p. 40.

The Moral Sense. — Finally, the feelings of approbation and disapprobation, like the feeling of obligation, may become wholly detached from all thought of the self-interest upon which they are originally founded. We then approve, or disapprove, simply and spontaneously, all conduct which we see to be directed in accordance with, or contrary to, the general welfare. We have developed a moral sense.

V. Concluding Remarks

Hedonism in the Three Schools. — Such, in outline, are the three classical English systems of ethics. All three systems, as we remarked at the outset, take for granted a hedonistic theory of values in general: that pleasure is the only ultimate good, and pain the only ultimate evil. For this very reason it is plain that hedonism (in this sense) has no *particular* connection with any one of the three. It is necessary to emphasize this fact, because during the nineteenth century hedonism came to be peculiarly associated with the derivative theory; so much so, indeed, that the terms 'utilitarianism' and 'hedonism' are often used as precise equivalents. The consequence is that nineteenth-century critics and historians, when they noted the signs of hedonism in the old intuitionalists and moral-sense writers, set this down to inconsistency or to mere carelessness of language.

What is really peculiar to the utilitarians is not hedonism in the sense of a general theory of values, but their peculiar *psychological hedonism:* the theory that all desire is originally for pleasure, and all aversion originally for pain, and that all new objects of desire and aversion are related to the old as means to end or cause to effect. This theory is earnestly repudiated by the opponents of utilitarianism.

Resemblance between Intuitionalism and Utilitarianism. — When we compare the three systems with each other, it is at once evident that intuitionalism and utilitarianism, despite the extreme opposition between them, bear a strong family resemblance to each other. Both are neatly worked-out logical schemes, based upon a minimum of direct evidence. The moral-sense theory, on the other hand, is thoroughly empirical in its temper and procedure, departing as little as possible from the observation of fact. The contrast may be partly explained by the fact that several influential members of the two first-mentioned schools were *theologians*, while the moral-sense school was led by men whose interests were essentially scientific. It may be noted that while the existence of God is an important presupposition of intuitionalism, and is absolutely essential to the utilitarian scheme, it plays no part in the moral-sense theory.

Social Evolution Overlooked. — The great weakness of all three systems, from our present point of view, lies in the universal neglect of the phenomena of social evolution. That moral standards had suffered extensive changes was admitted by some, denied by others. But, even when admitted, it was not regarded from an evolutionary standpoint. Even the utilitarians, who professed to give an account of the development of the moral sense, limited this account to the *individual consciousness*, and paid no attention to the means by which sentiments are transmitted from generation to generation and are progressively modified in the process. On the whole, we may say of the ethical theories of the eighteenth century that they are *individualistic* and *mechanical*.

REFERENCES

SELBY-BIGGE, L. A., *British Moralists: being Selections from Writers principally of the Eighteenth Century*. These selections are sufficient for the needs of elementary students; but Hume and Reid are not represented.

HUME, D., *Treatise of Human Nature*, Book III; *Enquiry concerning the Principles of Morals; A Dialogue*.

REID, T., *Essays on the Active Powers of Man*, Essay III, especially Part III; Essay V.
STEPHEN, L., *English Thought in the Eighteenth Century*, Ch. IX.
SIDGWICK, H., *Methods of Ethics*, Book III, Ch. XIII.
SETH, J., *Study of Ethical Principles*, Part I, Ch. II.
MEZES, S., *Ethics, Descriptive and Explanatory*, Ch. III.
DEWEY and TUFTS, *Ethics*, Ch. XVI, 3, 4.

CHAPTER XII

THE NINETEENTH CENTURY AND GERMAN INFLUENCE

I. The New Utilitarianism

DURING the nineteenth century all three lines of the classical English thought persisted; but utilitarianism came to possess an overshadowing importance. At the same time, however, it underwent certain decided modifications in its structure and temper; so that its new phase calls for a brief separate treatment.

Change of Emphasis. — Utilitarianism had lost its theological stamp. It was a theory of psychologists and of political reformers. Some of its most important adherents, including the most distinguished of all, — John Stuart Mill, — did not even believe in the existence of an omnipotent deity. The consequence was that less and less emphasis came to be placed upon the supernatural sanctions of morality, the rewards and punishments of a future world, and more upon the empirically observed sanctions.

Obligation. — But this meant that the old notion of obligation had to be revised; for without the assumption of an overruling Providence to make all things straight, the universal necessity of a given sort of conduct, at all times, in order to be happy, could not be proved. Instead of being an *external necessity*, therefore, obligation came to be regarded only as an *internal sense of compulsion* — the feeling that one cannot be satisfied to act except in a certain way. Thus it was admitted that right conduct might call for real and permanent self-sacrifice; and utilitarianism acquired a tone of sadness, if not of pessimism.

The Utilitarian Standard. — What is the standard of morality? There is no one standard. Every man of formed character has some standard, however crude, to which he feels himself bound. But what the standard is depends upon the circumstances of his upbringing. The utilitarian standard — the greatest happiness of the greatest number — is one which has been consciously accepted by many men, and half consciously by many more. When other standards of right and wrong are examined, it is generally (perhaps always) to be found that a regard for the general happiness underlies them; though it may be a mistaken regard, or a regard limited to the members of a restricted society. The utilitarian standard may therefore fairly be regarded as in some sort the logical outcome of all others: that to which men of insight and wide intelligence must naturally turn.

Theory of Sanctions. — What are the sanctions of morality, the sources of the sense of compulsion? These are of many kinds; but they may be divided into two main classes, according as they depend, or do not depend, on the expected attitude of other persons toward the conduct in question. In the first class belong the social and civil sanctions of the old utilitarians, as well as the divine sanctions (for all who believe in a God). In the second class belongs the natural sympathy of men for their associates or for men in general, by reason of which they are gratified at one another's happiness and distressed at one another's pain; and here also belongs the love of virtue for its own sake, which habit builds up in us. All these sanctions may attach to the utilitarian standard; and, indeed, it is peculiarly adapted to gain their support. For conduct which is intended to advance the general happiness will, unless it be misunderstood, win the good will of all except some few who may find their selfish interests threatened by it; and it is only rarely that such conduct can fall under the disapproval of the law —

especially under modern democratic conditions. The sympathetic sanction is, of course, in favor of the utilitarian standard; and the simplicity, clearness, and universal applicability of this standard make its incorporation into our ' second nature ' comparatively easy.

' **Original Altruism.**' — It is to be noted that in the nineteenth century utilitarians are no longer unanimous in insisting upon what was once the cardinal doctrine of the school: that all desire is originally for one's own happiness. This is now regarded as a debatable point, and some are inclined to the view that we have an original desire for the happiness of our fellow men; that is to say, that the idea of another's possible pleasure is naturally attractive to us, and the idea of his possible future pain naturally repugnant to us, altogether apart from any thought of further consequences to ourselves. This is a *rapprochement* with the old sentimental school, and is probably to be ascribed to the continued influence of the writings of David Hume.

Mill's Energism. — In this radical transformation of the old theory, John Stuart Mill is a leading figure. It should be mentioned here that Mill himself gave up the hedonistic theory of values that had characterized utilitarianism (in common with the other eighteenth-century systems) in favor of a crude energism, which he abstracted from Plato and Aristotle. He continues to use the general language of hedonism. The final good, he says, is happiness; and happiness consists of pleasure with the absence of pain. But he explains that by ' pleasure ' or ' pain ' he means, not the elementary affection of pleasantness or unpleasantness, but the total experience in which the affection is felt. For example, if playing tennis is pleasant to him, he does not speak of it as a *cause of pleasure* but as *a pleasure* — not as a source of happiness, but as a part of happiness. Furthermore, he declares that pleasures differ in quality, and that the quality affects their value, which is not dependent merely upon the amount. "Better to be Socrates dissatisfied than a fool satisfied." How, then, is the comparative value of two kinds of pleasure to be determined? By the preferences of those who have experienced both. The fool knows, for the most part, only physical pleasures. Socrates knows these; and he also knows intellectual and moral pleasure which he greatly prefers. If the *vast majority* of men of a similarly broad experience agree with him, we are warranted in rating intellectual and moral pleasures higher than physical.

All this has been generally felt to be a compromise with the old enemy, and other utilitarians have lent it but little support. On the other hand, the essential feature of the ancient energism — the notion of a harmonious functioning of the whole organism — is not appreciated by Mill. So that as we look back upon his system it is apt to strike us as a very promising — failure. There is another reason for this ill impression. Measured by our present standards of what explanation ought to be, the determination of values by a majority vote, even of a select electorate, seems very weak. But Mill, like the old utilitarians, has little conception of the method or significance of *social evolution;* and so he accepts his majority as an ultimate fact. Since his time, neo-Hegelianism, on the one hand, and Darwinism, on the other, have made social-evolutionary theory the central field of interest for ethics.

II. KANT

In the latter part of the eighteenth century, the center of ethical speculation shifted from England to Germany. With German ethics we shall not concern ourselves except in so far as their influence on later English and American thought has made them of peculiar importance to us. Accordingly, we shall confine our attention to Kant, Fichte, and Hegel.

Kant's Undertaking. — Kant's work in ethics is in origin an attempt to rehabilitate intuitionalism, and to demonstrate its reasonableness as against the moral-sense theory and utilitarianism. He tries, in the first place, to make plausible the doctrine that we have a consciousness of a universal moral law,[1] which is not derived from experience; and, in the second place, to show precisely what the moral law contains and what its acceptance as authoritative logically implies. In this latter part of his undertaking, he comes to results which issue in the inauguration of *a new self-realization theory*.

The Moral Motive. — In Kant's view the moral life consists of an incessant struggle between reason and the inclinations that spring from the sense of pleasure and pain. Whatever reason freely determines itself to do is right, and that alone. Whatever inclination effects is at best indifferent, and is wrong if it contradicts reason. The only moral motive is *reason's reverence for itself* and for its own commands. Even personal affection is no substitute. To serve your friends because you love them is not virtuous. It is virtuous only to serve them when and because you ought.

The Categorical Imperative. — The commands of reason — the moral law — take on an indefinite number of particular forms according to the conditions to which they are applied; but they all spring from a single principle which is entirely *independent of all conditions*, and which may therefore be called the 'categorical imperative.' This general principle is simply: *Revere reason*. This may seem

[1] We have tried to keep this account of the ethics of German idealism as free as possible from any reference to the underlying philosophical theories. It may be well, however, for us to observe here that according to Kant the consciousness of a moral obligation *is not knowledge* in the strict sense of the term, and is thus not analogous to mathematical knowledge. Our knowledge, he declares, can never extend beyond the limits of possible experience; and whatever can be given in experience is *conditioned*. A moral obligation, *i.e.* an *unconditional obligation*, cannot, therefore, be known. It can only be accepted. Moral obligation belongs to reason, not in its theoretical activity, but in its practical activity.

to be an empty tautology, as if it ran, ' Revere the command to revere reason '; or, ' Revere the command to revere the command to revere . . . ,' *ad indefinitum;* and many critics so regard it. But Kant, observing that the commands of reason are always *universal,* while the solicitations of sense are always *particular,* expands the statement of the law as follows: *Act always so that you can at the same time will that the maxim, by which you act, may be a universal law.* In other words, act always on principles that are really universal; and do not make an exception of the case in hand on account of the particular appeal to your inclinations which it makes. Ought I, for example, to lie to get myself out of trouble? Can I wish that everybody would do likewise? If they tried to, all faith in men's word would soon be gone, and so lying would be impracticable. Such a wish, therefore, contradicts itself; and hence my excuse for lying is invalid. This, says Kant, is precisely the test which all good men are forever applying: " What if everybody did the same? "

Virtue and Pleasure. — Kant's ethics is exceedingly austere, as austere in its way as that of the stoics. In one respect, however, his doctrine is milder than theirs. He does not, like them, maintain that virtue is the only good, and that the addition of all other so-called goods cannot swell its value. He does hold that virtue is the only unconditional good, and that pleasure is only good when it is the pleasure of the good man. But he admits that the virtuous man who is enjoying every pleasure is better off than the virtuous man who drags out an existence of privation and pain. For man is not simply a rational being, but a sensuous being as well; and though the demands of his sensuous nature should be subordinated, they cannot be altogether silenced. Nevertheless the fact that this eminent thinker ascribed to morality a value independent of pleasure and pain impressed powerfully many English readers who had been brought up on the unsatisfactory hedonism that prevailed in their own country.[1]

The Future Life. — Kant connects morality with the belief in immortality and in future reward and punishment in a manner analogous to that of the English intuitionalists.[2] His argument is substantially as follows (though involved in many complications). There can be no obligation where there is not liberty to comply.[3] The moral law commands us to be perfect; therefore it must be possible for us to be perfect. But the universal experience of mankind shows that we cannot be perfect. Any man who claimed to be so would at once be branded as a fool or a liar. How can this contradiction be resolved? It can be resolved only if it is possible for us, despite the weakness of our sensuous nature, *to become perfect through an everlasting process of approximation.* But for this we must be immortal. And since the process of our perfecting must go on in time, and must take place under natural conditions, the carrying-out of the process can only be assured if there exists a Moral Governor of the universe. Finally, although the moral law is unaffected by human inclinations, still we cannot think it right that, in the long run, the good man should suffer and the bad man

---

[1] Thus Carlyle exclaims over Schiller's Kantian essays: "Whoever reads these treatises of Schiller with attention will perceive that they depend on principles of an immensely higher and more complex character than our 'Essays on Taste,' and our 'Inquiries concerning the Freedom of the Will.' The laws of criticism, which it is their purpose to establish, are derived from the inmost nature of man; the scheme of morality, which they inculcate, soars into a brighter region, very far beyond the ken of our 'Utilities' and 'Reflex-senses.' They do not teach us 'to judge of poetry and art as we judge of dinner,' merely by observing the impressions it produced in us; and they *do* derive the duties and chief end of man from other grounds than the philosophy of Profit and Loss" (*Life of Schiller*, Part III).

[2] There is a difference due to the fact that he holds that the existence of God and the immortality of the soul life outside the field of possible knowledge. He does, however, maintain that the *belief* in God and in immortality is implied in the acceptance of any moral obligation.

[3] Cf. p. 55.

R

prosper. And hence we must expect the inequalities of the present life to disappear in the future.

III. FICHTE

The Everlasting Struggle. — Fichte, like Kant, looks upon the moral life as an everlasting struggle with sensuous inclination, in which we gradually approach an indefinitely distant ideal — the completed self (*das absolute Ich*). Indeed, he goes so far as to claim that that is the only value pleasure and pain have, the value of something to struggle against. To live rightly is to keep up the struggle. Every accomplishment institutes a new challenge to further endeavor. To live wrongly is to give up the struggle, to consent to be comfortable — in a word, to be *lazy*. All vice is, at bottom, laziness. On the other hand, a perfect moral being, that had no longer to struggle, would for that very reason cease to be. Fichte, therefore, does not believe in the existence of a God. God is, for him, an ideal eternally in the making, not a present entity.

The Vocation. — Fichte emphasizes, as Kant does not, the fact that man's moral life, in which his only true good consists, is essentially a social life — the *fulfilling of a vocation*, to which his actual relations with the society in which he lives call him. He is one of the first of modern philosophers to appreciate the ethical significance of marriage and the family: to realize that marriage is not a mere device for perpetuating the race and providing the state with citizens, but an all-important condition of ethical development and activity. And his further studies made him see that the like is true of the state: that the state is not merely an organization to provide for the common defense and to suppress internal disorder, but the sphere of tremendously important human activities. (Fichte was himself a patriot, one of the foremost spirits in the rehabilitation of Germany after the conquest by Napoleon.) Moreover, the state, too, has its vocation in forwarding the progress of humanity as a whole. For the ultimate ideal toward which all history moves — Fichte's God-in-the-making — is a moral order which embraces all humanity in one common life.

Influence in England. — The moral philosophy of Kant and Fichte influenced English thought less through the writings of professional ethicists than through the essays of such popular leaders as Thomas Carlyle, who found in the German rigorism an inspiration for their preaching. The traditional English hedonism, which found the good of man to consist in bits of pleasure no different qualitatively from those which the hog enjoys in his sty, seemed to them by contrast a 'swine philosophy.'

IV. HEGEL

Relation to Fichte. — But it was with the invasion of England and America by the Hegelian philosophy (which took place in the last quarter of the nineteenth century) that hedonism was first seriously weakened in its hold on English ethical thought. Hegel's system is a genial toning-down of Fichte's, under the influence of Plato and, especially, of Aristotle. Hegel, too, finds man's true good in a self-development which consists in a larger and larger entering into the life of society — the life of the family, of competitive industry, and of the state, and ultimately of the society of states which constitutes humanity. The difference between right and wrong cannot be reduced to any intuitively known formulæ, or felt by an inborn moral sense. It is the difference between performing one's part and not performing it, amid the actual social conditions and institutions that exist. What that part is can only be learned from society itself, by becoming in the fullest sense of the term a *citizen*.

Moral Development. — Hegel's great difference from Fichte is that he does not conceive of the process of development as essentially a struggle, though he is free to admit that struggle is constantly involved in it. For that against which we struggle is nothing alien or hostile to us. It is the narrowness of our own undeveloped nature. And in the process of development we do not set our old self aside — we do not even cease to be an animal in becoming a man — we preserve the old nature as a part, though only a part, of the new. Pleasure and pain, for example, are not to be contemned. They are for the lower life of feeling what the appreciation of good and evil is for the higher life of reason; and the higher life does not put an end to the lower. We often have to disregard particular pleasures and pains for the sake of more concrete interests; in fact no moral development can take place without many such a clash. And in that case the suppressed feelings appear to us as enemies. But we still continue regularly to find pleasure in good things and pain in evil things.

The Life of Humanity. — Hegel has a more positive view, too, of the social life in which the goods of humanity consist. For Fichte, morality was a struggle for the struggle's sake. For Hegel, it is the entering into the great inheritance of civilization — art, religion, and philosophy. Hegel, like Aristotle, finds man's supreme happiness in the contemplation of eternal truth. Only he does not think of this as a personal matter. It belongs to the life of humanity, in which the individual has but a passing share. It is significant that whereas Fichte speaks of his God (the perfect moral order) as an ideal whose existence would be a self-contradiction, Hegel thinks of his God (the developing reason of humanity) as existing eternally, though at any one time exhibiting himself in but one stage of his continual unfolding.

The 'Neo-Hegelians.' — This moral theory, with the larger metaphysical system in which it was contained, was carried over into the English-speaking world by a band of veritable apostles — men who were burningly convinced of the essential truth of its doctrines, and filled with pity or contempt for all who could continue to think along the traditional English lines. The success of their endeavors was most rapid. By the end of the century almost all the principal chairs of philosophy in Great Britain and America were filled by Hegelians. At the present time, though a strong tide of opposition to Hegelianism has arisen, the ablest critics recognize that there is much in the system, perhaps especially in its ethical doctrines, that is of permanent importance for science.

V. THE ENGLISH CONTROVERSIES

Subject of the Following Chapter. — In the ethical controversies of the last quarter of the century, the two chief points at issue were (1) the significance for ethics of the Darwinian theory of evolution (which is discussed in Chapter XVII) and (2) the hedonism which the utilitarian school still maintained as they received it from their eighteenth-century forbears, and which the Hegelians contemptuously repudiated. In the long controversy which raged over this latter point, a multitude of considerations were presented on both sides, in part repeated from ancient writers, in part new. The following chapter is intended to afford a general survey of the chief arguments.

Its Importance. — Such a survey cannot now claim the same interest that might have belonged to it fifteen or twenty years ago. Hedonism in all its forms is dead — for the present; though past experience may lead us to expect for it many another rebirth. But even if it were dead for good and all, it would still deserve our careful attention, for the reason that the ethical science of to-day never could have been what it is if it had not been for hedonism; and many of its chief doctrines can hardly be understood save in contrast to the hedonistic formulæ which they have replaced. A thorough discussion of hedonism is therefore of prime importance as an introduction to the direct presentation of theory which occupies the last part of this volume.

REFERENCES

KANT, I., *Fundamental Principles of the Metaphysic of Morals; Critique of Practical Reason;* both translated in Abbott's *Kant's Theory of Ethics*. The selections contained in Watson's *Philosophy of Kant* are a sufficient reference for beginners.

FICHTE, J. G., *Vocation of Man* (in *Popular Works of Johann Gottlieb Fichte*, translated by Wm. Smith, Vol. I), Part III, especially pp. 447 ff.

HEGEL, G. W. F., *Philosophy of Right;* best studied by the beginner in G. Morris's exposition, *Hegel's Philosophy of the State and of History*.

MILL, J. S., *Utilitarianism*.

SIDGWICK, H., *Methods of Ethics*.

SPENCER, H., *Data of Ethics* (Part I of *Principles of Ethics*).

STEPHEN, L., *Science of Ethics*.

HUXLEY, T. H., *Evolution and Ethics*, first two essays.

GREEN, T. H., *Prolegomena to Ethics*. The essential doctrines are best studied by the beginner in Muirhead's excellent text-book, *Elements of Ethics*, which is entirely in Green's spirit.

BRADLEY, F., *Ethical Studies*.

SORLEY, W. R., *The Ethics of Naturalism;* and *Recent Tendencies in Ethics*.

PRINGLE-PATTISON, A. SETH, *Man's Place in the Cosmos*.

DEWEY and TUFTS, *Ethics*, Chs. XVI, 1, 2, XVII, 1, 2.

CHAPTER XIII

THE HEDONISTIC CONTROVERSY

I. The Kinds of Hedonism

In an earlier connection we have briefly explained the various senses in which the term 'hedonism' (or its equivalent, 'the pleasure-theory') is used. Here it may be convenient to repeat this explanation more at length.[1]

(1) **Theory of Values.** — As we well know, one of the primary problems of ethics is to determine what the distinction between good and evil means; where 'good' and 'evil' are understood to be applicable to any sort of thing or circumstance that can interest us in any way. An answer to this problem is a *general theory of values*. Such a theory must be applicable in every particular field where values of

[1] The following outline may assist the student in threading his way through a tangled mass of distinctions:

Hedonism
- A general theory of values: good = pleasant, evil = painful.
- Theories as to the objects of desire and aversion
  - The selfish theory: all desire is really for pleasure, all aversion for pain.
  - The theory of original selfishness.
- Ethical hedonism: theories of moral values
  - Egoistic hedonism: right conduct means conduct that is most conducive to the pleasure of the agent.
  - Universalistic hedonism: right conduct means conduct that is most conducive to the pleasure of all concerned.

The student should observe that in the discussion which begins on p. 252 the two theories of desire and aversion are first considered.

any sort are recognized. It must hold equally of the virtuous and the vicious, the well-bred and the ill-bred, the beautiful and the ugly, the cheap and the dear, and so forth and so on.

One such general theory of values is *hedonism*. Put into few words it is the theory that 'good' and 'pleasant,' 'evil' and 'unpleasant' are the same. Set forth in a formal, systematic fashion, it embraces the following points.

1. A thing may conceivably be good or evil either in itself or as a cause of something else that is good or evil. We are familiar with things that are good or evil in the latter way. Corn is good to nourish our bodies; weeds are evil because they destroy the corn, or necessitate labor. But if nothing were good or evil in itself, nothing could be good or evil as a cause. There must, therefore, be an ultimate good and evil.

2. The ultimate good is pleasure; the ultimate evil is pain. Pleasure and pain are *simple* (unanalyzable) *feelings*, which we cannot define or describe, but with which we are all perfectly familiar. Every feeling of pleasure is good, every feeling of pain is evil, in itself, to him who feels it, independently of every other fact in the universe. Pleasure, with the absence of pain, is called 'happiness'; pain, with the absence of pleasure, is called 'misery.'

3. Pleasures are all *alike in quality*. They differ from each other only quantitatively (*i.e.* in intensity and duration) and in 'purity' (*i.e.* in freedom from admixture with pain). The like is true of pains. *Possible* pleasures and pains differ also in their degree of probability.

4. The *amount* of a pleasure or pain is the product of its duration and its average intensity. Pleasures and pains may be added to each other *algebraically*, the pains counting as negative pleasures. A sum of pleasures and pains is good or evil according as pleasure or pain predominates.

5. Everything that tends to produce pleasure is so far

good; everything that tends to produce pain is so far evil; that is, good or evil to him who may experience the pleasure or pain. It is good or evil, on the whole, according as it tends to produce more pleasure or more pain.

When it is thus set forth in detail, the hedonistic theory of values shows itself to be not quite so simple as might at first be supposed. Still it is at least as simple as any rival theory, and this has been a strong point in its favor. For, other things being equal, scientific men are always disposed to prefer the simpler of two alternative modes of explanation.

When we look to see the evidence that is offered for this theory, we frequently find none at all. It is advanced as if it were self-evident, or as if a slight examination of our habitual use of terms were sufficient to prove it; and those who deny it are regarded as if they were the victims of a stupid prejudice. Sometimes, however, a proof is given; and then it is almost always based on some theory of desire; that is to say, more precisely, *some theory with regard to the sorts of objects which excite desire and aversion* in men and other animate beings. Two such theories must now be distinguished.

(2) **Theories of Desire.** — A theory of values (such as we have been considering) is a theory as to what *ought to be desired*. We have now to deal with theories as to what men actually *do desire*. This is, of course, a very different question, since we often desire things that turn out to be undesirable; and a theory of desire must explain this phenomenon just as well as it explains desires for things that are actually good.

The Selfish Theory. — The theory of desire most widely held by hedonists in ancient times was this: that in all desire the ultimate object is the agent's own pleasure, in all aversion the ultimate object is his pain; and that whatever else may be desired is viewed as a means of getting pleasure and avoiding pain — whatever else is avoided is viewed as an obstacle to pleasure or as a source of pain. When we desire what turns out to be unpleasant, or are averse to a real source of pleasure, that is due to ignorance.

This theory is called 'psychological hedonism,'[1] the 'selfish theory,' or the 'theory of universal selfishness.'

It is easy to see why, if the selfish theory be true, the hedonistic theory of values follows from it. If pleasure is the only object that can ever be desired for its own sake, it is folly to say that anything else *ought* to be so desired. There is no sense in quarreling with a universal law of nature. One might as well say that $2 + 2$ ought to be 5. And as for secondary goods — would it not be absurd to hold that something which we only desire through ignorance of its true effects is good? No moralist has ever defended such an absurdity.

However, as we shall see, there are reasons for doubting the truth of the selfish theory, which do not directly affect the hedonistic theory of values; and in modern times the former has been very generally displaced among hedonists by an alternative theory.

Original Selfishness. — This second theory of desire is called the 'theory of original selfishness.' It may be outlined as follows:

It is not indeed true that in all our desires and aversions pleasure and pain are the ultimate object. We desire things and relations of many sorts without a thought as to their future effects upon our own feelings. For example, we can desire the happiness of a friend as an end in itself, beyond which our hopes do not reach. But this is an effect of *habit*. Originally we desire only our own pleasure and are averse only to our own pain. Then we desire, or are averse to, the things which we find bring us pleasure or pain. And, finally, with the repetition of the experience, the end

---

[1] This term is also used in a wider sense, so as to include the theory of original selfishness, mentioned below.

THE HEDONISTIC CONTROVERSY

drops out of our minds, and what was formerly a means becomes an end in itself. We at first love our friends (*i.e.* desire their happiness) for what they are worth to us; but with time we learn to love them whole-heartedly for themselves.[1]

(3) Theories of Moral Values. — So much for the hedonistic theory of values and its psychological supports. We must now take account of hedonism as a theory of *moral* values — 'ethical hedonism,' as we may call it. This is the application to moral values in particular, of the hedonistic theory of values in general. Character and conduct, like everything else (it is said), are good or evil according to their tendencies to produce pleasure or pain.

Egoistic and Universalistic Hedonism. — There are two particular forms which the hedonistic theory of moral values has taken. According to the one, when we speak of conduct as right or wrong, good or bad, we are referring to its value *to the agent*. According to the other, we are referring to its value *to all who are affected by it*. According to the former, the right thing for any man to do under any circumstances means the thing that will (barring unpredictable accidents) bring the greatest balance of pleasure to him. According to the latter, the right thing means that which will bring the greatest balance of pleasure to the group of persons concerned. The two forms of ethical hedonism are called 'egoistic hedonism' and 'universalistic hedonism' (or 'utilitarianism'), respectively. Roughly speaking, the former is the ancient, the latter the modern form of the theory.

The distinction between egoistic and universalistic hedonism is a little complicated by the fact that many hedonists (especially in modern times) have held that the conduct which is best for the agent and the conduct which is best for all concerned are *always the same*. (In fact, the attempted proof of this identity has been an important part of modern

[1] Cf. p. 225.

hedonistic theories.) In such a case it is sometimes difficult to classify the thinker one way or the other. A few recent hedonists have held that conduct to be right must be best for the agent and *also* best for all concerned. They are thus egoistic and universalistic at once.

We shall discuss the various hedonistic theories in the above order, except that we shall place first the two theories of desire: the selfish theory and the theory of original selfishness.

II. THE SELFISH THEORY

Its Plausibility. — The theory of universal selfishness is a typical piece of worldly wisdom — the sort of thing with which the disillusioned man of mature years damps the ardor of the romantic young enthusiast. In modern times this has been its chief significance, as few ethicists of any note have subscribed to it. However, it is exceedingly plausible, — it explains so many things so easily, — and the holder of it can flatter himself that he takes a cool and unprejudiced view of human nature, his own included.

Not Immoral. — To hold such a theory is no sign of wickedness or hardness of heart. The worst that its opponents can say of it is that it indicates a certain narrowness of mind or an inability to introspect clearly. The psychological hedonists have often been men of conspicuous generosity — constant friends, devoted philanthropists, and sturdy patriots. They have almost never thought of denying that love and benevolence exist, or of declaring that all pretensions to them are mere hypocrisy. They simply declare that if all these so-called 'unselfish' feelings be *analyzed*, they will be found to be nothing else than desire for various objects for the sake of one's own pleasure. The ultimate aim of all men is alike. They simply seek it in different directions.

Difference of Tastes. — According to this theory, then, if we wish for money or food or dress or books or music or love or virtue, we are, perhaps unknown to ourselves, really desiring the pleasure (or escape from pain) which the particular object brings. Men are, of course, of many different types. They inherit different tastes or capacities for pleasure; and education magnifies these differences still further. It is to this that their differences of conduct are due. Each seeks his pleasure where he expects to find it. In fact, to desire a thing and to expect pleasure from it, to feel aversion for a thing and to expect pain from it, are psychologically identical. Sympathy is no exception. Grant that there are sympathetic pains and pleasures, which we feel at witnessing the experiences of others, especially those whom we love. We cannot get outside our own minds. The pains and pleasures which we feel are *ours*, not theirs; and when we wish them to be happy, that is only because this will give us happiness. Benevolence simply indicates a capacity for deriving pleasure from a certain class of objects, and is at bottom no more disinterested than gluttony. The reason that the term 'selfishness' has an evil sound to us is that it is commonly taken to denote either lack of sympathy or lack of the foresight that would show how one's own interests and those of other men are bound up together. But, strictly speaking, the broadest mind and the broadest heart only go to make up an *enlightened selfishness;* and that is all that moral goodness means.

Proof of the Theory. — If the psychological hedonist is asked to prove his doctrine, he may simply appeal to the general experience of his questioner for confirmation; or he may put an imaginary test case as follows: If we consider anything whatever, which we are intensely desirous to have or to keep — fame, virtue, a place in heaven, or what you will — and then imagine that we are never to have the slightest pleasure from it, does not our attitude toward it lapse into utter indifference? Nay more, suppose that not only is it to give us no pleasure, but it is to be a perpetual source of agonizing pain; does not a positive aversion to it at once arise? Similarly of anything which we detest: imagine it to be a cause, not of pain, but of intense and unfailing pleasure, and can we then help longing for it? If an affirmative answer is given to these questions, the psychological hedonist regards the truth of his theory as granted.

Objections. — We shall have something to say with regard to this test later. Here let us consider some objections to the theory.

(1) Is there an Idea of Pleasure? — That we do at times desire our own pleasure is almost universally admitted, though in recent times some psychologists have denied it. Pleasure and pain, say these psychologists, are feelings (or affections), not sensations, and are not, like the latter, capable of being represented in the mind by the faint copies which we call 'ideas.' What we call the idea of pleasure is, then, really a vague general notion of the various sorts of experience in which pleasure is felt. But if there is no idea of pleasure, pleasure as such cannot be desired. If this be correct, psychological hedonism is false indeed; but there is no consensus of opinion upon the point. And, historically, the possibility of a desire for pleasure has not been seriously disputed.

(2) Not Pleasure but Pleasant Objects Desired. — What the critics urge is that the desire for pleasure occupies in most men a comparatively small part of their lives. What men ordinarily desire is not pleasure as such, to be gotten no matter how, but things and activities and all sorts of concrete experiences. The man who desires food desires food; the man who desires a game of billiards desires a game of billiards; the man who desires the conversion of the heathen desires the conversion of the heathen — not pleasure. The thought of pleasure may not enter into his mind at all. The reply of the psychological hedonist is, of course, that the idea of pleasure really is present, though not at the center of attention. The *immediate* object of desire is not pleasure, but the means by which pleasure is directly or indirectly to be had. But still it is pleasure that the man is consciously, if not self-consciously and attentively, seeking. And the fact that one man looks to one source of pleasure, another to another, is due (as was explained above) to the differences in their inherited and acquired tastes.

(3) *Ante Mortem* **Desires.** — But, say the objectors, men often desire events from which they cannot possibly expect any pleasure. A favorite example is taken from the conduct of Epicurus himself in his last hours of life. Epicurus, it will be recalled, was confident that at death both pleasure and pain cease forever. And yet, when he was about to die, he took care to make provision for his wards, the orphans of his friend Metrodorus. What pleasure could he hope to gain from the future welfare of these children? None, to be sure. But (says the hedonist) in the moments of life that were left to him, was not the imagination of their happiness pleasant, and would not the prospect of their unhappiness have been painful? — for we can have pleasure or pain even in a mere fiction. And was not the securing of this pleasure and the prevention of this pain a sufficient motive for his act?

(4) **Desire for Pleasure Defeats Itself.** — One favorite criticism is based upon the so-called ' hedonistic paradox.' The paradox, as alleged, is as follows: Men do sometimes desire particular objects only for the pleasure that they expect from them. Those who habitually do this we call ' pleasure-seekers.' Now our observation of such men constantly shows them to be unhappy. And when we look for the reason we see that *to desire anything merely for the sake of pleasure soon takes away our capacity for getting pleasure from that thing*. To get pleasure from billiards one must really care for billiards as an end in itself, and not simply as a means for which some other means might with perfect indifference be substituted. The proposition that all desire

is pleasure-seeking is, therefore, a manifest absurdity.[1] The reply of the psychological hedonist is simple. The melancholy pleasure-seeker differs from other men simply in this: that he does not know himself, does not understand his own capacities for pleasure. He tries to get pleasure in ways in which he sees some other men getting it; or, without reckoning upon the deadening effects of custom, he tries to get pleasure as he himself has often gotten it in the past. Naturally, the chances are great that he is disappointed. Moreover, the notion that you must have a specific desire for something before it can give you pleasure is false. Pleasure does not arise only from the satisfaction of particular desires. It may arise — and so may pain, too, for that matter — from a totally unexpected source. The suddenly wafted scent of a bed of unseen roses is none the less grateful because unanticipated. A game of billiards, which I enter upon against my will, solely to avoid some greater evil, may turn out to be surprisingly pleasant. Before a thing has been found to be a source of pleasure, it is not desired. Afterwards it is desired for the sake of the expected pleasure. That is the whole story.[2]

[1] The hedonistic paradox is often urged as an objection to other parts of the hedonistic program, and we shall touch upon it again.

[2] The paradox sometimes takes this form: *To experience pleasure you must not attend to it.* If you attend specifically to the pleasure itself (as distinguished from its source), its intensity is weakened, and it is soon blotted out altogether. Sip a glass of your favorite wine; and if your attention to the pleasure distracts you from the flavor, the pleasure vanishes. Hence the desire for pleasure, as distinct from the pleasant object, defeats itself. — The hedonist's reply is, first, that the facts are substantially as stated, and, secondly, that they do not militate against his theory. For what is described is not the natural effect of pleasure. It does not tend to monopolize the attention, but shares it with the source. It is *the analytical attention of the psychologist* that isolates the pleasure and so destroys it. And the only moral is: If you wish to be happy, do not introspect too much. The hedonist adds that, in his view, although pleasure is the ultimate object of all our desires, we seldom give it any high degree of attention; so that the whole argument of his opponent is badly misplaced.

Why Disproof is Difficult. — Psychological hedonism is thus not so easy to refute as may at first sight be supposed. On a closer examination we can easily see why. It is a theory with regard to the contents of consciousness to which we are not attending — the *field of inattention*. For whenever we analyze the object of our desire and find no expected pleasure there, the easy answer always is: It is there, but you do not notice it, because your attention is elsewhere — on the means of getting it. Now it is practically impossible to disprove a statement like that, for how can we tell what may not be where we cannot distinctly see? It transports discussion to the night, " where all cats are gray," as the French proverb has it.

Proof similarly Difficult. — But if it is hard to disprove, so also is it fatally hard to prove. If we cannot be sure that a given content does not lurk in the field of inattention, neither can we be sure that it always *does* lurk there. The imaginary test which we mentioned above is no real test at all, for it cannot be performed with any precision. We cannot in imagination subtract pleasure (or pain) from a given experience, and add pain (or pleasure), without changing the content of the experience otherwise. When, for example, we are told to think away all pleasure, we do more: we blur out the pleasant details upon which our attachment rests. When we are told to add pain, we add not pain as such, but *pains*, *i.e.* particular more or less definite sources of annoyance.

Uselessness of the Theory. — Now scientists have learned by a long experience that theories that cannot be brought to a test are seldom of any real service in explaining anything. The present theory is no exception. Every one admits that

At the present time many psychologists hold that it is impossible to attend to any affection of either pleasure or pain: that it is only on the sensational side of consciousness that attention is possible. The old hedonists would probably have regarded this theory as perfectly compatible with their own.

when things are (directly or indirectly) pleasant to us, we learn to like them, and that when they are unpleasant, we learn to dislike them. It makes this fact not a bit more simple to declare that on every occasion when we feel desire or aversion the idea of pleasure or pain is present in our minds, and that all our conscious activities are *planned* accordingly. Why should we make ourselves out to be so calculating? Why not say simply that the *past* pleasure or pain has modified our likes and dislikes, instead of lugging in the idea of a *future* pleasure or pain which introspection almost always fails to discover?

While, therefore, the selfish theory cannot be regarded as definitely refuted, no one in our time is inclined to regard it with favor. It is not a promising working hypothesis.

Idea of Pleasure *vs.* Pleasure in an Idea. — There is a further consideration which has told strongly against the selfish theory, a consideration which we here put last because it is based on a psychological analysis of the processes of desire and aversion, which is widely, but not universally, accepted. Desire is undoubtedly a complex process; and one component of it seems to be a feeling of pleasure, attached to the thought of the desired object. Some psychologists (including many modern hedonists) have held that this is all that desire is: pleasure in the thought of a possible future condition. Similarly, the complex process of aversion seems to contain a feeling of pain: some psychologists, again, going so far as to say that aversion is no more than pain at the thought of a possible future condition.[1] Now it should be observed that this pleasure or pain is not an idea referred to the future. It is not a *possible contingency* to which the man looks forward. It is an *actual present feeling*. It cannot, therefore, be regarded as a part of the desired or hated *object;* it is simply, as above said, a *psychological element in the desire or aversion itself*. Now the older hedonists, it is

[1] Cf. note, p. 225.

said, made just this mistake: they confused the *idea of pleasure* with *pleasure in an idea*. And because there can be no desire without pleasure or aversion without pain, they jumped to the conclusion that all desire is *for* pleasure and all aversion *for* pain.

The criticism is shrewd; very likely there is truth in it.

III. THE THEORY OF ORIGINAL SELFISHNESS

Its Advantages. — The theory of original selfishness is, as we have said, the modern substitute for the foregoing. It has the advantage of not being openly in opposition to our ordinary self-observation. It makes a slighter demand upon our ' scientific credulity.' Not all desire is for pleasure, not all aversion is for pain, but only *has been:* surely that is a very little thing to believe! And the theory has the further advantage of being in line with modes of explanation which have been found serviceable in the treatment of other problems of mind — the modes of explanation that are comprised under the general name of ' associationism.' Men who have held it could thus congratulate themselves that they were genuinely ' scientific.'

Empirical Evidence. — Besides, it is based on admitted facts. There is no doubt that we often do desire things first as means to further ends, and then (as these ends drop out of mind) for their own sake. The theory of original selfishness asks us to generalize this observation, to conceive that all our various desires have thus originated in one simple original desire — the desire for happiness. And there is this further direct evidence, which is generally admitted. We all desire pleasure, and are averse to pain, for its own sake, without ever having to learn; and our liking for particular objects increases as they give us pleasure, and decreases as they give us pain. What more natural, therefore, than to suppose that it is desire for pleasure and aversion to pain that have been the fundamental agencies in shaping all our particular tastes?

No longer Popular. — And yet, with all these advantages in its favor, the theory of original selfishness is now almost as much out of fashion as the selfish theory. And again it is not so much any direct refutation that has counted against it, as the emergence of a more 'economical' theory to account for the same facts: the theory that not desire for pleasure and aversion to pain are the agencies that form our tastes, but *pleasure and pain themselves*.

Objection: Desire for Objects comes First. — As for the direct refutation, that has always taken the form of trying to show that desire for particular objects must necessarily arise in the young animal earlier than the desire for pleasure. It is said, for example, that the *very first* desire cannot be for pleasure, because the animal has not yet experienced pleasure, and so can have no idea of it. The babe at the breast, when first he begins to suck, can have no idea of the pleasure the milk will give him. Only later, as he revives the experience in his mind, can a desire for a repetition of the pleasure arise in him. But the argument is almost unbelievably weak. If the babe has no expectation of pleasure, so neither has he any expectation of *milk*. His desire is not for any *object* at all. It is, for that reason, not what we properly term 'desire.' It is a blind, instinctive impulse, following with mechanical precision upon its peculiar stimuli. Now the hedonist is perfectly willing to admit that there are many such impulses, both instinctive and acquired by habit, which often move us to act. *His* theory has only to do with desire for an object; and he holds that the primitive object is pleasure. If the milk gave no pleasure (or relieved no pain), it would never become an object of desire. It is the pleasure that is desired first.

A Simpler Theory. — The theory of original selfishness has been generally abandoned, not because it has been proved to be false, but because it has been found to be *unnecessary*. For what hinders us from supposing that all objects of desire are particular from the start? Our first cravings are objectless; but as soon as we become aware of the objects of these cravings we desire them, not *for the sake of* the satisfaction, but *because of* the satisfaction. The actual pleasantness of the warm, sweet milk intensifies the sucking impulse and makes the infant pull the harder. And when the child has formed an idea of the milk, and the natural stimuli of sucking recur (the sensation of hunger, and the pressure of the nipple upon the lips), the idea of the milk will also arise, and by its pleasantness — its actually felt pleasantness — reënforce these stimuli. There is no need to assume an idea of pleasure, much less a distinct desire for pleasure. 'Pleasure facilitates, pain inhibits' — that is the only principle we need.

IV. THE HEDONISTIC THEORY OF VALUES IN GENERAL

Relation to the Foregoing Theories. — All this, however, may be regarded as a mere preliminary to the main problem, the nature of value. And it may even be set down as an unnecessary preliminary. For one may hold almost any theory you please with regard to the objects of desire; one may even hold that pleasure in the abstract — pleasure considered apart from any particular pleasant object or experience — never is desired, and that pain in the abstract is never avoided; and still maintain that pleasure is the sole ultimate good, and pain the sole ultimate evil.

For consider (it may be said) any object to which we ascribe great value; and let us admit that in thus valuing it no desire of pleasure as such is, or has been, active in our minds. If, now, for any length of time, the object is repeatedly found to give us no pleasure, its value gradually diminishes; and if it becomes a source of pain, its value eventually sinks below zero. The values of things are, in fact, constantly changing in this way. Pleasure and pain are thus the essential factors in constituting values. The good *is* the directly or indirectly pleasant; the evil *is* the directly or indirectly painful.

Objections: (1) **The 'Swine Philosophy.'** — The criticisms which have generally been urged against this view are quite as weak as the criticisms of the hedonistic theories of desire. For the most part they amount to a mere sentimentalism — a feeling that man is of too noble a nature to be born for nothing better than pleasure, since it is within the reach of the lower animals. So hedonism has been called the 'swine philosophy' — as if that were a sufficient refutation. Of course, if swine are capable in any measure of enjoying the highest good, so much the better for them; we as men are not worse off for that. But the epithet ignores the fact that hedonists are fully capable of recognizing the distinction between 'higher' and 'lower' pleasures. This distinction, indeed, plays an important part in their maxims for the guidance of life. The lower pleasures are those which, though they may for the moment be very intense, are not durable, and, when intense, are bound to be mixed with, or soon followed by, considerable pains. Such are the pleasures that arise from the satisfaction of sensual appetites. The higher pleasures, while less passionate, are purer and more durable, and are followed by no reaction. Such are the pleasures of refined social intercourse, and it is these that the wise man estimates most highly; while the pleasures of swine and the pleasures of swinish men belong to the other class.

(2) **The Good must be Permanent.** — Often it is objected that pleasure is transient, and that the supreme good must be something lasting that can permanently satisfy men's desires. But would not an unbroken succession of pleasures do this? After all, an unsatisfied desire is a pain, and in the hedonistic ideal this would not remain.

(3) **Real Values are Objective.** — Or, again, it is said that pleasure and pain are *subjective*, existing only as contents of an individual mind, and not directly cognizable by any one else; while values are *objective*, existing as qualities of things or circumstances, open to general observation. When, for example, we look together at a painting, each of us feels little waves of pleasure, or it may be of pain, as his glance flits from one detail to another or widens to take in a view of the whole; and these feelings are absolutely private, shut up within his own soul. But the *beauty* of the painting (its *æsthetic* value) is there for all to observe and appreciate. We set ourselves up as authorities to criticize it, and proceed to defend our criticisms, thereby treating the beauty as an objective fact, concerning which there may be difference of opinion but only one truth. The contrast between pleasure (and pain) and value is like that between the sensations of pressure, color, sound, etc., that enter a man's consciousness as he observes a physical object, and the physical object itself. The sensations have no existence save as the observer is conscious of them. The physical object is a part of our common world, to which all sound men have access. — The hedonist's answer to this objection is very simple. He points out that according to his own theory value is of two sorts, and that the objector confuses these. The one sort is *ultimate value*, which consists of pleasure and pain, and is, indeed, subjective. But the other sort, *relative value*, which consists in the capacity to excite pleasure and pain, is objective. No need to dispute this. We human beings are constructed, physically and mentally, on the same general pattern; so that the object which is capable of pleasing one sound man is, in general, capable of pleasing others. To be sure, there are exceptions, due to individual differences between men, ranging all the way from slight variations of taste to positive abnormality. But this is also true of physical qualities. Not all such qualities are observable by all

men. There are the deaf and the blind and the victims of catarrh, to whom more or less of the world is hidden. Furthermore, when one cannot appreciate the value of a thing directly, he can often become aware of it indirectly from the behavior of other men — just as the blind man learns of the different colors. He finds that his fellows are pleased or pained by things which affect him not at all. And thus he realizes that there may be in things a real capacity to please or pain, to which he himself has not the capacity to respond. The values exist for others, though they do not exist for him. Of course, if no one could ever respond, the capacity to please or pain would not be real — the value would not exist at all.

(4) **Common Good.** — Much the same answer is given to the allied objection, that the hedonistic theory is *individualistic:* that it treats each man as if he lived only for himself, and takes no account of any *common good*, whether it appertain to the welfare of the family, the community, the state, or humanity as a whole. To be sure, the hedonist may speak of the happiness of a number of men; but that is simply an external putting-together of the happinesses of so many individual men. — Again the hedonist replies that the distinction between ultimate and relative value has been overlooked. It is on the side of relative value — the capacity to give pleasure and pain — that all common goods and common evils belong. Some things must be enjoyed exclusively if they are to be enjoyed at all. But there are other things that a number of men, even a great multitude, can enjoy without mutual hindrance. A man's portion of food, his best suit of clothes, his toothbrush, he cannot share without some loss to himself. But his comfortable home is not less his, because his wife and children enjoy it also; indeed, were they removed, it would become a somber place for him. Good roads, a good water supply, good police protection are of value to every one in the community.

Good laws, good courts, a good army and navy spread their benefits nation-wide. The advances of science, the masterpieces of art, the encouragements and consolations of religious faith may be unlimited in the possible scope of their contribution to human happiness. These are common goods, and hedonism recognizes them as such.

(5) **Kinds of Pleasures.** — Sometimes it has been urged that there are *qualitative* (as well as quantitative) *differences* between one feeling of pleasure and another, and that these differences affect the value of the pleasure. Plato and Aristotle, as we have seen, are the authors of this view.[1] Sometimes it is even said that some kinds of pleasure are bad; but generally the objector is content with saying that the goodness of pleasure is not proportionate to its amount, but depends also upon the quality, or kind. It is admitted, then, that everything good is directly or indirectly pleasant, and, similarly, that all that is bad is unpleasant; but it is denied that ultimate goodness and pleasure can be *identical*, because they are not *proportional*. The important thing (it is said) is the quality; for a very little of one kind of pleasure may be worth more than a great deal of another kind. It is, then, essential to ethics to determine what kinds of behavior give rise to the higher kinds of pleasure, and what kinds impart only the lower. This is all very cogent if the initial observations upon which it is founded are correct. Does pleasure vary in quality? Hedonists have almost unanimously denied this; and up to our own day it may be said to be an open question, with the balance of scientific opinion on the hedonists' side. What we might be tempted to regard as qualitative differences between different kinds of pleasure — as between the pleasure of poetry and the pleasure of brisk exercise — are explained as belonging, not to the feeling of pleasure itself, but to the complex of sensations or ideas that accompany it in consciousness. Of course, even if it should

[1] Cf. pp. 143, 145.

be demonstrated that pleasure does vary in quality, the further question would still remain, whether different kinds of pleasure possess different grades of value. On the whole, it must be admitted that the hedonistic theory is still safe from attack in this direction.

(6) **Not Pleasure but the Pleasant Experience is Good.** — Sometimes it is said that the hedonistic view is one-sided: that we ought to consider as the ultimate good and evil, not pleasure and pain as such, but 'pleasures' and 'pains,' *i.e.* the *total experiences in which pleasure and pain are felt* — not the mere pleasantness of music, for example, but the music as heard and enjoyed. Such a view was held, in combination with the foregoing, by Plato and Aristotle, and it has been very popular in modern times. Taken by itself, however, it has not much controversial value. The hedonist can easily reply that the difference from his own view is merely verbal. We are, of course, so constituted that we cannot experience pleasure and pain except as elements in larger mental wholes. It is only as our senses or our imagination is stimulated in some way, that pleasure or pain can arise in us. They come as the accompaniments of tastes and shapes and sounds and fancies and expectations — we cannot isolate them. Let, therefore, any one who pleases attach the verbal tags, 'good' and 'evil,' to the total experiences and not to the pleasure and pain. These still remain essential constituents of the ultimate good and evil — the constituents upon which its value, positive or negative, depends, and with which the value is directly proportional.

The central point at issue between the hedonists and their critics is thus the *proportionality* of value and pleasure. Admit this, and the question of identity is not worth fighting over.

(7) **Are Pleasures and Values Proportional?** — Now at this central point the controversy becomes more technical

THE HEDONISTIC CONTROVERSY 267

than ever — and not a whit more conclusive. We shall content ourselves with noting one favorite line of attack.

Can There be a Sum of Pleasures? — If pleasures and values are proportional, then, since values are capable of being added together, pleasures too must be capable of being added together. (This, indeed, the hedonists openly assert.) But can there be a sum of pleasures? If there cannot, the hedonistic theory is at once demolished. It might still be true that pleasure is *essential* to value, but pleasure and ultimate value would no longer be *equivalent*, but would belong to two separate orders of facts.

Perhaps Not. — Now upon this vital question there is no general consensus of scientific opinion, though the balance is here probably somewhat against the hedonist. The question is really quite difficult and complicated. Of course, when we compare a number of pleasant experiences together, we may *value* one as much as we value two others taken together; so that if we had to choose between the one and the two, we should be uncertain which choice would be the wiser. But do we in such a case add together two quantities of pleasure and compare them with a third? A pleasure of a given intensity is not a whole that can be broken up into separate parts. One pleasure may be *more* intense than another, but can it be *twice* as intense?[1] In order to add together pleasures of different intensities and durations, we should have to reduce them to a common denomination; let us say, by multiplying the intensity by the duration. Do we ever do such a thing — not necessarily with any high degree of precision, but ever so roughly or approximately? Hedonists insist that we constantly do just this. The child who prefers the stick of 'sucking-candy' to the better tasting

[1] The same question has been asked with reference to the intensity of a sensation — say the sensation of warmth. One object may be warmer to the touch than another — a little warmer, or very much warmer. But can it be twice as warm? Or can one object be as warm as two others taken together? Psychologists are generally disposed to answer no.

chocolate cream, because the former lasts longer, is multiplying intensity by duration, is he not? And is not a great part of the rational planning of our lives precisely similar? The reply of the anti-hedonist is that we do nothing of the sort, for the simple reason that it cannot be done; the supposed operation is a psychological impossibility. The value of the candy does, indeed, depend on the pleasantness of its taste, and it does also depend upon its durability. Candy that pleased us not at all, or that pleased us but for an instant, would be worth nothing, or almost nothing. But to try to make this out to be a case of addition or multiplication of pleasures is to obscure the true limits of mathematical procedure.

The Dispute Inconclusive. — We leave it to the reader to form his own conclusion as to the merits of this dispute. But we venture this surmise: that no man was ever led by such considerations to change his attitude toward hedonism. The fact is that only very rarely in the history of the mental and social sciences has any important theory been overthrown by a frontal attack. In these sciences experiment has a narrow range of applicability. Men cannot repeat and control their observations as they will. And hence disputations may rage on endlessly. It does not follow that the disputations are idle. On the contrary, they are often most instructive. But they are usually inconclusive upon the main points at issue. For the most part, in these sciences, theories are set aside, not because they have been proved to be false, but because they proved themselves, in their attempted application, to be unhelpful — *unimportant if true.*

Futility of Hedonism. — Such is the case with hedonism. Suppose it true; and then there are comparatively few cases in which we can even pretend to show, by a calculus of pleasures and pains, why one good thing is preferable to another. One can always, to be sure, repeat the general formula, that the better thing is better because it gives rise to a greater net sum of pleasures; and one can generally point to particular pleasant and painful experiences which each thing makes possible. But anything like an estimate of their comparative value, in terms of pleasure and pain, is seldom so much as conceivable.

An Instructive Parallel. — Perhaps an illustration will help to make plain what we are asserting here, though at first sight the illustration may seem far-fetched.

At the beginning of the eighteenth century a theory with regard to physical laws was advanced, which has had advocates down to our own day; namely, that such laws are descriptions of the order in which our sensations come to us. The 'law of falling bodies,' for example, was held to be a description of the way in which certain visual (and other) sensations are accustomed to follow each other in our experience; and similarly of the law by which water expands in freezing, or the law by which the magnet attracts iron. The theory is plausible, because, of course, it is by means of our successive sensations that we observe the laws of nature. But it has this defect: that *no one has ever succeeded in expressing a single physical law in terms of sensations of any sort.* Make the attempt with the law of falling bodies, and you will soon see why. Try to fill out the formula, " Such and such sensations are invariably followed by such and such others," substituting definite kinds and intensities and combinations of sensations for each mere " such and such," and you cannot even begin. Physical terms, as distinguished from descriptions of sensations, must always be used. Or, better still, try to give a statement, in sensational terms, of the law of the indestructibility of matter, or of the law of the conservation of energy. The theory that physical laws describe the order of our sensations is, we repeat, plausible; but it has not to its credit one single definite application. No one in dealing with a physical law has ever found this theory of the slightest use. It is unimportant if true.

The Analysis of Values. — The case is the same, or almost the same, with hedonism. The value of a piece of candy — which has no use beyond the immediate enjoyment of it — ought to be conceivable as a sum of pleasures if anything is. But is it? As soon as one begins to be precise, as soon as a real analysis of the value begins, one finds oneself considering, not amounts of pleasure, but valuable details: the texture, the flavor, the contrast of the dry, bitter chocolate shell with the moist, sweet interior. And the value of the candy is not figured as a sum of increments of pleasure due to the various factors — so much to the texture, so much to the flavor, etc.; for, as a matter of fact, there is no amount of pleasure that is with any uniformity due to texture, flavor, or any other factor, or to any definable combination of factors. And so it is with everything else. I value my tennis racket for its weight and balance and improved shape, the resilience of the strings, the exactness with which the handle fits my grasp, etc. I value my friend for his moral courage, his generosity, his wit, his barytone voice, his affection for me. Now all these features and proportions are sources of pleasure: let that be admitted. (Even so, in our late illustration, the physical properties of things are admittedly the cause of our sensations.) But neither a tennis racket nor a friend is ever valued by a calculation of amounts of pleasure — even supposing such a calculation to be possible.

Conclusion. — The result of our discussion, then, is this: that although the hedonists are correct in saying that nothing is good except as it is capable of giving pleasure, or evil except as it is capable of giving pain; nevertheless, in claiming that the goodness and evilness are *proportional* to the pleasure and pain provided, they are indulging in an idle speculation, for no actual valuations are conducted upon such a basis.

Complexity of Value Systems. — This result may be viewed from a different point of view. The values of things, as we reckon them in our daily life, are of many different kinds, and the relations between these kinds are exceedingly complex and varied. The values of art alone — such as beauty, sublimity, comedy, and pathos — are subject matter for a science; and when we consider for a moment how the values of art are affected by economic, moral, and religious influences, the complexity of the subject is mightily increased. Such being the case, it is impossible to treat æsthetic values as reducible to amounts of pleasure and pain. No man of any critical appreciation at all would ever think of estimating the value of the simplest work of art in such terms. He might find it 'sweet' or 'quaint' or 'affecting' or 'commonplace,' but never 'good for so much pleasure.'

Sentiments and Institutions. — What we actually find among men is that the valuations of things are determined by a vast array of *sentiments* — sentiments which sometimes attach to particular things, as a favorite chair or a beloved wife, sometimes to types or kinds of things, as mission architecture or military valor. These sentiments vary more or less with the character of individual men and, more importantly, with that of communities and races; and they have their expression in *institutions* great and small, from governments and confederacies to the games of childhood. The study of values must be the study of sentiments or of institutions, or, in a comprehensive treatment, of both — their analysis and classification, and the tracing of the conditions and order of their development.

In such a study the hedonistic calculus does not enter.

V. Ethical Hedonism

Full Discussion Unnecessary. — After dwelling so long upon hedonism as a general theory of values, we need say little about ethical hedonism in either of its forms; for the same arguments are repeated upon both sides,[1] and the

---

[1] The argument against egoistic hedonism, based upon the 'hedonistic paradox,' deserves a footnote. If (it is said) to desire things only for the

outcome is very much the same: that neither egoistic hedonism nor universalistic hedonism can be definitely proved to be false, but that neither has any concrete application in the conduct of life.

One or two points of special interest must, however, be mentioned.

(1) **Are Moral Values Absolute?** — Many thinkers who have been quite willing to adopt the pleasure theory for all other sorts of values have balked at its application to moral values, for this reason: that moral values (as they have said) are absolute, or unconditional, while the conduciveness of any sort of conduct to produce pleasure or pain depends upon circumstances and may vary greatly. Thus, for example, it is always right to tell the truth, and wrong to lie; but there may well be occasions when the telling of a lie would make everybody concerned very happy. Again — to take the example which is of the greatest historical importance — it

---

sake of pleasure takes away the pleasure, how can it be true that a man *ought* always to aim at his own greatest happiness? Answer: Egoistic hedonism does not declare that a man ought always to *aim* at his own happiness. It declares that he ought to have *such aims* (both ultimate and proximate) *as will, in general, promote his happiness;* and that, indeed, this is the meaning of the word 'ought.' If the hedonistic paradox be correct, — if it be true that to aim at pleasure makes pleasure impossible, — then it simply follows that men ought not to aim at pleasure. This would be a somewhat pessimistic conclusion; for it would mean that the more clearly men understood the ultimate consequences of their acts, the less would be their capacity for happiness. It would involve men in a hopeless struggle to put out of mind the main concern of life. But it would not be a logically ridiculous conclusion. All that one can say is that if the paradox be correct, egoistic hedonism and the selfish theory are plainly incompatible. However, no advocate of the selfish theory would for a moment admit the paradox.

We may remark in this connection that universalistic hedonism does not declare that a man ought always to aim at the happiness of all concerned. It simply declares that his aims ought to be such as will, in general, promote the happiness of all concerned. In other words, universalistic hedonism does not reduce all morality to benevolence. However, it does undoubtedly tend to *encourage* benevolence, just as egoistic hedonism tends to encourage an 'enlightened selfishness.'

is never right to take from a man his property without due process of law; and yet the accumulation of vast fortunes, with the accompanying impoverishment of a great portion of the people, may be the cause of untold misery which a wholesale confiscation might easily remedy.

Radical and Conservative Views. — In the face of this contention we find hedonists taking two different positions.

(1) Some have simply denied that moral values are absolute. Truth-telling is sometimes wrong, and confiscation, or even stealing, is sometimes right. These men were moral and political reformers of the most extreme type; and they made of their hedonism the excuse for a general assault upon all manner of traditional prejudices and vested interests. And, as a matter of fact, though they sometimes seemed to lose their balance of judgment, hedonism has done a tremendous amount of good in the world through them.

(2) But hedonism has also had its conservatives, who have maintained the absoluteness of moral distinctions, and especially of the distinction between justice and injustice. In the first place, it has been said, the various rules by which right is distinguished from wrong have been laid down by God, whom we can trust to make all work out for the best if we obey him, and who will certainly punish us if we do not. This argument is, of course, very satisfactory to those who believe themselves possessed of a clear and unmistakable revelation of God's will in all the different circumstances of life. But to many other good and pious men it has seemed hard to believe that God could ever wish to punish us for doing what, *aside from his special interference,* was well calculated to promote the general happiness, And so they, in the second place, have advanced the following: We must govern ourselves by universal rules. In every particular case there are so many conflicting considerations that enter, that if we stopped to weigh them all, we should never get anywhere. It is easy to see in a general way that lying is

T

bad. But in each case when the temptation to lie arises, to calculate out all the possible effects of veracity and unveracity would be beyond our understanding. Besides, in the particular cases our private interests or our personal sympathy is apt to be aroused, and our judgment thus disturbed. And, finally, even if the rule were well broken on one occasion (supposing that to be the only exception), still the *habit* of breaking it, or even of *considering* breaking it, would be dangerous; and the *example* set to others, who perhaps had not the opportunity of considering all the special circumstances of the case, might easily be even more dangerous. Hence we ought never to make an exception. A stock remark of the conservative hedonists is this: that bad as the present division of property among men is, no man, and no assembly of men, would be wise enough to replace it by a better division.[1]

However, the first alternative has, on the whole, been the more popular, and hedonists have generally been content to give up the absoluteness of moral values.

(2) **Egoistic and Universalistic Hedonism.** — When one considers the two special forms of ethical hedonism — that which declares that a man ought always to act so as to promote his own greatest happiness, and that which declares that he ought to act so as to promote the greatest happiness of all concerned — one must not forget the assumption, that happiness is to be estimated *as an algebraic sum of pleasures and pains*. If this assumption be forgotten, the egoistic formula is easily interpreted as an exhortation to self-improvement; while the universalistic formula becomes practically an exhortation to benevolence. Now self-improvement and benevolence are, as we have elsewhere seen, two of the principal departments of morality. But, we repeat, it is not self-improvement or benevolence, as such, that is here in question, but two alternative *hedonistic* interpretations of moral values.

[1] This is the typical eighteenth-century *doctrinaire individualism*.

Either without the Other Unsatisfactory. — One very serious controversial difficulty that each of these interpretations lies under is — the other interpretation. For, somehow, there has been a strong and persistent feeling that *both* ought to apply. If we take the egoistic interpretation by itself, it strikes us as being heartless: to say that a man is justified in following his own pleasure regardless of the possible misery of every one else in the universe. To be sure most men are more or less sympathetic, and hence find it impossible to be happy when those about them are unhappy. But some men are very unsympathetic; and shall we say that their very hardness of heart is an excuse for every act of cruelty or neglect that policy may advise? Grant that prudence is an excellent thing: it does not seem to be all that we mean by morality.

But when we take the universalistic interpretation by itself, the case is not much improved. Have we the right to say that a man ought to promote the general happiness, even though his own everlasting misery should be the price? What if the net gain to the world as a whole were very slight, and the man's own misery exceedingly intense? If there be any possibility that virtue may demand such a sacrifice, we are moved to say, in the words of Bishop Butler, "that when we sit down in a cool hour, we can neither justify to ourselves this or any other pursuit, till we are convinced that it will be for our happiness, or at least not contrary to it" (*Sermons on Human Nature*, XI).

The Task of Reconciliation. — And so the task is set of showing that the two interpretations really coincide: that the same conduct which promotes the general happiness must also promote the happiness of the agent. A *general* coincidence is not hard to make out. We all know that as a matter of ordinary experience honesty is the best policy. But is the coincidence exact and complete? Are there no exceptions? Perhaps our religion assures us that in a future life all exceptions will be wiped out; and then this difficulty disappears for us. But if we have no such religion, or if, as scientific men, we prefer to rest our case on actual observations of men and manners, the difficulty remains. And, indeed, as controversy has gone on, hedonists have become more and more persuaded that the difficulty is insuperable. Of the two most distinguished hedonists of recent times, Herbert Spencer and Henry Sidgwick, the former declared that only in an ideal society could a man's life be made right both toward himself and toward his fellow men; while the latter threw himself into the study of 'spiritualistic' phenomena, hoping to find empirical proof of a future life in which the inequalities of earthly fortune might be healed.

(3) **Futility of the Calculus.** — Deeper than all such considerations, however, is the question of the *practicability of the hedonistic calculus* in ordering the affairs of life. We have already given our reasons for deciding this question in the negative. Leaving aside the question whether the calculation and summation of pains and pleasures is theoretically possible at all, the fact remains that our actual moral conduct is directed after a completely different fashion. And, indeed, in any situation that is complicated enough to call for a decision of conscience, the possible pleasures and pains involved are so multitudinous that a pretense of calculation is at once seen to be a mockery. We do respect our fellows' happiness, and we do have a prudential regard for our own; but this is not the *atomistic* happiness of hedonistic theory, made up of moments of pleasantness and unpleasantness, but an *organized* happiness, made up of all manner of interrelated goods. When, for example, I restrain an impulse to slap an exasperating child, think of the interests that are involved, which the hedonistic calculus would have to pull to pieces and put together again. The conceivable pain of the slap, the discomfort of the continued annoyance, are only a beginning.

Not to be too prolix, there is the order of the household, the prosecution of my work, the child's disposition, his sense of justice, the maintenance of affectionate relations between him and me — and each of these opens up vistas of cause and effect that stretch on endlessly.

Hedonistic Interpretation of Moral Standards. — Hedonistic thinkers have come more and more to see the force of this objection, and they have tried to meet it as follows. The calculus of possible pains and pleasures does not have to be performed each time afresh, as if it had never been performed before. We have the accumulated experience of mankind for many centuries to guide us. For this is precisely what the traditional moral standards represent — the standards that require of us truth and courage and obedience to authority, and all the rest of the long list of virtues. They represent precisely the sort of conduct which long experience has shown to be most conducive to the happiness of the agent himself or of others. On each particular occasion we have, therefore, only to consider how far any extraordinary special circumstances may modify the force of the general precepts.

Criticism. — Now this suggestion comes very close to what is now very generally believed to be the truth of the matter; and the reader should bear it in mind when he comes to consider our own account of the development of the moral sentiments. But as a defense of ethical hedonism it does not hold. For it virtually *refers back to the past the hedonistic calculus which we find impracticable in the present;* with this difference, indeed, that it is not imagined possible pleasures and pains that must, for the most part, be summed up, but the reported or dimly remembered actual pleasures and pains of multitudes of men. Now it will not do to dump our difficulties upon the past. They bulk as largely there as in the present.

Conclusion. — The truth is, ethical hedonism, like the whole hedonistic program, savors of what is called 'intellectualism.' By this is meant the tendency to explain men's perceptions, opinions, and sentiments, and their consequent conduct, in terms of supposed calculations or other reasonings, of which they are supposed to be the logical outcome. It is, for example, intellectualistic to suppose (as psychologists once did) that when a man meets a friend and recognizes him, he goes through a process of comparing the present perception with a revived image of his friend, and from their likeness concludes that they are to be referred to the same object. We know better than this now. The process of recognition seldom involves any such comparison or inference. And, more and more, scholars are becoming convinced that reasoning plays a much smaller part in human life than has generally in the past been supposed. How this reflection applies to the question of the nature and development of the moral sentiments will, we trust, be made sufficiently clear in the sequel.

REFERENCES

GREEN, T. H., *Prolegomena to Ethics*, Book III, Ch. I, 156–170; Book IV, Chs. III, IV.
SIDGWICK, H., *Methods of Ethics*, Book I, Ch. IV; Books II and IV.
SPENCER, H., *Data of Ethics*, Chs. III, IV, IX.
STEPHEN, L., *Science of Ethics*, Ch. II, 2, Ch. IX.
ALEXANDER, S., *Moral Order and Progress*, Book II, Ch. V.
SORLEY, W. R., *Ethics of Naturalism*, Part I.
RASHDALL, H., *Theory of Good and Evil*, Book I, Chs. II, III; Book II, Ch. I.
PAULSEN, F., *System of Ethics*, Book II, Ch. II.
SETH, J., *Study of Ethical Principles*, Part I, Ch. I.
MEZES, S., *Ethics, Descriptive and Explanatory*, Ch. XV.
MUIRHEAD, J. H., *Elements of Ethics*, Book III, Chs. I, III.

PART III
THE EVOLUTIONARY THEORY OF MORAL VALUES

CHAPTER XIV

THE SIGNIFICANCE OF MORALITY FOR SOCIETY

I. INTRODUCTION

Are the General Moral Predicates Definable? — At one time and another a good deal of space has been given by ethicists to the question whether the general moral predicates, 'good' and 'bad,' and 'right' and 'wrong,' are definable or indefinable. Just now less importance is attached to this question than formerly, for the reason that logicians have come to the conclusion that the distinction between the definable and the indefinable is not an absolute one. In a mathematical science, such as geometry, for example, it used to be thought that certain concepts — space, position, direction, distance — must be assumed as intrinsically indefinable, and the other concepts defined in terms of these. But it is now known that one may use the greatest freedom in choosing the terms that one shall treat as indefinable; so that the distinction in question is seen to be always relative to some particular arrangement of the subject. What is defined in one book may be assumed as indefinable in another.

They are Practically Indefinable. — But, putting the strictly logical question aside, we find that there are serious difficulties in the way of devising definitions of the moral predicates that shall be really illuminating and helpful, and at the same time shall not by implication involve a whole mass of disputed theories. 'Good,' we understand, is to mean 'morally good,' as distinguished from merely 'desirable,' or 'good' in the widest sense of the term. But, then, we have to explain 'morally'; and, moreover, it remains doubtful whether moral good is a *kind* of good, comprised under the general conception of good, or a special *meaning* of the term 'good,' as different, perhaps, from other goods as the bark of a dog is from the bark of a tree. 'Right' may be defined in terms of 'ought'; but how shall we define 'ought' except in terms of 'right'? The two motions are obviously correlative, one no more fundamental than the other.

The Question of Function. — Accordingly we must adopt some other mode of exposition, less direct but more practicable. Instead of asking at once what the meaning of the moral predicates is, let us ask what the *function* of morality is — what the part is that it plays in the life of the individual and in that of society. It will be convenient for us to consider the social aspect of the question first, the individual aspect being postponed to the following chapter.

II. Morality and Social Welfare

The General Rule. — It is a very old and trite observation, that morality is of great advantage to any society. Courage, honesty, and thrift defend it from enemies without and within. Other things being equal, the family or community or state in which temperate living is the rule is the successful rival, both in war and in peace, of that in which undisciplined self-indulgence prevails. Protagoras, it will be remembered, pointed out that without the moral sentiments of justice and self-respect no organized society can hold together; and the truth of this can easily be seen, even in the case of societies whose most prominent aims are immoral. "Honor among thieves" is proverbial; and the pirate crew, that flaunts the red flag in the face of all the laws of Christendom, must have laws of its own and an iron discipline in their observance.

Speaking generally, then, we may say that morality is very useful to society and that some degree or amount of it is absolutely essential to the existence of society. This general statement, of course, leaves room for all manner of particular exceptions. It may still be true that some comparatively bad men are more useful to society than some better men; or that some evil action may result in a higher social welfare than the right and proper alternative could have brought about; or, again, that in a struggle between two societies the less moral may triumph. Such cases may or may not occur. They often seem to occur, though some moralists have doubted or denied their reality. But whether they occur or not our general proposition is unaffected. *As a general rule*, the right is profitable and the wrong is unprofitable — if not to the moral agent himself, at least to the society of which he is a member.

The Case of Justice. — All this is strikingly clear where the alternatives of justice and injustice are in question. In the distribution of property, it often seems as if the interests of society would be much better served if one could simply ignore for a time the right and wrong of the matter. In a railway accident a wealthy man and his wife are killed, and a lawsuit over the estate arises between their relatives. If he died first, the property passed to her, and so goes now to her family; if not, it goes to his family. The former are worthy people in straightened circumstances; the latter are already immensely wealthy. The evidence in the case is scant and uncertain; but, in the judge's opinion, there is a slight presumption that the wife died first, and he decides accordingly. His action, we say, is just and right; but would not a more desirable distribution of property be secured if he silenced his moral principles and gave his decision the other way? There might, it is true, be some popular suspicion as to his motives that would tend to destroy confidence in him and perhaps also in the bench generally; but there might not. He himself might fall into a habit of allowing his judgment to be warped by his sympathies; but, again, he might not. But if judges in general should set their sympathies above the law, there would be no doubt about the social injury that their evil practice would cause. Beneficial as the single act of injustice might be or appear, widespread injustice would work ruin.

Are Some Moral Rules Hurtful? — Sometimes, however, the general observance of a moral rule seems to many observers to be exceedingly undesirable. Not only in particular instances, but in the sum total of instances, it seems to them as if conformity did more harm than good — or, at least, as if conformity to a different rule would result in a larger balance of good. In many instances the accepted rule works well enough; but the number and importance of the instances in which it works ill is so great that it seems incorrect to set them down as mere exceptions. They threaten the value of the rule itself.

Such a rule is this: *Give every man his due;* which is interpreted to mean: *Return good for good and evil for evil;* or, in the biblical phrase, *Thou shalt love thy neighbor and hate thine enemy.* It is a venerable maxim, which has been widely reverenced and followed. To thousands upon thousands of men its soundness and justice have been perfectly manifest. Yet thoughtful observers can see limits to its usefulness. To return evil for evil invites further retaliation. Hate increases hate, and the gust of passion becomes a deep and abiding rancor. But enemies must be constantly on guard against each other; and this is a strain upon the resources which they might otherwise devote to useful ends, and is thus a hindrance to normal social development; whereas friendship and mutual helpfulness are the most potent instrumentalities of culture. Can these facts be regarded as merely exceptional considerations?

Such Rules have once seemed Advantageous. — But it must be observed, with respect to these moral standards whose social value is called in question, that in times past the evil

SIGNIFICANCE OF MORALITY FOR SOCIETY

consequences which their observance entailed were much less in magnitude, or at any rate much less obvious, than has since been the case. Though ill adapted to present conditions, they were excellently adapted to former conditions; or, to speak more guardedly, their shortcomings were not such as the men of an older time readily appreciated. Let us return to the illustration which we have just used. In a military civilization — *i.e.* where war is always either actual or imminent — a good hater has a very evident value. The man who can be counted on to strike back and to put his heart into the blow is a man whom one hesitates to attack. A common hatred even brings men together, and indeed has been one of the great influences leading to the formation of the larger social groups. Enmity, though itself a form of disunion, may thus be a source of union and strength. On the other hand, a man who will not fight for his own rights can scarcely be expected to fight for his friends' rights, and so he will have few friends. The same is, of course, true of the family, the tribe, and the state. It is, therefore, not hard to see why a revengeful spirit should long have been counted among the virtues.

Their Influence is Declining. — Furthermore, when a standard has lost its real or apparent social utility, it tends to lose its hold upon men's respect, and to be gradually supplanted by some modification more in accordance with the finer requirements of the new conditions. Sooner or later some moral reformer cries out: " It has been said unto you by men of old time . . . but I say unto you . . ." And though many men may long continue to regard him as an impractical idealist, the consciences of an increasing number acknowledge the new claim which he has laid upon their obedience. The reform may be ultimately unsuccessful. It may never win general support. Or it may be so completely triumphant that men will no longer realize that the older, cruder moral standard ever held sway.

Summary. — Accordingly, the moral standards to be found at any time in a society may be divided into three classes: first, the great body of rules and ideals upon which the welfare, and even the existence, of society rests; secondly, those which have in times past been similarly useful, but now reveal serious shortcomings; and, thirdly, the newer standards which changing needs have brought forth, but which have not yet won general recognition.

III. Social Intercourse

Let us now ask the deeper question: In what does this social utility of morality consist? What manner of service does it perform? We have already anticipated the answer to this question, as, indeed, we could scarcely help doing; but it must be set forth explicitly. With this object in view we will here take note of a few important truths with regard to the nature of societies.

Society more than an Aggregate. — A society, as we well know, is not a mere aggregate of individuals that happen to be living together in the same place. It is true that, generally speaking, the members of a society must, at least at certain times, come together; but this requirement, though necessary, is not sufficient. This is easily seen in the case of any particular form of social organization. Take the family, for instance. It is possible for a domestic servant to live in a house for months or even years, and never become a member of the family; while, on the other hand, he or she may be ' taken into the family ' almost at the outset. Similarly in the case of polite society: one may long be a dweller in the midst of it, and even be constantly endeavoring to force one's way into membership, and yet remain permanently excluded. And so it is with society at large. French soldiers were garrisoned for months in the city of Moscow; but they did not become in any sense members of the community.

In the same way, the possession of a common language is commonly necessary for membership in the same society; but this, too, is seldom or never a sufficient condition.

Analogy of the Animal Organism. — A society is often compared to an animal organism, and social intercourse to the life of the organism. Few comparisons are more helpful and none is more dangerous. Just because it is so suggestive, we are easily tempted to carry it too far. We can find analogies for cells and tissues and organs; for nutrition, the circulation of the blood, nervous activity, reproduction, growth, and decay. For individuals are like cells; classes and conditions of men are like tissues; courts and schools and armies are like organs. Society transforms raw materials into forms suitable for its use; it has its channels of trade, and its lines of communication and control; it throws off colonies; it increases in size and strength and range of activity; and it shrinks and shrivels into significance. To follow out these analogies in detail is a most valuable exercise. The attention is sharpened, and is directed toward features of social organization which might otherwise be unnoticed; and, in fact, it is under the guidance of such analogies that a great part of our knowledge of society has been acquired.

Failure of the Analogy. — But let us note, in the first place, that the human individual stands in a very different relation to the classes and institutions of society, from that in which the body cell stands to the tissues and organs of the individual body. The cell is definitely of one sort or another, and of only one sort. It may be nerve cell or muscle cell, for instance; but it cannot be both at once. And, similarly, if it is a part of one organ, it cannot be part of another. But the individual man belongs to one class by his occupation, to another by his religion, to another by reason of his æsthetic culture, etc. And he may be at the same time member of a family, a business firm, a church, a musical club, a political organization, etc. Man, especially civilized man, is of a many-sided nature; and each side connects him differently with his fellows.

The Extent of a Society. — Let us note, in the second place, the ambiguity of the term 'society.' It may stand for any one of the many organizations to which a man may belong. Or it may stand for the organization made up of all these organizations, for the complex unity made up of a multitude of men bound together in any or all of the ways in which men are bound together. It is evident that in this latter sense one society is rarely marked off sharply from another. National boundary lines must not deceive us. In some respects the society to which a man belongs may be confined to a single village. In other respects it may overspread many nations. Here, then, is a second important respect in which the analogy with the animal organism breaks down. *A society extends as far as social intercourse extends.* Where means of transportation and communication fail, the society stops; and thus under primitive conditions societies are apt to be far more definitely separated than is the case with us. The railroad, the steamship, and the electric telegraph have so enlarged the possibilities of social intercourse, that the whole world is rapidly becoming one society.

Elements of Social Intercourse. — But what is social intercourse? An answer to this question would have positive significance for us — not merely the negative value of a distinction between society and the organism. Several elements can easily be recognized. First, there is interchange of *services*. We say 'interchange,' for although certain members of a society, the babes and the helpless invalids and the old men and women, are, during a limited period, merely recipients of services, yet normally some payment in kind will be or has been made. The idle rich may also be thought to be exceptions. But a moment's reflection recalls the fact, that, though such persons are of no use to the world at large,

SIGNIFICANCE OF MORALITY FOR SOCIETY 289

they do perform a variety of services for each other; and these strictly confined mutual services mark them out as a distinct class.

Secondly, there is interchange of *goods*. This, indeed, might easily be included under the first heading, as an indirect exchange of services. There is an important difference, however, for which our terminology ought in some way to provide. A man often works for a lifetime, without ever forming the least acquaintance with any one of those who enjoy the products of his labor. These pass from hand to hand indefinitely, and personal contact is utterly lost. Whereas, then, in the direct interchange of services the connection that is established is physical and psychical at once, in the interchange of goods the physical connection stretches on continuously, while the psychological connection is constantly broken. Still, the distinction is not a sharp one. There are public services of many kinds, both in war and in peace, where the personal acquaintance between those who labor and those who enjoy has a very limited range indeed — becomes, in fact, merely symbolic.

Thirdly, there is interchange of *ideas* — that is to say, of conceptions and beliefs. And, fourthly, there is interchange of *sentiments* — which is as much as to say, of the valuations habitually set upon things. Here, again, these two kinds might easily be consolidated into one; and we prefer to separate them only because the latter head is, as will soon appear, particularly important.

Importance of a Common Language. — It is, of course, for the communication of ideas and sentiments that a common language is so important. Translators and interpreters can effect much, but can never wholly wipe out a linguistic barrier. A religious movement, for example, like the spread of Methodism or of Christian Science, may assume powerful proportions in English-speaking countries, and cause scarcely a ripple of excitement outside. The Elizabethan drama ran its course in England, and nearly two centuries elapsed before its influence upon the German drama showed itself of decisive importance. By the time the demand for translation comes, a movement must have already gained considerable importance in its mother tongue; and the demand may never come. In Germany, in the half century following the publication of Kant's *Critique of Pure Reason* (1781), there was a philosophical activity such as the world has seldom known. But during that time its influence outside of Germany was very feeble; and even down to our own day the natural philosophy of Schelling and the metaphysics of Herbart (two of the greatest geniuses of the period) have been almost entirely without foreign influence.

In the interchange of sentiments, language is perhaps of less importance than conduct — the observable preferences which men display for one state of things as against another. At any rate, language alone can effect little. Our expressed admiration for a symphony will do little for its success, if we are not willing to stop and listen to it. Our outspoken condemnation of an act of injustice will go for naught, if we promptly commit a similar injustice at the first opportunity. This is in line with what the adage says: that "actions speak louder than words." They not only express one's sense of values more unmistakably, but they are far more likely to awaken a similar appreciation in others.

Interchange of Sentiments fundamentally Important. — All these four varieties of intercourse — the interchange of services, goods, ideas, and sentiments — are inseparable from the existence of society. But if any one is of predominant importance, it is the last. Trade and commerce are, as we have pointed out, an imperfect mode of union. Ideas to which no sentiments attach do not receive any persistent attention. And as for mutual services, it is easy to see that generally some common sentiment underlies them. Each man concerned must, in some way, take an interest in the others' welfare; and when one man does something for another, the doer must (in the vast majority of instances) think the favor worth the pains, and also expect that it will be appreciated by the recipient. We do not intentionally cast pearls before swine, or play sonatas for those who are tone deaf, or read poetry to one whose comment will be: "What does that prove?" We may further say that common sentiments are a direct cause of mutual services. The things and relations that men value may be divided into two classes: those which they enjoy in common or without mutual deprivation, such as good roads, good police protection, good literature, good religion; and those which they enjoy exclusively, and for the possession of which they compete. That the former may be possible to them, they must coöperate. But even for the latter, coöperation in some form is necessary, in order that the struggle for exclusive possession may not end in all being alike destitute. Common sentiments and mutual services are thus approximately coextensive, and the former are the prevailing cause of the latter. Thus the interchange of sentiments, by which community in them is established, may well be regarded as the fundamental part of social intercourse.

Sympathy. — How the sentiments are communicated from man to man is a question that we shall have to consider carefully in a later chapter. Here we must be content with the common-sense observation that it depends upon *sympathy*, the tendency which men show to feel emotions similar to those which are felt by others around them. Where men sympathize with each other in their joys and sorrows, their pride and fear and love and indignation, there somehow a community of sentiments extends and some form of social organization prevails.

The Common Good. — This doctrine, that the basis of social unity is community of sentiments, is often expressed in the equivalent form, that every social bond implies a common good. Perhaps in this form it is easier to trace it through its manifold applications. The common good may be a piece of material property; or it may be as abstract and impalpable as religious liberty. In the family the number of such goods is very great indeed — so great as to defy classification. In such a specialized institution as a school there is but one, or a few closely associated principal goods, although about these a variety of lesser goods are likely to cluster. In the huge and complex university, the unity of interests is in danger of being lost, unless the sharing of its name and the common pride in its student activities (in which members of all departments take part) suffice to hold it together. In the state there are a multitude of common goods, but all are centered in one: the maintenance of justice. When in any state a manifest injustice is done to any of its citizens, and remains unredressed, every citizen that is worthy of the name feels himself assailed. For though the original offense may affect the injured man alone, or perhaps some few who are moved to pity for the suffering he may have to endure, the miscarriage of justice is an evil to every man alike. A 'sentimental' evil? Yes; but not more sentimental than most of the other goods or evils that make life worth living or rob it of its sweetness.

IV. The Relation of Morality to Social Intercourse

Morality a Condition of Intercourse. — Let us now return to the question which was raised with respect to the nature of the social utility of morality, a question which we may now phrase: How does morality affect the interchange of services, of goods, and of ideas and sentiments? or, in the reverse form: How does immorality affect the interchange of these things? The answer is obvious. Immorality checks, retards, or puts an entire stop to social intercourse, while morality facilitates it.

Consider some examples. What effect has dishonesty upon

the interchange of goods? By impairing credit, it tends to limit exchange to the occasions when the goods can be immediately delivered on both sides, or an iron-clad security can be given for future delivery; and where this extreme is not reached, the added risk shows itself in exaggerated demands. What is the effect of intemperance upon the interchange of sentiments? The intemperate man, with his whole attention absorbed by a few overmastering desires, simply cuts himself off from the great mass of human interests. He inevitably impoverishes his life. In like manner, the coward is unfitted by his vice to take a normal view of a multitude of enterprizes to which powerful sentiments attach: war, sport, and even many business activities. What is the effect of lying upon friendship? What is the effect of selfishness and cruelty upon the relations of husband and wife? And, in a larger field, what is the effect upon a man's relations with his fellow-citizens, of a life of ruthless commercial brigandage? Such questions do not have to be answered one by one. Immorality of every kind *necessarily* produces isolation; and if we should stop to inquire about the effect of cruelty and ingratitude and insincerity upon the interchange of services and ideas, we should be led to an identical conclusion. The proverbial loneliness of the tyrant — lonely in the midst of his servants, his favorites, and his concubines — is simply an extreme instance of the workings of the universal law.

Incidental Exceptions. — It is true that incidentally a contrary effect may be produced. Any common interest whatsoever may bring men together, and the satisfaction of a vicious inclination will serve the turn. But the universal and necessary effect is not thereby eliminated. Though a little society is formed, the rupture with the larger society remains. And even within the little society of inebriates or gamblers or aristocratic parasites, it is the moral qualities which they possess that form the real connection between them. Drunkards, for example, may be generous and kindly men. Gamblers may be (according to the conventions of the game) honest and honorable men. The national vice of the Filipinos, against which their great leaders have ineffectually protested, is cock-fighting, with the attendant gambling. But they have no stakeholders. The man who wishes to place a bet simply goes about offering his money to any one who will take it, until some one accepts. If he loses, the money stays where it is. If he wins, it is handed back to him with the proper addition. An American soldier, who was out of cash, once accepted forty *pesos* from the mayor of a Filipino town, on a wager of this sort. By good fortune he won; but if he had lost, it would have made the name of American infamous throughout the countryside, and would have put a serious obstacle to further gambling between Americans and Filipinos.

"Only the good are friends," was an accepted principle among the Greek ethicists. True enough; except that good men and bad men are by no means so sharply distinguished as some of the ancients supposed. If we phrase it with an 'in so far as' — "It is only in so far as men are good that they can be friends" — it expresses an indubitable truth.

Incidentally, too, morality may cause division between men. Any marked difference in sentiments — æsthetic, religious, political, or what-not — which makes men disagreeable to each other, puts them out of sympathy, and so interferes with the interchange of sentiments of any kind; and a difference in moral sentiments may have this effect. "Be good, and you will be lonesome," said the great humorist; but he meant by being good, holding oneself severely aloof from the pleasures that men ordinarily consider innocent or nearly so. But in such cases what generally does the harm is not a mere difference of moral sentiments, but moral intolerance, priggishness. A man's unwillingness to smoke, because he thinks that smoking is wrong, will not necessarily

SIGNIFICANCE OF MORALITY FOR SOCIETY

put any bar between him and the common run of smoking men, provided he respects the sincerity of their contrary opinion. We must be on our guard, therefore, against attributing to morality an effect which is really due to a subtle form of immorality.

Conclusion. — After making due allowance for these secondary phenomena, we are brought back to the general principle: that the social significance of morality is that it facilitates social intercourse, while immorality checks or prevents it. A greater importance could hardly be ascribed to the distinction. For it makes morality an essential condition for the existence of any social values whatsoever, that is to say, of any common good; or, what amounts to the same thing, an essential condition of the existence of society itself.

REFERENCES

SPENCER, H., *Data of Ethics*, Ch. VIII.
STEPHEN, L., *Science of Ethics*, Chs. III–V.
CLIFFORD, W. K., *Lectures and Essays: On the Scientific Basis of Morals*, and *Right and Wrong*.
WUNDT, W., *Ethics*, Part III, Ch. I, Sect. II.
BOSANQUET, B., *Philosophical Theory of the State*, Chs. V, VII.
MACKENZIE, J. S., *Manual of Ethics*, Book III, Chs. I, II.
MUIRHEAD, J. H., *Elements of Ethics*, Book II, Ch. I.

CHAPTER XV

CHARACTER, SENTIMENT, AND VALUE

I. Morality and Individual Welfare

Effect of Morality on Other Individuals. — That, as a general rule, the better men are the happier they make those about them, is a proposition that no one seriously denies. Sometimes the good man interferes with the immoral pleasures of others, or (through an error of judgment) even with their innocent pleasures; and he may make a decided nuisance of himself by ill-advised attempts at discipline or charity. And sometimes, too, the bad man gives a good deal of pleasure to others by his very badness. But, when all such admissions have been made, we are well aware that the truth of the general principle remains unaffected. Some men (as we recall) have held that all morality is reducible to benevolence, the desire to make other men happier. Whether this is true or not, the general effect of morality is certainly to make others happier. To the direct working out of benevolent intentions must be added the indirect benefit that comes from the facilitation of social intercourse, and, above all, from the tendency of good men to make others like themselves, and so happier.

Are Good Men themselves made Happier? — For this also is true: that, in general, good men are happier than bad men, and that the better men are the happier they are. But this proposition is not nearly so obvious as the foregoing, and demands a thoroughgoing examination. It is easy to dispute, and is sometimes disputed; and to give a formal demonstration of it that carries any conviction is most difficult. We cannot compile graded lists of moral and immoral men, and of happy and unhappy men, and then by comparison determine how far the gradations run parallel. One of us cannot even prove in this fashion that he is himself happier when he is good than when he is bad; for nothing is more deceptive than our impression of our former joys and sorrows. These may be deepened or effaced or distorted to such an extent that it is dangerous to admit them into evidence. Propositions of this sort, maxims of common human wisdom, are the net result of an age-long experience of untold multitudes of men, — now confirmed, now contradicted, and again confirmed or contradicted, — so that the judgment that prevails is the resultant of innumerable petty forces which no pen can record. That is why they are so easily disputed; for while the (real or apparent) exceptions may be unimportant in the great total, they are very numerous in themselves; and a few striking instances can always be cited to make out a case for the dissentient.

A favorite ancient example of a good man made miserable by his excessive goodness is Regulus, tortured by the Carthaginians. He would not advise the Romans to make peace (as his Carthaginian captors wished), and he would not break his promise to return to Carthage if peace were not declared. The latter course, since it could not be kept concealed, would have brought him into public contempt, and so might well have made him miserable — though hardly more miserable than the awful tortures. But he might easily have concealed his opinion. It was easy to argue for peace; in fact the great majority of the Romans were strongly inclined to favor it. And though his secret conscience might still have troubled him for a time, that sting would eventually have died out, and he would have ended by persuading himself that very likely he had acted for the best anyhow. An unscrupulous man could cheerfully have chosen the easy and comfortable course, and would not even have had to pay the penalty of a restive conscience afterwards.

Are the Good necessarily Happy? — However, when we look carefully into the dispute, we find that the general truth of the principle is seldom called in question. It is the number and importance of the exceptions that disagreement turns on. Certain extremists, like the stoics, have held that moral goodness and happiness are absolutely coextensive, or rather are simply different names or different aspects of the same thing; while many others, though admitting the distinction, have maintained that in the long run virtue must lead to happiness and vice must lead to misery. But the arguments (where there are any) for these contentions are either metaphysical or religious; and hence are restricted in their appeal to men of a similar metaphysical or religious bias. Common experience does not support them. Even were the extreme position perfectly true, our observations are so far from being full and exact that we should never be able to demonstrate its correctness. To be sure, we cannot refute it. The dogmatic believer can always refer to secret pangs of remorse or to a purgatory or hell awaiting the wicked in the hereafter; and so one can prove that he is wrong. But such considerations lie outside the field of science.

Let us see what light can be thrown upon the principle by a study of the significance of morality as a factor in individual life.

II. CHARACTER

The Unity of Character. — Character may be roughly defined as the whole body of tendencies in a man, to act in various ways in various circumstances; each such tendency being called a 'trait of character.' But one must beware of regarding these traits as making up a mere *aggregate*. Any trait that one might mention is apt to be inextricably involved with many others. Of the infant, indeed, this is hardly true. He is a bundle of uncorrelated instincts. But his education consists mainly of the correlation of instincts, the fusing of them into what we call character. It is like the forming of a handwriting. The unformed hand sprawls its line in all sorts of ways, now at one angle, now at another, as the uncontrolled impulse of the hand determines. On the same page different portions may seem to be utterly dissimilar to each other. But the formed hand has its distinctive 'character,' recognizable at a glance. All the twists and curlycues are somehow brought into relation with each other, so that they form one whole. So the infant is at one moment a fretful hunger, at another a cooing contentment, and at yet another a wailing pin prick; and there is no connection between these various phases. But the man of formed character, though he may be hungry, is seldom merely hungry; and into his deepest contentment pin pricks find their way. He scarcely ever acts from mere instinct. He eats with knife and fork, handled as society directs; or, if he be a savage, holds (say) his corn in his left hand and his meat in his right. He drinks his soup without making a noise — unless, being a Japanese, he makes a very loud noise indeed. When he fights to the death with his worst enemy, he avoids using a foul stroke. And his whole mode of conduct, from eating and drinking to fighting and dying, is somehow bound together to make up his unitary personality. It is only under the disintegrating influence of disease or drugs, or of some overwhelming passion, that the work of education may be swept away, and he be reduced again to the condition of the infant — a single incarnate want.

How Character Develops. — The development of character is thus *not* a mere intensification or weakening of inherited traits, whereby, for example, jealousy, cupidity, and irascibility may be strengthened at the expense of joviality and talkativeness. Such strengthening and weakening do, of course, occur, but they are not the distinctive feature of the process. It is essentially a *complication*, a weaving together of traits into composite wholes. It is brought about by the conflict of impulses, instinctive or previously acquired; that is to say, if each instinct could operate in complete independence of every other, the development of character would never take place. To adopt a well-known analogy (of Gabriel Tarde), it is the *cross-fertilization* of impulses that is responsible for the result.

Habitual Preferences. — Suppose a situation arises, in which the agent is impelled toward two ends between which a choice must be made. One or the other of the impulses shows itself the stronger by issuing in action. If the choice proves unsatisfactory — which may depend upon many factors, such as the attitude of the bystanders and the persistence of the ungratified impulse, as well as upon the direct outcome of the action itself — then, in a similar situation, the impulse that triumphed before is less likely to triumph again. The unpleasantness of the after-effects adds its force to the contrary tendency; and by a cumulation of such results the direction of choice may be reversed. But let the consequences of choice be satisfactory, and the chance of its repetition is increased. Thus the repeated conflict of impulses leads to the regular subordination of one to the other. In other words, a *habitual preference* (or *volitional disposition*) is built up. It is important to note that such a preference has a force of its own that is measurably independent of the relative strength of the two impulses as they come into conflict. If on some occasion the subordinated impulse is unusually strong, and the dominant impulse weak, the latter will promptly increase in strength, as if from some inner reservoir, and will probably carry the day. The habitual preference has thus a stability which the uncoördinated elementary impulses do not possess; and the conduct which it controls has a higher degree of regularity. It is of habitual preferences that what we call 'character' is mainly, if not entirely, composed.

The establishment of habitual preferences must be carefully distinguished from the further stage in the process of habituation, in which the consciousness of preference is lost; and action becomes as simple and spontaneous as if it were prompted by a single original instinct. The result is then a *habit* in the proper sense of the term; though in general literature ' habit ' is often used to include habitual preferences. However, it is not only in active choice that habitual preferences show themselves. When situations that *would be* preferred (to their common alternatives) are met with, the habitual preference manifests itself in the acceptance of the situation, that is to say, in pleased relaxation. And again, in situations which would generally be avoided, no suggestion of escape may present itself; and then the habitual preference shows itself in an unpleasant tension. Perhaps for this reason ' volitional disposition ' (the literal translation of the German *Begehrungsdisposition*) is a better term. But it is even more cumbersome; and so, with this word of explanation, we shall continue to use the other.

Complexity of Habitual Preferences. — The earliest habitual preferences are very simple. The situation that calls for choice contains but one or two relevant features that tend to awaken any feeling. But as the development proceeds, this is no longer true. We prefer, let us say, blue to red, but not as the color of a house. Most of our neckties are blue or gray; yet we like a brighter flash of color for a change — though many men would rather see it on another than on themselves. We like a red dressing jacket; it looks so warm and cozy. A young woman can wear red on many occasions where in an older woman it would give offense. To a person of cultivated taste the question whether red or blue is in general preferable may well appear ridiculous, the preference depends upon so many possibilities. The choice is no longer between A and B simply, but between A and B, if C, when D, provided E, and so on to the end of the alphabet; or, even so, not between A and B, but between such and such relative amounts of the one and the other. The factors may easily be so numerous as to defy enumeration; nay, even the most careful analysis may fail to reveal more than a very few of them. The situation is somehow taken in as a whole. It belongs to a *type* with which he has gradually become familiar; and it is his acquired preferences with respect to the type that determine his choice in the matter.

Different Sides of Character. — As habitual preferences of greater and greater complexity are formed, they group themselves into fairly distinct masses. For, in the ordinary course of life, we do not have to choose between a smile and a sunset, a bow and a second cup of coffee. But between the smile and the bow (or both, or neither) we do have to choose if we are to display good manners. The various occupations that make up the day and the year, — the various relations into which we are brought with our fellow men, — business, sport, domestic life, social entertainment, art, science, politics, religion, — each have their hosts of delicately shifting situations in which different sides of character display themselves. And very commonly the different sides function in virtual independence of each other. A man's good taste has nothing to do with his buying or selling railroad stocks. His religion has nothing to do with his accepting an invitation to dinner. In some men the cleavage is so complete that they seem almost to be multiple personalities — like Jekyll and Hyde. Between (say) the corrupt politician and the faithful and tender husband, between the social leader and the religious devotee, there may seem to be only the accidental connection of their being lodged in the same body.

Moral Habits and their Function. — And yet, as we know, it is only in peculiar cases of mental disease that this cleavage of the personality is really thoroughgoing. In the sane man there are a body of habitual preferences that run through all the many different departments of conduct and serve to unite them into a whole. These habitual preferences are called *moral habits*, and taken together they make up the *moral character*. It is their function to reënforce, hold in check, harmonize, control all the other habitual preferences. A financier, let us say, is endeavoring to rehabilitate a weak concern. His conduct in so doing is for the most part simply controlled by his character as business man. But let him grow wearied or discouraged, and his *industry* and *perseverance* keep him to the task, and *self-respect* makes him still strive to do his best — moral habits which would be of equal service to him if he should undertake to learn to play the violin. On the other hand, his plan involves the selling of an issue of bonds, the value of which is largely speculative; and when an elderly woman, attracted by the high rate of interest that is offered, proposes to invest her savings in them, he cannot advise her to do so. His moral character will not let him, just as it would not let him filch her purse from her pocket. In order to succeed in his undertaking he needs the support of some man of great wealth. The wife of one such man, whose antecedents are humble, has been vainly trying to make her way into society. By asking his own wife to call upon her, he can easily conciliate the husband's favor. Shall he do so? His gentlemanly 'instincts' are outraged at the thought. But the condition of his affairs is now desperate. Failure, besides the great loss of time and money involved, would seriously injure his prestige. *Ought* he to let slip such an opportunity of relief? It belongs to his moral character to decide.

Non-moral Unity of Character. — Sometimes a kind of unity is given to character by the dominance of some body of habitual preferences other than the moral habits. A man may be an artist in all things — in love, in religion, in politics, and so on. Not that his æsthetic tastes are always active, but that when an important clash occurs, these decide the issue. And a man may be a politician in all things, or a man of business, or the father of a family. But when this happens, the development of the other sides of the character is seriously dwarfed. The man who is first and last an artist cannot be a very good husband. The mere business man is a poor patriot. The unity that results is a one-sided unity. Now, to be sure, something analogous may happen as a result of the dominance of the moral habits. It may, for example, very well be that a man's moral nature interferes with his development as an artist. Lowell thought that this had been the case with himself. But this result is relatively infrequent and unimportant. As a rule a man's morality does not injure his taste — quite the reverse. But the dwarfing produced by the dominance of the other sides of character is inevitable and far-reaching.

Unity of Character Imperfect. — After all, it must be remembered, the unity of character which the moral habits produce is never perfect. No man is ever completely at one with himself. Again and again situations arise in which the conflict of the different elements of character is irreconcilable, and, whatever choice is made, a persistent regret remains. The disconnected instincts from which education sets out are not wholly fused at the end. The moral habits themselves sometimes clash with one another; and though there is in each man a certain amount of subordination among them, the order is by no means clear and fixed. Complete unity of character is simply an ideal limit toward which the more strongly knit characters tend. We are all more or less creatures of impulse. Perhaps we shall find reason to think that this is not an unmixed disadvantage.

III. The Sentiments

Character as Seen from Within. — We have been looking at the structure of human character from the outside; that is to say, we have thought of character simply as that which controls conduct. What is it from the inside? What is it in the direct experience of the man himself?

The inner, conscious side of an habitual preference we shall call a *sentiment*. The usage of this term varies greatly, among both popular and scientific writers. As here defined, it has a somewhat wider sense than is common. It would generally be restricted to cases where the habitual preference was highly developed and applied to very complex types of situations. One little girl's predilection for red and another's for blue would not ordinarily be called sentiments. However, the point is of little importance to us, as the sentiments with which we shall be especially concerned belong to a much higher grade of development.

An Organization of Feelings. — Now, with the possible exception of the very simplest cases, a sentiment is *not one certain conscious process*, but a system of interconnected processes, that can never occur together in one moment of time. The sentiment of the tragic, for instance, is not just one peculiar feeling; nor is the sentiment of justice one peculiar feeling. They are organizations of feelings that can at most follow each other closely in consciousness. It is not even true that there is some one feeling that must always arise if the sentiment is to be experienced, while the others accompany it or not as the case may be. The sentiment may be represented by any one of a host of feelings, between which little, if any, universal resemblance may exist.

Analogy of the Concept. — The sentiment thus plays a part in the affective life of man similar to that which the *concept* plays in his cognitive life. Suppose I take a child's building block in my hand, and look it over on all sides. As I place it at each new angle, my visual image of it takes a different shape. At no time do I see the six square faces at once; and, indeed, it is only by limiting my view to a single face that I can make its four sides equal ' to the eye.' But I never for a moment doubt that I am looking at a *cube*. Each different view of the object conforms perfectly with this conviction. It *belongs* to such a solid to present just such

x

varying appearances under just such conditions, — and I should be mightily surprised if it behaved otherwise. If, for example, I should see at one time six faces, all of whose sides were equal ' to the eye,' I should be instantly convinced that the block was not a cube. Now by my concept of the block's shape I mean the whole organization of ideas (of which only a vanishingly small part is ever present to consciousness at one time) which underlies my present experience — the organization by virtue of which so many different visual images *mean* the same thing. For, let it be observed, however unequal the sides may be ' to the eye,' I *see* them equal. However oblique the angles may become in perspective, I see them as right angles.

The great superiority of the concept to the unorganized sensuous image rests upon its far greater stability. The image may vary within exceedingly wide limits, while the concept remains unmodified, and, whether for purposes of pure theory or for practical guidance, its efficiency is undisturbed. The cube, seen from whatever angle, is still a cube; and it will not fit into a round hole. So it is with the sentiment. Our feelings with respect to all manner of things vary almost without limit from day to day or even from hour to hour. But our sentiments remain comparatively constant. The occupation which now fills me with enthusiasm, a few hours later bores me. If I were a little child, I should drop it immediately. If I do not, it is because my conduct is controlled by something more than a feeling of the moment — by a persistent sentiment organized by many years of habituation.

Standards. — Something was said above (p. 302) with regard to the types of situations in which habitual preferences display themselves, and in which, accordingly, sentiments are experienced. What is preferred in typical situations is called a *norm*, or *standard*. Whatever conforms to the standard is (in the most general sense of the term) *right;* whatever fails to conform is *wrong*. Thus a printed wedding-card, a Democratic victory, a rhyme of 'human' and 'common,' are right or wrong according to the standard that prevails. It is evident that the concept of a standard of right and wrong develops with the growth of the sentiment itself. It is, in fact, its intellectual content.

Sentimental Feelings. — When feelings become organized into sentiments, — 'sentimental feelings' we may call them then, — they themselves become modified in the process. One very common modification is the diminution of intensity. This fact has led some psychologists and ethicists (notably Hume) to regard sentiments as simply one class of feelings, distinguished from the other class (the passions) by their generally lower intensity. A more important modification, however, is the *fusion* of feelings into complex wholes. Indeed the loss of intensity is generally a mere incident to the fusion. Violent feelings do not easily fuse; they rather exclude one another from consciousness. For example, the feelings belonging to the sublime generally contain an element of fear. But if the fear becomes intense, it occupies the whole of consciousness, and the effect of sublimity is destroyed. The storm at sea is sublime — to the man on shore. It may also be sublime to the ship's passenger, but not if he becomes sensible of imminent danger. In the same way an element of cruelty — the peculiar delight that comes from inflicting pain upon a helpless victim — is a common element in the feelings of the comic; but if this element becomes too strong, the comedy is lost in mere brutality However, for many men the limit is a high one; the cruelty must be great indeed before the comic effect is impaired.

Feelings of Obligation. — When feelings of any kind are impelling men to action, and are resisted in their expression by contrary feelings, they are very apt to be greatly intensified, at least temporarily. When a sentimental feeling is thus resisted, it becomes what is called a feeling of *obligation*. Obligations are thus of as many different kinds as sentiments, or as the habitual preferences of which sentiments are the internal aspect. Thus they may be professional, social, artistic, religious, moral, and so on. And these may conflict. The painter, for example, who is finishing a miniature, and whose eyes are heavy from the strain of months of close application, feels keenly the obligation not to let it go till he has made it as beautiful as his skill will permit. It may be that as a matter of business any further work upon the miniature will not pay. The patron is more than satisfied, and the public is little educated in such matters; so that the artist's reputation would not suffer if he dropped the thing at once. Now dollars and cents are not everything, but they are certainly something; and the painter feels a certain obligation not to neglect them. Besides, while he keeps making scarcely discernible strokes with tiny brushes, his family in the hot city are suffering for the outing which he cannot afford to give them. The tints on his little girl's cheek, as well as the tints in the miniature, have their importance.

Supremacy of Moral Obligations. — We have spoken of the manner in which the moral habits bring together the various departments of character into a unitary whole, harmonizing and controlling the conflicting tendencies. In terms of the feelings of obligation, this means that in the well-developed individual the moral obligations are *supreme*. Where these clash with obligations of other kinds, they are apt to supersede them; where other obligations clash, a moral obligation arises and subordinates them to itself; or, if not, the unity of character in so far breaks down. The moral obligation is thus, in a certain sense, the obligation of the man as a whole; the others belong only to fractions of the man. Take the case of the painter above. He feels the obligations of the artist, the business man, the father of a family. It may be that these will continue to pull and haul him without decisive issue, or until some one overwhelms the others and remains in sole control. But if his is a well-organized personality, something different is likely to happen. His moral sentiments assert themselves, and he feels an obligation in which the others are at once included and subordinated. Some one (or some combination) of the inferior obligations is reënforced at the expense of the rest. Which one is thus distinguished, is a matter which the strength of the original feelings does not ordinarily affect. It is the moral sentiments of the man that decide the issue. It may be, for instance, that the monetary consideration strikes the painter as an ignoble temptation; and that, as far as his family are concerned, if he leaves them the heritage of his fair name, the loss of a summer's vacation is of little concern. He ought to be true to his art. Or he may decide otherwise — that depends upon the man.

Because of this normal supremacy of the moral obligations, they stand in common usage as *the* obligations, without need of qualifying adjective; and the equivalent verb ' ought,' as well as the adjectives ' right ' and ' wrong,' also belong especially to the moral domain.

Separation of Obligations: (1) In Business. — Lack of unity in character, as well as the unnatural dominance of character by one of its inferior aspects, may also be viewed to advantage in its effect upon the feelings of obligation. The division between business, on the one hand, and home, polite society, and religion, on the other hand, is a very common phenomenon. The phrase, ' Business is business,' implying that in this sphere no other than commercial obligations have any weight, is proverbial. Thus, for example, a retail merchant, who in the other relations of life is strictly truthful, and would regard a lie as ungentlemanly as well as immoral, does not hesitate to print lying advertisements of his goods; or, if he does hesitate, it is because he is inclined to think that in the long run truthful advertising brings in better returns. Moral considerations are simply excluded. He would be ashamed, let us say, not to give up his seat to a woman in a crowded street car; but he keeps his clerks, men and women alike, standing for ten hours a day — or, if he gives them a chance to sit, it is pressure upon his pocketbook that makes him do it. At the same time, he would not let his wife assist him in the business in any capacity. Not that he doubts her ability. But she belongs to home and children. And, if business is business, it is none the less true that home is home.

(2) **In Art.** — But perhaps the most striking illustrations of the divided personality and its separate obligations are to be found in the life of the artist, and especially in that of the poet or novelist. 'Art for art's sake' — in this field no other sentiments than those of the beautiful must have any but a subordinate place. If the demands, say, of realistic truth and those of morality seem to clash, morality must be firmly ruled out of the inclosure. Chaucer in his *Canterbury Tales* tells some capital funny stories, certain of which have the defect of being (in many men's opinion, at any rate) shockingly immoral. He himself frankly acknowledges this, but, in his humorous way, insists that he could not have written otherwise. It is, for example, the Miller and the Reeve (in whose mouths two of the stories are placed) that are to blame. These are coarse men; and he but repeats their stories as they told them. In plain prose, he writes only as a due and proper realism demands. If the interests of morality suffer thereby, so much the worse for morality. The interests of art are paramount here.

Now appended to all the best manuscripts of Chaucer's poems is an earnest prayer to the public, not to read these tales. Literary critics of a certain sort have been free to condemn this prayer as a monkish forgery; but so far as we are aware there is no sound reason for doubting its genuineness. Chaucer was a deeply moral man; and however thoroughly, in the enthusiasm of creation, he could persuade

CHARACTER, SENTIMENT, AND VALUE

himself that art is its own sufficient excuse for being, the afterthought could not fail to arise, that human life is far more than art, and that the obligations of the poet are inferior to the obligations of the man.

Compare the case of Scott's *Ivanhoe*. When this romance first appeared, a protest arose from thousands of readers, which has not yet wholly died out, that the hero ought not to have married the lady Rowena but the interesting Jewess Rebecca. In the preface which he published some years later, Scott justified his course in the matter. One would have expected him to urge æsthetic considerations, and no doubt he might have done so. But what he emphasizes is this: that a marriage between the young knight and the Jewess would have been untrue to life, and hence would have tended to give false ideas of the world to many young men and women — perhaps to their moral detriment. Even though, therefore, his story might have been improved, he was unwilling to improve it — at such a risk.

For examples of the dominance of conduct by the æsthetic sentiments (as distinguished from their supremacy within a restricted field), we are accustomed to look to the Italian renaissance. Browning's *The Bishop Orders his Tomb* is a remarkable study of this type. Tennyson's *Romney's Remorse* illustrates a different but closely allied phenomenon — the sacrifice of the closest of personal ties in order to realize more favorable conditions for æsthetic creation.

IV. VALUATION

Orders of Preference. — One noteworthy consequence of the formation of stable sentiments is a certain classification, or rather ordering, of the contents of our world, according to the way in which they are preferred or rejected in comparison with each other. Things and their relations are *good, bad,* and *indifferent;* or, where a more elaborate division takes place, they may be *excellent, very good, good, fair, tolerable,* *poor, bad, very bad, abominable,* etc.; and sometimes even a quantitative scale is developed, according to which one thing is, say, twice as good or three times as bad as another. The so-called ' null-point ' of indifference is fixed by our not caring whether a thing (or a relation) exists or not.

Their Complexity. — There is not merely one such order. The orders are as various as the sentiments themselves. Where a consistent preference is impossible, the things are said not to be comparable. We do not ordinarily try to rank Shakespeare, Beethoven, and Titian, artists though they be; nay, we should hardly try to compare the merits of *Othello* and *Cymbeline,* dramas though they be, and though they contain many elements that may well enough be compared. Nor would we be apt to weigh in the balance one man's courtesy against another man's wit. But the point is too obvious to be insisted upon. At the same time, the multitudinous orders of preference are not *wholly* distinct and independent. There are more comprehensive sentiments which connect them. We have wider as well as narrower standards of comparison. There are occasions when we are called upon to compare courtesy and wit, or even one man's religious orthodoxy with another's bank account; and sentiments are formed by which our choice on such occasions is controlled. So that, after all, the many orders of preference do form one order, though a very ill-defined one; whatever ultimate unity there is being largely due, generally speaking, to the most comprehensive class of sentiments, the moral sentiments.

Valuation and Evaluation. The process by which the objects of our experience are thus grouped and ordered is called *valuation,* and the place which any object takes in the scale is called its *value.* Values are *positive* or *negative,* according as they stand above or below the null-point of indifference, to which the *zero value* corresponds. Valuation is thus something more than merely liking or disliking things, or even than habitual preference. It is the formation of a system of concepts, the concepts of the various grades of valued objects. As a matter of fact, when a man is called upon to assign a given object to its proper place in the scale, — in other words, to form a *judgment of value*, or an *evaluation*, — the process is often a purely intellectual one. He observes that the thing is of a familiar type, which he remembers as being characteristic of objects of a certain grade; and he classifies it accordingly. Not that this is always the case. Sometimes the judgment is inspired by an actual present sentiment. Perhaps most often the judgment is partly dictated by sentiment and partly by external marks. In any case, however, it must not be forgotten that, however large a part purely intellectual processes may play in the particular evaluation, it is only through sentimental feelings that the scale of values, upon which the judgment is based, has itself been built up.

Judgments of these various kinds are familiar to us in all the different spheres of valuation. The marking of an examination paper affords some apt illustrations. This may be done without any sentiment whatsoever — so many per cent off for each mistake. Or the examiner may have in his mind a certain body of facts which he expects each answer to contain; and he may take off so many points for each omission. Every once in a while, however, he may have a feeling that the grade he has given is unjust, higher or lower than it should be; and if this impression is strong enough, he disregards his formal estimate and alters the mark. Or the operation may be guided by active sentiments throughout — not so much a matter of counting as of weighing. Generally speaking, the better the criticism, the more fresh sentiment has gone into it. To trust to general criteria, without spontaneous feeling for the individual case, is to display a low order of judgment.

Obligation and Values. — The relation of valuation to the feelings of obligation is very simple. One ought always to choose the more valuable in preference to the less valuable.

It is an obligation of the merchant to buy as cheaply and sell as dearly as he can; just as it is an obligation of the society woman to cultivate the 'best' people, of the politician to nominate the most popular candidate, of the scholar to devote himself to the most significant problem, and so on. To get less than one might of any kind of good is in so far wrong, and can only be made right by becoming the condition of obtaining a greater value of another kind.

A Condition of the Subordination of Sentiments. — A noteworthy consequence of this relation is that in any complex situation, where one sentiment is subordinated to another, the possible values of the kind appreciated by the lower sentiment must be less than those appreciated by the higher sentiment. Poe, in his account of the writing of *The Raven*, tells us that if any of the earlier stanzas of the poem had turned out "more vigorous" than that which contains the climax, he would " without scruple have purposely enfeebled them." Now if, in the writing of a poem, one's feeling for the beauty of stanzaic rhythm is to be subordinated to the sense of the climacteric effect of the whole, it must be possible to make the poem better by insisting on the climax than it could be made by letting each stanza have its own maximum rhythmical value. This does not necessarily mean that in *every* poetic composition the details ought to be subordinated to the whole — though Poe, indeed, thought so. Sometimes the general structure may be a mere excuse for bringing together the details. What we are urging is simply that *when* the poet is under obligation to subordinate the details, he must be able to make the poem in hand a better poem thereby.

The Range of Moral Values. — This principle applies most strikingly to the most comprehensive sentiments and the supreme obligations: the moral. It means that in any situation the possible moral values are greater than any others *with which they there conflict* — or, if this is not the

CHARACTER, SENTIMENT, AND VALUE 315

case, the moral sentiments fail to perform their proper function. And if (as seems probable) the complexity of human life is such that there is no non-moral value which may not in some situation conflict with a moral value, it follows that for the well-organized individual the moral values are capable of higher degrees than any others.

When different scales of values are combined in one, it is generally to be observed that the highest positive values and the lowest negative values belong together. Greater potentialities of beauty, for example, go with greater potentialities of ugliness. If the best tragedies stand upon a level which comedy cannot reach, the worst tragedies sink to depths of dullness and brutality which the worst comedies cannot approach. And similarly, if good breeding is more desirable than good birth, ill breeding is a greater defect than lowly birth. This applies to the relation of the moral values to all others. Just as, in common estimation, virtue is capable of heights to which no other type of good can be exalted, so vice is capable of depths to which no other type of evil can descend.

V. THE VALUE OF A SUM OF THINGS

Addition of Values. — When the values of a number of things belong to the same scale, and the scale is a quantified one, the value of the collection as a whole is, as a general rule, simply the (algebraic) sum of the values of the several things. This is illustrated by economic values, and, again, by the credit marks on a student's examination paper. Six points in each of ten questions means sixty points on the whole.

Addition generally Impossible. — It is, however, only exceptionally that a scale of values is quantified. It is far more apt to be like a scale of intensities — the scale of the intensities of warmth and cold, for example. The sensations may be arranged in an ordered series, with a null-point of insensibility in the middle. But one warmth cannot be twice as intense as another, or equal to the sum or difference of two others; and it is only very roughly that we can say that a warmth is as intense as a given cold. So it is, we repeat, with most scales of value. One painting is more beautiful than another; but it scarcely makes sense to say that it is twice as beautiful, or that its beauty is equal to the sum of the beauties of two others. We must, then, be careful to avoid the error of assuming that the value of a sum of things is necessarily a sum. It generally is not, even though the values all belong to the same scale.

It is true, indeed, that the value of such a sum is generally greater than the value of any of the particular things; but there are exceptions even to this. The value of Coleridge's poetry would be in no wise diminished if three fourths of his verses had never been written, though none of them are entirely without merit. A very few are so much better than the rest that the latter shrivel into insignificance beside them.

Subordination of Sentiments Involved. — But we are often called upon to value combinations of values of widely different kinds. The young woman that hesitates between two suitors does this. And the distinguished lawyer who hesitates before accepting an appointment to the bench must do this also. Consider some of the factors in the latter situation. As a lawyer he earns ten times the amount of the judge's salary; and this larger income provides many advantages for himself and his family. He is to a considerable extent free in the choice of his interests and activities, while the judge is bound to his calendar. But the appointment is a great honor, and brings with it a great increase of power — power which is attractive both in itself and as a means of public service. Now, of course, either the young woman or the lawyer *may* be carried away by passion, and may choose even without coming to any conclusion as to the comparative merits of the case. But if a conclusion is reached and an

CHARACTER, SENTIMENT, AND VALUE

evaluation is effected, it is obvious that some correlation and subordination of sentiments is involved, such as we have already studied.

Happiness. — In like manner a *whole condition of life* may be recognized as having a value. This value, positive or negative, is called ' happiness ' or ' unhappiness.' (We have in English no word that covers both. In Greek πρᾶξις is used in this sense.) These conceptions involve no new theoretical difficulties; but it is obvious that so complex a synthesis cannot possess any high degree of accuracy. It is often difficult for a man to decide whether he is happy or not, not to speak of deciding how happy or how unhappy. And yet such decisions play an important part in the conduct of life.

The Greatest Happiness. — The ideal of the greatest happiness (*bonum consummatum*) is the combination of all the good things in life, so far as they are compatible with each other; where they are incompatible, the worse being sacrificed for the better. Needless to say, this ideal changes greatly with change of character, and is at all times exceedingly vague. It contains elements of widely different nature, each of which is open to wide variation; for example, physical health, a certain standard of living, affectionate relations with wife and children, social success, a good conscience. Sometimes a single element, such as a woman's love or a great fortune, outweighs all the rest. The man believes that if he had this one thing, nothing else would matter much. Such a valuation (when it persists) is, of course, indicative of a very one-sided character. The normal man includes in his ideal of the greatest happiness a great number and variety of elements. Among these a good moral character is bound to have an important place; for, as we recall, it is the habitual ascendancy of the moral sentiments that is the essential condition of unity of character — that is to say, of the harmonization of one's desires for different things.

The Essentials of Happiness. — Men also form conceptions of what they regard as essential to happiness — that without which they would necessarily be unhappy. These conceptions also vary greatly from man to man. And here again, in the estimation of normal men, a good moral character has an important place. The habitual ascendancy which the moral sentiments have in their minds makes it impossible for them to conceive of happiness with the moral values left out.

VI. Virtue and Happiness

Two Considerations. — On the basis of the above account of the place and function of the moral sentiments, can anything definite be said with regard to the question from which we set out, the question of the sufficiency of morality as a condition of happiness? There are here two distinct considerations to be borne in mind: (1) the relation in which morality stands to the other elements in happiness; and (2) the estimate that is due the moral values as such — the value of a good or a bad conscience.

1. *Indirect Value of Morality*

Immorality Prevents Content. — In the first place, as we have so often had to repeat, the supremacy of the moral sentiments in deciding the issues of life is a general condition of the harmonization and unification of our desires. But where desires are not unified every important choice contains the seeds of disappointment. From this point of view it appears obvious that while the moral man may often be unhappy, the immoral man can scarcely avoid a great deal of unhappiness. He is well-nigh doomed to a deep and abiding discontent.

The Contraction of Life. — We have admitted, to be sure, that in an exceptional case some other class of sentiments (the æsthetic, for example) may perform the work of unification. In such a case, as we have pointed out, the other sides of a man's nature are of necessity starved and stunted. This means, of course, that numerous sources of happiness are cut off. Hence it is probable, that, even though upon the one abnormally developed side an unusual sensibility to its peculiar values may arise, the possibility of happiness on the whole is seriously reduced. At the same time, however, the possibilities of unhappiness are similarly reduced. The man who could not rejoice at a victory does not sorrow at a defeat. From this point of view, then, we cannot say that such an exceptionally immoral man is probably less happy than a moral man. We can only say, somewhat as we would say in comparing a brute and a man, that the former has less capacity for both happiness and unhappiness. What further conclusion is drawn from these premises depends, of course, upon our optimistic or pessimistic attitude toward life in general. If, as a general rule, life is worth living, — if, to point the question, it is better to live the wider life of a man than the narrower life of a brute, — then it is better to be a good man than a mere æsthete.

Effects of Isolation. — A similar conclusion may be reached when we recall to mind what was said in the last chapter with regard to the social significance of morality. Morality, we there found, is an essential condition of social intercourse, and, in particular, of the communication of sentiments, from man to man. Immorality, therefore, means so much isolation, means the being cut off to a greater or less extent from the common interests and occupations of one's fellows. Now in most bad men this undoubtedly gives rise to considerable unhappiness. They cannot help yearning for the society from which they find themselves excluded. In the extreme case of the thoroughly abnormal individual, who cares little for any other society than that of those who share his own narrow interests and who are bound to him through these interests alone — in this extreme case, life simply proceeds upon a smaller scale. A vast multitude of joys and sorrows are alike unfelt. The possibilities of happiness and of unhappiness are reduced together.

The Winning of Sympathy. — There is another consideration, however, that points more decisively to the advantage of the better balanced moral man. The ability to sympathize is a potent means of gaining sympathy. The man whose one-sided development deprives him of interest in his fellows loses their good will and hearty coöperation. Whatever ills come to him, he has the greater chance of bearing their full brunt, even if he escapes active enmity. And however powerful he may be, he cannot compel or purchase the loving consideration upon which many of life's most substantial charms depend.

2. *Direct Value of Morality*

Moral Values as Such. —But aside from the indirect value of morality as a condition for the attainment of the other goods of life, it has a peculiar value of its own, which is appreciated by the moral sentiments themselves. It may be that in *origin* these two kinds of value are closely connected together; but as elements in the happiness of the individual they are so distinct as to require a separate appraisement. Every sane man feels and believes that it is worth something just to be good; and we have to consider how far this condition may compensate for the various ills of life.

Their Relative Magnitude. — Now, in the first place, we are confronted by the fact, that moral values, like values of other kinds, vary on both sides of the null-point of indifference. It is not a single value, or a pair of opposite values, but a whole range of values that we are called upon to place. Sometimes moral teachers have urged that *any* positive moral value, however low in the scale, is greater than any value whatsoever of any other kind. Such a statement does not ring true. It seems to express a species of fanaticism. And when we look for evidence in its support, we find none. For

CHARACTER, SENTIMENT, AND VALUE 321

the plain fact of the matter is that such a comparison as the formula suggests cannot be performed. We have no mental machinery for performing it. What does appear to be true is that (for reasons above given) *in any particular situation* the possible moral values must be greater than any other values with which they come in opposition.

Let us take an illustration. A Jew, walking though a field of grain on a Saturday, feels hungry. To pluck a few ears and thereby satisfy his hunger is a breach of a rule to which a powerful moral sentiment attaches. The question arises whether it is better for him to observe the rule or to eat. But this itself is a moral question. For in order to bring together and compare values of diverse kinds, a more comprehensive sentiment is necessary; and where a moral value is concerned, only a moral sentiment can do this. If the function is usurped by a sentiment of any lower kind, the moral value in question is simply neglected and left out of account. Hence, to return to our illustration, a decision that it is better to eat is equivalent to a decision that in the case in hand the strict observance of the Sabbath would be immoral; and to pluck and eat becomes a moral obligation. The conflict is removed. If, on the contrary, the decision is that it is better to follow the rule, the man's hunger is not thereby stilled and the conflict persists. But the moral value now is not simply that of obedience to the rule. It is that of obedience to the rule despite urgent temptation to break it. The value of right conduct is not only judged to be superior, but it is enhanced by the act of judgment itself, and enhanced in proportion to the conflicting value which is foregone.

General Conclusion. — Putting this conclusion with the former one (as to the indirect effects of morality upon happiness), we may say that morality is an exceedingly important factor in the production of happiness, doubtless the most important; that good men have far greater chances of happiness than bad men. Does this leave no room for individual exceptions? Certainly it does. A man's character in general and his moral character in particular may well be the most important condition of happiness. But there are numberless other contributing factors — all that goes together under the inclusive name of good or evil 'fortune'; and nothing that we have said warrants the conclusion that a good man cannot be unhappy, or a bad man happy. Morality and immorality are matters of degree; and how far either can go in counterbalancing the effects of extraordinary external conditions we have no means of determining with any assurance. We can only say that under *any* external conditions, the better a man is the happier he is at all times likely to be; and in a lifetime of ordinary length the total likelihood amounts to a practical certainty.

A simple illustration may help to make this point clear. The most important conditions for success in agriculture are, let us say, skill and industry in the farmer, a fertile soil, and a fair rainfall. The better farmer with the better farm has every chance of having the better crop. But in any particular year he may not. A stroke of lightning or a spark from a passing engine may undo all his toil. The sciences that deal with human affairs can never make universal predictions that exclude the possibility of exceptions. They must be content, as Aristotle said, to set forth the important general *tendencies* — what is true for the most part (τὰ ὡς ἐπὶ τὸ πολύ). It does not lie within the scope of ethics to guarantee any man happiness.

The Universal Policy. — It is to be observed that the supremacy of moral obligations is not here called in question, any more than the farmer's obligation to cultivate his fields to the best of his ability is called in question when we admit the possibility of the unpredictable and unescapable lightning stroke. We must guide our lives according to that which we expect and by means of that which is within our control. The supreme practical problem is not, *What* *condition, if it were possible, would insure happiness?* but *What mode of conduct is most favorable to happiness?* A supernatural revelation, which promises eventual happiness to all good men, may greatly strengthen the hearts of those who accept it; but it cannot alter the content of a single moral obligation.

The Single Act and the Persistent Character. — In conclusion, there is one ancient and frequently revived misconception that must be noticed. When we ask ourselves whether Regulus was the happier for going back to torture and death at Carthage — whether a less scrupulous man would not soon have soothed the pangs of conscience and lived on in perfect comfort — we should not forget the deeper question: Is it likely that Regulus, being the sturdy patriot that he was, got more or less out of life as a whole than he would have gotten had he been of poorer moral fiber? Had the very traits of character that made it impossible for him to advise his people to their hurt — had these traits throughout his life made him more or less capable of enjoying the glories of that country for which at last he died? It is one thing to say that a particular good act has brought misery upon the doer. It is another thing to say that the persistent character behind the act has on the whole contributed to the man's unhappiness.

REFERENCES

GREEN, T. H., *Prolegomena to Ethics*, Book II, Ch. II.; Book III, Ch. I, 171–179.
STEPHEN, L., *Science of Ethics*, Ch. II, Sects. I–III; Chs. VIII, X, XI.
TAYLOR, A. E., *Problem of Conduct*, Ch. III.
MACKENZIE, J. S., *Manual of Ethics*, Book I.
IRONS, D., *Psychology of Ethics*.
SHAND, A. F., *Character and the Emotions*, in *Mind*, N. S., Vol. V.
STOUT, G. F., *Groundwork of Psychology*, Ch. XVII.
MCDOUGALL, W., *Social Psychology*, Ch. V.
MEZES, S., *Ethics, Descriptive and Explanatory*, Chs. IV, V.

CHAPTER XVI

THE SOCIAL CHARACTER OF SENTIMENTS AND THE OBJECTIVITY OF VALUES

I. INTRODUCTION

The Social Factor in Character Formation. — In the foregoing account of character, sentiment, and value, we have limited ourselves, as far as possible, to the standpoint of individual psychology. We have studied these phenomena as if they pertained to a single mind, leaving out of account the influence of one mind upon another. This was to commit an enormous abstraction, to omit from consideration the very features of the phenomena which are of most illuminating significance. Now an abstraction is not an error; and in every exposition of a complex subject one must begin by an abstraction of one sort or another. But to leave an abstraction unsupplemented is indeed error, and error of the most dangerous kind.

In treating of the development of character, we observed that it is the pleasant or painful consequences of action that determine the formation of an habitual preference; and we noted in passing that the attitude of other men toward the act is one factor that goes to determine whether the consequences are on the whole pleasant or unpleasant. It is the influence of this factor that must now occupy our attention.

Sympathy: Pride and Shame. — Among the various ways in which we may be affected by the feelings of others, there are two which are of especial importance for ethical theory. In the first place, we may *sympathize;* that is to say, when we perceive the situation in which the other persons stand and the outward expressions of their feelings, similar feelings tend to arise in us.[1] It is probable that any feeling whatsoever may in some degree be communicated or strengthened by sympathy, though some are much more communicable than others. In the second place we are sensitive to their expressions of *admiration* (or *respect*) and *contempt* for ourselves, which awaken in us the responsive feelings of *pride* and *shame*. This is not a mere case of sympathy, though sympathy may be involved; because admiration and contempt are very different qualitatively from the pride and humility that are awakened.

II. THE EXCITATION OF SYMPATHY

(1) The Direct-action Theory. — The process by which sympathetic feelings are aroused has been eagerly studied by psychologists and ethicists, and a variety of theories have been offered in explanation of it. Some have held that our inherited psychophysical structure is such that *the perception of the signs of emotion in others directly produces similar emotions in us*. There is no doubt some truth in this. What we sometimes call 'instinctive sympathy' is no doubt thus to be explained. The sympathy which our animal pets show for us must generally be caused in this way; for they can seldom have any notion of the situation in which we stand. It is, however, to be observed that when feelings are thus directly aroused by the expression of others' feelings, the former need not be similar to the latter at all, or, if similar, need not be directed toward the same objects (*e.g.* they may be *reciprocal*). Thus anger may give rise to fear, or to anger against the angry person. A baby that cannot yet understand a single word, and has never in his whole

[1] The student should note that in ethics the word 'sympathy' is used in its etymological significance: to *feel with* another, whether in joy or in grief. It is *not* a synonym for 'pity.'

life been cruelly used, cries when I speak to him in a threatening tone of voice. Thus we see that the direct stimulation of feelings by the expressions of feelings in others may or may not be sympathetic. Instinctive sympathy is thus but one sort of case of a far more general phenomenon — the awakening of emotion by the signs of emotion in others — and is remarkable only for the special circumstance that the stimulus is more or less like the response.[1]

Criticism. — But it is evident that most human sympathy is of a more intricate nature than this. Thus it has been remarked that to see some one angry at some one else, when we are not aware of the cause, has little or no tendency to move us to sympathetic anger. The signs of anger interest us, and we look to see the why and wherefore; but it is only when we have seen the *situation* that we begin to be angry ourselves. And though the signs of deep grief or suffering may easily affect us when we do not understand the occasion, our sympathy is apt to be greatly increased when we are enlightened. On the other hand, when we are unable to perceive any expression of emotion at all, but the situation is one in which we cannot imagine a man existing without his feeling some emotion, our sympathy may be even greater than it would be if his cries of joy or grief were ringing in our ears.

(2) The Substitution Theory. — Now just what part does the knowledge of the situation play in the matter? It has been widely held that in order to sympathize we must ' put ourselves in the other man's place ' — *imagine ourselves enjoying or enduring what he enjoys or endures.* Various evidences have been adduced in support of this theory, and

---

[1] It is much the same with the so-called *instinctive imitation*. The act of pecking in a young chick is aroused in various ways: by the sight of a small moving object; also by the sound of his mother's pecking. When the latter is the stimulus, we call the act imitative, because the chick is doing what its mother does; but the phenomenon is very different from the attentive, discriminating imitation of a child.

the usages of common speech are obviously in accordance with it. "When we see a stroke aimed and just about to fall upon the leg or arm of another person, we naturally shrink and draw back our own leg or our own arm; and when it does fall, we feel it in some measure, and are hurt by it as well as the sufferer. The mob, when they are gazing at a dancer on the slack rope, naturally writhe and twist and balance their own bodies, as they see him do, and as they feel that they themselves must do if in his situation."[1] Furthermore, in so far as lack of experience or the peculiar circumstances of one's life make it difficult or impossible for one to imagine himself in the given situation, sympathetic feeling is greatly weakened. The rich of the third generation — those who have inherited wealth which they have not seen their fathers earn — are seldom charitably inclined.

Criticism. — This theory is a very useful one, because it accords well with the conditions under which sympathetic emotion arises. But it is a misinterpretation of our experience, and careful introspection at once refutes it. It is very seldom indeed that we imagine ourselves in another man's place. We see him struck and we quiver at the blow. But this is not imagination. It is a real quiver, and it is directly aroused by the sight of the blow; and it forms one of the elements into which our perception of the *other man's* experience may be analyzed. We do not first see the blow, then imagine the smart, and then shrink away. We see and shrink; and instead of imagining pain we really feel the disagreeable tension into which our bodies have been thrown. And in so far as imagination enters into the experience it is *his* condition we imagine, not a supposed condition of our own. The sympathetic observer is not thinking of himself at all. To be sure he does feel very much as if he were in the other man's place, but not because he imagines himself there.

[1] Adam Smith, *Theory of the Moral Sentiments*, Part I, Sect. I, Ch. I.

(3) Emotions Arise from the Situations as Such. — However defective this substitution theory may be, it is doubtless right in emphasizing the part that the perception of the situation plays in exciting sympathetic feeling. But the true explanation of the phenomenon is probably much simpler. Our emotions are not in the beginning so self-centered as is often supposed. They attach rather to the situations as such than to ourselves as the center of the situations. We are afraid, let us say, to cross a field where a bull is at large; but the resulting situation is terrible in itself and not simply as *our* situation. Why, then, do we feel it so much more keenly when we ourselves are running the danger? In the first place, we may not. Our terror may be immeasurably less than it would be if it were a wife or child that was in peril. A person in whom we had less interest otherwise would of course give less interest to the situation as a whole;[1] and if the course of our mental development has been such as to make us so self-centered that we are deeply interested in nobody but ourselves, then most assuredly our capacity must be very limited. Even a hearty hatred (if there were no actual anger at the moment) would be more favorable to sympathy than this. But, in the second place, if we do feel greater fear for ourselves, that is largely because when we are the center of the situation, we are generally in a better position to be impressed by it. For example, the nearness of the charging animal, the noise of his hoofs, the sense of his impending bulk, are large factors in our terror of the bull.

Conclusion. — If we are right, sympathy is of two kinds: first, the direct excitation of feeling by the perception of the signs of like feeling in another; and, secondly, the excitation of feeling by the perception of the situation in which another stands. However, in common experience the two kinds of

[1] It must not be forgotten that the person in danger is an essential *part* of the situation. If he were not present, the situation would not exist.

sympathy are not clearly distinguishable. On the one hand, the other man's expressions of feeling help us to comprehend the situation. If he were insensible (or, rather, if we felt him to be insensible), the situation would disappear, just as it would if the man himself were snatched away. On the other hand, to perceive the general situation often helps to fix our attention upon the expressions of feeling, or even causes us to imagine them; and in this way the effect may be greatly heightened.[1]

III. ADMIRATION AND CONTEMPT, PRIDE AND SHAME

Pre-human Origin. — So much for the theory of sympathy. We need speak only briefly of the feelings of admiration and contempt, and pride and shame. These are very ancient feelings. They are, in fact, pre-human in origin, as is shown by their being found in many of the higher animals; with this difference, to be sure, that in the animals they are occasioned only by a narrow range of natural stimuli, while in us they may be awakened by almost anything good or bad with which any one can be associated.

Interrelations. — The four feelings stand in a peculiar rectangular relation to one another. Pride and shame are opposites, and so are admiration and contempt. One feels pride (or shame) on account of the same things in or belonging to oneself, as arouse admiration (or contempt) when they are found in or belonging to another. We are in some degree moved to admiration or contempt for a man by anything connected with him that arouses our feelings of approval or disapproval, *i.e.* that strikes us as being in any way good or bad. Any notable quality of mind or body, any external advantage or defect, will serve. And similarly we are stim-

[1] The above account deals explicitly only with emotion that is felt for another. But it can be applied without difficulty to the stimulation or strengthening of emotion that is felt on one's own account. The cry of fear is itself fear-inspiring; and furthermore it forcibly draws our attention to the particular danger in which we too may stand.

ulated to pride or shame by any such quality or circumstance connected with ourselves.

Furthermore, pride is easily awakened or strengthened by the perception of another's admiration; and this relation also holds between shame and contempt; in fact, in secret concerns, where admiration and contempt are out of the question, pride and shame are seldom intense. Pride might almost be described as the expectation of admiration, and shame as the expectation of contempt. For these and similar reasons it has sometimes been held that admiration and contempt are of earlier origin. It seems, however, that if the one admired or despised were not in some way susceptible to being influenced by the fact, the emotion would have much less excuse for being. The probability therefore is that the four emotions have grown up together. At any rate, they are all far older than humanity.

The Exaggeration of Values. — A point which is of especial importance for ethical theory is this: that pride or shame, when once aroused, reacts powerfully upon our estimate of the thing or quality to which it attaches. To feel pride in anything is to feel its excellence with redoubled intensity; to be mortified because of it is to be doubly conscious of its shortcomings. This does not mean that a man necessarily thinks better of a thing because it is his own. Some men do have a tendency in this direction; but many others show just the opposite tendency. But *any* man thinks decidedly better or worse of a thing through which his self-respect has been flattered or hurt.

IV. THE EDUCATION OF THE SENTIMENTS

Operation of the Social Factor. — It is easy to see how sympathy affects the formation of sentiments. It makes of them not so much individual affairs as common possessions of the social group. Every peculiarly individual tendency to feeling is discouraged. Every tendency that is in accord with the sentiments of one's companions is exaggerated. The effect on each occasion may be slight; but for most men the process is incessant throughout their whole lives, and its shaping influence is not to be escaped.

Similar, but much intensified, is the effect of admiration and contempt.

The Determination of the Environment. — Before the education of the individual begins the sentiments of other men have already done much *to shape and select the environment* in which he is to live and grow. The objects by which he is surrounded have almost without exception been changed or moved in response to some one's valuation. And the human environment, the characters of men and institutions, are tissues of sentiments. The individual's experience is thus from the beginning a select one; and the standards which he forms must be built up from the material with which existing standards have provided him. He cannot choose his world. It has been chosen for him. He may have his peculiar preferences; but their range is limited from the outset by the preferences of others.

The Contact of Tastes. — But even in the environment thus provided the individual's preferences are not due to his inherited constitution alone, or to his own experience of the qualities of men and things. At every turn he has impressed upon him the feelings of his associates. He is constantly the witness of their likes and dislikes, and is moved to sympathetic likes and dislikes himself. And, more than that, the likes and dislikes of others are manifested toward himself and all that is connected with him, and the powerful influence of pride and shame is thus thrown in the direction of the common sentiment.

How Sentiments are 'Communicated.' — We speak elsewhere of the 'communication of sentiments.' The phrase is useful; but from our present standpoint we can see how inexact, or at least compressed, it is. A sentiment is not communicated as a whole. It must grow up in each man under the influence of his associates.[1] An example may be taken from the æsthetic sentiments. There is no direct means by which one man can impart to another his taste in singing. He may sing to him, or take him where songs can be heard; and he can express to him his own varying appreciation of the composition and rendering. And when the pupil asks for a song or criticizes it, or (better still) sings it or composes it himself, the teacher can express his approval or disapproval of the choice, the criticism, the performance, the creation. In this way the pupil grows into the likeness of his master, and becomes, as we say, a typical member of his 'school.' If such a process as this is fairly to be called the 'communication' of sentiments, we may let the phrase stand. At any rate we have no right to mean anything more by it.

Analogy of the Concept. — The like is true of the communication of concepts, and the analogy may perhaps again be of service to us. No man can directly impart a concept, whether it be the concept of a particular thing or of a type of things. All that can be done is to provide a certain environment and to direct attention to the important features of the resulting experience. The organization of images into concepts is a process the necessity of which in each individual mind cannot be obviated, though by appropriate suggestions it can be spared many useless deviations. This is the essential function of the teacher. And yet, limited as this function at each moment appears, its gross results

[1] In the last two chapters we have given two strikingly different accounts of the function of morality. First it was the essential condition of social unity; then it was the essential condition of unity of character. We can now understand how these two functions are combined. It is through social intercourse that the human personality grows. The rupture of that intercourse on any side means inevitably an arrested development on that side — either malcoördination or downright atrophy. Hence it is that only the supremacy of the moral sentiments can insure a well-rounded personality.

are very great. The little boy of two does not even recognize a policeman; and yet some day he and his father may be gravely discussing such topics as the attitude of socialism toward the institution of private property!

Individual and Social Differences. — In what we have said we must not be understood to imply that individual differences in sentiments (or in concepts) do not exist among members of the same social group. They do, of course, as we are all well aware. But where men's sentiments have been formed by the same tradition, the greatest individual differences are small, compared with differences that are common between representatives of different traditions. A lover of Wagner and a lover of Meyerbeer may fancy themselves at opposite poles of the musical world; but, if so, they little know how wide that world is. They are next-door neighbors when it comes to a comparison with a Japanese critic. Yes, and greatly as the Japanese musicians may differ among themselves they will all look alike to the student from Paris or Vienna; they are so far away that they show but as a single point. The differences within the limits of a common musical tradition (like the differences within a common religion) appear striking to us, because they bring us into active opposition with one another. But, as a matter of fact, it is only because there is a large fund of sentiments shared between us that opposition is possible. And besides, when we seek to compare individual differences with social differences we must not forget a point that is emphasized in another chapter: that there are societies upon societies within societies. The lover of Wagner and the lover of Meyerbeer, who cleave to the one and despise the other, *may* very well have had characteristically different individual bents from the start. But though they are both inheritors of a common European tradition, the family and local influences under which they have been brought up will probably account for most of the contrast between them.

Social Character of the Sentiments. — The consequence is that it is possible to give a connected and intelligent account of the analysis and development of important classes of human sentiments without paying any attention to individual peculiarities at all — except, perhaps, to brand them as peculiarities and set them aside as of no interest to the discussion. In such an account the individual is not regarded as a *cause;* he appears only as a more or less typical *illustration* of social conditions. There is inevitable inexactness, no doubt, in this sort of procedure. The individual *is* a cause, as well as an illustration. But every large view must be had at the cost of inaccuracy of detail; and our natural human interest in striking personalities is so great, that the danger that lies in overlooking the importance of individual differences is far less likely to be serious than the danger of overestimating them.

For, indeed, a developed sentiment is almost beyond individual control. It seems so impalpable, so shadowy a thing, that many a bold innovator has thought that he could banish it at a word. But his words and his blows and his tears leave scarcely a trace upon it. The chances are that in his own heart of hearts, in depths of his nature beyond his introspection, he is as much subject to it as any one; and in some sudden crisis he is astonished at his ' weakness.' He believes, let us say, in free love — is outraged at the thought of a legal or religious marriage. But despite himself he makes an exception of his daughter's case, and feels surprisingly relieved when she is united in the conventional way to the young man of her choice.

Summary. — To resume: Among the factors which go to determine the development of character and sentiments, the feelings of one's associates have a commanding place. Sentiments are not directly communicated; but by means of sympathy and the excitation of pride and shame they are constrained to develop in each individual in general conformity with the sentiments of those around him. They thus present the appearance of being a social rather than an individual function.

The Moral Sentiments. — In all this no special mention has been made of the moral sentiments. This was by design, with the thought that by not referring to them in particular we might emphasize the fact that in these respects there is nothing peculiar about them. For they, too, are 'communicated' by the instrumentality of sympathy, reënforced by pride and shame; and the uniformity of sentiment that results is so great that it has often been explained as due to inborn human nature. If the moral sentiments call for any special remark, it is that they exhibit the social control of sentiment-formation at its *highest intensity*. The suggestions are, as a rule, more frequent and more forcible than in any other department, especially during the formative period of life. The moral character of each individual is constantly finding expression in action by which the attention of his companions is attracted, and their approval or disapproval aroused; and hence any divergence from the accepted type stands the greater change of being promptly suppressed.

V. THE OBJECTIVITY OF VALUES

Values as Relative to the Individual. — We must now look to see what effect the social nature of the sentiments has upon valuation in general and upon moral valuation in particular. In our previous treatment, we have looked upon values as relative to the individual character. As habitual preferences are formed, the objects of preference are sorted out and given a serial order; and their place in the series is their value. To be very good is to belong to a type that has been ranked high; to be excellent is to belong to a type that has been ranked still higher — the ranking being a function of the individual consciousness. From this point of view, what is good with reference to one man may well be bad with reference to another, not because of any difference in its effects upon the two men, but because of some difference in their character-development. Now this view is not wholly false, and we shall have occasion to return to it; but it needs serious supplementation.

Values as Relative to the Society. — Since, despite individual variations, sentiments are, in the main, social functions, it follows that values are, in the main, relative not to individuals but to societies. Polite and impolite, beautiful and ugly, just and unjust, cheap and dear, are not subject to personal desires — even though, of course, if *all* personal desires were taken away the values would be gone also. They are *superindividual*, and hence *objective;* that is to say, they stand to each man as a reality outside himself, by which his judgments may be criticized as *true* or *false*. His own subjective scale of values is, so far as it *is* his own, regarded as a mere representation (which may be more or less accurate) of the real values of things. That he congratulates himself upon his deportment may not prevent his being utterly 'impossible'; that he adores Meyerbeer does not prove that that composer was a genius; that he condemns the acquisition of California may still leave it an amply justified piece of statecraft; and his satisfaction with his new suit of clothes may simply indicate how thoroughly he was cheated.

Are Values Subjective or Objective? — We are thus brought to the consideration of one of the good old paradoxes that has formed the staple of so much controversy, popular as well as learned. From one point of view nothing seems more obvious than the subjectivity of values. "There's nothing either good or bad but thinking makes it so" — is not this true? "There's no disputing about tastes" — has not that become proverbial? And yet the very fact that men *do* dispute about tastes is sufficient to prove that

THE SOCIAL CHARACTER OF SENTIMENTS

there is another side to the question. When some one says that the Bay of San Francisco is beautiful, he is recording, to be sure, an individual impression. But he means to do more than that. He means to say that the bay *is* beautiful, no matter what you or I may think about it — yes, no matter though he himself had not had the sense to appreciate it. He means that its beauty is a *fact*, as palpable as the fact that the waters of the bay are salt. And hence if this fact is denied he insists upon it, and even endeavors to prove it.

The case of economic values illustrates the general problem very well. Has a thing a real value, independent of what its owner can get for it, or is such a ' real value ' an idle abstraction? On the one hand, an affirmative answer seems necessary, because, if there is no real value, how can we ever speak of a price as being too high or too low, or of a market as being inflated or depressed? Or consider the case of a manuscript ascribed to Oliver Cromwell and easily salable for several hundred pounds. A prying expert notices that the loop of a certain letter is such as Cromwell never made, and proves the manuscript to be the work of a humble secretary; and its market price drops to a few shillings. Was not the manuscript really worth exactly as much before as after the discovery? — But, on the other hand, if there were not, and never would be, any demand at all for an article, it would surely have no economic value. And things surely do rise in value as the demand for them increases.

Is there a real beauty, or is the beauty of a thing only what men take it to be? Is there a real moral good or evil, or are these too only projections of men's fancy? When this last question is boldly put, the full import of the controversy comes into view. Morality is a species of value for which men are not seldom called upon to sacrifice wealth and reputation and health and life. Now if they become convinced that it was merely subjective, heroic resolution or even ordinary right living would become impossible. To be sure, if the moral values were illusory, there would be the same reason for regarding every other kind of value as illusory. But, in the first place, men never *can* bring themselves to a complete skepticism of values; and when the higher kinds lose their appeal they simply yield it to the lower. And in the second place, in so far as values of every kind are rejected, and the individual reverts (in this respect) to the condition of his earliest infancy, there still remain the inhibiting power of pain and the attractive power of pleasure, which precede and underlie the whole development of valuation. Men need to believe in a something beyond themselves; they need an external support upon which to stand. Turn thoughts and efforts inward, and they are dissipated in the melancholy hedonism of the grown infant.

Reconciliation. — Now, if our view of the social nature of sentiment is correct, the escape from all this difficulty lies in observing that the issues as thus presented are not clear. It is not *fair* to ask whether values, economic or moral or what you please, are relative to human feeling or objectively real. They are both. The question would not be wholly fair even if human sentiments were not essentially social. For, even so, a man's formed character is a pretty stable organization; and to be relative to that means something very definite. Even if tastes did differ as endlessly as has sometimes been supposed, it remains a very real quality of the object that it can win A's approval and cannot win B's. It is a quality that at least reaches out beyond the individual's momentary impulse and includes his past and future, so long as his character (in the relevant respect) remains substantially unchanged.

But, we repeat, when the social nature of valuation is considered, the alternative between objective reality and relativity to human feelings is doubly unsound. For here the standard of reference transcends the character of the individual as such, and is measurably independent of the most radical changes in his tastes and preferences. It is the character of the society that fixes the distinction between good and evil; and this, for the individual, throughout the whole course of his life, makes it for most intents and purposes an objective distinction. The ugly girl does not simply seem ugly. She is ugly; and the thought that in various foreign climes she might be greatly admired does nothing to mitigate the awful fact. A comedy that fails is a failure. The poet cannot (as Lamb suggested) " write for antiquity." And though remodeling the truth is a polite art in Canton and Singapore, it is plain lying nearer home.

Apparent Skepticism. — The dependence of values upon the sentiments prevalent in a society is generally not present to men's consciousness. So long and so far as the society remains unitary and the sentiments remain substantially unanimous, the values are looked upon as self-subsistent. Even an economic value, when it has persisted for some time, seems to be no product of human demand, but a part of the established order of nature. And when divisions and dissensions arise, they are very commonly settled in each man's mind by his identifying his own standards with the objectively real ones, and condemning the standards of his adversaries as false; or, if modesty and a due sense of human fallibility forbid, both standards are confessed to be probably more or less false, and the true standard remains in the unknown, perhaps unknowable, beyond. In either case, the independence of values from all relativity to human feeling, whether individual or social, is not called in question. Hence when the notion of such a relativity does come to men's minds, it is only natural that it should present itself as a sort of skeptical disillusionment — as if no value that did not transcend all human preferences could possibly be real.

VI. The Function of the Élite

Values Relative to the Élite. — But there are certain important facts with regard to social standards, of which due account has yet to be taken. Society, as we have so often repeated, is not a simple organization; and as civilization advances it becomes increasingly complex. But this means that it may contain, and, indeed, as a rule it does contain, a diversity of traditions and a conflict of sentiments upon every important subject. This is glaringly evident in the case of the division of classes, with their characteristically different notions of honor and propriety. It is evident, too, in the divisions of creeds and parties and æsthetic cults. And there are innumerable minor divisions, the traditions of family, school, office, etc., etc. To say, therefore, that it is the sentiments of the society that fix values is not a sufficient statement. Each value is fixed by the sentiments of a *select society*, a body of *élite;* and to recognize this value as a true one is at the same time to recognize this body of élite as being the proper and competent judge of the matter. (If an individual is thus distinguished, it is generally as a representative of his class or coterie.)

Relation of the Élite to the Larger Society. — This is no more than must needs follow from the acceptance of values as objective facts. To believe the fact is to credit the witness. On the other hand, the observation that we do credit some men as being better judges than some others is often accepted as conclusive proof that values cannot have a subjective reference. For if values depended on the judge — it is said — how could one judge be better than another? Each would simply be right in his own opinion. It should be noticed, however, that when the limits of a common social tradition are left behind — as, for example, in the comparison of Japanese and European painting — the subordination of judges stops; a *double standard* of excellence is recognized.

When, say, a Parisian critic sets himself the task of learning to appreciate the Japanese art, his problem is substantially this: to initiate himself into the tradition of the cultivated Japanese public — to grow into their likeness, that he may perceive and respond even as they do. It is *only within a larger social organization* that a select society can occupy its favored position as a superior court. It acts (to use the old simile) *as an organ* of the larger society, performing its critical function with far greater efficiency by reason of its special adaptation, but performing it always within, and with reference to, the society as a whole.

Have the Élite Extraordinary Faculties? — In what consists the superiority of the élite? It is not easy to reply. Sometimes an exclusive circle has attributed the superiority which they profess to a peculiar endowment of sensibility or extraordinary faculty of intelligence — as in the case of the mutual-admiration society of the Romanticists in Germany. But though men of this stamp are confident of their own distinction, and though they often impose on the general public for a time, their standing is insecure, and they soon fall into contempt. Now, to be sure, it may seem to be abstractly possible that such a body of men are right in their estimate of themselves. But if this is the case it will nevertheless be impossible for us to take account of it in our theory. For we, like the rest of the academic world, are plain workaday folk, not singular beings with peculiar feelings. So, even if the singular beings are right, we have no means of verifying the fact. And an unverifiable fact might as well be no fact at all. Consequently, for the purposes of science, it is an inevitable working assumption that the exclusive circles are wrong, and the ultimate popular judgment right. The men who sincerely claim to have extraordinary faculties must be set down as self-deceiving charlatans. Besides, there is always this to be said: in so far as these men *are* singular, their singularity sets them apart from us, makes them to all intents and purposes foreigners in our midst. They are not part of our society, and hence cannot function as our élite.

They are Well Developed. — But if this be so, what can constitute the superiority of the true élite? If, just as the only facts worth talking about are generally verifiable facts, so the only values worth talking about are generally appreciable values, then is not everybody of the élite? No, because few men are what they might be. The élite have been fortunate in a special *development* of powers which originally were no more remarkable than those of many humbler men. They have had an education beyond the common lot of their fellows. They represent in actuality what in others has remained only a half-developed germ. That is why they can speak for the society as a whole. They *are* the society at its best.

Let us take a concrete instance. There exists at the present time a comparatively small body of men who believe that an offensive war is never justifiable. They do not base this belief on any special intuition of their own. They do not claim to possess an experience of moral values which none of the rest of us can ever know. On the contrary, they attribute their peculiar belief to the fortunate circumstances of their own upbringing, that has made them feel what others have not yet felt. And they believe most heartily that in the course of time all men of sound mind will come to feel as they do; so that their judgment, which now to most men seems so extreme, will be a commonplace. Now a position like this is worth considering. The pacificists may be wrong; but at least they have not condemned themselves in advance. They are such as the true élite might well be.

How are the Élite to be Recognized? — But how are we, from the impartial standpoint of the outsider, to determine whether the pacificists have indeed reached a higher morality or no? Answer plain and short: *there is no impartial standpoint* except that of ignorance. I either think with the pacificists or against them, or I know not what to think. In no case is there any absolute test by which I can get behind myself and them.

The Test of Time. — There is, indeed, an ulterior test; but it does not lie within our volition to apply it. It is the test of time. If the pacificists are right, and it is true that they represent a grade in advance in the general evolution of morality, the actual progress of that evolution itself may be counted on to confirm that judgment. At any rate, there is no other possibility of an impersonal confirmation.

Its Wide Application. — The test of time, which we cannot apply, but which is forever applying itself, is familiar in all departments of life. At that recent auction of old books was too high a price paid for the First Folio of Shakespeare? Not if at future auctions as high a bid is reached. Is Browning or Tennyson the greater poet? Leave the question to the year 2000. Is the Emperor William a great man? That is for future historians to say.[1] The test is perhaps of rarest but most profound significance in the sphere of morals. There it is the appeal of martyrs of all degrees, who look beyond the petty inflictions or the greater torments which the judgment of their own day visits upon them, to

---

[1] In the discussion of particular examples the student must be careful to make allowance for several considerations which lie outside the scope of our argument. (1) Things are constantly changing in value by reason of changed conditions, without any change in the standards of value themselves. Our interest is in the *standards*. (2) Valuations of things are constantly changing by reason of improved knowledge of them and of their effects — again without change in the standards. One reason why we must postpone judgment on the character of William is that the facts are not all in, or, if in, are not yet arranged and systematized and thus made available for our judgment. What we have to note is that even when all this has been accomplished, his place in history will not be definitely fixed. The development of the standards themselves may still exalt or degrade him to a degree which we can at present scarcely imagine.

the heartfelt approval of the time to come. For even the deeply religious minds, that look only to a hereafter where God is the supreme judge, expect a *public* vindication. They would scarcely be content with the thought that their fellow-saints should continue to condemn them throughout all eternity.

There are, of course, values which the future is left no part in determining. That is because the standards upon which they are based are themselves consciously restricted to the present. What seems fashionable now, is fashionable. Next year has nothing to say about it. For though a year hence the thing may no longer be fashionable, it will remain true to the end of time that it *was* fashionable to-day. Yet even here there are limiting cases where the test of time does apply. The perfection of fashion is that which just outruns, and hence can hope to guide, the prevailing mode. The most distinguished success, therefore, involves a certain anticipation, a certain risk, which a brief lapse of time can alone altogether justify.

Is the Test Superficial? — But why should we thus be dependent on time for the sanction of our judgments? Why should the future know more than we? On the face of it the test of time seems superficial and unfair, to say the least, and in theory we are sometimes tempted to reject it; but in general practice we constantly fall back upon it with the utmost confidence. Is our confidence justified, or is the test as superficial as it appears?

Historical Continuity of Society. — The answer to this question depends upon the fact that the society to which values are relative is not a creature of to-day alone, but embraces a past, and looks forward to a future which will be what the past and the present have made it. In a word, it has had, and will have, a *history*. The society of to-day, considered apart from all this history, is an abstraction, a mere *temporal cross section* of the real society; for the real society has a temporal as well as a spatial extension. The acceptance of a value as objectively real implies that it is real for the society as a whole, comprehending its past and its future. The older generations may not have been sufficiently developed to appreciate it; the future generations may be so much farther developed as to have a much richer and fuller appreciation than our own. But the former needed only the further development of the sentiments they possessed, not any extraneous addition; and the latter, though they may feel more than we, will never give our feelings the lie — if the value in question is indeed real.

Consider, for example, the moral value of such conduct as that of Abraham Lincoln in the reëstablishment of the federal power in the South. The general opinion among intelligent men throughout the world, then as now, has been that he followed the only course honorably open to him; that it was his paramount duty to maintain the Union, even as he did. A very different view, however, is occasionally met with. It is held that 'to maintain the Union' is a misleading name for Lincoln's policy, and that the war was essentially a war of conquest. The Confederate government, it is urged, was an accomplished fact. All the law and order that existed south of the Potomac was its law and order. Its legislatures and its courts, its administrators of high and low degree, and its armed forces were alone there. What Lincoln did was to send hundreds of thousands of soldiers into a peaceful country, bringing with them untold havoc and desolation, in order to bring it into subjection. So, we repeat, a few critics believe as against the almost universal opinion to the contrary. Now it is no part of our purpose to discuss whether this criticism of Lincoln's conduct is valid. Our concern is only to ask what it would mean for it to be valid. And we answer that if it be valid it must express even now the inevitable outgrowth of our deepest convictions, which our past history has securely implanted in us; and that, for this reason, it is bound to spread among thoughtful men and eventually to become an established judgment.

Historical Continuity and the Objectivity of Values. — As we now perceive, the test of time is anything but superficial. *The passing of this test is an essential part of what the possession of value means.* As the élite within a given society function, in the pronouncing of their judgments, as representatives of the whole society, even so the present society, and in particular its élite, functions in its judgments as a representative of the society's past and future. It is *the historical continuity of the development of the sentiments* that gives to values the objective character of reaching out beyond the limits of the present, just as it is sympathy that gives to them the objective character of reaching out beyond the experience of the particular individual.

The Breach of Continuity. — What happens when the historical continuity is broken? In strict literalness, of course, this does not occur. Society, like nature, makes no leaps. But just as in the history of the earth's fauna there are periods of revolutionary change, during which the old monarchs of the earth and sea and air are swept away, and their places are taken by the descendants of animals which occupied a much humbler place in the scale; so there are revolutions in human sentiment, so profound and so far-reaching, that the new age exhibits the most striking contrast to the old, exalting much that was despised and despising much that was exalted. And again, even when no single startling revolution has occurred, the slow course of imperceptible modifications may bring about total changes of the utmost magnitude; so that as the later society looks back upon the earlier it finds many of its ideals utterly foreign. In such a case the older values are viewed much as are the values that obtain in foreign societies of one's own day. Their objective character is lost, and they present themselves as mere reflections of the changing sentiments of men. It becomes a distinct problem for the critic to find his way back to the ancient modes of thought and feeling — to make himself an ancient, as it were — in order that he may be able to form a just judgment of the ancient deeds and works.

Historical Position of the Élite. — The distinguishing mark of the true élite is that they are closer than the mass of society to the past and the future of society. Because they often rate very low some things which the mob rate very high, they are often regarded as narrow men. It is, on the contrary, the breadth of their sympathies, the catholicity of their appreciations, that makes them what they are. Not all change is progress, or even decadence. Much of it is aimless fruitless fluctuation. The petty changes of fashion are of this sort — little eddies upon the surface of the great current of tradition. The élite, in so far as they are properly to perform their representative function, must be too deep for fashion to touch, moved only by the larger trend.

VII. ABSOLUTE VALUES

Absolute Values as Limits. — In relation to the evolution of human sentiments, the notion of a real, objective value of things takes on a new significance. If sentiments were uniform and changeless, the values which they recognize would be indisputably real. When sentiments are found to be discordant and changeful, real values seem to exist only with reference to the particular phase of the particular society. But the conception of an evolution of sentiments provides for real values in the further sense of the *ideal limits* toward which the actual evaluations of things are indefinitely tending. Such limits may be called *absolute values*.

Have They a Real Existence? — But is it a fact that there are any definite limits toward which actual values tend? Is there a system of absolute values? We have no evidence that makes this probable. If we try to trace the history of any kind of value, we find the continuity of the development constantly broken into through the influence of new valuations of other sorts, and ultimately by new physical conditions. A religious revival may inaugurate a new school of comedy, which may profoundly influence the standards of polite manners. The exhaustion of a source of metal supply may cause a change in economic conditions, which has its effect on morality and taste. And if we try to conceive of a development of the whole system of values, comprehending them all in all their interrelations, it simply passes our comprehension. We do, indeed, find certain progressive differences, which, despite innumerable exceptions, hold generally as between savagery and civilization. But these are far from sufficient to constitute a unitary development; and if they were sufficient, we have no reason to suppose that the process would have a definite and final limit. At the same time we must admit that if there *were* a unitary development of the system of values, it would be upon so vast a scale that we might well be utterly unable to detect it, much less predict its course.

Regulative Use of the Conception. — However, the question whether there is an ultimate goal to the evolution of values in general or of any particular kind of values is not of any great significance. Few, if any, unanswerable questions are significant. Our use of the conception of the goal or limit is (as logicians say) *regulative*. It helps us to analyze and comprehend the particular periods of evolution that interest us. For to single out any particular period as a distinct object of inquiry is to treat it *as if it were* somehow complete in itself; and that means that it must be conceived as having a certain end of its own. If the evolution lies wholly in the past, we pick out some phase which seems to us especially typical or significant, and treat the whole process as the evolution *of that phase*. We write of the evo-

THE SOCIAL CHARACTER OF SENTIMENTS

lution of English tragedy, and close with *King Lear;* of the evolution of the French monarchy, and close with Louis XIV; of the evolution of German philosophy, and close with Hegel and Schopenhauer. The commonest terminus is of course the present state of things. The evolution of the orchestra is the evolution of the orchestra of Richard Strauss and Debussy. The evolution of American politics is the evolution of the politics of Bryan and Roosevelt, Murphy and Barnes. But often the development presents itself to us in the light of a story whose plot is not yet worked out; and we figure to ourselves as well as we can what the outcome of the story is bound to be. In such a case the anticipated outcome is thought of as rounding off the evolutionary process, just as in other cases the present or past outcome is thought of. It would ill suit the ends of our imperfect thinking to be always endeavoring to think of the processes of evolution as infinite in scope and duration. We are bound to take it in periods, and to regard each period in turn as if its conclusion were indeed a logical stopping place.

Now as applied to the evolution of values this means that it is often necessary for us to think of values as if they were absolute. They are, so to speak, absolute *for us*, bounding our field of vision as effectually as if there were indeed nothing beyond. We believe, for example, that under civilized conditions slavery is morally wrong. We are perfectly ready to trace the evolutionary movement by which this conviction arose in ourselves and in others like us, until it became practically universal. But here, so far as our present outlook is concerned, the evolution ceases. It has come to a full stop. The evilness of slavery is absolute matter-of-fact, as plain and clear as $2+2=4$. We say, perhaps, make a lip confession of the fallibility and mutability of human judgments, but this does not imply the least skepticism as to the ultimate truth of our own creed.

VIII. Historical Continuity

Let us now observe more closely the nature of that *historical continuity* upon which, as we have said, rests in part the kind of objectivity which values in general possess.

Its General Meaning. — When anything of an organic nature is subjected to influences that tend to modify it, it does not yield to those influences with equal readiness in all its parts and functions. It yields first in its more superficial features; that is to say, generally speaking, in its more recently acquired features, that have not yet been intricately interwoven with others, and upon which still later developments have not yet been based. It yields where it can yield with the least disturbance of its constitution as a whole. The modification follows, as we say, the 'path of least resistance.' Only when a superficial change does not suffice to restore a stable equilibrium does the change strike deeper and deeper; and only the most extraordinary and persistent exigencies can disturb its most ancient and fundamental traits. This is what is meant by 'continuity.'

Illustrations. — It would lead us too far afield to attempt to illustrate this conception in all the various fields in which it is applicable. Let a few examples suffice: (1) Some sentimentalists have suggested that the course of evolution might perhaps some time do away with the distinction of sex. According to the principle of continuity, no change could well be more improbable. The distinction of sex has existed from the very origin of the many-called forms of animal life. *Anything* will go sooner than that. (2) Similarly, in social evolution, the abolition of private property is almost inconceivable. But private property in land is comparatively recent, and under long and severe stress might go. Franchises for the operation of various public utilities are still more recent, and might easily go. (3) The history of science exhibits a similar continuity. When a strange

THE SOCIAL CHARACTER OF SENTIMENTS 351

phenomenon is observed, which contradicts our preconceptions, we make room for it most grudgingly, giving up as little of our old ideas as possible. An investigator exhibits test tubes containing low forms of animal life, and declares that the test tubes were carefully sterilized after being hermetically sealed. Ninety-nine out of a hundred of us declare that the sealing must have been faulty, or the sterilization insufficient. It is easier for us — it requires a less profound unsettling of our conceptions — to suppose that the investigator is incompetent, than to admit that fresh living matter can originate in a test tube. Sometimes, to be sure, the readjustment of ideas has to go pretty deep; as when the conception of permanent species of organisms was given up; or as when the phenomena of radioactivity compelled the admission that the chemical atom is not absolutely undecomposable. But in such a case the evidences must be overwhelming, and they are subjected to the most critical tests; and, if these tests are passed, all manner of compromises are tried before the radical explanation is accepted as necessary.

Continuity in Changes of Valuation. — Now this same continuity obtains in the realm of values. In the standards of good manners, only a little change would be necessary to make it proper to drink soup from the tip of the spoon, or to keep one's hat on in an elevator; for not much else would be affected. Such changes take place constantly. But to make it proper for women to smoke in public, much more is required. Smoking has long been taboo to the sex. A host of associations and prejudices have clustered about it, that tend to keep it so. If women are to smoke in public it must involve a widespread movement among women to break the bonds of their ancient taboos. This movement must itself be in the first instance unfashionable. Smoking might then be symbolic — like the red necktie of the socialist. By the time it was good form for women to smoke on the streets, our most deep-seated notions of seemly relations between the sexes might well be changed. Men might no longer be doffing their hats or resigning their seats or assuming petty burdens.

Application to Moral Values. — We need not delay longer with preliminary examples. We know that the principle is universal in its application; and we have already considered its significance for the general theory of values. What we have now to consider is its special significance in relation to moral values, by reason of the fundamental and comprehensive character which these values possess.

In the last two chapters we dwelt at some length upon the function of the moral habits in unifying character and in facilitating social intercourse. In view of the facts there laid down, we can see that an alteration of moral values can hardly occur without far-reaching effects. The organizing force being shifted, the organized material must needs undergo a notable rearrangement.

The Standard of Veracity. — What would be the effect if we were no longer to hold it wrong to tell a lie to a stranger? We are not without grounds upon which to base a reply. There are peoples among whom a lie to a stranger is considered quite innocent. These peoples do not stand high in the scale of civilization. They are incapable of any complex form of social organization. Their industrial and commercial policy is of the crudest. Their religion is limited to local and family cults. Scientific procedure is unknown to them. It is not hard for us to see why this must be the case. If the stranger, as such, is to be deceived at will, so also he is not to be trusted. No alliance with him can be more than temporary, and all the maxims of tribal craft must turn on the expectation of treachery; credit is so narrowly restricted that the standards of good business, as we conceive it, are incomprehensible; the stranger's god is suspected and feared as the stranger is. How impossible science must be without the sentiment of universal veracity we can see from the importance with which the duty is invested by scientific men to-day. Many of them hold it in a religious, not to say superstitious, reverence.

If, now, we look at the reverse process — the process by which actually our ideal of veracity has arisen, we see at once that it must have been impossible except as an essential part of the whole development of civilized society. There are, to be sure, many uncivilized peoples who regard a lie as intrinsically shameful. But, indeed, these are almost as far from the conception of the civilized 'man of honor' or merchant or scientific investigator, as the peoples who regard the lie as innocent, especially if told to a stranger. For observe how different these civilized men are from each other. The man of honor will die rather than be guilty of a falsehood for his own benefit; but he will lie without scruple in order to protect the honor of a friend. The merchant's word is for him the entering into of a contract. For him the highest praise is that 'his word is as good as his bond.' If he was honestly mistaken in his statement, that does not release him from it; he must make his word good. Moreover, he feels a certain obligation, if not to tell the whole truth, at least not to endeavor to conceal any part of it. The man of science cannot make his word good if it was not good. He is bound not only to absolute veracity, but to the utmost care in making his observations and in verifying the reports of others. He must set down with the same fidelity the fact that contradicts as the fact that confirms his theory. In the presence of the truth, friendship counts for nothing. And he is bound, so to speak, to advertise the faults of his goods.

Continuity of Moral Evolution. — Now, we say, the development of such standards as these cannot be a thing apart. The development of the integrity of the cavalier's, the merchant's, the scientist's integrity is inseparable from the development of chivalry, of commerce, and of science. And for that reason, we repeat, the process must be slow; and, what is more, it must be gradual. Our moral sentiments, upon which the unity of individual and social life depends, cannot vary without manifold and extensive consequences; and hence in them the continuity of history is exhibited in an especial degree.

This is the form which the dogma of 'eternal and immutable morality' takes for us to-day. For the men who framed that dogma there was no alternative between absolute fixedness and unrestricted change. The only universality of which they could conceive was an abstract identity of type. We have learned of another sort of universality, which admits of degrees, and into which change enters as a factor. And this sort of universality we recognize as belonging to moral values as to no others within the compass of our knowledge.

IX. INDIVIDUAL DIFFERENCES

They must be Admitted. — And now let us return to the individual differences which we have so long neglected. That there are marked individual differences in men's valuations of things is as evident as the fact that men differ in character; or rather these are but two aspects of the same fact. Grant that sentiments are, in the main, social functions, — just as concepts are, in the main, social functions, — it remains true that sentiments, like concepts, vary almost without assignable limit, from man to man, within the given society.

Their Character. — But let us not exaggerate. The individual is not capable of developing by himself any type of valuation that is radically different from that which obtains among his associates. The differences which he exhibits are for the most part not strictly personal, but belong to the narrower social circles in which he has grown up — as we remarked a while ago in speaking of the lover of Wagner and the lover of Meyerbeer. The strictly personal differences are: (1) differences in elementary (congenital) susceptibility to pleasant and unpleasant excitation; (2) exaggerations and minimizations of accepted values, due to such differences in elementary susceptibility; (3) arrested development in one or another direction, due to a more thorough lack of feeling; and in some few directions, perhaps, (4) a further development of the customary valuations — though it is only a very little way that even the greatest genius can go by himself, without sympathy from some source. All told, the individual differences that we find are such as may be described as *divergences from a type*. The most striking peculiarities are the cases of arrested development.

Are Values for the Individual Real Values? — Well, then, such as they are, what are we to say of the individual differences? Are things, or are they not, really good, when some man finds them good; and are they, or are they not, just as good as he finds them? Grant that other men judge differently, is not his valuation as much of a standard as any one's else, or as all men's else, so far as he is concerned? And if a thing pleases him, does it not just as truly please him though all the rest of the world are pained by it? And if it displeases him, what does it matter if everybody else is charmed by it?

In questions like these there are generally implied two misconceptions which must be removed before a fair direct answer can be given.

In the first place, the last two sentences are probably guilty of the common hedonistic confusion between pleasantness (and unpleasantness) and value. It is not the isolated feelings as such, but organized sentiments, that are the basis of value. The fact that a thing pleases a man generally causes him to regard it as valuable; but it may not. For example, he may be amused by a trashy novel, and still regard it as trash. Of course, if the same sort of novel were a frequent resource of his leisure hours, he would soon come to ascribe a certain value to it. Value must always have some degree of permanence, and a passing pleasure does not necessarily indicate it.

In the second place, the questioner wholly forgets the systematic nature of sentiments, and hence of values. A sentiment, no matter how strong, can hardly be said to be correct, unless it harmonizes with the general system of the man's sentiments. For otherwise it must lead him into contradictory judgments. But with respect to the systematic connections between the feelings (as distinguished from the original elementary susceptibilities to feeling) the individual is almost entirely dependent upon social influences. *Generally speaking,* the external harmony of a man with his fellows and the internal harmony of his own sentiments coincide. Sentiments that are without public support are very likely to be without a very broad foundation in the individual's character.

The Question Restated. — All this, however, is simply narrowing the exceptions, not denying them. What of the cases where a man's character does show an independent, and yet internally consistent, development? And what of the more numerous instances where the divergence from the type is (as we have phrased it) one of simple exaggeration or minimization? Are the values thus recognized real or not? We are accustomed to say that they are real *for the man himself;* but that means only that his experience repeatedly confirms the judgment of their reality, and contains nothing that contradicts it. *For us,* we say, they are not real; which means that our experience does belie their reality — that if we try to get any satisfaction out of such things, we are disappointed. Are values, which in the above sense are real for one man and not for others, real or not?

Let it be constantly borne in mind that the question is not whether the man's sentiments are real. It is supposed that they are. But no one regards one of his sentiments as being identical with the value which he sets upon a thing, any more than he regards his concept of the thing as being identical with the thing. The question relates solely to values.

The Negative Answer Formally Required. — If, now, we are to use language with formal accuracy, we must answer shortly and plainly in the negative. Real values, like other realities, must not only be characterized by coherence with the experience of the individual, but they must be generally verifiable. As a rule (we have seen) these two characteristics go together, so that the former alone may be taken as a sufficient indication of reality; but where they are separated we are logically bound to say that the reality is destroyed. As we urged in another connection, when a man asserts that San Francisco Bay has a certain æsthetic value, he is not referring merely, or necessarily, to experiences of his own. He is alleging an objective fact, that reaches out beyond himself, and would remain if his whole consciousness of the matter ceased to be, or, indeed, had never been.

Its Futility. — But we must beware of trying to give a greater accuracy to our language than our thoughts possess. We should remember that ' external ' and ' internal harmony,' the ' systematization of the sentiments,' etc., stand only for matters of degree. No man has a thoroughly unified character, and no man is thoroughly at one with his social environment. Consequently, if we wished to hold ourselves to perfect accuracy we should have to say that *no values*, at least as we experience them, *are real*. But this is futile — as futile as the contention that all of our concepts are imperfect, and that we know nothing as it truly is. Science is human and it makes no pretences to perfection. The differences in our valuations of things exhibit an endless gradation. Everything is a departure from type; and when we try to fix it rigidly, the type — that is to say, the reality — eludes us and vanishes into the unknown.

If, therefore, we say that values that exist only for the individual are unreal, we must say it with the reservation that *all* our valuations are to an undetermined extent marked with individuality. We must not be understood as if we were contrasting these unreal values with others that were entirely impersonal.

X. Values Peculiar to Minor Social Groups

Their Impermanence. — There is another question of similar import, which must be disposed of in an analogous fashion. When a value recognized by a smaller social group is at no time recognized by the larger group of which it is a part, is the value real? On the whole we must answer no. The fact that the larger society gives the valuation no support, but, on the contrary, with every contact tends to weaken it, means that it is doomed to an early disappearance. The tastes and ideals of cliques and coteries, when they fail to reach the great public, are without permanence. The test of time condemns them.

Most of the apparent exceptions are only apparent. When, as happens, for example, in aristocratic or priestly circles, a set of valuations persists and develops through the centuries, despite the prevalence of a different set outside, this does not indicate an entire lack of sympathy from the outside. Though the populace keep their own standards for themselves, they think it well enough that nobles should be nobles and priests be priests; and they would be scandalized to see a member of the privileged classes doing what they themselves do without scruple. And in the few remaining cases, where an entire lack of sympathy exists, we can generally say that the smaller society is not really a part of the larger, but a parasite upon it.

The Logical Extreme is Futile. — But here again we must not think ourselves bound (or entitled) to an absolute accuracy in our distinctions. The spatial boundaries, the temporal origins and dissolutions of societies, are seldom precisely marked. If we push our principle to the uttermost, we can scarcely stop short of the assertion that no value that is not destined to universal and permanent acceptance is real. But this too is futile; for science knows nothing of eternal destinies.

REFERENCES

STEPHEN, L., *Science of Ethics*, Ch. III.
BALDWIN, J., *Social and Ethical Interpretations of Mental Development*.
COOLEY, C. H., *Human Nature and the Social Order*.
ROSS, E., *Social Control*, Part II, especially Chs. XIII–XV, XXIV, XXVII.
MCDOUGALL, W., *Social Psychology*, Ch. VI.
WESTERMARCK, E., *Origin and Development of the Moral Ideas*, Ch. V.
BOSANQUET, B., *Philosophical Theory of the State*, Ch. XI.
ROYCE, J., *Outlines of Psychology*, Ch. XII.
READ, C., *Natural and Social Morals*, Book I, Ch. III.
MEZES, S., *Ethics, Descriptive and Explanatory*, Chs. VII, VIII.

CHAPTER XVII

THE SIGNIFICANCE OF DARWINISM

I. Evolution in General

Relation of Ethics to Organic Evolution. — Ethics, in common with all the other sciences of life and mind, was profoundly affected by the publication, in 1859, of Darwin's great work on the *Origin of Species*. For a time it seemed as if the whole science must be recast in the light of the principles which he there laid down. We know now that this expectation was groundless — that the theory of organic evolution has no direct bearing upon the problems of ethics. This very truth, however, is itself of no small importance; and we shall feel warranted in turning aside from the direct prosecution of our theme in order to make this truth clear.

Definition of Evolution. — Evolution is *gradual increase in complexity*. — By 'complexity' we mean: to consist of many parts, which (1) are of unlike nature or activity, but which (2) are closely dependent upon one another for their continued existence or activity. Evolution, as an increase in complexity, thus includes: (1) an increased variety in the parts, and (2) their more intimate mutual dependence. These two aspects of evolution are called 'differentiation' and 'integration,' respectively.

Complexity. — Examples of complexity are so numerous that it is difficult to choose among them; but perhaps the carpenter's kit of tools affords as instructive an example as any. The kit consists of scores of tools, which differ among themselves enormously, and almost any one of which would be useless without the others — or so nearly useless

THE SIGNIFICANCE OF DARWINISM 361

that there would be no sense in manufacturing it. The plane, for example, is an admirable thing; but it has to have its surface prepared for it by some other tool. One would never accomplish anything if one started to plane a rough block of wood. Each too has its own function, and is ill-adapted to replace any of the others. Now consider, by way of contrast, the kris of the Filipino peasant. Aside from its use as a weapon, he can cut down trees with it, trim off the branches, shape timbers, build himself a house and fill it with furniture, without employing any other tool. It cuts with impact, like an ax, and with pressure, like a knife or a plane. The owner can turn it over and drive in a nail or a peg with the back of it — a peg which he has perhaps whittled out with the kris itself. The kris is *independently useful*, as the several contents of the carpenter's tool chest mostly are not. The kit of tools is a single complex thing. A chestful of krisses would not be a complex thing at all. It would be a mere *collection*.

There is the same difference between the Filipino village and a more highly civilized community. In the Filipino village every man is a farmer, a carpenter, a smith, a cook. When he needs a rope he makes it on the spot. He cuts his brother's hair, and his brother cuts his. He has not lost the barbaric art of making a fire by rubbing two pieces of wood together. Separate him from his fellows — set him, like Robinson Crusoe, alone upon an uninhabited island — and he would get along beautifully. But do the same with the average New Yorker or Philadelphian, and the man would perish miserably. Our communities are exceedingly complex, consisting of men of widely different training and abilities, who supplement one another admirably, but who cannot live without one another. By contrast, the Filipino village might be said to be a mere collection; though, indeed, this would be an exaggeration. For though every man is, say, a carpenter, there are in each village one or two men who are known as having special skill as carpenters, and who are likely to be called in to do difficult work in that line — when they happen not to be busy in their own fields.

Universal Evolution. — Now historians are well aware that American and European society has gradually arisen out of a condition analogous to that of the Filipino village; and that the carpenter's tool kit is in like manner descended from a very few tools that were analogous to the kris. They are *products of evolution*. And we have come more and more to suspect that all the complexity that is anywhere observable in the world has come into existence by evolution. The system of chemical elements, the solar system, the surface of the earth, the vegetable and animal kingdoms, societies and their customs and institutions, production, transportation, exchange, religion, science, art, morality — all these now exhibit a high degree of complexity, which we believe they did not always possess and did not suddenly acquire. The most conspicuous example of evolution is, of course, the development of the individual plant or animal from the single cell in which it invariably has its beginning.

Theories of Evolution. — A *theory of evolution* is either *descriptive* or *explanatory*. A descriptive theory sets forth in a generalized form the various phases of the process, as it is observed to take place. An explanatory theory attempts to point out the conditions under which evolution occurs, the various causes, or factors, which contribute to the result, and the manner in which they affect each other. Some theories of evolution have been devised to apply to *all* evolution, wherever it may occur. The most important recent instance of a universal explanatory theory is that of Herbert Spencer (*First Principles*, 1861), who tried to show that evolution is an inevitable consequence of the conservation of energy. It is an exceedingly ingenious and impressive theory; but the advance of physical science has already made it somewhat antiquated; and (a far more serious matter) it was never of the least service in explaining organic and social evolution.

Other theories of evolution apply only to particular fields: government, say, or language or religion. In many important fields we have only the beginnings of an explanatory theory. This is notoriously the case with respect to individual development. It is also the case with language and art.

Scope of the Darwinian Theory. — Darwin's theory of evolution is an *explanatory theory*, applying only to *plant and animal species* — their structure, functions, and general behavior. It is an attempt to explain *how* all these species, complex as many of them now are, may have originated from one, or a very few, single-celled forms, as many lines of evidence have convinced us they have in fact originated.[1] It does not pretend to apply to individual development, whether physical or mental; and it applies only indirectly, if at all, to the various phases of social evolution.

II. DARWINISM

Artificial Selection. — The Darwinian theory was suggested by the experience of breeders in producing new varieties of pigeons, rabbits, sheep, cattle, and other animals, by a process of *selection*. If a sheep owner wishes to produce sheep of a certain sort, which he has in mind, he picks out for breeding those that come nearest to his wish; and again from their offspring picks out those that come nearest; and so on. In this way, in a very few years, surprising changes in size and shape and in the yield and quality of wool can be brought about — all as the effect of the *constant preference of the breeder* for sheep that possess certain traits.

Natural Selection. — Darwin observed that a very similar thing happens when no human contriver is at work. As we

[1] By far the best popular account of this evidence is that given in the first part of Joseph Le Conte's *Evolution*.

all know, every species of plants or animals produces far more new individuals than can possibly reach maturity and themselves leave offspring. This fact is called the 'struggle for existence.' Even the slow-breeding elephants, if not thinned out by premature death, would in a few centuries encumber the earth. And many species produce thousands of young for one that reaches maturity. What determines which that one shall be? Accident, largely. But also, it may be, the peculiar size or strength or some other characteristic of the individuals. In the long run, those survive that are *fittest to survive.* Now it seems to be the case that every new individual is, from the very beginning of its development, different in many ways from the parent organisms, though the differences are generally very slight; and it also seems that these so-called 'congenital variations' are themselves inheritable. Sometimes a variation is such as to give the plant or animal a greater chance of reaching maturity and perpetuating itself. The variation is then said to have *survival value.* In any particular case this survival value may count for nothing; an untoward accident may stamp it out. No doubt many favorable variations are thus lost. But the same cause (whatever it may have been) that produced the favorable variation in one individual has very likely produced a similar variation in many others. Now when great numbers are considered, the effect of accident tends to be eliminated. A greater proportion of the individuals that exhibit the favorable variation are apt to survive, than is the case with the species generally; and they transmit to their offspring the same advantage. Hence, in the course of time, the variation is likely to spread itself throughout the whole region; and, what is more, any further variation in the same direction, that may occur, will add itself in cumulative fashion to the original variation. Thus a *continued advantage in the struggle for existence,* enjoyed by those individuals who vary from their fellows in a certain

THE SIGNIFICANCE OF DARWINISM

direction, has an effect like that of the *persistent preference of the breeder*. These individuals are, as it were, selected by nature for the purpose of breeding. Hence the phrase 'natural selection.'

Environmental Changes. — If external conditions remained the same, it is conceivable that the modification of species by natural selection might come to a stop in a condition of universal equilibrium. But, as a matter of fact, environmental conditions are constantly changing, both by reason of the slow transformation of the earth's surface, of which geology treats, and by reason of the migrations of species. Thus the coming of the lion into South Africa or of the white man into America brought about a tremendous change in the environment of many plants and animals. But a change in the environment means generally a disturbance of adaptation. It means that there is further room, and further need, for variations that may prove to have survival value. For if the maladaptation is great, and favorable variations do not soon appear, the unfortunate species becomes extinct. The *necessity of adaptation to the changing environment* thus makes the modification of species perpetual.

Why Evolution is Produced. — But why has this modification been in the direction of greater complexity? Why has it been an *evolution?* [1] It has not always been. Natural selection has sometimes brought about evolution, sometimes devolution, sometimes neither. All depends upon whether increased complexity has survival value or not. Increased complexity is in one way apt to be advantageous. When, instead of a single tissue or organ's having to perform several distinct functions, these functions can be distributed among a number of different tissues or organs, a higher efficiency is

---

[1] The reader should note that many biologists use the term 'evolution' to denote *any* modification of a species. This usage is unfortunate, and has given rise to much confusion. Thus the question which we ask above has often been completely overlooked.

made possible. Differentiation, in other words, has the advantage that lies in all *specialization.* There is, however, another way, in which increased complexity may be disadvantageous. The more complex organism has more *complex needs.* All of its many diverse parts must be kept in repair, and kept in adjustment to each other. Now sometimes this increased difficulty of maintenance more than balances the advantage of specialization. Then devolution takes place. For many millions of years, since the cleaning up of the atmosphere by the forests of the coal age, evolution has on the whole been limited to land animals and flowering plants. And thousands of species of one-celled organisms, both animal and vegetable, still dwell in our midst.

Is Natural Selection Sufficient? — Biologists have been seriously divided over the question whether the natural selection of slight congenital variations is sufficient to account for all the evolution of species that has taken place. When we compare two widely separated forms — as man and his fish ancestor — this seems impossible. But the more we consider the long series of forms that intervened, analogues of many of which still exist, the difficulty greatly diminishes if it does not wholly disappear. For the most striking transformations, such as, for example, the origin and development of the limbs, seem to have been brought about by insignificant quantitative steps: slight changes in the size, shape, number, and arrangement of minute structures. The question is still an open one, with the burden of proof upon the opponents of Darwinism.

Inheritance of Acquired Characters. — There are two chief points upon which the controversy has turned. The first of these seemed at one time to have momentous consequences for ethics, which we shall consider in another place. Are not only *congenital variations* (it was asked), but also *traits acquired during the course of individual life*, inheritable? For example, does the blacksmith's exercise of his right arm make his child's biceps any bigger? The question has not been decisively answered; but the evidence goes to show that if any effect takes place it is quite as slight as the congenital variations which the Darwinian theory in its extreme form alone assumes. The reproductive cells, from which the new generation arises, are always distinct from the organism which contains them, and from which, in parasitic fashion, they draw their nourishment. So far as can now be seen, the only way in which the blacksmith's exercise can affect his child is by somehow modifying the constitution of the blood upon which the reproductive cells feed, and thus indirectly affecting them. But there is no reason to suppose the effect, whatever it might be, would show itself in the child's right arm rather than elsewhere.

Mutations. — Upon the other point we shall say just a word. Has evolution been due to the selection of slight variations, or to the *larger variations* which sometimes occur and which are called 'mutations'? Careful observation has shown that new species and varieties may, indeed, arise by mutation, but that it is scarcely possible that any evolution (as we have defined the term) should be thus produced. For the evidence goes to show that mutations are caused by the combination and dropping-out of different hereditary tendencies ('unit-characters,' as they are called), which *persist unchanged* throughout all the combinations into which they enter. It is by the slow accumulation of slight variations that the origin of the unit-characters must, in all probability, be itself explained.[1]

III. Application of Darwinism to Ethics

The Conception of Moral Instincts. — When men inspired by Darwin's ideas undertook to explain the evolution of moral sentiments, it was natural enough that they should

[1] *Cf.* Castle, W. E., *The Method of Evolution*, in *Heredity and Eugenics*, University of Chicago Press, 1912.

overlook one striking difference between sentiments and the different structures and functions with which Darwin had been occupied. He had been dealing with traits which are passed on from generation to generation by *heredity*, and modified by variations which are themselves perpetuated by heredity. And the early investigators of moral evolution treated moral sentiments as if they too were transmitted in this way. In other words, they treated moral sentiments as *instincts*, similar in nature and origin to the animal instincts of migration and of protection of offspring. They thought of them as having been acquired by natural selection and transmitted to each new generation in the shape of a peculiar inborn arrangement in the nervous mechanism. They supposed that a child inherits the tendency to approve of temperance and condemn untruthfulness, exactly as a kitten inherits from its parents the tendency to play with a mouse.

Their Survival-value. — They looked, therefore, to see what the survival-value of the 'moral instincts' might be. Do justice, chastity, truthfulness, kindness, loyalty, courage, and temperance make a man 'fitter' to survive? By this is meant, let it be remembered, not *more worthy* to survive, but *better equipped* to survive, and hence *more likely* to survive. Interpreting the question thus, the evolutionists had little difficulty in coming to an affirmative answer. Accidents sometimes happen; but generally speaking it is the moral men that live long in the land and leave it to their children as a heritage.

Heroic Virtue. — And yet a difficulty arose. We find men almost universally admiring as the very height of virtue characteristics that seem more apt to lessen than to increase the individual's chance of leaving offspring. It is well to be just; but if you are too scrupulous you will never be rich. It is well to be brave; but if you are too brave you will never go back to the girl you left behind you. When virtue amounts to heroism or self-sacrifice, how can it have survival-value?

Group-selection. — Perhaps this difficulty was never felt to be very serious; but, at any rate, Darwin soon made a suggestion that completely nullified it. He pointed out that among social animals traits may have a survival-value, not because they are serviceable to the individual, but because they are serviceable to the social group. The industry of the worker-bee has survival-value, even though the workers are all barren; for it maintains the *hive*. The warning-calls, by which many birds and mammals arouse their companions to the presence of danger, have a double value: first, to their own young, who may be present, and, secondly, to the flock or herd as a whole. Now is not this the case with the virtues? Altogether apart from their usefulness to the individual in increasing his chance of leaving offspring, are they not of manifest value to the community? Without chastity the family falls apart; without honesty commerce comes to a standstill; without mutual good-will coöperation for the common defense or for public improvements is impossible; without temperance the resources of the community must be wasted; without courage its liberty cannot be maintained.

Evolution of Moral Instincts. — Supposing, then, that the moral sentiments are instinctive, it is easy to see how they have been developed and spread abroad. Every variation in their direction would have survival-value and hence would tend to be selected. The more virtuous a society is, the more formidable it is both in war and in economic rivalry, the more apt to spread its borders and send out vigorous colonies; while the less virtuous dwindle away and perhaps wholly disappear. In that way, it may be conceived, the virtues have grown to their present degree of perfection and have become a general characteristic of the whole species. The *vicious man is simply an instance* (in respect of his vices) *of atavism,* or reversion to an earlier type: the type of the primitive savage, or perhaps even of the ape-man who was still in the condition of a brute.

Difficulties. — Allowing its first assumption, the theory seemed on the whole to work very well. But two serious difficulties manifested themselves.

(1) **Natural Selection too Slow.** — The first difficulty was of wider scope than the theory of moral evolution. It attached to the application of Darwinism to social evolution generally — not only in the field of morals, but in that of language, art, commerce, religion, etc. Natural selection of minute congenital variations is a very slow process. Social evolution is a relatively rapid, and, what is more, an increasingly rapid process. And while changes in moral sentiments are slow as compared with other social changes, yet the lapse of a century or two can work wonders. But even the whole time of recorded history would be too short for natural selection to make any effectual impress. Geological periods are needed.

Spencer's Theory. — It was partly for this reason that many scholars insisted that the fruits of individual experience must be in great measure inheritable. Herbert Spencer declared that moral instincts must have arisen from the experience of generations of our ancestors, as to what sorts of conduct brought pleasure to the agent and to others, and what sorts brought pain; the experience being inherited by each generation in the form of a vague, unanalyzable aversion to certain sorts of conduct, and passed on, intensified by fresh experiences, to the next. He cited as an analogy the rapid growth of an instinctive terror of man, in the birds of newly peopled lands. The birds at first view him without the slightest timidity; but they soon exhibit great fear, especially when he carries a gun. Unfortunately for the theory it was soon shown that this fear is not, and does not become, instinctive. It is *traditional.* It is originally acquired by experience, and is diffused and transmitted from generation to generation by means of *warning cries*. A bird, hatched by a female of another species, to whose warning cries he is unable to respond, grows up as fearless of man as the birds of a desert island.

(2) **Immorality not Atavistic.** — The other difficulty arose in the study of the immoral man, and particularly the *criminal*. Taking seriously the notion that the criminal is a reversion to a primitive type of man, anthropologists set themselves the task of analyzing and describing this type. For a time all ran smoothly. They found that a great number of abnormalities, ranging from left-handedness and color-blindness to imbecility (which are known or suspected to be atavistic), were far more common among criminals than among law-abiding men; so that, when they cast up the averages, they were able to describe the criminal as a pretty definite type of man. But, as the critics soon pointed out, the fact remained that great numbers of law-abiding men are far more abnormal than the average criminal. The true explanation of the facts was then forthcoming. Habitual criminals are, in great part, men who either have not *learned how to work*, or have not been *habituated to work* so as to make it seem a natural part of their lives. Any constitutional defect, whether atavistic or not, that makes it more difficult for a man to take training — as left-handedness does, of course, in a slight degree — makes him just so much more likely to become a criminal. But there is no criminal type.

The Initial Assumptions False. — Weighed down by these and similar difficulties, Darwinism in morals collapsed — at least so far as the opinions of ethicists are concerned; among educated men in general, it still has a considerable following. And as it failed in the field of ethics so it failed in all the other departments of social science. For the initial assumptions were false. Social traits are not transmitted by heredity; and it is only to traits so transmitted that the theory of natural selection applies. A language, for example, is not transmitted by heredity. A child whose ancestors have for a thousand years spoken nothing but English learns to speak English or Greek or Japanese indifferently, according to the circumstances of his upbringing. A religion is not inherited. A child is not born a Christian or a Buddhist. The Janizaries, famous for their fanatical Mohammedanism, were recruited from the children of Christians. An art is not inherited. It is not by intermarriage with the Spaniards that the Filipinos acquired their taste and skill in European music; for such intermarriage has been comparatively slight. And a morality is not inherited. Few social changes have been more striking than the stop which Christianity, both in ancient and in modern times, has put to the toleration of infanticide.

IV. Congenital Basis of Morality

The Congenital Basis. — Darwinism in the social sciences has had, however, one permanently good effect. It provided an explanation of *those congenital human endowments that lie at the basis of all our acquisitions.* Men used to speak of a religious instinct — thinking, the while, that they were glorifying religion by putting it upon the psychological level of the migration of the swallow or the web-construction of the spider. We know now that there is no religious instinct. But there are, of course, instincts out of which the religious sentiments grow; for example, the combined fear and curiosity which strange phenomena excite. Art in general and the several arts in particular have their basis in inherited traits. The pleasantness of various colors and color-combinations, and of various proportions and curves, belongs to our common human nature. The consonant intervals between notes are the same for all mankind.[1] And thus it

[1] Differences in the instrumental scales of various peoples long obscured this point; but the evidence is now overwhelming.

is with morality. Though in its developed form it is not inherited, it grows out of instincts and other congenital tendencies which are indeed inherited, and which, if they are absent from any individual, leave him a *moral imbecile.*

(1) **Sympathy; Pride, Shame,** etc. — We have spoken in another connection of the part which the *tendency to sympathetic feeling* plays in the development of all sentiments. In the same connection we spoke of the similar part played by the instinctive feelings of *pride* and *shame, respect* and *contempt.* Here we may add that these feelings not only influence the development of the moral sentiments, but persist as a very common and important factor in them. For the moral sentiments have as their objects types of conduct and character. And, as we recall, pride and shame are easily awakened by a valuation set upon anything connected with oneself; while respect and contempt are as easily stimulated by a valuation set upon anything connected with another. But nothing is closer to a man than his own moral character and the conduct by which it is expressed. Hence in moral emotions which we feel about ourselves pride and shame generally enter, as respect and contempt enter into those which we feel about others.

(2) **Retributive Emotions.** — Account must also be taken of the retributive emotions, *resentment* and *gratitude*. Some thinkers have held that these feelings, and especially the former, are *the* real instinctive basis of morality. This extreme view is easily suggested by the sort of documents from which the history of morality must in great part be studied: documents of a *legal* character. For laws not only set forth a moral standard but attach *penalties* to non-performance; and the practice of punishment undoubtedly has its source in the instinctive feeling of resentment. Some ethicists have regarded moral approval and disapproval as generalized forms of gratitude and resentment: gratitude and resentment on behalf of the community. It may be

noted that these are primarily *other-regarding* feelings. They may at times be directed toward oneself, but this is clearly not their normal tendency. Hence ethicists who treat these feelings as the sole (or principal) basis of morality are led to treat the moral emotions that attach to other persons as primary, and those that relate to oneself as a sort of inward reflection of these. On a general survey, there can be little doubt that this view is one-sided. Our moral attitudes toward ourselves obviously contain more of pride and shame than of gratitude and resentment; and in our attitudes toward others respect and contempt often enter where the more active feelings of gratitude and resentment have no place.[1]

(3) **Hostility to the Abnormal.** — Another instinctive feeling which should be mentioned on account of its strong *conservative* influence upon moral as well as æsthetic standards, is that of *hostility to what is abnormal*. The part which this instinct plays among animals in weeding out tendencies to degeneration is well known, and can in fact be observed in every barnyard. In man it is a protection, not only against congenital abnormalities, but against abrupt departures from established usage.

(4) **Instincts of Family Life.** — Furthermore, various instinctive tendencies of human nature have played a direct part in the shaping of particular moral standards. We had reason to mention several of these in Part I, Chapter V. Especially worthy of notice are the instincts out of which

---

[1] Closely connected with the erroneous view here criticized is another error which has caused untold evil. This is the widespread opinion *that punishment is the essential agency in moral education*. Now the fact is that only under a narrow range of conditions has punishment any *direct* effect upon the moral sentiments; namely, when it excites shame, and shame not at the punishment but at the fault which occasioned it. It has, of course, an important indirect effect through the maintenance of order. But it is safe to say that you can no more beat morality into a boy than you can beat æsthetic taste into him.

THE SIGNIFICANCE OF DARWINISM

family life arises: sexual love and the jealousy which so readily attaches to it; the love of the mother for her newborn child [1] and (more particularly) for the nursing child; the love of the child for its nurse; and those vaguer, but, in the long run, not less effective tendencies by which the care and companionship of the child bind the whole family together. In former times it was generally believed that the community was an outgrowth of the family; and no doubt if one goes back far enough that is true. But it seems probable that while man was still at the ape-level the hunting-group (the community) and the reproduction-group (the family) existed together.

Human Values Products of Culture. — But there is no moral instinct. None of the feelings which constitute, as it were, the raw material of the moral sentiments are in themselves distinctively moral; they are, as a matter of fact, widely shared by the higher animals. This observation need not, however, be confined to morality. Just as, physiologically, man has no new tissues or organs, so psychologically man has no new sensations, or (as it would seem) instinctive feelings. The elementary differences that we find are differences in degree. What is peculiar to humanity is the *complex organization of the given elements* that belong to the common heritage of man and the higher animals. The distinctively human values of art, religion, and morals are products of *culture*. In Kant's words, though in a somewhat altered sense, " Man becomes a *man* only by education."

[1] We do not wish to suggest that there is in women a specific instinct of this sort. Probably there is not, but only an instinctive love for children in general, intensified by the feeling of personal relationship which the months of pregnancy and the pains of childbirth have inspired. It has been observed that women in whom the love of children in general is weak, feel little love for their own new-born children, although they may later become passionately attached to them. There is, of course, no specific paternal instinct. Men, like women, feel a love of children in general, but generally in a much weaker degree; and from this beginning has arisen one of the most powerful sentiments known to humanity — that of fatherhood.

Necessity of Education. — In fact, as we compare man with the higher brutes, one of the most striking contrasts lies in the utter insufficiency of his instincts alone to direct his behavior, even under the simplest conditions of savage life. Human instincts are for the most part fragmentary and vague. They require much practice and experience to develop them to a point where they become useful. The baby grasps by instinct; but his early efforts to grasp are pitiful to see. He creeps by instinct; but he is months in learning how, and many babies do not learn. He walks and runs by instinct; but he must learn to do both. He says *ngă* and *dă* by instinct; but he must learn to talk.

V. THE ANALOGY OF LANGUAGE

This last remark suggests an instructive comparison.

Simple Sounds and Combinations. — How much of language is inherited, and how much is traditional? Certain of the consonant and vowel sounds occur in the instinctive cries and exclamations of the infant. Others almost inevitably come to him as he amuses himself by making noises with his mouth, and, when they catch his attention, are repeated until he has a mastery of them. As a matter of fact many more sounds thus occur than any language has use for. A selection is thus instituted which varies widely from one language or family of languages to another. Thus the Filipino dialects are generally lacking in the sounds of *f*, *v*, *th* and *sh* (hard and soft), *ch*, *j*, and *z*. Moreover, the sounds selected are fixed and standardized in a way that varies greatly. The French *l* and the English *l* are not exactly the same, the one being a dental, the other a palatal sound. The permitted combinations of sounds are also fixed by tradition. We find the Greek initial *kt* and *pt* awkward. In many languages no two consonants ever come together, and every syllable ends with a vowel. In others no two consonants can come together except at the end of one syllable and the beginning of the next. Thus it is fair to say that the vocal elements of any language are in no part merely inherited. All, as we have it, is traditional.

Speech-melodies, etc. — Again, the so-called melodies of speech — such, for example, as the marking-off of a parenthetical phrase by a lower pitch, or as the rising inflection characteristic of the question to be answered by 'yes' or 'no' — are instinctive. There are even instinctive words, such as 'huh-huh' and 'm-m,' for 'yes' and 'no.' But these too are given their specific local forms by tradition. Nothing seems more senseless to an American (before he gets used to it) than the sing-song of an Englishman's speech. And, as we well know, the sentiment is reciprocated. The varieties of 'huh-huh's' and 'm-m's' have never been counted. And the instinctive meaning is probably not exactly yes and no, but consent and refusal.[1] Add to the list a few exclamations, also standardized and greatly modified by variations of tradition — 'ouch' and 'ah' and the like — and the instinctive part of language seems to be fairly summed up. Almost the whole vocabulary, the parts of speech, the distinctions of case, number, person, voice, tense, and mood, the order of words (except, perhaps, the subject-predicate order) are traditional. There is no natural grammar. And of that which is beyond grammar — the soul of the language — all lives only in tradition.

Conclusion. — Now we may venture to say that in morality the instinctive and the traditional — or, if you please, the animal and the human — are similarly related. What belongs to instinct is essential, of course; but it is only a bare beginning. Even what is directly due to instinct is subject to selection and standardization. (The example of the prohibited degrees of marriage recurs to us.) But the instinctive contributions are at best but slight in comparison

[1] The shake of the head is originally a refusal to take offered food. The nod seems to be an expression of determination.

with the developed sentiments which have grown out of them, and which are transmitted from generation to generation, not by heredity, but by the sympathetic contact of man with man.

REFERENCES

DARWIN, C., *Descent of Man*, Chs. IV, V.
HUXLEY, T. H., *Evolution and Ethics*.
SCHURMAN, J. G., *Ethical Import of Darwinism*.
FISKE, J., *Outlines of Cosmic Philosophy*, Part II, Ch. XXII.
SORLEY, W. R., *Recent Tendencies in Ethics*, Ch. II.
STEPHEN, L., *Ethics and the Struggle for Existence*, in *Contemporary Review*, Vol. LXIV, reprinted in *Popular Science Monthly*, Vol. XLIV.
DEWEY, J., *Evolution and Ethics*, in *Monist*, Vol. VIII.

CHAPTER XVIII

THE EVOLUTION OF MORAL STANDARDS

I. CONDITIONS OF MORAL EVOLUTION

Moral Evolution Affected by Non-moral Sentiments. — There is a sense in which the separate study of the evolution of morality is impracticable. For morality is dependent throughout its evolution upon religion, art, politics, and scientific inquiry — nay, even upon such pettier concerns as sport and social entertainment. All these, it may be said, are similarly dependent upon one another and upon morality. But the peculiar double function which morality performs, as the essential condition of social unity and of the unity of personal character, makes it especially open to modifying influences from every quarter. Not that moral sentiments change easily. On the contrary, their stability is extraordinary. But it is the almost endless complexity of the interests which they correlate that gives them this stability. And, contrariwise, if one is to understand the moral evolution that has taken place, no class of interests can be safely neglected.

And on Economic Changes. — Meanwhile the moral sentiments, in common with every other class of sentiments, have been dependent in their evolution upon conditions of another kind. We have elsewhere pointed out that social intercourse comprises the interchange of services and goods, as well as of ideas and sentiments. Social evolution thus involves as an essential factor the evolution of industry and commerce. And we must not disguise the fact that the history of morality, like that of religion, art, and politics, cannot be adequately studied without a parallel study of economic history.

Let us note, by way of illustration, a few of the most obvious effects of the evolution of industry upon morality.

Primitive man does no *work*. He gets food for a meal or two at a time; he provides himself with rude clothing and shelter; he makes a few tools and weapons. But all that he does is for the *immediate support* of himself and his family, or, perhaps, his companions in the chase. In civilized society the vast majority of men must work — must devote the greater part of their waking life and the utmost limits of their energy to tasks which contribute nothing directly to their own support. The necessity of learning to work involves the modification or suppression of powerful human instincts. Hence the virtue of *industry*. Among primitive men there is no wealth, and consequently no war; for there are neither the motives nor the means for carrying on war. With the accumulation of wealth war begins, and with war arises the relation between chief and common man, and the military duty of *obedience*. Necessarily bound up with the organization of work is the exchange of goods; and this cannot proceed far without the institution of contracts and the commercial virtue of *honesty*.

Is this ' Materialism '? — These are but a few hints of the close and constant influence which economic conditions have had upon morality. Sometimes ethicists have been inclined to minimize this influence, feeling that it gave too ' materialistic ' a tone to the subject. But this was ill-advised; for the reciprocal influence of morality upon economic conditions is no less real. And, indeed, if the development of morality had not been constantly controlled by non-moral conditions, it would stand to-day out of relation with such conditions, an ineffectual mass of prejudice.

Now this is not to deny that moral evolution presents a

THE EVOLUTION OF MORAL STANDARDS

certain inner continuity. It does. It makes a very interesting story. But if any one imagines that, taking this story as it stands, it presents a complete causal sequence, in which the earlier events sufficiently account for the later, he is woefully mistaken. And yet he is no more mistaken than the man who supposes that economic history is a complete causal sequence, in relation to which morality is but an unsubstantial 'epiphenomenon.'

II. THE PROBLEM OF MORAL EVOLUTION

The Problem Stated. — Nevertheless there is one line of questions with regard to moral evolution which may, and indeed must, receive separate treatment. As moral standards arise and are modified in response to changed conditions, how is the particular mode of response determined? For though morality may develop in an economic environment, it is morality none the less; and the adjustment to external change is *its* adjustment. There is a real development of morality as it has been, not a mere accretion or substitution from without. It always remains true that a different morality, under a like economic stress, would develop differently. And we therefore ask: *In what characteristic way is the adjustment of morality to external conditions determined?*

Analogy of Organic Evolution. — The problem which is thus set before us is comparable to that which Darwin asked with reference to organic evolution, and for the solution of which his theory of natural selection was offered. How is the adaptation of the species to changing environmental conditions directed? Of the nature of the particular environmental changes he had in most cases very slight knowledge; and of the causes of these changes he had almost no knowledge at all. Even so recent and extraordinary a phenomenon as the glacial epoch remains to-day very imperfectly explained. Yet Darwin was able, from his survey of the conditions of organic life, to propose a general theory of the way in which organic evolution at all times proceeds.

The Æsthetical Problem. — A similar problem may, of course, be raised with respect to every distinct class of sentiments and values. For example, we may ask how the changes of æsthetic sentiment are determined. In the last third of the seventeenth century the English stage developed an exceedingly fine ' comedy of manners,' which culminated in the masterpieces of Congreve and Farquhar. Suddenly it was swept away; and though a half-century later it enjoyed a brief revival (at the hands of two Irishmen), this was only to be followed by a new and permanent collapse. Why these changes in public taste? A religious revival is pointed to as the first destructive agency, and the French Revolution as the second. Such an account may satisfy the literary historian. But the great question of evolutionary theory remains: *How* does public taste change?

The General Problem. — A similar question may also be asked with reference to sentiments and values in general. No doubt different classes of sentiments have their own characteristic modes of evolution. But it is at least open to inquiry whether there is not a generic resemblance among them all; and, if this be the case, the establishment of this resemblance is a scientific *desideratum* of great magnitude.

As a matter of fact little has yet been accomplished toward the upbuilding of a general evolutionary theory of values. Some few points will be noted here.

III. THE MODIFICATION OF STANDARDS OF VALUE

(1) **The Canoe: the Accepted Type.** — A most suggestive illustration — because of its visible concreteness — of the mode of change which standards of value exhibit, is to be found in the successive modifications by which useful implements are gradually brought to perfection. Among savages of a low grade the standard of a good canoe is very

THE EVOLUTION OF MORAL STANDARDS

simple. Roughly shaped from a single log, the canoe is heavy, slow, and awkward, of small carrying-capacity, and easily swamped in stormy weather; and yet its owner is quite content with it. One specimen after another is constructed after a traditional pattern, without thought of possible improvement. Of course, the uses of such a boat are limited; but so long as there is no need to use it beyond these limits, their presence is unfelt; just as we do not feel it to be a defect in an ordinary steamship that it could not survive an arctic winter. If the savage fisherman's boat is swamped, he blames the rough weather, which might have been different. It never occurs to him that the boat might have been different, unless, perhaps, it might have been more *lucky*. The type of boat he accepts as implicitly as if it were a natural species.

Discontent and Invention. — But gradually the demands upon the canoe increase. We need not here ask the reason why. It may be war, or sport, or the failure of a usual food supply. But, for whatever reason, more is required. The canoe must bear heavier burdens, in rougher waters, and with greater speed. As it is pressed into this more exacting service, its deficiencies are soon manifest. Mishaps are increasingly common and serious. Discontent begins to be felt, not now with the weather — for equally bad weather must often be met — but with the boat; and discontent is the mother of invention. When one boat is accidentally better than another, discontent sharpens men's eyes to see the essential points of difference. Various analogies suggest improvements, and discontent supplies the initiative that gives them a trial. Thus, let us say, the sides of the boat are built up, the seams are stopped with pitch, outriggers are added, and the general lines are so modified that the resistance of the water and of contrary winds is decreased. And as discontent prompts the inventor, so discontent in those about him makes them welcome his suggestion and imitate it in their own new boats.[1] Moreover, just as changed external conditions first brought new demands upon the boat, so its improved form leads to new uses — let us say, to a more extensive commerce — and the change in social conditions thus arising may react in increased demands upon the boat. Thus a widened commerce, which was at first a convenience, may easily become a necessity by reason of the increased population or higher standard of living which it helps to bring about.

Acceptance of the New Type. — Now it should be observed that when a man makes a boat according to a customary pattern, he need have little or no idea of the significance of the various proportions which he follows. He may very likely see why the sides are built up, but not why they are built up just so high and not higher. He sees clearly that the bow cuts through the water; but it does not occur to him to ask why it should not be sharper. His appreciation of the pattern is thus vague; and we must add that it is very superficial. The general type of the boat is simply taken for granted, accepted without question, even by the cleverest constructors; and when one does not question, no reasons appear. As each modification is suggested and accepted, its significance must be in some measure understood. But as soon as the modification has become incorporated in the accepted pattern, any understanding of it is no longer necessary. Imitation now suffices. Thus, *while there may*

---

[1] Psychologists have sometimes reasoned as if an invention had only to be made, in order to be appreciated and imitated. This is so far true, that the discontent that stirred in the inventor was almost certainly not confined to him — he has a public prepared for him. But the prepared public may be small; and it may be years and years before the larger public is ready. As far as mere imitation goes, the traditional mode of doing things offers a thousand models to the inventor's one. The imitative tendency alone would seldom suffice to lead men aside into the new ways. This is sometimes strikingly evident when the attempt is made to introduce a foreign invention among a people who are entirely content with their own methods — American tools among the Mexican peons, for example.

be no significant feature of the boat that has not at some time been understood — namely, when it was introduced — *the boat as a whole never has been understood.*

Mental Simplification. — In this respect the boat exemplifies a very general law of mental and social evolution. The results of experience are not conserved, in the individual or in the race, in the form in which they have been acquired, but in a more or less simplified or abbreviated form. A boy learns to play a piece on the violin. The accomplishment is a very different thing in his experience, from what it will be when it has become a familiar habit. A woman meets on the street a man to whom she was introduced the evening before. The mental process of recognition is far more complex than it will be when he has become an intimate friend. In the acquiring or modifying of a function, consciousness is present in forms and degrees that are superfluous when the acquisition or modification has been effected; and in so far as consciousness becomes superfluous, it drops out. The same principle probably applies also to the evolution of instincts; though precisely how it works here is still uncertain.[1]

The modification of the standard of a good boat may now be paralleled by examples of modifications in other kinds of valuation.

(2) The Accepted Price. — In a certain Filipino village the price of eggs was a penny (*i.e.* $.006$\frac{1}{4}$) apiece. If you asked why, the only answer was that such was the custom in those parts. When one had eggs to sell, one sold them at a penny an egg, if at all. If one wished to buy, one offered a penny an egg; and if none could be procured at that price, one simply went without.

The New Market Price. — But a change came. A little American colony grew up in the neighborhood. The Amer-

---

[1] *Cf.* C. Lloyd Morgan, *Habit and Instinct*, especially the concluding chapter.

icans bought eggs for a penny apiece; and when the supply ran short they offered twopence, and, on occasion, even more. This the townsfolk set down as weak foolishness — as the European cabdriver sets down as folly the extravagance of the American who gives him an over-large tip. But if Americans were foolish, all the more reason for plundering them with a good conscience. So the Filipinos saved their eggs to sell to the Americans at twopence. Between themselves the old price still subsisted. They were ashamed to ask a fellow-townsman more than the 'real value' of the eggs. But the consequence was that more and more often the Filipino who needed eggs could not buy them. The egg-owner would declare that he had none to sell.

The Change of the Standard. — The situation was thus a strained one. Not to be able to buy eggs occasionally was to be expected and endured; almost never to be able to buy them was not so easily endurable. Gradually sales at the new price began to be made between Filipinos, though with some grumbling. A few conservatives long continued to declare that they would never consent to be robbed; and perhaps they kept their word. But eggs were now by general consent worth twopence apiece. *Their value had changed.* And the reason was plain. The extravagant Americans had raised the price at which they could be bought and sold; and the popular valuation had gradually come into accordance with the new conditions. But we may venture to predict that if the two-penny rate endures, it will, in popular estimation, soon be an axiomatic principle.

Comparison with Previous Example. — It need hardly be said that the change in economic valuation is a much simpler process than the change in the standard of a good boat. The element of invention scarcely enters. The value of the eggs (*i.e.* the price at which they are thought to be neither 'cheap' nor 'dear') simply accommodates itself to the market price (*i.e.* the price at which they can be freely bought and sold).[1] In this respect economic valuation is exceptional. But the generic resemblance to the case of the boat is still evident. There is the same transition from one customary standard to another, brought about by dissatisfaction with ills that were once endured as occasional accidents, but can now no longer be so regarded.

(3) **Art-forms.** — We may add a few general remarks with regard to the modification of art-forms. The modifications occur in many ways which we cannot now attempt to enumerate or classify. Always, however, there is the customary standard to begin with, which is commonly followed with only the shallowest appreciation of its limitations; and when the modification has been effected it soon forms part of a new custom, as little understood as the first. Why, for example, should the sonnet have fourteen lines, rather than fifteen? The rhyming scheme is pretty; but why should this one scheme be perpetuated in hundreds upon hundreds of poems? One common source of dissatisfaction with old art-forms is this: that they are applied to a new material or a new content or a new useful end, by which their limitations are emphasized. A beautiful example is to be found in the adaptation of the English iambic pentameter verse, originally (in Chaucer and his followers) a narrative form, to the uses of the Elizabethan drama. On the stage its stiffness and formality became a nuisance; and little by little the regularity of its rhythm was relaxed until it had almost the freedom of prose. Long before the closing of the theaters (with the establishment of the Commonwealth) the new dramatic versification had become an accepted type.

---

[1] It should be observed that the science of economics either takes no account of what we here call the *value* of the eggs (the term 'value' being applied to the market price), or else looks upon it as a merely *individual* matter. Economics seems not to suffer in consequence; but from the standpoint of the general theory of values the confusion of thought that results is most unfortunate. The standards of cheapness and dearness are certainly no more individual than the standards of good taste in dress or deportment.

IV. Conventionality in Moral Standards

We have now to examine how this general mode of evolution exhibits itself in the particular case of moral standards.

(1) **In Standards of Duty.** — It is not difficult to observe that in a great part of our moral judgments the standards applied are quite as conventional, quite as empty of understanding, as the penny-an-egg standard or the fourteen-line-sonnet standard have ever been. That it is wrong to steal or tell a lie; that suicide is worse than larceny — judgments such as these are accepted and applied to particular instances without a thought that there may be a rational ground for them, much less that a rational ground is needed. Indeed, to some men it has seemed to involve a gross misconception of the nature of moral values to ask for a ground for them. What is wrong is wrong (they have said), and that's the end of it; what is right is right, and any attempt at further justification only belittles its essential character.

(2) **In Standards of Benevolence.** — Do these remarks apply only to the morality of duty? They apply most widely and most obviously there; but they have also their application to the morality of benevolence and to that of virtue. To speak first of benevolence, we recall that its direction is laid down by standards of duty — we are not called upon to squander our kindnesses indiscriminately — and, in so far, benevolence is apt to be as conventional as any accustomed duty. Moreover, the goods of various kinds which benevolent men bestow — money, education, social prominence, political liberty, and the rest — are in great part conventionally estimated. It may be objected that this does not affect the character of the benevolence itself that it may in its own sphere be equally intelligent, whether the non-moral valuations upon which it rests are conventional or not; much as an argument may be perfectly valid,

irrespective of the truth or falsity of its premises. But the objection is not wholly sound. When one unquestioningly accepts the conventional valuation of the objects of a benevolent enterprise — universal suffrage, for example — this valuation is raised to the rank of a moral principle. It helps to define what altruism *means*. And the consequence is that where other equally estimable objects conflict, a spirit of *intolerance* shows itself, as blindly irrational as any Pharisaism.

(3) **In Standards of Virtue.** — And the virtues, too, are conventional. We might infer this from their dependence upon the standards of duty and altruism; but a direct examination shows it very clearly. The virtues, taken strictly, are monstrosities, as indeed all ideals are. For human imagination can never set up a standard of perfection in one respect, except at the cost of a sacrifice of essential values in other respects. The just man of our idealizing fancy is a machine; the merciful man is a weakling; the brave, the temperate, the wise, are fools and ascetics and cads. No ideal could be endured, or rather no ideal would be possible, if it were not to some extent conventional; and, as a matter of fact, moral ideals are often thoroughly conventional. We see this in the heroes of other times: in the Hebrew prophet who slew with his own hands the prisoner whom the king had wished to save in the extermination of an accursed people; in the Spartan father who butchered his daughter to prove that she was a virgin; in the Christian saint who passed his life upon a pillar. And we have to expect that the day will come when the like will be as obvious of the heroes of to-day. In practice we distrust the virtues, as we distrust all extremes. We *temper* them with each other: justice with mercy, courage with wisdom. It matters not that logically they are but various aspects of a single whole. We see the aspects as if they were wholes, and can only fit them together by prunings-off and compromises.

The Conventional Element is Indispensable. — At this point a warning may be in place. To point out that our moral standards are in great part conventional is not necessarily to criticize our morality in a hostile fashion. It is not necessarily to decry it in comparison with an imaginary morality that is rational through and through. For the truth is that, unless human intelligence were enormously increased, such a morality as that would have to be very limited and superficial. The appreciation of values is in this respect like the understanding of external things. Much of our understanding is in terms that are conventional, and, while they are grossly unclear, derive an apparent clearness from the very fact that they are uncritically taken for granted. For two thousand years one of the fundamental conceptions of science was 'the wet.' Every one thought that he knew what was meant by it, so no one asked. Finally Bacon exposed it. "The word 'wet,'" he said, " is nothing else than a mark loosely and confusedly applied to denote a variety of properties which cannot be reduced to any consistent meaning." And now men of science agree that he was right. But, in different degrees, the same is true of all (or almost all) of the fundamental scientific conceptions of to-day, not to speak of the conceptions of ordinary common sense. If they seem crystal clear, it is only because they are uncritically accepted. Space, time, energy, and the transformation of energy are all nests of vague assumptions. Now is this to say that science (or common sense) would be improved by a banishing of the vague? No indeed. Unless human intelligence were enlarged so as to be truly divine, we need the conventional, we need the vague. Limit us to what is ideally rational and clear, and the cleverest of us would never be able to understand the manufacture of an omelet. And so, we repeat, it is in the matter of valuation: we need the conventional, the irrational, the vague; and not less in morality than in art or politics.

THE EVOLUTION OF MORAL STANDARDS

It is not Diminishing. — But, it may be asked, as science advances are not vague conceptions cleared up? And is not this, at least in part, what the advancement of science means: that its working-conceptions are more and more stripped of the 'accidents' of conventionality and set forth in their plain, intelligible truth? And must not the like be true of moral progress: that, at least in part, it consists in the rationalization of moral standards? No doubt all these questions must be answered in the affirmative. Vagueness and conventionality are not advantages but defects, and every successful reduction of them is an improvement. But we must not forget that while they are reduced in one and another quarter, the *totality* of the vague and the conventional is not reduced. For with progress there comes, too, an immense broadening of the fields of knowledge and appreciation. More and more is being added that has yet to undergo the process of rationalization. The bulk of our unclear conceptions, of our naïve standards, becomes greater, not less.

In pointing out, therefore, that our moral standards are largely conventional, we intend no hostile criticism. We are, indeed, admitting that there is scope for improvement; but after every improvement there will be more scope for improvement than before.

V. DOUBT AND REFLECTION

Let us return to the subject and observe that while the standards of morality are in process of change we become keenly aware of their significance, at least so far as the successive modifications themselves are concerned.

The Passing of Wifely Obedience. — There was a time, not long ago, when obedience in a wife passed as a virtue. We do not now generally so regard it. The promise to obey is more and more commonly dropped from the marriage service; and where it is retained it is regarded as an empty formula, not as the acceptance of a serious life-long obligation. And we know very well why this is so. It is because we have become acutely conscious of the fact that when women are kept under a perpetual tutelage they cannot develop their full possibilities of intelligence and character, and hence are worth less to themselves as well as to their husbands and children. We see too that as a matter of fact the virtue of wifely obedience, while in the abstract it still received a lip-homage, had lost most of its influence in the particular issues of everyday life. It did not go far toward assuring a man the mastery of his household. It had, indeed, the baleful influence which false and hollow ideals always have: that of hindering the development of a true, living ideal — in this case the ideal of loyal coöperation.

The Real Basis of Obedience. — At the same time, let it be noted, we are put in a position to see more clearly what the real significance of the old ideal was. Just because we do not accept it dogmatically, we can distinguish the limits within which it had a valid basis. Obedience goes with dependence for protection and support; and in so far as that relation has existed, or still exists, between men and women, obedience is due. That is why the thoroughgoing feminist is the loudest to declare that the wife ought not to be a dependent; that all the obligations of husband and wife should be those of equal partners in the business of life. And those of us who are not prepared at present to go so far as this — those of us who say that now and for an indefinite period to come the vast majority of women must continue to be dependent upon men to a considerable extent — say also that man's responsibility cannot be effective without a right to command. Are we, then, just where we were before? Not by any means. For the husband's authority, just because it is put upon a rational ground, extends no farther than that ground extends. If, for example, as in many circles of society is still the case, a man is responsible for his wife's honor — if he must resent, at the jeopardy of his own body, any affront that is put upon her — he has a right to require her to refrain from any conduct which he may deem shameful. Since she is not her own protector she cannot be her own judge. But that does not give him the right to dictate her course in obviously innocent affairs. The authority must match the responsibility, not exceed it. Quite similarly, if he is the wage-earner of the family, he has a right to forbid what he may deem extravagance in expenditure. Otherwise he is his wife's serf. But that does not give him the right to demand that she spend nothing without his sanction. Within the limits of economy the freedom of choice may be unrestrained. And, furthermore, the argument works both ways. In so far as the husband is dependent upon the wife — in so far as she is responsible for his comfort and well-being — she has a right to demand his acquiescence with her wishes. The like holds of their relations to the children whom they have undertaken to bring up. Any special responsibility thrown upon one parent lays an obligation of at least passive conformity upon the other.

Criticism and Appreciation. — Perhaps this example will suffice to show how, as the shortcomings of any feature of the accepted moral code are brought to light, its real grounds are also disclosed; and the demand for change, though it may at first be a mere outcry of rebellion, becomes directed by a more or less intelligent appreciation of the real relations involved. Our time offers many such examples, and, indeed, exhibits them in striking fashion to us, as contests arise over proposed amendments to the laws of the land. The divorce-problem, the limitation of property-rights, the treatment of criminals and prostitutes, all involve familiar moral issues. And I dare say that if we were to consider any one of these issues we should find that the radicals of to-day have a better appreciation of the real grounds upon which the older standards rested — I do not say, than the conservatives of to-day, but — than almost any one had before the radical agitation began. Even as Socrates, in the *Apology*, declares that he believes in the gods as none of his accusers do; so it often happens that the innovator in morals believes in the established code far more deeply than its dogmatic defenders. But, on the other hand, the defenders cannot remain dogmatic. They are shocked into reflection.

Limits of Reflection. — In saying this, we must not forget what we lately insisted upon at such length: that after all possible rationalization of moral standards, their conventionality is merely pushed back, not abolished. Authority, we said, must accompany responsibility. Ought a younger child to obey an older one? Only if, and in so far as, the older child is responsible for the younger child's behavior. An enlightened doctrine, is it not? But it takes for granted the conceptions of *authority* and *responsibility;* it takes for granted a whole social structure in which these conceptions operate. The enlightenment reaches only a little way beneath the surface of things, and beneath it the shadows reign undisturbed.

Increase of Plasticity. — Such as it is, however, the enlightenment is the necessary condition of a reform of the conventional standards. It arises in and through conflict, and it brings about a new readjustment. The blind convention, so long as it remains blind, has no power to change itself. The state of enlightenment is the state of instability of convention. The more deeply rationalized a morality is, the greater is its plasticity.

VI. THE RISE OF DISCONTENT

The Attitude of Dogmatism. — Has there ever been a time when evils incident to the subjection of women have not been evident? Probably not; just as there certainly

THE EVOLUTION OF MORAL STANDARDS 395

never was a time, since boats were first used, that the swamping of a boat has not been a perceptible misfortune. Why, then, were these evident evils so long unable to modify the conviction that women ought to be subject to their husbands? For the same reason that thousands upon thousands of boats may be swamped without impressing men with the fact that the type of boat is radically faulty. The evils are regarded as *misfortunes*. One husband is a brute; another is a fool; another is an idler; still another is a rogue. So much the worse for the poor women! Perhaps they ought to have known better than to have married such men. Perhaps their youth and inexperience absolve them from blame, and they deserve only pity. *But* these men are now their husbands, and women ought to obey their husbands.

We are all familiar with this way of thinking, because we all continue to follow it in the application of standards which we dogmatically accept. Perhaps, for example, we accept in this way the command, "Thou shalt not commit adultery." Then how do we judge the case of George Eliot? Lewes's wife was living; and though she had been unfaithful to him, he was unable (because he had once forgiven her) to obtain a divorce. Why should he and this other gifted woman suffer for no fault of their own? Why should they not defy convention and make each other happy? We answer (let us say) that they have no right to such happiness. They were unfortunate, to be sure; and so are thousands of other men and women, who show their courage by patiently enduring their misfortunes without thinking of violating the moral law.

Its Legitimacy. — So far as it goes, this way of thinking is perfectly sound. If a given moral standard is accepted as absolute, then any evils that are incidental to its rigid application are misfortunes; and no misfortune, however great, however pitiful, can affect the eternal standard. It is sound thinking, and the moral conduct which it controls is indispensably precious to us. There are radicals to whom George Eliot is a glorious heroine. But even they can scarcely deny that the thousands of men and women who have buried their love and gone on grimly with their appointed life are not to be despised.

Limits of Foreign Influence. — How, then, is the standard ever brought under suspicion? Sometimes by contrast with foreign standards that are radically different. But the suspicion thus engendered is likely to be at least as irrational as the dogmatism which it disturbs. The observation, that standards differ, and that therefore none is really authoritative, simply leaves us with no standard at all. The common effect of the contact of two moralities — as in the oriental seaports of to-day — is the deterioration of both. This is not to deny that foreign influence may be important for good. It may be highly beneficial. But when it is so, it is because the internal conditions have become such as to make assimilation of the foreign ideals possible. Similar observations are made in the field of art. The English literature of the Elizabethan age shows a strong Italian, and then a Spanish influence; while the literature of the Restoration period is even more strongly marked by French influence. But why? The real question is: What difference had come over England, that in the later period it found its inspiration in French, rather than in Spanish or Italian sources? Even so, when the revival of letters is attributed to the recovery of the Greek and Latin classics, we should ask: What change had come over men, that their hearts were now open to the beauty and power of the classics? Petrarch, you say, ransacked the monasteries of Italy for their forgotten literary treasures. But why were men like Petrarch and those who so eagerly greeted his discoveries produced at that time? The truth is, the explanation of social movements, whether ethical, artistic, political, or religious, in terms simply of external influence is almost always shallow.

THE EVOLUTION OF MORAL STANDARDS

What, it may be asked, of Japan's rapid appropriation of European civilization? But why Japan, rather than Korea or China? The deeper reasons lie within.

Inner Causes of Change. — So we are driven back upon our former question: If the misfortunes incident to the dogmatic acceptance of a moral standard are not sufficient to call it into serious question, how is this ever brought about? The answer lies in the fact that what have been regarded as incidental misfortunes may cease to be so regarded. If, under altered social conditions, their frequency greatly increases; and especially if, among the increased evils, there are some of a new and deep seriousness, depending upon a sensitiveness to hitherto unfelt aspirations and a conception of hitherto unformulated standards of happiness, so that they become a matter of vital public concern; then they present themselves as *consequences* of the moral standard itself, and hence as constituting a defect in it. The case is again like that of the dug-out. So long as swamping is rare, it may be, and is, set down to bad luck. But when the conditions of boating have so changed, that the possibility of the swamping of boats is felt as a real menace to the general welfare, the dogmatic faith in the type of boat is shaken. Something is the matter, though the boatman knows not what, and he is open to suggestions of improvement — if these be not too radical. So with the wife's duty of obedience. Many women may be made miserable, and the duty still hold. Anything, everything except the standard itself is blamed. But let the frequency of these evils greatly increase, and — as the greater frequency probably indicates — let them be felt as an impediment upon newly developed ideals of life, so that they constitute a standing menace to happiness; then the moral standard itself becomes chargeable with them, and society is ready for some change.

Conservatism. — We do not mean by this that change comes quickly and easily. On the contrary, any amendment that may be suggested is bound to meet with resentful protest. Though the standard be felt to be imperfect, anything else is very likely worse. The evils which the standard entails are not infinite. After all, society has endured them thus far; so why not farther? But the suggested change invokes horrid images of all manner of ill-defined evils. If wives do not obey their husbands, what will society come to? And the protest has generally a good deal of sound sense on its side. Reforms, in morals as elsewhere, almost never work out as their early advocates expect. It takes time and many failures to achieve success. Well is it, therefore, for society, that the old standards are not easily given up, that a storm of protest arises when they are assailed.

The Two Parties. — Every phase of moral evolution thus brings about, and depends upon, a division of society into its *conservative* and *radical* elements. To the conservative, the radical is an essentially unsound man, who neglects obvious truths in favor of vain, deluding theories. To the radical, the conservative is one who is essentially stupid or blinded by selfish prejudice, so that he is unable to follow the guidance of reason. As between the two, the sympathy of the student is naturally on the side of the radical. There must be conservatives; but, then, we may rest assured that there always will be; so that it is the champions of reason for whom we feel a real need. But when we are inclined to charge a great part of our fellow-men with stupidity, it is well for us to remember the words of a certain wise American: "Let us be thankful for the fools. But for them the rest of us could not survive."

VII. Duty and Benevolence in Evolution

Modification of Duty by Benevolence. — As we remarked upon an earlier page, the standards of benevolence, as well as those of duty and virtue, are always in some degree conventional, both because the direction of benevolence is fixed by duty, and because the goods conferred by the benevolent are themselves of necessity more or less conventional. But to say this is virtually to confess that benevolent conduct is conventional only in so far as its character is given to it by other than benevolent motives. And now, as we reflect upon the account which has just been given of the development of moral standards, we see that the development consists in a continual remolding of the standards of duty in conformity with the requirements of benevolence.

Morality not Reducible to Benevolence. — It is in this sense that charity may be said to constitute the whole of the law. Viewed as an analytical matter of fact, this simply cannot pass muster. As the hard-headed Bishop Butler pointed out, it is evident in the case of some of the most monstrous acts of injustice, such as treason, that we cannot resolve our condemnation of them into regard for the welfare of any body of men. We hate and despise such acts with a naïve spontaneity that does not wait for the weighing of consequences. And, as the worthy bishop further remarked, it is well for us that all our morality is not exhausted in benevolent impulses. We have not brains enough to play the part of Providence. At every turn of life we need external guidance, the guidance of a rule suited to the limitations of our capacities. If, in disregard of convention, we should attempt to shape our conduct by what we conceive to be the greatest good of men, we should be perpetually bringing about the most serious evils. Our vision is limited at its best, and it is seldom at its best. At one time we are blind to possibilities which at another time would absorb our whole attention. A pure benevolence, if it could exist, would doubtless look very much like madness.

Benevolence the Shaping Power. — Analytically considered, the reduction of morality to benevolence is thus palpably unsound. But from the genetic standpoint it is plain and simple truth. Our deepest moral convictions have a history; and that history is what men's struggles for the common welfare have made it. Benevolence, though not the whole of morality, is its essential *raison d'être*.

Benevolence not Earlier than Justice. — This is not to say that in the order of time benevolence came first and justice afterwards. If only from the intimate relation in which they stand to-day, we know that this is not possible. Natural affection is, no doubt, older than justice; but so is natural aversion to the abnormal older than benevolence. Both benevolence and justice spring from sources that are older than humanity; and they have developed together, with constant interaction. As we noted in an earlier chapter, benevolence is directed, not simply toward individuals, but toward institutions and toward abstract causes; and even when it is directed toward individuals, these often owe their selection to the fact that they stand for institutions or causes. But the institution, though it must have its roots in human instincts, is not, as it stands, a 'natural' phenomenon — not even of the family can that be truly said. It is an expression of sentiments of justice. And this is obviously true of the cause. Hence, rather than claim that benevolence, as such, is prior to justice, we should prefer the paradox, that justice is the *raison d'être* of benevolence. For the ends of all benevolence are at least based upon justice; and many of the noblest and most devoted benefactors of humanity would say that all that they were striving for was what simple justice required.

Justice the Basis of Benevolence. — Moral reform, therefore, is by no means so simple a matter as the reformer is apt to conceive it. The problem is not to make new laws for a new race in a new world. The reform can only proceed upon the basis of justice as it is; and if the foundation is disturbed at one point, we must lean the more heavily upon the remainder. We wish, let us say, to make men happy, as happy as possible. But, then, it is men who are to be made happy, not two-legged animals; and what it is that can make them happy is determined, not simply by their instinctive traits, but by complex bodies of sentiments that have grown up during hundreds of centuries. And, furthermore, the very existence and perpetuation of those sentiments — the very possibility of man's being happy, except as the orang-outang may be happy — depends on the system of justice. If this seems like an over-statement, we have only to apply it to a few concrete instances to make it seem like a paltry truism.

Conclusion. — The relation between benevolence and justice is thus a type of the general relation between progress and conservatism. All that is conserved has been won by former progress; and every movement that is made depends for its possibility upon the conservation of past results.

But, paradoxes aside, why cannot we say (1) that the real purpose of all morality is the welfare of mankind, and (2) that benevolence is simply morality that has become conscious of its purpose, directly intending that to which all morality tends? If by 'real purpose' is meant 'function,' we have already committed ourselves to the first proposition (in the chapters on the significance of morality in society and in the individual); and we are ready to admit the truth of the second, provided it be understood as a matter of *degree*. No morality is entirely self-conscious. Nothing human is. But in proportion as morality becomes self-conscious, the more is its abstract, impersonal justice qualified by human charity.

VIII. THE PROGRESS OF BENEVOLENCE

Convention subordinated to Benevolence. — This leads us to repeat with emphasis what we have already noted in passing: that the evolution of morality is not merely a transition from one convention to another, mediated by sentiments of benevolence. It is marked by an increased self-consciousness, an increased subordination of mere convention to benevolence; hence, also, by an increased plasticity of convention, and by a greater and greater rapidity of movement.

The contrast between the old and the new is well brought out when we consider the inflexibility of military justice, which, for various reasons, has been retarded in its development, and set against it the action of Abraham Lincoln in pardoning man after man who had been guilty of sleeping at his post, or even of deserting in the presence of the enemy. Lincoln, of course, was a civilian, and thus naturally far less subservient to the military tradition than his generals could be. And, on the other hand, the army with which he was dealing was — as he clearly saw — different from the armies in which the military tradition had grown up and persisted. It was made up of free, intelligent volunteers, who, even though the rules were broken, and broken repeatedly, would still appreciate their significance and respect them accordingly — men who were guided, not by laws alone, but by free ideals of human welfare.

Why does not Benevolence become Superfluous? — It may be asked why this is so: why, as the conventions of justice are modified to accord with the demands of benevolence, conscious benevolence does not fall into abeyance. Indeed, have we not already admitted that this does happen? How, then, is a progressive increase of benevolence possible?

An Analogous Question. — Let us match this question with another. Men think, when they have questions to solve. When a problem is fairly solved, a certain amount of thinking becomes superfluous. How is it, then, that as problem after problem is solved we find men thinking not less but more? Obviously, because there is no fixed fund of problems to be solved, which can gradually be exhausted till none are left for us to think about. Every advance of human knowledge opens up new fields of investigation, gives us more and more to think about. The most learned man has not fewer questions to ask than the most ignorant — quite the reverse. The great men in the history of science are signalized, not only by the discoveries they have made, but also, and perhaps more importantly, by the problems they have raised.

Justice does replace Benevolence. — Similarly, there is no fixed sum of human goods to be achieved. If there were, one might with some cogency argue that as more and more was secured by the regulations of justice, less and less would be left to the direct action of benevolence. Thus, for example, in lands where a man has a right to marry several wives, he may, out of a pure regard for the happiness of the first wife, refrain from marrying a second. But with us any such benevolence has become superfluous. The wife can claim her exclusive relations with her husband as a right. Turning toward the future, we note that one of the great promises of the socialists is that their scheme of society will eliminate not only the necessity but even the possibility of a vast amount of benevolence. Socialism, they declare, will give men as their right well-nigh all that private charity can now bestow. We, of course, do not care in this discussion whether the claim of the socialists is well founded or not. We are interested only in the nature of the claim as such. For this once more illustrates the truth, of which we wish to take account: that one essential aspect of the progress of humanity consists in the substitution of justice for benevolence.

Infinite Possible Scope of Benevolence. — Why, then, is the scope of benevolence not restricted? Simply because there is no fixed maximum of good that benevolence can bestow. The more men possess, the more they can and do aspire unto; and the more, therefore, the well-wishers of humanity can desire for them. The wife, we said, has now a claim upon the fidelity of the husband. But the actual scope for personal consideration on the husband's part has not been lessened. Isaac, according to the Bible story, loved his wife Rebecca, and took no other beside her. The modern man cannot show his love for his wife in just that way. But there are a thousand others in its place. The happiness of a wife *means* vastly more, it contains an almost infinitely more complex content than Rebecca dreamed of. And, no doubt, we can predict as much with reference to the socialist's ideal state: that if all he previsages should indeed come to pass, there would in consequence be not less room for kindness and devotion, but immeasurably more.

IX. Relation of Virtue to Duty and Benevolence

How the Evolution of Virtue is Determined. — It is not necessary for us to undertake a special study of the evolution of ideals of virtue. For since, as we have seen, these ideals are simply the standards of duty and of benevolence seen under a new aspect, — as a directly appreciable possession of the virtuous man, instead of as conformity to an external standard, or as the neglect of one's own good for another's, — it is clear that the evolution of virtue follows closely that of duty and benevolence. When a given type of conduct is regarded as obligatory or as benevolent, the type of character that can be counted upon to display such conduct is regarded as in so far virtuous; and courage, temperance, and wisdom take their direction accordingly.

Virtue as a Higher Stage of Morality. — In an earlier chapter we noted that, for the morality of virtue, conduct that is marked by a keen sense of obligation or of personal loss is of comparatively little significance. What this morality emphasizes is a sure insight and an unhesitating decision. From this point of view, the morality of virtue may be regarded as constituting a higher stage in individual or social evolution. Morality that is but half-won and not yet firmly established appears as duty or as self-sacrifice; but as a thoroughly secure possession it is virtue, the free self-expression of the agent's character.

Are Duty and Benevolence Superfluous? — During the latter part of the nineteenth century, the theory was frequently advanced, that obligation and self-denial are wholly unnecessary for morality, and, indeed, that they belong only to a low, or false, type of morality. A higher type would consist simply in self-assertion. Nietzsche and Guyau are the chief representatives of this way of thinking. The former regards the Christian morality about him as essentially a slave-morality, a conspiracy of the under dogs to mitigate their wretchedness and, if possible, hold in check the tyranny of their oppressors. This is well enough for them; but for their masters, the aristocracy of art, science, and war, unscrupulous egoism is the only sane principle of life.[1] Guyau's theory is less sensational. The true end of life, he declares, is the limitless expansion of life itself; and the only motive which it needs is its own inherent energy. The sense of compulsion, like the need of external rewards and punishments, is a mark of weakness. The strong will do what is good just because they are strong.

According to our principles all such theories must be set down as fundamentally in error. The virtues owe their whole content to men's experience of duty and self-sacrifice. The abstract individual has no character to assert — nothing more than the impulses of "the ape and the tiger." The necessary consequence of Nietzsche's program or Guyau's would be, first, an arrest of development, and then disintegration. For if (as we have said) present virtue may be regarded as the higher product of past duty and benevolence, it is equally true that the duty and benevolence of to-day represent the beginnings of the higher virtue of to-morrow.

[1] Compare the sophistic theory outlined on pp. 110-111

Moral Progress has no Visible Limits. — Fortunately we have no reason to suppose that moral progress is fated to bring itself to naught. As old duties lose their oppressiveness, we acquire new ones, which may be no less oppressive than the old. As our selves expand so as to take in the objects of our former sacrifices, so the sphere of our benevolence expands to take in more and more that was formerly indifferent to us. If there is any limit to the process, it lies beyond the present horizon of science.

REFERENCES

GREEN, T. H., *Prolegomena to Ethics*, Book III, Chs. III-V.
STEPHEN, L., *Science of Ethics*, especially Ch. II, Sect. IV; Ch. III, Sects. I, II; Ch. IV, Sects. I, II, V.
ALEXANDER, S., *Moral Order and Progress*, Book III.
WUNDT, W., *Ethics*, Part I, *The Facts of the Moral Life*. (An account of the non-moral conditions of moral development.)
TAYLOR, A. E., *Problem of Conduct*, Ch. V.
HOBHOUSE, L. T., *Morals in Evolution*, especially Part I, Ch. I, and Part II, Ch. VIII.
ROSS, E. A., *Social Control*, Part II, Chs. XXV, XXVI.
TUFTS, J., *On Moral Evolution*, in *Studies in Philosophy and Psychology by Former Students of Charles Edward Garman*.
MEZES, S., *Ethics, Descriptive and Explanatory*, Ch. VIII.
SETH, J., *Study of Ethical Principles*, Part II, Ch. III.
MACKENZIE, J. S., *Manual of Ethics*, Book III, Ch. VII.
MUIRHEAD, J. H., *Elements of Ethics*, Book V.

CONCLUSION

Relation of the Foregoing Theory (1) to Hedonism. — It scarcely needs to be pointed out that the evolutionary theory of values in general and of moral values in particular, which has been set forth in the preceding chapters, is an *energism*. It has, to be sure, its bonds of sympathy with the rival classical theories of hedonism and rigorism. It is allied to hedonism, because, while it does not regard pleasure and pain as absolute value (positive and negative), it does regard them as the ultimately shaping influences to which the development of standards of value is due. It differs from hedonism in its insistence upon the complexity of the system of values — in its rejection of the assumption that such a system can be reduced to terms of more or less of a single pair of qualities.

(2) **To Rigorism.** — On the other hand, evolutionary ethics finds itself foreshadowed, though only vaguely, in the stoic theory of the genetic relationship between moral values and the lower kinds of value, with their ultimate dependence upon the instincts of the human species; more clearly in the stoic insistence upon the social nature of man, as affecting not only his lower, but also his very highest functions. But we find ourselves repelled to-day by the conception of the evolution as a finished process. We see no 'sages' in the world. To us, the shallowest of all distinctions is that between good men and bad. And that universal society of rational beings, in which the stoic thought to move, and by whose life he felt his own life to be continually sustained — that society is, for us, in the making. Again, we feel that the stoic does virtue no true honor in

separating it, so soon as it exists, from the other values of human life, as if it alone made up all possible happiness. For his position quickly reduces to a mere verbalism. " The good man, though on the rack, is happy." Why? Because it is no fault of his that he is there! This is simply playing with words. It is true that a good man may be happy though on the rack. For he has great resources. At any rate, he is far more likely to be happy there than a coward or a libertine. A good man might conceivably be happy even if his wife or child were on the rack — though there, it is to be confessed, a bad man would very likely have the advantage of him. But, indeed, from our point of view, the man that is always happy is as unreal and idle an abstraction as the absolutely good man. If he could be found, we should not greatly admire him. Under the actual conditions of human life, to be always happy is to be less than a man.

(3) **To the Ancient Energism.** — Our theory, then, is an energism. According to us, happiness is a value belonging to a condition of life as a whole. Our quarrel with the ancient energists rests upon the fact that we no longer conceive of life as the activity of a certain given set of faculties. We know too well that all the activities of civilized men are the content of an ever varying tradition; that human nature, as heredity leaves it, is capable of all manner of different modes of development and of all manner of different modes of happiness. What happiness is for any man depends upon the man; and the man is the child of his time and place. The ancient formulas, according to which one kind of activity — that of contemplation of eternal truths — is superior to all others, appears to us, not only as false, but as grotesque. We do not think in such terms.

(4) **To the Modern Energism.** — The modern energists, on the other hand,— Fichte and Hegel and their English-speaking followers, — are an inspiration and a challenge to us. They inspire us by reason of the conception of social

solidarity which they set before us. The idea of the function of morality as the basis of organized unity in both social and individual life is theirs. The idea of historical continuity is theirs. But these conceptions, as they present them, are to our mind an assemblage of problems rather than of solutions. These men saw far and saw profoundly. But we now feel it incumbent upon us to reinterpret their speculative vision in such terms as are afforded by a plain, workaday empirical method. And in doing this we must, no doubt, reconstruct as well as interpret, if only because within the limits of our method much that to them seemed crystal-clear is left as tentative. We cannot pretend to explain the world by reference to a metaphysical reality underlying and determining it. For us, there is nothing truer than history.

(5) **To Utilitarianism.** — As between the English classical schools our allegiance is even more divided. We know nothing of moral axioms, or of an innate moral sense, or of a hedonistic calculus. But, to speak first of utilitarianism, we sympathize with it as a genuine and courageous attempt to explain the development of the moral individual. Especially in the form which it owes to John Stuart Mill, it strikes us as being the direct forerunner of the scientific ethics of to-day. To the last, however, utilitarianism remains individualistic and mechanical, a characteristically eighteenth-century product. The association, shuffling, and dropping-out of conscious elements remain its whole machinery of explanation. Social psychology is almost unattempted. The nature of the sentiments and the manner of their communication is most superficially studied. The conception of historical continuity is practically unknown. These things we owe to other sources.

(6) **To Intuitionalism and Sentimentalism.** — As between the rival nativistic schools, the intuitionalists and the sentimentalists, we have to thank each for upholding an impor-

tant fraction of the truth. The sentimentalists have to their credit a worthy service, in insisting upon the affective basis of valuation. The accusation of their enemies, that they humanized morality, does not now seem to us a damaging one. On the other hand, the rationalists are abundantly justified in maintaining that to judge an action to be right or wrong is not simply to feel a peculiar emotional thrill. The rationality of moral judgment is not a superficial after-development. It belongs to its essential nature. There is no valuation, much less moral valuation, without stable concepts.

Is Morality Immutable or in Evolution? — There remains, of course, the fact that for the ethicists of the eighteenth century morality is 'eternal and immutable,' while for us it is in process of evolution. The difference, however, is far less from our point of view than from theirs. From their point of view we have simply given ourselves up to anarchy. But, as we see the matter, their position is a fair 'first approximation' to the truth. It is, at any rate, far nearer the truth than the skeptical position, that morality is whatever convention makes it.

The Preëvolutionary Standpoint. — The contrast between the ethics of to-day and that of the eighteenth century is, in fact, typical of the relations between our science and theirs. Men had not yet learned to think in evolutionistic terms. And so long as they were limited to a choice between eternity and immutability on the one hand, and capricious change on the other, they were generally right in choosing the former alternative. When, for example, it was suggested that once upon a time man went on all fours, the sober science of 1750 could not do otherwise than reject the theory as ridiculous. The manner in which the head is joined to the body; the disproportionate length of the legs as compared with the arms; the structure of the feet and ankles; these and a host of other considerations made it reasonably certain that man had always been a biped. Shall we nevertheless say that this was a mistake? If we do, our judgment is a shallow one. It is true that in the dim geological past our ancestors were quadrupeds; and this the eighteenth century did not know. But the modification that has taken place has been no superficial change of habit, but a continuous and profound evolution of the human organism.

The Classical Theory Right in the Main. — Quite similar must be our attitude toward the classic theory of the immutability of moral standards. When readers of ancient and modern literature declared that the standards of morality varied without limit and without reason from age to age, it was proper enough for the ethicist to reply: "The original principles of praise and blame are uniform." From our present standpoint we can, indeed, see that this will not strictly hold: that if the original principles of morals appear to be uniform, it is partly because the terms in which they are stated are themselves shifting in their significance. But, for all that, the position was right in the main — as nearly right as was possible with the conceptions of society and of history that were then current.

Identity in Change. — A real evolution is more than change. It involves an identity persistent through change. We began this study by quoting some passages illustrative of different types of morality, the first two of which have come down to us from proto-historic times. Let us glance back at them in closing, and feel once more how, after the lapse of centuries, we are still of the same fiber as the patriarchs: "How shall I go up to my father, if the lad be not with me?" — "I have opened my mouth unto Jehovah, and I cannot go back."

INDEX

Absolute values, 206 f., 272 ff., 347 ff.
Animals, judgments on, 27 f.
Anniceris, 125 n.
Antisthenes, 123, 133, 158 ff.
Aristippus, 123, 124 ff., 128 n., 133.
Aristotle, 4 n., 8, 14, 15, 29, 43, 61, 102 n., 113, 132 f., 144 ff., 265, 266.

Bacon, 13, 390.
Beauty, relation to goodness, 8 f., 114, 143, 208 ff., 222 f.
Benevolence, 80 ff., 398 ff.
  contains all morality (?), 193, 218 f., 399.
  conventionality in, 388 f.
  grades of, 82.
  relation to duty, 81, 83, 398 ff.
  universalized, 85 ff.
Bentham, 200.
Butler, 200, 218 f., 275, 399.

Cambridge Platonists, 177, 189 f.
Character, 24 ff., 298 ff.
Clarke, 200.
Common good, 115, 171, 194, 264 f., 291 f.
Conservatism and radicalism, 397 f.
Conventionality, 72 f., 110, 384, 385, 387, 388 ff.
Courage, 89 ff.
Cudworth, 189 f.
Cumberland, 190 ff.
Custom, 69 ff.
Cynics, 16, 158 ff.

Darwin, 27, 360, 363, 369.
Darwinism, 363 ff.
  in ethics, 367 ff.
Deliberation, 29, 31 f.
Deodand, law of, 28.
Descartes, 62.
Desire, theories of, 113, 179, 225, 249, 252 ff., 298 ff.
Determinism, 58 ff.

Diogenes, 159, 161 f.
Divine laws, 78 f., 176, 191 f., 204, 227 f.
Duty, 67 ff., 81 f., 398 ff., 404 ff.

Effort, 96 f.
Élite, function of the, 340 ff.
Empiricism, 13, 14 f., 199 n., 207 f.
Energism, 102, 104, 131 ff., 237 f., 408 f.
Epicurus, 126 ff., 255.
Ethics, definition of, 3 f.
  methods of, 13 ff.
  problems of, 101 ff.
  relations of, 8 ff.
Euclid, 123, 161.
Eudoxus, 126.
Evolution, 360 ff.
  of moral standards, 379 ff.

Fatalism, 56 f.
Fichte, 242 f., 408.

Gay, 200, 226.
Genetic method, 16 ff.
Grotius, 176.
Guyau, 405.

Habitual preferences, 300 ff.
Habituation, 119, 150, 300 f.
Happiness, 3, 9 f., 102, 147 ff., 317 f.
Harmony, morality as, 135, 150, 165, 218, 302 ff., 308 f.
Hedonism, 102, 123 ff., 142 ff., 147 f., 232, 245 f., 247 ff., 407.
Hedonistic calculus, 126, 266 ff., 276.
Hedonistic paradox, 255 f., 271 n.
Hegel, 243 ff., 408.
Hegesias, 127 n.
Hippias, 106 n., 108.
Historical continuity, 344 ff., 350 ff., 410 f.
Hobbes, 62, 177 ff.
Hume, 200, 211, 219, 221 f., 223 n., 237.
Hutcheson, 200, 218.

414 INDEX

Imitation of ideal, 97 f.
Indeterminism, 51 ff., 56 ff.
Individual, utility of morality to, 116 f., 125 f., 127, 143, 215 f., 275 f., 296 ff., 318 ff.
Individual differences, 35, 46 f., 212 ff., 333, 354 ff.
Intention, 32, 40 f., 231.
   to do right, 42 ff.
Intuitionalism, 16, 103, 200 ff., 207 ff., 222 f., 232 f., 409 f.

Justice, 88, 115 f., 151, 186, 219, 283 f., 400 f.

Kant, 30, 55, 238 ff.

Law, authority of, 77 ff.
   of nature, 78, 173 f., 175, 181 f., 185 ff., 191 f.
Locke, 193 f., 198, 200.

Mill, J. S., 235, 237 f., 409.
Moral act, analysis of, 31 ff.
Moral agent, 26 ff.
Moral feelings, 23 f., 109, 203 f., 211, 217, 220 f., 228 f., 235, 239.
Moral habits, 302 ff.
Moral judgments, subjects of, 23 ff.
   indirect, 29, 37, 48 f.
Moral sense, 151, 155, 209 ff., 224, 232.
Moral standards, 66 ff.
   evolution of, 379 ff.
Motive, 32, 39 ff.

Nature vs. convention, 108 f., 161 f.
Nietzsche, 405.

Obligation, 204, 205, 215 ff., 226 f., 235, 307 f., 313 f.
Original selfishness, theory of, 129, 250 f., 259 ff.

Paley, 200.
Personal authority, 73 ff.
Plato, 14, 15, 27, 61, 92, 102, 123, 126, 132 ff., 149 n., 152, 154 ff., 165, 216 n., 219 n., 265, 266.
Pleasure; see Hedonism.
   kinds of, 143 f., 145, 237 f., 265 f.

Price, 200.
Pride and shame, 324 f., 329 f., 373.
Prodicus, 106 n., 107.
Protagoras, 106 n., 107 n., 109 f., 112 n., 124 n., 133.
Punishment, 39, 54, 374 n.

Rationalism, 13, 16, 155, 200 ff.
Responsibility, 50 ff.
Retributive emotions, 373 f.
Rigorism, 102, 104, 158 ff., 407 f.

Sanctions, 68, 226 f., 236.
Selfish theory, 129, 249 f., 252 ff.
Self-realization; see Energism.
Sentimentalism, 103, 199 f., 207 ff., 409 f.
Sentiments, 304 ff.
   education of, 330 ff.
Shaftesbury, 198, 218.
Skepticism, 73, 110 f., 156.
Smith, Adam, 219 ff., 327 n.
Social intercourse, 286 ff., 292 ff.
Social nature of man, 133, 171, 195.
Society, utility of morality to, 109, 281 ff.
Socrates, 13, 14 f., 112 ff., 133, 134, 135, 136.
Sophists, 105 ff.
State of nature, 174, 182 ff.
Stephen, 94.
Stoicism, 16, 61, 163 ff.
Sympathy, 219 ff., 291, 324, 325 ff., 373.

Temperance, 91 ff.
Theodorus, 125 n.
Thrasymachus, 106 n.
Time, test of, 343 ff.
Tradition, 109 f., 277, 370, 376 ff.

Unforeseen consequences, 33 ff.
Utilitarianism, 103 f., 223 ff., 232 f., 235 ff., 409.

Values, theory of, 9 f., 114, 135, 143, 147, 164 f., 179 ff., 192, 261 ff., 311 ff., 335 ff., 382 ff.
Virtue, 88 ff., 115, 135 ff., ·149 ff., 165, 389, 404 ff.